William Beckford's FONTHILL

William Beckford's
FONTHILL

ARCHITECTURE, LANDSCAPE
AND THE ARTS

ROBERT J. GEMMETT

FONTHILL

Fonthill Media Limited
Fonthill Media LLC
www.fonthillmedia.com
office@fonthillmedia.com

First published in the United Kingdom
and the United States of America 2016

British Library Cataloguing in Publication Data:
A catalogue record for this book is available from the British Library

ISBN 978-1-78155-483-8

Typeset in 10pt on 13pt MinionPro
Printed and bound by CPI Group (UK) Ltd, Croydon, CR0 4YY

Contents

Introduction

Fonthill, referred to in early records as Fountel, Fontel, or Funtell, is believed to have derived its name from the variety of springs that came forth from the hillsides of the manor of Fonthill Gifford located in the south western division of Wiltshire. The name Gifford came from the baronial family of Gifford who held the property at the time of the completion of the Domesday Book, or general survey of property holdings in 1086. Andrew Gifford then sold the lands in 1209 to Sir Robert Mauduit and his heirs, one of whom was Robert de Mandeville. From the Mandevilles and Mauduits, the demesne lands passed by marriage to the Moleyn family. When Sir William Moleyn died, a portion of the manor passed to his daughter and only surviving heir Eleanor, who would marry Robert de Hungerford giving him the legal authority of possession. Hungerford then appears to have lost the estate through an act of attainder in 1461, whereupon the lands went to Lord John Wenlock, who was killed during the Battle of Tewkesbury in 1471. It was by purchase and another portion by inheritance that the Sir John Mervyn acquired the Fonthill lands in 1533. In 1620 the land was sold to Mervyn Tuchet, Earl of Castlehaven. When he was beheaded in 1631 for a felony, the estate was granted in the following year to Sir Francis Mervyn, also known as Lord Cottington, who was Chancellor of the Exchequer. It was his heirs that sold the Fonthill domain in 1745 to William Beckford, the Lord Mayor of London, and father of William Beckford, the author of *Vathek*.

The architectural history of Fonthill began with the house built for Sir John Mervyn and then modified and restored due to a fire in 1624 or 1625. This house, called Fonthill *Antiquus* by the Wiltshire historian Richard Colt-Hoare, was reproduced in a *c.* 1700 painting which hung on a wall in Fonthill Abbey. John Rutter, who wrote a history of Fonthill, described the view of the house from the painting as an edifice that

> formed three sides of a quadrangle, having the fourth occupied by a sort of screen or cloister of one story, in the centre of which was the entrance to the court … . The windows were large … the fronts terminated in gables along the whole line. A large advanced court enclosed, occupied a considerable area in front of the whole edifice … and parallel to the house, ran a canal, crossed by a bridge. In the middle of the front line of the court, at a great distance from the house, stood a detached gate-way or barbican of two stories in

height, highly decorated, and having a turret of three stories, crowned by a cupola at each angle. Beyond all these … [were] detached offices, gardens, fish ponds, &c.; and adjoining the principal building on the right, was a wing of lower elevation; and to the left was the plaisance, having a small piece of water with an island in the centre (pp. 105-6).

Lord Cottington ordered major changes in the building during the period of his ownership including a refaced front in the classical style, as evident in George Lambert's painting of the house in 1740, now in the UK Government Art Collection. This is the way Fonthill *Redivivus*, as Hoare dubbed it, appeared when Alderman Beckford purchased it in 1745. He in turn made his own alterations to the structure and the grounds with the addition of a five-arched bridge over the canal, a church with a Tuscan portico on a higher elevation, a pagoda and a small temple. But on 12 February 1755 a great portion of the building burnt to the ground from a chimney fire in the centre of the house leaving only the two north wings, the great kitchen and the brew house behind. A dramatic account of the fire that consumed the whole building in three hours appeared in the local newssheets:

> It was discovered about Two o'Clock by the old Gardener, George Jewer, who lay in the Garret over the Kitchen, and was awak'd by the rattling of the Fire, which he first thought to be a Hail-Storm, but looking out of his Window saw the Flame bursting through the Chamber Window in the North Front; upon which he instantly alarmed his Fellow Servants (only three in Number, Mr. Beckford being in London) by firing off his Gun, and immediately afterwards the Neighbourhood by ringing the Stable Bell; but it was Three o'Clock before any Assistance came, by which Time the Fire had consumed the great Hall, the fine Organ, with the rest of the Furniture, and all the North Apartments with every Thing therein: However the Neighbours now, to a considerable Number, were got together, and with the utmost Hazard of their Lives, saved most of the rich Furniture in the South Apartments by Four o'Clock, when the whole House was a Blaze, and soon after the Roof fell in. This very melancholy Misfortune and great Loss, more perhaps to the Publick than the Owner, was occasioned by the Workmen (who were finishing a Ceiling) making a Fire in a Closet Chimney in the North Apartment, in the very Centre of the House, in which Chimney the Hearth had been taken up, and express Orders given to make no Fire in it; but notwithstanding all this, a Fire was afterwards made there, which, 'tis supposed, communicated itself to a Beam that lay under or near it, and so on 'till it broke out. (*The Derby Mercury*, 28 February 1755, p. 1)

The total loss was was estimated to be £30,000, which would be equivalent to £5,400,000 today. Only £6,000 was insured, but despite the considerable loss Beckford proceeded to build a new house in the Palladian style identified in time as Fonthill *Splendens*. The construction began *c.* 1757 and was not completed until *c.* 1770. Howard Colvin identified the architect and builder of the new Fonthill house as 'a man named Hoare', from the city. If Hoare indeed prepared the designs for the new building, he may not have followed through on the task since William Moulton (d. 1803), a master-builder who set up a business in nearby Salisbury identified himself in 1768 as the person who superintended and completed the construction of the Alderman's house (*Salisbury and Winchester Journal*, 26 December 1768, p. 2).

It was in this house that the young Beckford grew up and spent a good portion of his life before the idea of a new building in a different style loomed in his mind and became an obsession that led to the creation of one of the great wonders of its day—Fonthill Abbey.

This book extends my first study of Fonthill published in 2003 under the title *Beckford's Fonthill the Rise of a Romantic Icon*, which was essentially an anthology of source material on the Abbey published between 1797 and 1844. The sources included newspaper accounts, magazine articles, visitors's descriptions, professional assessments, satires, eulogies and original poems that I was able to uncover over the years. This new study provides a considerable amount of new material based on more extensive research since 2003, including chapters on Fonthill Splendens dealing with the four major auctions in 1801 and 1807 that caused a general stir throughout England and abroad. Earlier versions of Chapters six and seven, dealing with the household sales of 1801 and 1807, appeared in my articles in *The Burlington Magazine* (June 2008) and the *Journal of the History of Collections* (no. 2: 2010). These were the important sales that led to the final destruction of the celebrated mansion where William Beckford spent forty-seven years of his life. They help to complete the story of two of the greatest estates in England, the one whose architectural style and contents looked back to the classical age and the other that looked forward to the Romantic era.

Having access to the wealth of documents among the Beckford's Papers, in the Bodleian Library at Oxford, was essential to the telling of the Fonthill story as I have attempted to do. Important also were the collections relating to Fonthill at the Beinecke Library at Yale as well as smaller archival holdings in museums and libraries in England. Research for this book also included an extensive investigation of the newspapers and journals of the period starting with 1796, the year that marked the beginning of the construction of Fonthill Abbey, to Beckford's death in 1844, to uncover news accounts, letters, original essays and other information about both Fonthill estates that would be relevant to this study

William Beckford's prominence, immense wealth, and inaccessibility created an interest in him and in both Fonthill estates that reached legendary proportions during the time he lived there. The Fonthill sales of 1801 and 1807 made the Fonthill Splendens estate fully accessible to the public with thousands descending upon the grounds to witness the opulent offerings put up for sale and perhaps catch a glimpse of its elusive owner, by then one of the most famous men in England. This interest reached a fever pitch in 1822 when the newspapers of the day announced that Fonthill Abbey, it contents, and the surrounding property would be sold. For the first time in its history, the Abbey and its grounds became accessible to the public and a visit to this second estate became an even more dramatic social event, developing into what became dubbed as the 'Fonthill fever'. Thousands of people responded to the announcement and in their eagerness to see Fonthill eventually clogged all roads that led to Beckford's 'Holy Sepulchre'.

Numerous artists were among the visitors, anxious to paint the Abbey in its setting, along with the interior rooms and their contents. Before long, engravings of their work began to appear in books and periodicals that served to stimulate the public appetite for even more access to Fonthill. During the two public openings in 1822 and 1823, prominent authors published original essays, verse, and descriptive accounts about the Abbey, the artistic treasures it held, and the surrounding grounds in major magazines and newspapers throughout England. These written works and engraved 'views' now provide an historical record of the popularity of Fonthill in its day and the extent and nature of its artistic achievement.

Utilising all of these materials, this study provides an extended account in fourteen chapters of the origin, design and development of Fonthill. It assesses both Fonthills within the context of the aesthetics of the picturesque and sublime as defined by such eighteenth-century theorists as William Gilpin, Uvedale Price and Edmund Burke. It makes a case for appreciating Fonthill Abbey as an artistic totality that included an imposing Gothic residence, an impressive collection of art works and a dramatic landscape garden. This study also provides evidence of the younger Beckford's extensive landscaping activities in Old Park, the grounds surrounding Splendens prior to turning his attention to the Fonthill Abbey estate.

The anthology in *Beckford's Fonthill* included unrecorded or unattributed works about Fonthill by John Britton, Charles Knight, Thomas F. Dibdin, Abbé Denis Macquin, John Lettice, William Garbett, Isaac Reed and Alaric Watts. In this new book, I provide in Appendix I an extended list of the prominent visitors who visited the Abbey estate in 1823 and in Appendix II the identity of J. Sidney Taylor who published a series of significant and well written articles published in the *Morning Chronicle* in 1823. I also include a selection of the more important critical observations he made on this experience. His collection of essays join the works of other contemporary writers—Hazlitt, Dibdin, Macquin, and Charles Knight—as some of the most important records of the sights and sounds of the experience of being there when the London auctioneer Harry Phillips raised his hammer to disperse the riches of Fonthill.

Central to the rise of Fonthill Abbey as enduring work of art were six public sales in 1801, 1807, 1822 and 1823. This book examines the public impact of these sales, the reaction of the press, the behind-the-scene negotiations that led to the sale of Fonthill Abbey, and the controversies that erupted during the auction of its contents. It discusses in detail some of the most important appraisals of the Abbey that appeared in the press, particularly original works by John Britton, John Rutter, William Hazlitt, Peter Patmore, William Garbett, and J. C. Loudon. Finally, it concludes with an examination of the critical assessment of Fonthill Abbey to the present time.

Of particular importance to this study are the numerous views of the Abbey in its setting and the interior views of the rooms within the Abbey by such artists as John Martin, Thomas Higham, Charles Wild, George Cattermole, and J. M. W. Turner. Since Fonthill was primarily a visual experience, their works appear within this book as essential iconographic documents. The book concludes with an extensive Fonthill bibliography devoted to sources relevant to a study of Fonthill—books, guide books, auction catalogues, an extended list of articles published on Fonthill from 1797 to the present day and a list of secondary source material that was helpful in this study.

I am indebted to the Department of Western Mss., Bodleian Library, University of Oxford, where the Beckford Papers are located, for the use of unpublished material over the years and for this study. The Beckford Collection of the Beinecke Library at Yale University also provided invaluable information, which aided this study, as did the Britton Collection in the Library of the Wiltshire Archaeological and Natural History Society, Devizes, England.

I also wish to acknowledge and express appreciation to the following individuals who supplied me with important information about Fonthill paintings and drawings included in this volume: Alex Kidson, Walker Art Gallery; Jean Bray, Sudeley Castle archivist; Andrea Gilbert, Librarian and Archivist of the Wallace Collection; Mark Wisbey, Bolton Museum and Art Gallery; Charles Nugent, The Whitworth Art Gallery; Ian Warrell, Tate Britain; Alison Fuller and Anna Harrison, The National Trust; Mara Meikle, the Art Gallery of Ontario; Jenny Ramkalawon, British Museum, Department of Prints and Drawings; Scott Wilcox, Yale Center for British Art; Moira Thunder, Victoria and Albert Museum; Jane Standen, the Salisbury Museum; Jennie Macve, Hafod Trust, and Danielle Blanchette, Musée des Beaux-Arts de Montréal.

To my children, Steve, Scott, David and Kerry and grandchildren, Hannah, Lilah, Riley and Mark, for all of their contributions, given wittingly and unwittingly, I am very grateful. Last but not least, to Kendra for her unfailing support since the beginning of all of this in 1964.

When a colleague first suggested Beckford to me as a subject of investigation in the early Sixties, I knew very little about him. The one thing that did come to mind, however, was the image of Fonthill Abbey which I had remembered from an engraving I had seen—it was a brooding architectural presence sitting in a commanding position overlooking the downs of Wiltshire—its tall tower reaching heavenward. I felt that it had a compelling quality and that it seemed emblematic of a period of time that had already captured my imagination. I decided to pursue the matter.

The Background for Fonthill

William Beckford's Fonthill Abbey stands today as an enduring icon for a period of history when the aesthetic experience in the arts was shifting towards an emphasis on self revelation, sensory appeal, and emotional values. Beckford's oriental fantasy *Vathek* had already revealed the romantic sensibilities that represented a significant break from the restrictions of classicism. This distinctive literary work broke new ground as a *tour de force* of imagination with the creation of a Beckfordian persona in the form of a caliph who was allowed to relish unorthodox behaviour and indulge in a world of sensory opulence. It placed Beckford among the 'Devil's party', as William Blake would characterise it, as a pioneer writer who exposed the undermind of a repressed European society in an amoral world of Romantic aestheticism, celebrated later by such writers as John Keats, Lord Byron, and Edgar Allan Poe. The Fonthill Abbey estate, considered as an artistic totality which included an imposing Gothic residence, an impressive collection of art works, sumptuously bound books and a dramatic landscape setting, was a kindred creation to *Vathek*, a piece cut from the same artistic fabric and also inextricably associated with the creator's complex personal life. Both works were constructs of imagination in the new mode of artistic expression that cultivated self-dramatization and a taste for sensational effects; both were in accord with the newly formulated aesthetics of the picturesque and the sublime that fused sensory appeal with emotional transport. But it was Fonthill, despite the influence of *Vathek* in the literary world, that Beckford felt was the 'great work of his life' in which he displayed his taste and knowledge more conspicuously than in 'anything he had ever done besides'.[1]

The background for Fonthill Abbey and the factors that led to its creation can be traced in Beckford's early life. The wealth that made such an extravagant scheme possible came from his father, the owner of Jamaican sugar estates and a political figure of national prominence as Lord Mayor of London. It was reported that he left an estate that totalled £48,000, equivalent to £8,200,000 today, which made him the richest commoner in England next to Lord Clive.[2] Young Beckford inherited the bulk of the estate when he reached majority in 1781.

When Beckford's father died in 1770, he was celebrated and mourned throughout the land as a signal patriot of the country and a champion of liberty. His body was interred at the church he built at Fonthill. The church was hung in black for the occasion and 'six country labourers' in suits of grey coarse cloth carried the cedar-wood coffin covered in black velvet with a gold plate attached. *The Manchester Mercury* reported that his heart was enclosed in a leaden urn and sent to Jamica, where he was born.[3]

It was not just his peers who expressed their deep respect for him on this occasion. The *Kentish Gazette* noted that a group of college youths who never met him demonstrated their own feelings by tolling a minute bell at the Mother church at Bow at the time his body was removed from London and then when they believed it had arrived at the Fonthill estate, they ordered the bell to be tolled again at about ten o'clock at which time they supposed the body to be interred; they then followed with ringing a dead peal until midnight 'testifying , by every means in their power, the deep sense they entertained of the loss of one of the greatest ornaments, not only of the city of London, but of his country in general'.[4] In the same issue of this paper it was noted that the young Beckford looked very much like his father and bore the lineaments of his face, and then added: 'Time only can discover if he will imitate him in his conduct'.

Beckford greatly admired his father, but his death when Beckford was only nine, left him exposed to other shaping influences. In particular, his mother Maria Beckford tended to be autocratic, fiercely possessive of her son's affection and desirous of having him follow in his father's footsteps as a prominent political figure. A strong influence on his life, she instilled in him a Calvinistic sense of fate and sin which pervaded so much of what he later wrote and which cultivated a taste for religious art that ultimately manifested itself most dramatically in the artistic design of Fonthill Abbey as a monastic residence. She was a contributing factor in another way by turning his attention to a study of his own ancestry, which increased his self-centredness and bred in him a vanity of birth that led to the celebration of his lineage as a central motif for Fonthill Abbey and its interior decoration.

The preoccupation with his own solitariness that developed in Beckford as a young man might have been mitigated by sending him away to school where he could have had the opportunity to be in contact with persons his age, but Mrs Beckford refused to allow it, educating him instead at home, where he was constantly subjected to the pressures of a family council composed of dowager aunts and people removed from his generation. She did this despite the fact that her husband left £1,000 per year for his son's education. It was a stifling atmosphere, which made him lonely and secretive, and prone to long periods of exaggerated introspection. Before long, he began to show signs of growing rebelliousness. The dull civilities of polite society bored him, dampened his spirits, and sometimes stirred in him a sense of outrage:

> Delivered up to a Sword, Bag and pretty Cloathes, I am obliged to go dangling about to assemblies of sweet, dear, prim, tulipy, variegated Creatures, oppressed with powder and pomatum, and tired with the lisping nonsense I hear all around me … .At home I am infested with a species which, like mathematical points, have neither *parts* nor magnitude—Alas, fat Bulls of Basan encompass me around—Tubs upon two legs, crammed with Stupidity, amble about me. Some of them mere trivets and Footstools, supple, pliant, and complaisant.[5]

His private education did little to make his existence bearable; it was rigidly classical in character and in accord with the expectations for gentlemen of the day. The regimen of discipline required was not always nurturing to his artistic temperament. Beckford was precociously intelligent, but he was also intensely emotional and wilful by nature—a mercurial personality who sought other gardens of delight. These he soon found in the more volatile imaginative literature of the day, particularly the *Arabian Nights* and its imitations. This became evident as early as the age of eleven when he made his first-known book purchase, a five-volume set of Pétis de la Croix's *Mille et un Jour, Contes Persians* (1711–13).[6] There was food for daydream in the colourful tales he pored over in the isolation of his chambers, an outlet to escape the heavy demands at home. Once aware of the depth of this unclassical interest, the family took steps to curb it. On one occasion, the guardian tutor, the Revd John Lettice, forced the boy to burn a 'splendid heap of oriental drawings', but the repressive effort failed partly because of another tutor, Alexander Cozens, who consistently encouraged the young Beckford's exotic tastes and escapist longings. A widely travelled water-colourist, he stimulated the young boy's lively imagination with extravagant stories from his own past. Beckford also enjoyed sharing with Cozens his readings of Ariosto, Milton, Dante, Spencer and the 'melancholy Gray', all of whom had fired his imagination and cultivated his taste for dramatic representation.

Cozens also taught him much of what he knew about the graphic arts in the 1770s, the depth of which would become apparent in his Beckford's first published work *Biographical Memoirs of Extraordinary Painters,* which he wrote when he was seventeen. Under Cozens's tutorship, Beckford developed his pictorial sense of the natural landscape and a highly picturesque literary style. Almost from the date of his relationship with Cozens and as a consequence of his training in the pictorial arts under this teacher, Beckford was in the habit of making observations about the world around him as if he were examining a painting in one of the galleries in his father's house. The young writer's letters to the water-colourist, especially those from Switzerland in 1777 and 1778, where Beckford spent some time as part of his private education, provide evidence of his ability to describe Alpine scenery from the perspective of a painter. As he wrote from Thun:

> The Mountain from whose summit I wrote my last letter, is my chief comfort, and I resort to it once every Fortnight. It consists of two huge masses of Rock, separated by a chasm, the one called the Great, the other the Little Salève. No sooner do I reach the Summit than I leap off my Horse and spring into a Valley concealed as it were in the Bosom of the Mountain. There, two stupendous Rocks present an uninterrupted Range of Cliffs for about a quarter of a Mile, and the Vale between is formed by a smooth Lawn nicely fitted by the hand of Nature into every crevice. The opening at the farther end discovers a plain, at the foot of the precipice, quite even for the space of 15 Leagues and level all the way with the Lake, that together with a chain of Azure Mountains terminates the vast Horizon.… I think I behold you charmed with hearing nothing but the trickling of a small *Rill* that oozes out of the Rock, quite an Hermit's Spring.… Then the fresh Underwood that extends on the right of the Dell under the lofty Cliffs would please you

beyond expression; so green, so flourishing and mellowed by the gleams of the setting Sun.[7]

Or, as he wrote the following year from Aix en Savoy on another excursion:

> After crossing a cultivated Plain I heard the roar of some considerable Torrent, and approaching nearer and nearer to the woodlands from whence the Sound proceeded, was startled at the sight of a deep cleft dividing another wide extended valley probably rent by some dreadful Earthquake. A Stream rushes turbulently from the distant Hills and fills this rocky Channel along which it hurries with a loud bellowing.
>
> The Slender withered Trees which hang over it on one side and the tall Mountain Ash which springs from the Cliffs on the other have a fine effect, nor is the dark colour of the rocks opposed to the Silver brightness of the Stream less pleasing. I leaned a long while on the barrier of a Bridge which crosses the Precipice and gazed on the dark Gulph, on the foaming waters and the Lights reflected from the variegated Sky with great delight and wished you was with me to enjoy them. A few miles on we came to the Bridge of Cope consisting of one bold Arch, thrown over the same torrent we had crossed before and soon after passing thro' *Rumilly* traversed a beautiful plain bounded on every side by Mountains as varied as a picturesque Eye could desire and above whose Summits rise the distant Glaciers in all their majesty.[8]

Reading these letters, it is apparent that Beckford was making a studied effort to reconstruct a natural landscape in prose by incorporating the elements needed to fill and frame a picture, similar to the efforts of many of his contemporaries who were using a convex mirror called a 'Claude glass' to study a landscape scene. They also provide evidence of Beckford's growing interest in the aesthetics of the picturesque that laid the groundwork for the creation of Fonthill.

While it may seem improbable that Beckford at the early age of seventeen was contemplating anything remotely connected with Fonthill, a remarkably prophetic essay-letter, which he wrote to Cozens in 1777, recapitulates a dream they shared of creating a solipsistic retreat that would allow them to indulge their 'romantic inclinations' in an English countryside separated from the world. This retreat, as Boyd Alexander first noted, suggests Fonthill in a rudimentary form:

> Yes the time will arrive when we may abstract ourselves at least One hundred Days from the World, and in retirement give way to our romantic inclinations. There we will sit on the banks of the river which flows by my native walls and looking up amongst the Shrubs which surround them fancy ourselves on Hesperian ground. There we will execute those plans you have imagined and realise in some measure the dreams of our Fancy. We will obey no other Sovereign than Nature and follow no other guide than pure simplicity.[9]

It is also interesting to note that a central element in this plan, as Beckford described it, is a tower constructed on a hill:

Sometimes, when our minds are exalted by the sublime reveries of philosophy we will ascend a lofty Hill which till lately was a Mountain in my eyes. There I hope to erect a Tower dedicated to meditation on whose summit we will take our station and survey the vast range of countries beneath.… At midnight when the planets roll brightest, and universal stillness prevails we will recline on stately couches placed on the roof of our Tower and our eyes shall wander amongst the stars' (pp. 27-8).

So important was Beckford's relationship with Cozens that it is believed he kept Cozens's letters in a bedside table to the end of his life. 'All your Letters', he wrote to the artist, 'were deposited in a Drawer lined with blue, the colour of the Aether'.[10] Unfortunately, these letters to Beckford have never been found and may have been destroyed after Beckford's death. They would have given a fuller picture of the thoughts these two individuals shared regarding this plan for a romantic retreat. They would have helped to clarify, for example, a tantalising reference to a scheme that Cozens had laid out in a letter in November 1777, involving a romantic garden that could have been a stimulus to the writing of the prophetic essay. 'Reserve with care your System of sentimental Gardening', Beckford wrote, 'the time may come perhaps when we shall execute it'.[11]

The similarities to the future Fonthill in the essay to Cozens do not end with the construction of a tower in pursuit of seclusion. Beckford also managed to weave his taste for things medieval into the fabric of his fantasy by providing a description of the sumptuous interior of the building as decorated with armorial bearings, religious images, and priceless objects; he even forecasted the inclusion of a Baronial hall noting that the:

… painted windows of a Hall high above in the Tower will gleam with the light of many tapers and summon us to our evening's repast. We shall ascend the hundred steps which lead to the spacious Hall wainscoted with Cedar, whose arched roof will be strangely sculptured with gothic devices. The pavement is ruddy marble and the seats are painted with achievements, the tall windows are crowded with gorgeous Figures coloured in antient times. Here are Knights, and Sovereigns clad in rich mosaic, Saints, distinguished by their glories and divers quaint forms unintelligible to modern Ages. Above the great window and below the others, is a broad and ample Gallery inclosed with gilt Lattices and supported by thin wasted pillars fretted with scrupulous dexterity. The Doors of old oak are large and folded; in the huge Chimney, useless in this Season, will be placed grotesque vases of antique china filled with Tube roses and on the Gallery you will find stout coffers of Cedar whose laborious carvings will amuse you for some moments. Open them and you will discover, robes of state, rich chalices and censers, glistening apparel, coral rosaries and uncouth Trinkets, the treasure of the imaginary Lady of the Tower (p. 31).

At this very early stage of his life, Beckford was also exhibiting a strongly romantic characteristic in the way his imaginings tended toward concrete realization. His tendency to particularise bears a resemblance to Blake whose quest for 'strong and better lineaments' gave his own art a distinctive quality. But the character of Beckford's imaginings suggest an even stronger relationship with Keats, since he tended to transport himself imaginatively in order to indulge his senses more fully. In the dream-state developed in this essay, for example, Beckford inevitably paused to savour the pleasing appeal of the Baronial hall as Keats did later in the 'The Eve of St Agnes': 'We shall gaze at the Objects in our sight, admire the rich imagery of the plate, the tapers flaming with the wind and diffusing so grand a lustre about the Hall and all its barbarous magnificence' (p. 32). Turning to the landscape setting for his imaginary tower, he continued: 'Every object will convey to us some agreeable sensation, the richness of the Herbage which we tread, the bleating of the sheep that graze it, the contentment and innocent hilarity of those that tend them and the vivacity of the Birds that flying from bough to bough and warbling upon every spray, seem to revel with the rest of nature in the beams of the morning Sun … .' (p. 34). Finally, in the midst of this landscape of imagination stood one of the most important ingredients of his later creation—the ruined Monastery, a germinal element in the Fonthill plan: 'The shadows cast by the declining Sun on the meads beneath and the reflection of a ruined Monastery in the water at this hour when the Merit of every little circumstance is enhanced, are exquisitely agreeable. A rising ground on the other side covered with inclosures, whose hedges are filled with Broom in blossom and a little Glen shaded with Underwood where the stream loses itself and gurgles unseen terminate the prospect characterised by a calmness and serenity that will sooth[e] our minds' (p. 37). More than twenty years would pass before the young Beckford's preoccupation with sensory appeal, love of unspoiled nature and the aesthetic qualities of the religious experience would be realised in another, more dramatic artistic form, but it is evident that the groundwork was laid for it at this early stage of his life.

The impact of Cozens on Beckford is also evident in two additional writings of this period: *The Long Story* (published as *The Vision* in 1930) and *Dreams, Waking Thoughts and Incidents*, both of which were addressed to the artist. 'Your approbation', he wrote to Cozens, 'is the approbation of a Multitude. It is all I desire and all I seek for in venturing to commit to writing the inspirations of my Fancy, those pleasing Dreams in which perhaps consist the happiest moments of the Life of WILLIAM BECKFORD'.[12] *The Long Story* seems to be an extension of the prophetic essay-letter to Cozens, carrying forward some of the same romantic subject matter of dream fantasy expressive of the search for prelapsarian innocence and voluptuous seclusion. It is an initiation story, which plays out Beckford's own desire at this time for self-determination, which he finds in the interior world of imagination. At one point in the story, the narrator seeks refuge with the beautiful Nouronihar in a sequestered cave, which turns out to be a sumptuous apartment carved in rock of yellow jasper and lit by a myriad of crystal lamps which engulf the room in a continuous glow of evening light:

> The pavement was intirely covered with mats of the nicest workmanship, on which some skillful artist had imitated fruits and flowers with so much success that at first sight they could not be distinguished from bunches of real ones.… A pile of aromatic wood, neatly cleft, was placed by the side of a cheerful fire, fed with the same fuel and three large

baskets heaped with cocoa nuts and all the variety of fruits the valleys produced stood on the other side. The fountain I heard in the dark trickled from a nook in the interior grot and was received in a cavity on the brink of which were placed a variety of clear crystal vases, some empty, others filled with cinnamon and wild roses in full bloom.[13]

As the storm rages in the valley outside, these two delicate beings enjoy the 'perfect security' of their cell. The story, in short, constitutes the Beckfordian dream of separation from the kinds of responsibilities that were being imposed upon him. Instead of dabbling in the world of politics, he sought self-realization in the realm of aesthetics—the self-indulgent world of Edgar Allan Poe's theme of the artist as monarch. Beckford desired to 'immure' himself, a word that he and Cozens shared frequently together, which expressed his own solipsistic longing for seclusion and private happiness and which would ultimately lead him to his own palace of art at Fonthill.

Dreams, Waking Thoughts and Incidents demonstrates Cozens's influence in other significant ways. In this early work, Beckford appears to be purposely appealing to the reader's eye, as we have seen in his early letters from Switzerland.[14] By now, however, his writing style is more developed and displays an even stronger alliance with picturesque aesthetics. Page after page of the book demonstrates an eye eager for colour, lights and shades, surface textures, distant lines, perspectives and picture-like views. 'Beyond, in the centre of this striking theatre', he wrote from Bonn, 'rises a romantic assemblage of distant mountains, crowned with ruins of castles, whose turrets, but faintly seen, were just such as you have created to compleat a prospect' (p. 68). His picturesque orientation also explains why he reveals in *Dreams* his partiality for seeing objects in the 'dubious visionary light' of dusk, and why in the fashion of the picturesque theorists he is consistently drawn to the paintable qualities of rough, rugged surfaces and irregular lines. Nor is it a coincidence that his own descriptions are frequently linked to the works of famous painters, so that irregular hills, clumps of cypress and pastoral cottages, become the ingredients for a scene that 'Zuccarelli loved to paint', or rocks and grottoes 'half lost in thickets from which rise craggy pinnacles crowned by mouldering towers' constitute 'just such scenery as Polemburg and Peter de Laer introduce in their paintings'. Aside from its psychological interest, *Dreams, Waking Thoughts, and Incidents* remains one of the best illustrations of 'literary picturesque' to be produced in the declining years of the eighteenth century with its heavy emphasis on visual imagery and pictorial composition.

While Cozens was an important influence, Beckford's European travels promoted his artistic interests even further in support of the development that led to Fonthill, particularly his visit to the Grande Chartreuse. Having read the life of St Bruno, the founding father of this Carthusian monastery, and inspired by Thomas Gray's poem on the subject, Beckford made an excursion to this remote site in 1778. Once there, he admitted to its profound effect on him: 'It is more wonderfully wild than I can describe, or even you can imagine. It has possessed me to such a degree, that I can at present neither think, speak, nor write upon any other subject'.[15] The details of Bruno's life obviously struck a responsive chord in Beckford. Bruno was a man of noble descent and of great wealth. Known for his remarkable qualities of mind and for being 'poetical, singular, and visionary', he became disenchanted with the world and the 'charms of society', thereafter seeking retirement from it in claustral life. In short, Bruno's biography mirrored many of Beckford's own longings and feelings about himself at this time with which he easily identified.

Beckford's ownership of a sister monastery in ruins on one of his properties in England, called Witham Abbey, promoted an immediate bond with the resident monks who urged him to preserve Witham: 'The Secretary, almost with tears in his eyes, beseeched me to revere these consecrated edifices, and to preserve their remains for the sake of St Hugo, their canonised Prior. I replied greatly to his satisfaction; and then declaimed so much in favour of Saint Bruno, and the holy prior of Witham, that the good fathers grew exceedingly delighted with the conversation, and made me promise to remain some days with them' (p. 217).

The Grande Chartreuse appears to have captured Beckford's imagination partly because it represented a realization of his dream of protective security apart from the vicissitudes of the world. But there was also a strong aesthetic attraction. The Grande Chartreuse symbolised the fusion of religion and art in its visual appeal and evocation of feelings of awe that Beckford would recreate at Fonthill. As he examined the interior of the monastery, he was deeply affected by its ambience as he passed from the chapel 'in which two altars with lamps burning before them, on each side of a lofty portal' to the 'grand coved hall, adorned with historical paintings of St Bruno's life and the portraits of all the Generals of the order'. It was a setting he would not forget. 'I could, in some moments', he wrote, 'fancy myself capable of plunging into the horrors of a desart, and foregoing all the vanities and delights of the world, to secure my memory so sublime a consecration' (p. 218). The internal scenic effects also had an enormous appeal to him when during a service he observed: 'The illumination of so many tapers, striking on the shrines, censers, and pillars of polished jasper, sustaining the canopy of the altar produced a wonderful effect; and, as the rest of the chapel was visible only by the faint external light admitted from above, the splendor and dignity of the altar was inconceivable … the sparkling of several lamps of chased silver, that hung from the roofs, and the gleaming of nine huge tapers … began to be visible, just as I left the chapel' (pp. 219-20).

Besides the monastery itself, the remote and sublime setting in which it was located presented another unforgettable experience. At one point, as he explored the external grounds, he witnessed an event involving the approach of storm clouds and their modifying effect on the surrounding landscape. It became an ecstatic moment that had such a potent effect on him that he re-created it in prose:

> … Escaping from the courts and cloisters of the monastery, all hushed in stillness, [I] ascended a green knoll, which several antient pines marked with their fantastic shadows: there, leaning against one of their trunks, I lifted up my eyes to the awful barrier of surrounding mountains, discovered by the trembling silver light of the moon, shooting directly on the woods which fringed their acclivities. The lawns, the vast woods, the steep

descents, the precipices, the torrents, lay all extended beneath, softened by a pale blueish haze, that alleviated, in some measure, the stern prospect of the rocky promontories above, wrapped in dark shadows. The sky was of the deepest azure; innumerable stars were distinguished with unusual clearness from this elevation, many of which twinkled behind the fir-trees edging the promontories. White, grey, and darkish clouds came marching towards the moon, that shone full against a range of cliffs, which lift themselves far above the others. The hoarse murmur of the torrent, throwing itself from the distant wildernesses into the gloomy vales, was mingled with the blast that blew from the mountains.

It increased. The forests began to wave, black clouds rose from the north, and, as they fleeted along, approached the moon, whose light they shortly extinguished. A moment of darkness succeeded: the gust was chill and melancholy; it swept along the desert, and then subsiding, the vapours began to pass away, and the moon returned: the grandeur of the scene was renewed, and its imposing solemnity was increased by her presence. Inspiration was in every wind; I followed some impulse, which drove me to the summit of the mountains before me; and there, casting a look on the whole extent of wild woods and romantic precipices, thought of the days of St. Bruno: I eagerly contemplated every rock, that formerly might have met his eyes; drank of the spring which tradition says he was wont to drink of; and ran to every withered pine, whose appearance bespoke a remote antiquity, and beneath which, perhaps, the Saint had reposed himself, when worn with vigils, or possessed with the sacred spirit of his institutions. It was midnight: the convent bell tolled; for the most solemn hour of prayer was arrived. I cannot, nor would I, attempt to unfold to you, in prose, half the strange things, of which I thought; and which, I seemed to see, during this wild excursion (pp. 224-5).

Beckford left after a few days, but the total experience of the Grande Chartreuse, the vision of a secluded monastery set in Alpine scenery, was forever imprinted on his mind, providing substance to the dream he had shared with Cozens. It was one of those 'spots of time', as Wordsworth would later describe the indelible personal experience. Even in the latter years of his life he underscored its importance to him: 'There never was a finer field for poetry—a more striking scene. I have a vivid recollection of its grand solitudes'.[16]

While travelling in the years that followed, Beckford's artistic interests and ideas began to mature. His grand tour of Europe, of which *Dreams, Waking Thoughts and Incidents* is a record, is a case in point. There are times in this work when Beckford combines pictorial accent with a poetic sensibility linking him in another vital way to the full-blown Romanticism that was emerging in Europe and in his own country. If Beckford had the facility for portraying with accuracy the genuine aspect of things, he also began to merge the exterior world with the interior landscape of the self. There are occasions in *Dreams* when he does not stop with a mere literal transcription of objective reality, but goes beyond to render the mood and feeling associated with it. There is a sense, as Richard Garnett once pointed out, in which some of Beckford's pictures become 'equally objective and subjective ... brilliantly clear in outline ... yet steeped in the rich hues of his own peculiar feeling'.[17] Beckford's sunsets, in particular, partake of this combination of pictorial and emotional values. Whether the closing scenes of day are described in terms of a final blush of crimson in a darkening sky, or as the last sunbeams purpling the sails of ships at rest in the harbour, or as a glow lingering on the verge of a landscape, which slowly fades into a variety of warm hues, and then into a deeper, more melancholy blue—these scenes, with their emphasis on colour, take their meaning from the feeling observer, the self actively blended with the scene.

This shift from topographical description to the landscape of sensibility can also be seen in the paintings that John Robert Cozens, the son of Alexander, made for him on his second Grand Tour in 1782. Beckford commissioned these works as a pictorial record of this journey. Recent research has shown that their importance as a group of paintings lies in the extent to which they reflected Beckford's own personal taste since he exercised considerable control over the subjects selected and the style of the finished works.[18] The evidence indicates that the end result was a collaborative effort between the patron and the artist involving ultimately a series of ninety-four watercolours. Cozens, in other words, modified his own style to illustrate Beckford's response to a visual experience, resulting in an unusual extension of *ut pictura poesis*. The diminishment of the distance between Beckford's descriptions and the medium of paint called for extraordinary empathy and produced an advancement in Cozens's work that may have had an impact on the evolution of English landscape art. Cozens employed colour enrichment and sometimes storm scenes to capture Beckford's emotional responses and growing taste for sublime effects as in the case of a painting entitled *Between Brixen and Bolzano: Storm* or the dramatically realised *Storm over Padua* with its depiction of lightning over the city of St Anthony, Beckford's chosen patron saint. It is evident that the placid landscape of Claude Lorrain was no longer sufficient; Beckford's growing interest in dramatic effects required a more intense transaction, one that elicited pleasurable emotions of awe in the face of nature in a state of turbulence. Beckford's explanation was that 'a thunder-storm gave character to a landscape' [19] revealing his interest in emotional impact and his shift toward the agenda of Romanticism.

That the formulation of the aesthetics of the picturesque and the sublime deepened during this period in Beckford's mind is also apparent in his interest in Giovanni Piranesi, particularly in the artist's architectural fantasies displayed in the *Carceri d'invenzione* (*Imaginary Prisons*). Beckford's fascination with Piranesi may have started with his father who collected the dramatic prints of this artist. When Beckford visited Venice and encountered the Bridge of Sighs, it was Piranesi who came immediately to his mind, as he explained in *Dreams, Waking Thoughts and Incidents*:

> I left the courts; and, stepping into my bark, was rowed down a canal, over which the lofty vaults of the palace cast a tremendous shade. Beneath these fatal waters, the dungeons I have been speaking of are situated. There, the wretches lie marking the sound of the oars, and counting the free passage of every gondola. Above, a marble bridge, of bold, majestic architecture, joins the highest part of the prisons to the secret galleries of the palace;

from whence criminals are conducted over the arch, to a cruel and mysterious death. I shuddered whilst passing below, and believe it is not without cause, this structure is named PONTE DEI SOSPIRI. Horrors and dismal prospects haunted my fancy upon my return. I could not dine in peace, so strongly was my imagination affected; but, snatching my pencil, I drew chasms and subterraneous hollows, the domain of fear and torture, with chains, rocks, wheels, and dreadful engines, in the style of Piranesi (pp. 102-3).

On another occasion, as he approached the town of Bonn and was struck by a set of irregular mountains that bounded his view, he imagined that he was transported to their summits and there, he wrote: 'I shot swiftly from rock to rock, and built castles, in the style of Piranesi, upon most of their pinnacles. The magnificence and variety of my aerial towers, hindered my thinking the way long' (p. 67).

Piranesi, who first published the *Carceri* in 1745, defied the artistic conventions of the time by giving full play to his imagination in creating scenes of gigantic architectural proportions and spatial complexity that dwarfed the human figures within a landscape of the mind. Highly original in their display of structural forms that overwhelm and control the viewer, these innovative architectural scenes derive their reality from the realm of dreams and nightmare. The confinement of prison is not simply visually realised but presented so dramatically that it is experienced as both physical and psychic imprisonment. The enormous masonry forms resist penetration and contribute to the heavy weight of the experience; the dominance of curvilinear arches symbolises the state of oppressive entrapment; and the series of stairs presented at various levels add to the spectator's deep sense of claustrophobia by leading nowhere. Significantly, the second edition, published in the early 1760s, Piranesi made even darker in tone with the addition of shadows, wheels, pulleys, winches and other instruments of torture, modifications that prefigured the development of the Gothic novel. Here Beckford could experience the sublime in another form besides the Grande Chartreuse and the melancholy works of Thomas Gray. Piranesi's art represented the new aesthetics of pleasing terror that Edmund Burke defined in *The Origin of Our Ideas of the Sublime and the Beautiful* in 1756, particularly in the emphasis on obscurity, vastness, and magnificence, which the theorist identified as constituent elements of the sublime. The appeal of Piranesi's art had to do with the way it fostered a freer expression of imagination by rendering explicit the images of fear and the aesthetic power of darkness. It was art freed from the shackles of the conventional tenets of artistic taste in the eighteenth century, which would naturally appeal to Beckford's own proto-Romantic imagination. Moreover, behind Piranesi's theatrical display was also a psychological dimension that must have had a catalytic effect on Beckford's own introspective art. The subterranean passages and web-like complexities of Piranesi's architectural dreams are revelatory of the repressed self finding expression in the world of dream while simultaneously recording the nature of the forces working against that freedom.

The influence of Piranesi's potent architectural imagery on Beckford can also be seen in a description of a Christmas party held at Fonthill in December 1781, following the first

European tour. For the occasion, Beckford hired Philippe Jacques de Loutherbourg, the famed scene designer and master of lighting effects, to create a *mise en scène* that would bathe the rooms in a 'necromantic light' producing a mysterious and other-worldly effect. One of the rooms in Fonthill Splendens was called the Egyptian room which Beckford described in terms remarkably similar to Piranesi's prison scenes:

> The solid Egyptian Hall looked as if hewn out of a living rock—the line of apartments and apparently endless passages extending from it on either side were all vaulted—an interminable stair case, which when you looked down it—appeared as deep as the well in the pyramid—and when you looked up—was lost in vapour, led to suites of stately apartments ... the mystic look, the vastness, the intricacy of this vaulted labyrinth occasioned so bewildering an effect that it became impossible for any one to define—at the moment—where he stood, where he had been, or to whither he was wandering— such was the confusion—the perplexity so many illuminated storys of infinitely varied apartments gave rise to. It was, in short, the realization of romance in its most extravagant intensity. No wonder such scenery inspired the description of the Halls of Eblis.[20]

What happened shortly after this unusual Christmas gathering has been told many times: Beckford left Fonthill for his London residence; and sometime in January, 1782, with the visions of the festival still swirling in his head, he composed his masterwork *Vathek*. In this tale, Beckford's dissident imagination frequently found expression in strange architectural structures of no known human order that one might experience in a dream. At the very beginning of the story, Beckford tells us that the Caliph Vathek constructed an immense tower of fifteen hundred stairs where 'he cast his eyes below, and beheld men not larger than pismires; mountains, than shells; and cities, than beehives'.[21] The perspective here is Piranesian, with the created effect of spatial immensity designed to promote a sense of awe and power. Piranesi's visual idiom seems even more obvious near the end of the story, when Vathek visits the vast ruins of Istakhar with his mistress Nouronihar:

> A death-like stillness reigned over the mountain and through the air. The moon dilated on a vast platform, the shades of the lofty columns which reached from the terrace almost to the clouds. The gloomy watch-towers, whose number could not be counted, were covered by no roof; and their capitals, of an architecture unknown in the records of the earth, served as an asylum for the birds of night.... On the right rose the watch-towers, ranged before the ruins of an immense palace, whose walls were embossed with various figures. In front stood forth the colossal forms of four creatures, composed of the leopard and the griffin, and though but of stone, inspired emotions of terror.... [As they proceeded into the Palace of Eblis] the Caliph and Nouronihar beheld each other with amazement, at finding themselves in a place, which though roofed with a vaulted ceiling, was so spacious and lofty, that, at first, they took it for an immeasurable plain. But their eyes, at length, growing familiar to the grandeur of the surrounding objects, they extended their view to those at distance; and discovered rows of columns and arcades,

which gradually diminished, till they terminated in a point radiant as the sun (pp. 107; 109).

There are many threads of influence in the creative fabric of *Vathek*, but Piranesi's surrealistic vision reinforced the distinctive visual quality of Beckford's literary vocabulary, and was a powerful stimulus to Beckford's own architectural visualizations which would ultimately find expression in the creation of Fonthill Abbey.

Beckford's visit to Portugal in 1794 also played an important role in shaping the interest that led to Fonthill. At that time, he saw the Gothic monasteries of Alcobaça and Batalha, an experience that led over forty years later to the publication of his *Recollections of an Excursion to the Monasteries of Alcobaça and Batalha*. The first monastery he saw was Alcobaça. 'The first sight of this regal monastery is very imposing', he wrote, 'and the picturesque, well-wooded and well-watered village, out of the quiet bosom of which it appears to rise, relieves the mind from a sense of oppression the huge domineering bulk of the conventual buildings inspire'.[22] Once inside the building, he found it gloomy and somewhat austere, but he was affected by the soft light that relieved the darkness 'where the perpetual lamps burning before the high altar diffused a light most solemn and religious' (2: 273). The quality of subdued light became a sustained interest throughout his lifetime and a dominant element in the interior designs at Fonthill and in Lansdown Tower in Bath. It was the light of repose and the 'true light of devotion', as he explained in his later years to Cyrus Redding. 'It is an excitement in itself to solemn thoughts and prayer—the dim religious light of the sanctuary'. He also believed that it was the interior light most characteristic of the older Gothic cathedrals, observing that the 'Bath abbey-church is of the later Gothic—too light for such an effect'. [23]

Here Beckford accented the religious associations of subdued light, but as a young man he was strongly drawn to the aesthetic qualities of the interior lighting effects of cathedrals he visited during his travels. Although he never embraced Roman Catholicism, he felt that this religion devoted more attention to the aesthetics of the interior world of the cathedral than did the Protestant religion. Comparing the two religions, he once told an artist friend, 'the one is the opera and the other the dress rehearsal'. His fascination with the Roman church was always more secular than religious despite attempts on the part of some of his contemporaries to link him to it. In response to an accusation in the *Sunday Times* that he had 'apostatised to the Catholic religion' while in Portugal, he wrote: I plead guilty of almost unbounded extravagance, but not of having apostatised in Portugal, or any where else. I never took the trouble. At Lisbon I warmly admired the picturesque pomp of its patriarchal Church & felt its sublime music at my heart's core, but between a *professor* & an *amateur* there exists an essential difference. I never belonged to the former *description God knows*.[24] It was simply good theatre; the pageantry of religion that he indulged as art. Anglicanism was too austere and coldly intellectual to appeal to Beckford's artistic temperament, as he once made clear: 'Gracious God! the Roman Catholic religion is filled with fine stage effects, glittering crosses, censers, mitres, crosiers, dresses, candles, pictures, banners, processions, perfumes, dolls, and music from the deep tones of the organ to the delightful squeakings of the pope's eunuchs'.[25] It was for this reason that he sought paintings that depicted the devotional imagery of the Christian Church and such Renaissance panels, for example, as the triptych attributed to Nardon Penicaud representing in three panels the *Descent from the Cross, the Entombment,* and *Christ in the Garden,* which he thought about selling in 1822 (Christie catalogue, lot 101) but withdrew when the sale was cancelled and kept for the rest of his life believing that it was too important to leave his hands.

Besides the lighting effects at Alcobaça, the apartment where he stayed had walls that were naked, but 'the ceiling was gilt and painted, the floor spread with Persian carpets of the finest texture, and the tables in rich velvet petticoats, decked with superb ewers and basins of chased silver, and towels bordered with point-lace of a curious antique pattern' (2: 275). Elsewhere, there were gilded ornaments, effigies of kings, a full-size portrait of St Thomas à Becket, a glistening sacristy, carvings in rock crystal, and golden reliquaries, all of which were to constitute the antiquarian and religious motifs of Fonthill.

Proceeding to Batalha, Beckford again was led to comment on the picturesque quality of the Gothic architecture, noting 'the great church, with its rich cluster of abbatial buildings, buttresses, and pinnacles, and fretted spires, towering in all their pride, and marking the ground with deep shadows that appeared interminable' (2: 289). After passing through a sculptured gateway, he stood in front of the grand western façade of the church with a portal fifty feet in height, an awe-inspiring sight that may well have inspired the western entrance to Fonthill Abbey that was fifteen feet shorter but equally impressive. 'As soon as we drew near', he wrote, 'the valves of a huge oaken door were thrown open, and we entered the nave, which reminded me of Winchester in form of arches and mouldings, and of Amiens in loftiness' (2: 297).

A dominant scenic effect that Beckford would strive to create within the interior of Fonthill was once again the ambience of subdued light that would accent a sumptuous interior scene, utilising stained glass, drapery and candlelight to achieve a heightened emotional response. He had observed this play of light and colour before at the Grande Chartreuse. The transmutation of light in the nave of the cathedral at Batalha into rich golden hues seemed to have had a profound impact on his imagination as well: 'No tapestry, however rich—no painting, however vivid, could equal the gorgeousness of tint, the splendour of the golden and ruby light which streamed forth from the long series of stained windows: it played flickering about in all directions, on pavement and on roof, casting over every object myriads of glowing mellow shadows ever in undulating motion, like the reflection of branches swayed to and fro by the breeze. We all partook of these gorgeous tints—the white monastic garments of my conductors seemed as it were embroidered with the brightest flowers of paradise, and our whole procession kept advancing invested with celestial colours'. (2: 297-8).

Batalha provided another connection to the different stages of development of Fonthill in Beckford's mind. Following his attendance at the cathedral service at Batalha, he visited the mausoleum where he saw the effigies of John I and Philippa on their tombs in the middle of the chapel, along with their children. Philippa was the granddaughter of Edward III to whom Beckford would dedicate a wing of Fonthill. This experience very likely inspired him to consider incorporating his own tomb in the early plans of the Fonthill design. He was also deeply impressed by the armorial bearings that displayed historical associations with English nobility, which became another constituent element of Fonthill. 'I withdrew from the contemplation of these tombs with reluctance', he explained, 'every object in the chapel which contains them being so pure in taste, so harmonious in colour; every armorial device, every mottoed lambel, so tersely and correctly sculptured, associated also so closely with historical and English recollections—the garter, the leopards, the fleur-de-lis, "from haughty Gallia torn"; the Plantagenet cast of the whole chamber conveyed home to my bosom a feeling so interesting, so congenial, that I could hardly persuade myself to move away, though my reverend conductors began to show evident signs of impatience' (2: 299). Batalha, in short, impressed Beckford to such an extent that the first design of Fonthill as a residence was based on the monastery, and when that plan was rejected for another, he maintained the connection by incorporating three great stained-glass windows in the Octagon room that were copied from windows at Batalha.

One other formative influence that fuelled Beckford's architectural ideas was the house he leased in Sintra after he left the monasteries of Alcobaça and Batalha. This residence, called Monserrate, was owned by a London merchant by the name of Gerard de Visme who built it in 1789. It continues to this day to have historical importance because it is considered to be the earliest example of Gothic revival architecture in Portugal. Beckford was attracted to the place because of its elevation, which permitted expanded views of the countryside surrounding it. He once described it as 'a beautiful Claude-like place, surrounded by a most enchanting country'.[26] But its medieval architectural style also had a strong appeal to him, flanked on two sides by twin towers with a principal entrance that led to an octagonal room, permitting extended internal vistas looking down the wings radiating from it, a principal feature that Beckford would incorporate at Fonthill. While in residence there, Beckford made his own improvements in the house and the gardens. He liked the place well enough to acquire it when de Visme died in 1798.[27] This was the site that inspired Byron to pen some reflections of Beckford when he saw the house and gardens in a neglected state in 1809:

> There thou too, Vathek! England's wealthiest son,
> Once form'd thy Paradise, as not aware
> When wanton Wealth her mightiest deeds hath done,
> Meek Peace voluptuous lures was ever wont to shun.
>
> Here didst thou dwell, here schemes of pleasure plan,
> Beneath yon mountain's ever beauteous brow:
> But now, as if a thing unblest by Man,
> Thy fairy dwelling is as lone as Thou!

> Here giant weeds a passage scarce allow
> To Halls deserted, portals gaping wide:
> Fresh lessons to the thinking bosom, how
> Vain are the pleasaunces on earth supplied;
> Swept into wrecks anon by Time's ungentle tide!

Sir Francis Cook acquired this estate in 1856, and with the aid of an English architect orientalised the exterior in a Moorish design. The interior, however, remained unchanged and continues today to be in the character of Beckford's residency.[28]

While Beckford's early visual training and travel experiences helped to forge his artistic interests, there were other critical events in his personal life, to which Byron alluded in the above lines, that led to the decision to devote himself to the development of Fonthill. It was during his tour of England in 1779 that he met and developed almost instantly a 'strange wayward passion' for William Courtenay, the feminine eleven-year-old son of Lord Courtenay of Powderham Castle. Initially, the relationship appeared to be innocent enough, falling more in the category of adoration fantasy. In the end, however, it would be a fateful moment in Beckford's life that would ultimately lead to his social ostracism in England and affect the way he led the rest of his life. 'I grew sensible', Beckford wrote, 'there was a pleasure in loving something besides oneself and felt there would be more luxury in dying for him than living for the rest of the Universe'.[29] Following the initial contact, Beckford experienced constant anxiety in his efforts to keep in touch with the 'little C'.; he was also frequently agitated by the efforts of his family to dissolve what they felt was an unhealthy relationship.

While the relationship with Courtenay has been subject to varying interpretations, there can be little doubt about its profound emotional impact. It marked an awakening of latent homosexual feelings of which Beckford became fully aware a year later, when on his Grand Tour he became involved in the decadence of Venetian high society, largely through the help of the adventuress Countessa d'Orsini-Rosenberg and her lover Count Benincasa; and, before long, was drawn into a homosexual entanglement with a young member of the aristocratic Cornaro family which left him in a feverish state of mind. Years later he attempted to explain the relationship in discreet terms as a 'passion of the mind—resembling those generous attachments we venerate in ancient history, and holy writ. What David felt towards the brother of his heart, the son of Saul'.[30] But the immediate impact on him was traumatic; and, for the rest of the tour, he was haunted by one object: 'One image alone possesses me and pursues me in a terrible way. In vain do I throw myself into Society—this image forever starts up before me. In vain do I try to come up to the great expectations formed of me—my words are cut short and I am halted in mid-career. This unique object is all I hope for—and I am dead to everything else'.[31]

By the time he reached Naples in November, he had worked himself into such a state that he could no longer contain his feelings and unloaded all his emotional freight upon the shoulders of a new friend and confidante Lady Hamilton, the first wife of Sir William Hamilton, the English ambassador to the Court of Naples. Beckford stayed with the Hamiltons for a month during which time Catherine Hamilton acted as a positive influence; and, disapproving completely of his Venetian affair, she made him aware of the dangers he might be led into if he continued it. On his return trip to the 'pestilential air' of Venice, she pleaded with him to 'resist nobly a Sentiment that in your soul you cannot approve, and which if indulged must end in your misery and in the destruction of a Mother that dotes on you'.[32] In Venice at the end of December, he wrote assurances that he would not yield to the 'insinuating whisper of a soft but criminal delight',[33] and she answered with a letter imploring him to continue the resistance: 'Every day you will find the struggle less—the important struggle! What is it for? No less than *honor*, *reputation* and all that an honest and noble Soul holds most dear, while Infamy, eternal infamy (my soul freezes while I write the word) attends the giving way to the soft alluring of a criminal passion'.[34] Beckford surmounted the temptation, because by 10 January 1781, he had abandoned his 'Venetian state' and with it the 'fatal connection'.

There followed another complication in his life at this time, involving an intense relationship with the unhappily married Louisa Pitt-Rivers, wife of Beckford's cousin, Peter. She was another confidante with whom he could share his deepest feelings and anxieties. In reality, however, the relationship was lopsided. Louisa was desperately in love with Beckford, which he encouraged but never to the extent that would involve an equivalent commitment. Still, the liaison between the wealthy heir of Fonthill and his cousin's wife became the source of considerable rumours among the social set that added to the alarm of the dowagers at Fonthill and increased concern about Beckford's behavioural patterns.

If the culmination of the emotional experiences with Courtenay, Cornaro, and Louisa did not wear him thin mentally, the prospect of entering public life did. As he neared majority in 1781, he began to exhibit increasing signs of psychological stress over the thought of embarking on a political career as his mother had expected. He was also faced with a major financial threat from Chancery proceedings involving a bastard brother which he would have to address before his twenty-first birthday, or risk losing control of some profitable sugar estates in Jamaica. 'I am fated, it seems', he wrote to Lady Hamilton, 'to return to a country where sober, sullen realities must put ["my happy fantastic imaginations"] all to flight—where I have no friend like you to sustain my spirits and receive my ideas except Mr. Cozens…. Not an animal comprehends me. At this disastrous moment, too, when every individual is abandoned to terrors and anxieties, which way can I turn myself? Public affairs I dare not plunge into. My health is far too wavering. Whilst I write my hand trembles like that of a paralytic Chinese. Strange colours swim before my eyes and sounds keep ringing in my ears for which I can hardly account'.[35]

Increasingly, Beckford turned to writing as an escape from the sullen realities he knew he would have to face. In fact, the period following his twenty-first birthday on 29 September 1781, marked a particularly fertile literary phase of his life despite the psychological strain. Never again would he write at such a productive pace. While *Vathek* was composed in a great rush in January 1782, he did spend a portion of the spring refining it. In the same year, he began writing a long Eastern narrative called the *Histoire de Darianoc, jeune homme du pays de Gou-Gou*, readied *Dreams, Waking Thoughts and Incidents* for the press, and wrote to Samuel Henley that additional 'Arabian Tales' were springing up like mushrooms all over the downs of Fonthill. Before the winter season ended, he had embarked on the *Episodes of Vathek*.

But when he attempted to place five hundred quarto copies of *Dreams, Waking Thoughts and Incidents* on the market in March 1783, Mrs Beckford and several members of the family moved in and forced him to order their withdrawal and confiscate most of the copies. To publish a book which began with the words, 'Shall I tell you my dreams?—To give an account of my time, is doing, I assure you, but little better. Never did there exist a more ideal being', seemed to run counter to the *gravitas* expected of a future member of the House of Commons. The suppression of an important literary work, however, was not enough to satisfy Mrs Beckford; she took even sterner action to ensure her son's entrance into the political world by arranging his marriage to Lady Margaret Gordon, the daughter of the fourth Earl of Aboyne. On 5 May 1783, the couple recited their vows under the mother's watchful eye.

Beckford's marriage was a triumph for the family; and it seemed for a time that he was ready to settle down to the practical affairs of life. He even wrote to his family friend Lord Chancellor Thurlow in the following spring that he was inclined to sit in Parliament; and, before the year was over, he had obtained the seat for Wells in Somerset. But the romance with politics was short-lived. He had no taste for sitting through the tedious proceedings of the House and sought freedom from these responsibilities by means of a peerage with the title of 'Lord Beckford of Fonthill'. He tried to obtain it through Thurlow and might have been successful had it not been for the scandal that erupted after a visit to Powderham Castle, Devonshire, where William Courtenay resided. Following his stay there with Lady Margaret in 1784, a series of stories began to circulate about a sexual liaison between Beckford and Courtenay which spread to the London newspapers by the end of November. One of the most damning reports appeared in the *Morning Herald*: 'The rumour concerning a *Grammatical mistake of Mr. B--*and the *Hon. Mr. C--*, in regard to the genders, we hope for the honour of Nature originates in *Calumny*! For, however depraved the being must be, who can propagate such reports without foundation, we must wish such a being exists, in preference to characters, who, regardless of Divine, Natural and Human Law, sink themselves below the lowest class of brutes in the most *preposterous* rites'.[36] The instigator was Lord Loughborough, husband of William's aunt Charlotte Courtenay, and a man who harboured a personal dislike for Beckford. Loughborough considered Thurlow his major political rival and was jealous of Beckford's potential for a peerage with the Lord Chancellor's support. Destroying Beckford would be a way of undermining his political enemy as well.

While the charges were never substantiated, they effectively eliminated the sought-after barony and marked Beckford as a pederast for the rest of his life. Throughout the furore of these reports, Beckford protested his innocence. He solemnly declared to both friends and relatives that the sordid tales were groundless, but he never publicly refuted the charges. The result was a shadow of suspicion that persisted in the mind of the public. From time to time, the subject would emerge in the press, reminding the readers of Beckford's 'depravity', as in the case of a piece that appeared in *The Monthly Visitor* in October 1797: 'When the character of an individual has been publicly understood as degraded to the foulest practices of the most foul and unnatural *times*, it is not sufficient to assign such a belief to the efforts of "detraction", "malice", "ignorance", and "ingratitude", it is necessary to prove, that individuals have been slanderous and ungrateful—that a nation has been ignorant and malicious. By a sophism which our laws permit—TRUTH IS A LIBEL; and we dare not explain to the public, the wretched enormities of certain men'.[37] With the Powderham event unanswered, Beckford became a marked figure in British society. It began the process of marginalization that has prevented him from being taken seriously even to the present day.

As the word of the 'Courtenay affair' spread throughout England, Beckford plunged into despair which soon gave way to bitterness. Reaching a breaking point, he finally decided, at the suggestion of his wife, to return to the 'tranquil pure atmosphere' of Vevy on the shores of Lake Geneva where he had found solace before. He was there less than a year, however, when he suffered another serious setback: the death of Lady Margaret on 26 May 1786, after she had given birth to their second daughter. To Beckford, her death was a severe shock, an abrupt loss of someone he had grown to love and respect. She had been one of the few individuals who stood by him during this very dark period of his life. To make matters worse, when the news of her death reached England, a few newspapers claimed that it was due directly to his brutal treatment of her. It was an unwarranted and gratuitous attack that caused a wound that would never heal. As he wrote to a friend years later: 'You was in Turkey or in Lubberland when the storm raged against me, and when I was stabbed to the heart by the loss of Lady Margaret. And what was the balm poured into my wounds—a set of paragraphs accusing me of having occasioned her death by ill usage. Allowances were to be made for former attacks but none for this; and I will own to you that the recollection of this black stroke fills me with such horror and indignation that I sigh for the pestilential breath of an African serpent to destroy every Englishman who comes in my way'. [38]

It was a traumatic period of Beckford's life. His beloved wife was now gone; his barony had been lost; his mother's political dreams for him were unquestionably dimmed and a major literary work had been suppressed. Mocked by those who did not know him and feeling abandoned by some of his friends and relatives, he spent the next ten years of his life, from 1786 to 1796, on the Continent in virtual exile from England.

It was then during these years that Fonthill began to play a significant role in his life. Chastened by self-examination while abroad and sobered by the grim realities of his early manhood, he began to think that he might make Fonthill his home. Often during his travels, his thoughts would return to his birthplace. 'I have been haunted all night with rural ideas of England', he recorded in his Portuguese journal in 1787, 'the fresh smell of my pines at Fonthill seemed wafted to me in my dreams. The bleating of my sheep and lowing of herds in the deep valley of Lawn Farm faintly sounded in my ears … shall I banish myself forever from these happy scenes of my childhood?'[39] If he were going to be ostracised, he decided it would be on his own terms. Throughout the countryside of this large estate, he could find another challenge to his artistic imagination. It began with a tower as a feature in a landscape, then gradually developed into a work of art on a grand scale with a magnificent Gothic residence as the crown in a well-conceived setting and whose scenic interior, displaying some of the most impressive works of art ever to be gathered in one place, combined with the exterior scenic effects to create a total aesthetic experience that made Fonthill not only a sensation in its day but one of the major contributions to the visual arts in nineteenth-century England.

The Educated Eye

It is important to recognise at the outset that Fonthill began as a landscape design and that any structure that was considered within it, whether a tower or a ruin, was to be a feature of a broader artistic plan. This is not surprising when one considers the important role of landscape architecture as one of the 'sister arts' in eighteenth-century England and the extent to which cultivated gentlemen before Beckford, from Alexander Pope to Horace Walpole, carried out garden experiments on their own estates. Fonthill was also located in an area of such great estates as Stourhead and Longleat which had achieved notoriety as great examples of this art. It is telling of Beckford's interest in gardening that he often purchased land to accommodate his landscape plans, that he continued his gardening and building efforts throughout his later years in Bath, and that he told his first biographer, Cyrus Redding, that his greatest artistic achievement was the creation of the picturesque wilderness about the Abbey.

It is clear that Beckford from a very early age was drawn to the beauty of the natural landscape. The knowledge of painting he obtained as a young man gave him insight into the possibilities of 'nature unadorned' as a subject of pure aesthetic enjoyment. His early travels continued to educate his eye in seeing by providing him with opportunities to analyze European scenery often in relationship to his knowledge of eighteenth-century landscape paintings. As in the case of many of his contemporaries, he appreciated the beauty of the asymmetrical line. Formal patterns and geometric design, he would complain, dulled his senses and 'yawned' his 'soul out'. Although he never formulated a systematic theory of landscape gardening, it is clear from his letters and travel books, where he commented on the gardens of others, and from his own practical experiments, that he believed garden composition should be created by subordinating art to nature, while the natural elements of the layout had to be carefully massed and shaped into a harmonious whole in accordance with the basic principles of composition in painting.

There is evidence that Beckford received some formal training in the principles of architecture and landscape design under the tutorship of Sir William Chambers. It is based on Beckford's own account as he told an artist friend later in life that he was a 'pupil of Sir W. Chambers when he was building Somerset House'.[1] Chambers began work on Somerset House in 1775 and was known to be one of the busiest architects in England at the time, which has led to some dispute over the possibility of having enough time to tutor the young Beckford.[2] Under the circumstances, Chambers contribution to Beckford's architectural education may have been limited, but there is no reason to doubt Beckford's account. There is, furthermore, an additional piece of documentation that Beckford's biographers have overlooked and that is a presentation copy of the second edition of the *Dissertation on Oriental Gardening* (1773) which Chambers gave to Beckford. It contained the inscription 'From the Author, 19th March 1773',[3] which supports the existence of a relationship. Chambers was regarded in England at the time as an important architect whose professional accomplishments led to his appointment as Comptroller of the Works in 1769. Chambers could also have provided additional inspiration for Beckford's later interest in garden design since it was in the seventies when he was expressing his strongly held views on the art of laying out grounds in contradistinction to the work of Lancelot 'Capability' Brown and his followers.

Beckford's knowledge of the principles of architecture developed as he became more widely read in this area and had an opportunity to examine various building styles throughout his travels. Over time, he amassed a respectable collection of books and prints as an academic reference library on this subject. While it would be unrealistic to claim that Beckford's knowledge of architecture ever reached a professional level, he could claim at least a scholarly knowledge of the subject and came to be known as an individual who was quite capable of producing competent architectural drawings. A contemporary architect, who once shared with him a plan for a public building, conveyed his own astonishment at Beckford's understanding of architectural principles. 'I should have thought him', he exclaimed, 'a regular architect! When he saw the ground plans, he told me in a moment the intended size of all the apartments'.[4]

Following the tradition of naturalism in garden design, Beckford criticised the taste illustrated by the formal gardens of the Restoration and supported a freer, more open style of garden planning. When he visited the country house of Count Bentinck in The Hague in 1780, he complained that 'the walks and alleys have all that stiffness and formality our ancestors admired'; and on the road between Amsterdam and Utrecht, he recorded scornfully: 'We beheld no other objects than endless avenues and stiff parterres, scrawled and flourished in patterns, like the embroidery of an old maid's work-bag'.[5]

Seven years later, he discovered examples of a similarly abhorrent architectural style in Portugal. A garden attached to the Pagliavam villa moved him to write: 'A great flat space before the garden-front of the villa is laid out in dismal labyrinths of clipped myrtle, with lofty pyramids rising from them, in the style of that vile Dutch maze planted by King William at Kensington, and rooted up some years ago by King George the Third. Beyond this puzzling ground are several long alleys of stiff dark verdure, called *ruas*, i.e. literally streets, with great propriety, being more close, more formal, and not less dusty than High-Holborn'.[6]

For Beckford excessive art was too fastidious and disciplinary to be pleasing. His typical reaction was that it 'suffocated him'. He felt strongly enough about this subject to make it a central theme in his first published work *Biographical Memoirs of Extraordinary Painters*, where he attacked Dutch and Flemish painters for their strained and artificial mannerisms.[7] He also complained in the opening chapters of *Dreams, Waking Thoughts and Incidents* about the 'whimsical buffoonery of a Dutch imagination', and even chastised Rubens for becoming 'lost in the flounces of the Virgin's drapery.'[8] Behind these criticisms was Beckford's preference for breadth and freedom, which he often found in the natural landscape and sometimes in a garden, like that of the Negroni in Rome. 'There I found, what my soul desired', Beckford wrote, 'thickets of jasmine, and wild spots overgrown with bay; long alleys of cypress totally neglected, and almost impassable through the luxuriance of the vegetation; on every side, antique fragments, vases, sarcophagi, and altars, sacred to the Manes, in deep, shady recesses; which I am certain the Manes must love. The air was filled with the murmurs of water, trickling down basins of porphyry, and losing itself amongst over-grown weeds and grasses. Above the wood, and between its boughs, appeared several domes, and a strange lofty tower'.[9]

In extreme reaction against the formal garden, some eighteenth-century landscapists, particularly Capability Brown and his followers, had laid too much stress on simplicity and smoothness in the garden scene. Beckford disliked both extremes. On this issue he was in agreement with Chambers, who argued in *Dissertation on Oriental Gardening* (1772), that 'neither the artful nor the simple style of gardening is right: the one being too much refined and too extravagant a deviation from nature; the other, like a Dutch picture, an affected adherence to her without choice of judgment'.[10] Beckford clearly disliked gardens designed in the style of Brown, such as the one he saw in Aranjuez in 1795. 'I was sorry to see', he lamented, 'many, very many acres of unmeaning shrubbery, serpentine walks, and clumps of paltry flowers, encroaching upon the wild thickets upon the banks of the Tagus…. The King, the Queen, the favourite, are bitten by the rage of what they fancy to be improvement, and are levelling ground, and smoothing banks, and building rock-work, with pagodas and Chinese railing. The laburnums, weeping willows, and flowering shrubs, which I admired so much seven years ago in all their native luxuriance, are beginning to be trimmed and tortured into what the gardener calls genteel shapes. Even the course of the Tagus has been thwarted, and part of its waters diverted into a broad ditch in order to form an island, flat, swampy, and dotted over with exotic shrubs, to make room for which many a venerable arbele and poplar has been laid low'.[11]

What was essential for a beautiful design, Beckford felt, was a proper mixture of both art and nature. Bare nature often lacked sufficient variety to amuse the spectator, so a limited assistance of art was needed to include in the plan the provocative elements of surprise and contrast. 'No one', Redding once observed, 'understood the force of contrast better than Mr. Beckford'.[12] In the case of the gardens of Aranjuez where nature was bountiful and little art was necessary, Beckford would follow Uvedale Price's dictum of 'knowing where to leave off'. 'If they would but let Aranjuez alone', he argued, 'I should not care. Nature has lavished her with charms most bountifully on this valley; the wild hills which close it in, though barren, are picturesquely-shaped; the Tagus here winds along in the boldest manner, overhung by crooked willows and lofty arbeles; now losing itself in almost impervious thickets, now undermining steep banks, laying rocks bare, and forming irregular coves and recesses; now flowing smoothly through vast tracts of low shrubs, aspens and tamarisks; in one spot edged by the most delicate greensward, in another by beds of mint and a thousand other fragrant herbs'.[13]

Beckford's ideas on the landscape garden were not particularly unique or extraordinary in the 1780s and 1790s. His specific disdain for the formal garden as an illustration of false taste, his belief in the principle that nature must ever be followed, and the view that a good landscapist was essentially a painter were, after all, major themes in the rise and development of the informal garden in the eighteenth century.

In terms of his specific interest in landscape gardening, Beckford was familiar with the works of almost every garden theorist, both French and British, in the seventeenth and eighteenth centuries. Of the books related to gardening theory, some containing his own manuscript notes on the flyleaves, the following were in his libraries at Fonthill and Bath: Batty Langley's *New Principles of Gardening* (1728); A. J. De Lille's *Les Jardins* (1732); J. Serle's *A Plan of Pope's Garden* (1745); William Chambers's *Dissertation on Oriental Gardening* (1773); Joseph Heeley's *Letters on the Beauties of Hagley, Envil and The Leasowes* (1777); Horace Walpole's *Essay on Modern Gardening* (1785); Thomas Whately's *Observations on Modern Gardening* (1793); William Gilpin's *Three Essays: On Picturesque Beauty; on Picturesque Travel; and on Sketching Landscape* (1794); R. P. Knight's *The Landscape* (1794); Humphry Repton's *Sketches and Hints on Landscape Gardening* (1794) and George Mason's *An Essay on Design in Gardening* (1795). This is only a partial list; he owned many others that were equally important in the history of the movement.[14]

Besides these specialised treatises, one of Beckford's interests had always been literary descriptions of Fortunate Isles and other paradisiacal gardens. Not restricting himself to the classics, he also studied the descriptions of legendary gardens in Milton's *Paradise Lost* and Ariosto's *Orlando Furioso*, and the enchanted gardens and palaces in Tasso, Spencer, and Camoens.[15] He used to cite the following passages from Tasso and Milton as direct sources of inspiration for his ideas on garden design:[16]

> Faire trees, high plants, strange herbes and flowrets new,
> Sunshinie hills, dales hid from Phoebus' raies;
> Groves, arbours, mossie caves, at once they view,
> And that which beautie most, most wonder brought,
> No where appear'd the arte which all this wroughte.

> So with the rude, the polisht mingled was
> That natural seemed all and every parte;
> Nature would crafte in counterfeiting pas,
> And imitate her imitator, Arte. [Tasso]

> Flowers, worthy of Paradise, which not nice Art
> In beds and curious knots, but Nature's boon
> Pour'd forth profuse on hill, and dale, and plain,
> Both where the morning sun first warmly smote

The open field, and where the unpierc'd shade
Embrown'd the noon-tide bowers. [Milton]

But to a man of Beckford's taste, the direct appeal of these descriptions was, of course, in their insistence that nature was most attractive in its wild and unadorned state, and that the real serpent in the garden was art that was obvious, such as was represented in the clipped hedge, the geometrically shaped tree, or the embroidered parterre. This is not to say that Beckford believed that art had no place in garden design, but only that it should never be intrusive.

It was this view of 'professed art' as an encroachment upon the living landscape which ultimately led Beckford, as it did other early romantic artists, to the recognition that the integrity of a specific landscape must never be violated. Once irregular nature was appreciated for itself, without the intrusion of excessive art, the respect for the 'character' of an individual scene was inevitable and led to the study of topography as a prelude to landscape design.[17] There are no surviving statements by Beckford addressing this approach to laying out a landscape, but Redding furnished an example of how an appreciation of the topography of an area on the Fonthill estate became the basis for achieving a unified effect. Describing a section of the estate near Hindon that Beckford developed, Redding wrote: 'The character of the scenery here its owner had studied to render as wildly natural as possible. All was rustic. Even the lodges were common, and the twisted trees, meeting overhead, carried on the deception, until, emerging on a sudden, the Abbey, in all its imposing mass, came suddenly upon the eye'.[18] In relation to the history of the gardening movement, this course of action represented an important shift away from the neo-classical technique of creating gardens according to a pre-established formula towards the more romantic approach of allowing the character of a particular setting to dictate the design. Interestingly, it was Alexander Pope who laid the groundwork for this important principle of garden design in his 'Epistle to Burlington' in 1731:

Consult the Genius of the Place in all;
That tells the Waters or to rise or fall;
Or helps th' ambitious Hill the heavens to scale,
Or scoops in circling theatres the Vale;
Calls in the Country, catches opening glades,
Joins willing woods, and varies shades from shades;
Now breaks, or now directs, th' intending Lines;
Paints as you plant, and, as you work, designs.

One of the essential characteristics for a garden setting that Beckford always insisted upon and took advantage of was its natural advantages for a prospect. He was aware of the possibilities a good location provided for an extensive view and considered it a principal ingredient in the garden design. When he walked the entire twelve miles of green walks at Highclere, it was the magnificent prospects which moved him to exclaim that he wanted 'nothing more beautiful than this'. All four of Beckford's residences containing garden scenes were located in elevated regions with commanding views. In Portugal, he resided at Ramalhão, in 1787–1788, about twelve miles from Lisbon, 'on an eminence under the pyramidical rocks of Sintra, an exposed situation over-looking a vast stretch of country bounded by the ocean';[19] he selected Monserrate in 1794, for its lovely grounds and views. The Fonthill Abbey estate was located in one of the highest regions of Wiltshire, and the tower he had constructed as part of his garden in Bath, the residence of his final years of life, provided an extended view of the surrounding countryside. 'I am partial to glancing over a wide horizon', he once told Cyrus Redding, 'it delights me to sweep along an extended landscape. I must elevate myself to do this'.[20]

Beckford's interest in prospect was inextricably involved with his passion for towers. A tower presented an image of both authority and seclusion for Beckford—an appropriate symbol that expressed the way he saw himself and that he transferred to the central character of his major literary work, the Caliph Vathek. At an exhibition of paintings, he always ran first to look at those works which contained towers. The drawings he made of landscape scenes or from imagination invariably had in them a tall tower perched on a mountain-top over-looking a deep valley below.[21] We have already pointed out how the essay-letter to Cozens in 1777, manifested the same obsession with the sweeping prospect from a lofty tower, where he and the artist could look down upon the world below. It was a compelling interest that remained with him throughout his life. At least five years after he left Fonthill, he could not resist making note of the arresting character of a tower in a landscape, as he revealed in his copy of Gilbert L. Meason's *On the Landscape Architecture of the Great Painters of Italy* (London, 1828)[22] where he recorded in the flyleaf the following passages that captured his interest in the book:

> Among the paintings found at Pompeia are some supposed to be of villas, each of which has its tower of safety hard by

> A tower was a necessary appendage to the vinyard or garden, in the east, at the most remote area

> On the reverse side of a silver coin, fished up from the Euphrates, close to the ruins of the palace of Babylon, are five embattled towers, and one outward wall

> In the villa of Ventidus Bassus, the tower was sixty paces square; that of the palace of Maceanas was still larger

> Attached to the palace of the Duke of Braschi on the lake of Nemi, is a tower of great antiquity. It is one hundred and twenty feet high, thirty feet in exterior diameter, and the wells are five feet in thickness

A visitor to Beckford's tower in Bath once asked him how he managed to adjust to the loss of his great estate at Fonthill. His eyes brightened as, sweeping his fingers across the Welsh mountains, the estuary of Severn, and the rolling Downs of Wiltshire, he answered: 'This! this—the finest prospect in Europe'.[23]

Beckford's need for a 'view' as an important element in the garden plan was a natural outcome of his years of European travel, but it also developed from his knowledge of painting. His early studies in painting, as already mentioned, had helped him to observe nature with the careful eye of the painter. Thus, when he walked through the garden attached to the Elector's residence in Bonn, it was the prospect that he highlighted and went on to describe because it reminded him of one of Alexander Cozens's landscapes:

> It was so dusky, that I was a minute or two seeking in vain the entrance of an orangery.... At length I discovered it; and passing under an arch, found myself in the midst of lemon and orange trees, now in the fullest blow, which form a continued grove before the palace, and extend, on each side of its grand portal, out of sight. A few steps separate this extensive terrace from a lawn, bordered by stately rows of beeches. Beyond, in the centre of this striking theatre, rises a romantic assemblage of distant mountains, crowned with the ruins of castles, whose turrets, but faintly seen, were just as you would have created to complete a prospect.[24]

As this interest in the natural landscape grew, he inevitably recognised the essential interrelationship between gardening and painting: he came to understand that the basic principles of the one art readily applied to the other. This picturesque orientation ultimately manifested itself in his own highly visual style of writing, in his obsessive interest in collecting books with engraved illustrations, and, most dramatically, in his landscape designs.

Beckford never elaborated any technical theory of the picturesque, but it is clear from his writings that he understood the doctrines espoused by the picturesque theorists. He often spoke of himself as a man with 'a picturesque eye', and, like William Gilpin and Uvedale Price, he believed that certain objects had intrinsic qualities which made them picturesque. 'The situation is striking and picturesque', he wrote in Verona, 'a long line of battlement-walls, flanked by venerable towers, mounts the hill in a grand, irregular sweep, and incloses many a woody garden, and grove of slender cypresses'.[25] He described exposed tree-roots as 'picturesquely fantastic'.[26] Old, gnarled trees, ruined fountains, mutilated statues 'variegated by the lapse of years with innumerable tints of purple, green and yellow' were 'picturesque beauties'.[27] In *Modern Novel Writing* (1796), he portrayed Lord Mahogany's seat as essentially picturesque, utilising a lengthy passage from his half-sister Elizabeth Hervey's novel *Melissa and Marcia; or the Sisters* (1788), to provide the descriptive details. From the beginning of this description, Beckford employed Hervey's exact words but where she identified 'Brown' as the improver of the estate in her book, he substituted the name of Brown's adversary—Richard Payne Knight—in his work. 'In the distribution of the grounds', Beckford wrote, 'the hand of KNIGHT had assisted but not forced nature; each masterly stroke of his art had only served to bring to light beauties that lay concealed before'.[28] The substitution of 'KNIGHT' in full capital letters could have been done in recognition that the park Hervey described (essentially based upon scenes around the Fonthill Splendens estate) as 'beautifully irregular; wild and diversified' was more in accord with Knight's taste than Brown's:

A gradual descent carried you from the house, through a winding path irregularly planted with firs and forest trees, skirted with laurels and flowering shrubs. Here and there the eye caught thorns in all the pride of blossom; their reign of beauty but short, yet they stood alone on distinguished spots and wreathed their trunks into many fantastic shapes.

The purple lilac in lovely clusters, and the unsullied white, vied with the Portugal laurel, and gelder rose, in beauty. Here festoons of libernum, and there the elegant acacia pleased the eye, while the air was perfumed with the united fragrance of sweet-briar and violets …

In wandering thus through a labyrinth of sweets, sometimes you caught a view of the adjacent country, and saw the water glitter through the trees; but often the closing branches confined the eye to the delightful spot around. As you advanced, the shrubs gave way entirely to forest trees—majestic oaks, elms, chestnuts, and beeches formed into a spacious grove. At first their tall straight stems appeared like columns set at convenient distances from each other; by degrees they pressed together; their bright tints disappeared; the deep recesses of the grove were darkened with the solemn gloom of cedars, and mournful cypresses, now quite impervious to the rays of the sun (p. 131).[29]

Beckford could also have been using this opportunity to allude to the controversy between the Brown-Repton school of landscape practice and the adherents of the picturesque led by Knight and Price. Only two years before the publication of *Modern Novel Writing*, Knight launched a strong invective against Brown's 'levelling' and 'clumping' in his poem *The Landscape* (1794).

Beckford returned to this subject in his next satire *Azemia* published in 1797. Here he described the simplicity and utility of the grounds surrounding a vicar's country seat in opposition to the more dominant taste in the 1790s for the picturesque landscape. 'There are neither rising grounds nor hedge rows', Beckford wrote, 'to relieve the wearisome uniformity of common fields on one side; on the other the eye turns with disgust from a dreary moor, intersected by sluggish streams, and apparently the abode only of the otter and the heron; discouraging as these appearances are, the general character of the country is that of fertility. It would have suited the taste of Dr. Johnson; but the poet, the painter, or the enthusiast in picturesque beauty, would undoubtedly travel through it as fast as they could'.[30]

It is not surprising, then, that when Beckford set about engaging in the practical activities that he followed the principles of picturesque design—not in any strict academic sense but as a concomitant quality of his own individual style. His early travels, his training with Cozens, his knowledge of painting, his predilection for painting landscapes in prose, and a writing style with a strong visual accent—all helped to shape his taste for a landscaping style that would culminate in the creation of a dramatic landscape composition on his own property at Fonthill. At the age of twenty-one, when he assumed proprietorship of Fonthill, he had a sophisticated grasp of the important visual principles of separation, selection, and composition, possessed a strong feeling for colour and contrast, and understood how all of these elements could be carried into practice working with the canvas of the living landscape.

Landscape Improvements on the Fonthill Splendens Estate

The vast estate of which Beckford became proprietor when he reached his majority in 1781, together with his own purchases of surrounding land, comprised an area of almost 6,000 acres. On its long side, the ground stretched from the village of Fonthill Bishop south-west along the downs as far as Knoyle Corner, where it turned south-east and proceeded to Castle Town. From there it moved in an irregular north-easterly direction to unite again with Fonthill Bishop. On the western side of the boundary lay the original estate, the mile-long river and the family mansion called Fonthill Splendens. The major approach to Splendens was by way of a public road which passed through the grounds from Fonthill Bishop on the way to Semley. Following this route, the visitor first came upon the grand stone gateway, said to be modelled after a seventeenth-century design by Inigo Jones and possibly constructed by the architect John Vardy (1718–1765) in the mid-eighteenth century on the orders of Alderman Beckford. From this point, one could see the four-hundred-foot façade of the family mansion, nestled to the left of a hill which led to higher ground and to the scene of Beckford's later endeavours.

The mansion, constructed in the Palladian style, consisted of a four-storey main block, four hundred feet wide, with a classical portico, resembling Houghton Hall in Norfolk. Flanked by two elliptical colonnades with square pavilions of two storeys at each end, it was situated near a river, at a right angle to it, facing south. The river, crossed by a very large stone bridge with five arches, passed the east wing in a slight curve before losing itself in the distant woods. There was also a vaulted boathouse contemporary with the entrance gateway at the north end of the park and also likely to have been constructed by Vardy. A large stone quarry, which provided some of the materials for the construction of the mansion, lay partially concealed by trees and shrubs on the eastern shore of its banks. For almost twelve years, Beckford restricted his landscaping activities to this comparatively small family estate called Old Park.

It is not well known that Beckford engaged in any landscaping activities on his father's estate. Boyd Alexander, for example, believed that Beckford's gardening activities at Fonthill began in 1793 with the construction of a barrier wall which enclosed the Abbey estate and that his contributions to landscape features were confined to this area.[1] Timothy Mowl, Beckford's most recent biographer, claims that 'much of what survives today in the park at Fonthill is of the Alderman's time'.[2] But there is documentation to show that Beckford was heavily involved in planting activities before he turned his attention to the Abbey and its surrounding grounds. In a letter he wrote on 9 March 1787, revealing the extent to which he paid attention to such matters, he directed his agent to enhance the conservatory at Splendens in support of planned improvements by securing plants at an upcoming auction of the collection of Princess Amelia, the daughter of George II: 'Let me enjoin you, as you love Fonthill & believe in the excellence of its conservatory, to buy fifty or a hundred pounds worth of the grandest orange, oleander & myrtle trees'.[3]

Furthermore, an important article entitled 'Account of the Works Now Executing at Fonthill', published in February 1797 by the editor of *The European Magazine and London Review*, reveals that Beckford had been actively engaged in making improvements on his father's estate 'from the time he attained majority in 1781'.[4] This report was actually a follow-up to a previous account of Christmas festivities at Fonthill, published in January 1797, by an unidentified 'correspondent' who was present at the affair. This correspondent was obviously an insider, almost assuredly John Lettice, whom the editor considered to be an authoritative source of information about Beckford's activities. At the end of the correspondent's piece, the editor inserted the following paragraph announcing his forthcoming account 'through the same channel by which we have procured the above account':

> As some interesting circumstances relative to Fonthill, and the works which have been carrying on there for these last sixteen years, are little known to the public, much the finest parts of the place being never shewn but to Mr. Beckford's particular friends, and the primary motives of these great projects being little understood, we hope to be able, in our next, to gratify our readers, through the same channel by which we have procured the above account, with a communication of some particulars, which will, perhaps, be thought more valuable, as they are of a less temporary nature than those we have now presented.[5]

In the next issue, the editor began by indicating that the 'following details will, as their authenticity may be depended upon, not appear unworthy of attention, nor ill calculated to gratify that curiosity which is still much alive on the subject of Fonthill'. The importance of this account lies in the fact that it documents some of the significant improvements Beckford made on his father's estate prior to his later efforts on the Fonthill Abbey grounds. Unfortunately, it has been overlooked in almost all attempts to describe Beckford's landscape gardening activities on his father's estate.

It is clear from the information available that Fonthill Splendens was never developed as a unified composition of house and grounds. While the mansion was a magnificent piece of architecture, strikingly displayed against a background of dark hills and rising forests, the surrounding grounds in conjunction with the building did not form a well-harmonised composition. There were several reasons for this incongruity. John Rutter, in his study of Fonthill, noted that the grounds were not 'constructed upon one pervading principle of art; but have in many parts a wild and uncultivated character, and derive their attraction from the beauty of their situation, rather than from the taste of their embellishment'.[6] William Gilpin, on one of his picturesque tours, expressed dissatisfaction with the 'sumptuous bridge' that crossed the river. 'If the bridge had been more simple', he observed, 'the scene about it would have been more pleasing'.[7] Another problem was the intrusive public road which passed in front of and close to the residence itself. Adjacent to the road was a river, looking more like a canal from the engraved views of the period. Rutter also reported that the view was 'circumscribed in its limits, and though beautiful, extremely monotonous in character'.[8] It proximity to the water in such a low location was a constant source of dampness in and around the building. Then, there was the matter of the white stone quarry, near the shore line, which was used in the construction of Fonthill Splendens. Several acres had been left open upon completion of the mansion, leaving 'large naked masses of white stone and ugly excavations'.[9] Earth was brought in to fill in the excavations and cover the exposed stones. Trees and shrubs were also planted to mask this unsightly area. However, this area, the imposing stone bridge, the public road and the serpentine river failed to blend with the stately simplicity of the Palladian mansion. Based on the record provided in *The European Magazine and London Review* and some other contemporary accounts, it is evident that Beckford attempted to correct some of the glaring faults of this situation after he assumed proprietorship, and his experiments during this time provide an interesting prologue to his later work on the Abbey estate.

One of the first changes Beckford made was to fill in some of the barren, unplanted areas throughout Old Park with trees, exotic plants, and shrubs to avoid the monotonous effect of the flat, rolling style of landscape that Capability Brown had made so popular. This effort continued every year after 1781 on a grand scale in conjunction with other improvements. Some years he planted as many as 'several hundred thousand trees'; other years he planted 'not less than a million'.[10] He removed the bridge that Gilpin had found so unsightly around 1781,[11] and thereafter ordered a partial damming of the river to enlarge it into a lake. The result was a larger, deeper body of water which greatly enhanced the beauty of the place. As the editor of *The European Magazine and London Review* wrote, 'The different form of the shores and extension now given to the breadth of the water have entirely changed its former aspect and character, and rendered it worthy of its present appellation of a Lake'.[12] All of these changes constituted an effort to 'harmonise Fonthill', as Beckford explained to Sir William Hamilton in 1796.[13] Even after 1797 Beckford was still planning to enlarge the lake further and to vary its form: 'Further improvements … are in due time to be made upon this water; its size to be still enlarged and its form more varied'.[14] Years later, after the completion of the Fonthill Abbey estate, *The Times* reported that 'there is nothing at all about the grounds of the Abbey to compare with the broad lake which flows in front of the old mansion'.[15]

An undated landscape design by James Wyatt among the Beckford Papers reveals a more ambitious plan for Old Park than has hitherto been known.[16] This drawing shows an attempt to eliminate the public entry from the grand stone gateway through the property and to create an alternate route east of the existing road on the opposite side of the lake with the new road proceeding south and then crossing the water over a new iron bridge whereupon it would run directly past Splendens and reconnect with the original public road. The elimination of a great part of the public road would not only create more privacy in the park but would also provide the opportunity for a more unified natural design in relationship to Splendens. Included in this configuration was an approach to the house from the bridge that Wyatt sketched 'in case the present road ... cannot be made private'. Other new features included a cascade on the western side of the lake and a series of small islands in the lake, one of which was identified as a 'Stew for Fish in the middle of a large island', a holding place for keeping fish fresh for the table. Wyatt also provided sketches for additional plantations and described the eastern side of the lake as a 'Marsh Common'. Another less detailed landscape sketch by Wyatt in the Beckford Collection at the Beinecke Library at Yale shows a three-arched stone bridge crossing a body of water with two roads, one to the house and the other to rejoin the public road.[17] On the back of the Yale drawing is a note to Wyatt from Beckford and Beckford's London address as '12 Wimpole Street'. Since Beckford moved to Portman Square from Wimpole Street sometime during the spring of 1782, these drawings were very likely made in 1781 as possible replacement designs for the original bridge that was removed in the same year. This appears to be corroborated by John Britton who, in 1801, referred to a 'plan drawn by Mr. Wyatt' involving a 'fishing seat'.[18] Neither of these designs was ever carried out, but they underscore the extent of Beckford's interest in landscaping his father's estate. Beckford's failure to obtain the privacy he sought in Old Park may have been a factor in his decision in the end to construct another residence more removed from the eye of the public.

Looking at the lake more closely, it is evident that Beckford's was committed to naturalistic effects in the way he insisted on heavy planting all the way down to the edges of the lake to avoid the hard line between water and land. When Britton first saw it, he pronounced it a superior achievement in the beauty of irregular design: 'The lake, which always produces the most brilliant and captivating effect in a landscape, is here a beauty of the superior order. Free from the formality of straight outline, its banks are thickly wooded, and its head concealed by clustered islands'.[19] While there is no record of the actual dates of initiation and completion of this particular project, Beckford seems to have made an allusion to it in two letters to Samuel Henley in May and July 1784, encouraging him to come to Fonthill to view the results of recent work. In the first, he wrote: 'If you are to visit D[evonshire] this summer I trust you will not pass by Fonthill without casting an eye upon my rocks and water, which is wonderfully expanded'. And in July, he followed up with a similar reference: 'I should not have let your last kind letter have remained so long unanswered had I not been engaged with packing up & preparations for Fonthill, where I now am amidst hay & roses perfectly tranquil and solitary. If you could stretch your excursion as far as Fonthill you would greatly oblige me, & we should enjoy my new creation of wood and water'.[20] While Henley is known as the individual who translated *Vathek* into English for its first publication in 1786, he was also a student of picturesque design and would have been keenly interested in Beckford's creation. He was sufficiently sophisticated in this area to have conducted a correspondence on the fine points of the principles of the picturesque with William Gilpin in the late 1760s, following the appearance of *The Essay on Prints* in 1768.[21]

Further indication of Beckford's gardening interests in Old Park was the creation of a new kitchen and flower garden in a protected area north-east of the house 'upon a scale four times larger than the old one'.[22] Beckford's taste for picturesque effects in landscaping was also evident at this time in the type of improvements he advocated for the quarry scene on the eastern shore of the lake. Beckford's father had taken steps to conceal the exposed stones and excavation marks with soil and plantings of beech, larch, and fir and even allowed some of the rough-hewn pieces to show through the foliage to improve the scene.[23] According to *The European Magazine and London Review* article, Beckford capitalised on this situation by considerably extending this plantation 'along the adjoining hills which hang over the Lake; on the side of which has been formed a Grotto trickling with perennial springs; the surface of its Rock-work variegated with many-coloured mosses, and its crevices filled with aquatic plants and flowers'. By 1797 the quarry area, with the wood having attained a considerable growth, produced a scene that in 'point of beauty and original effect' would 'challenge any garden scenery in the kingdom'.[24]

Beckford also insisted, as in the case of the shore line, that the edges of any walkways that were added in this area should be broken with flowers and shrubs to eliminate any signs of regular lines. In these cases, the improvement was always dictated by Beckford's own sense of design and taste. How successful he was can be measured by Britton's comments in his description of this part of the Fonthill estate in 1801. He found the 'many bold inequities' of this particular part of the estate captivating to the eye:

> Mr. Beckford, in a very early stage of his minority, discovered that feeling for the picturesque, for which he is so much celebrated, and caused this ground to be planted with every sort of forest wood; adventitious soil was brought in, where natural earth was wanting. This plantation having wonderfully succeeded, and after some years attained a most luxuriant growth, walks and scenes of lawn, rocks, etc. were opened in several parts, where the nature of the place suggested that improvement. These first walks, and consequently the more open parts, were made of sufficient width to admit of borders of flowers and exotic shrubs, so adapted to each season as to delight the spectator with their successive bloom and fragrance through eight or nine months in the year.[25]

These grounds became known as the 'Alpine Garden' in 1796, when new walkways were added and additional planting executed under the supervision of John Lettice.[26] This work was carried out, according to Britton's account, for the purpose of procuring the pleasing effects of successive contrasts 'between the lowest, the intermediate and the highest ground'. Openings were made to emphasise particular views of the estate and the whole was so managed 'as to present to the moving spectator a continual variety of scenes, each marked with a different, and generally some striking character', and all designed to inspire particular sentiments or emotions in accordance with the new aesthetics of the romantic landscape garden.[27] Lettice commemorated the scene in an original poem he penned in 1800:

Written in an Arbour of the Alpine Garden Fronting the Lake

In every Season, every Day, each Hour
Save when rude Wind, or rougher Tempest blows,
Yon Scene is character'd by pure Repose.
But on this favour'd Eve, as from this Bow'r,
I view the Lake's Expanse, what heavnly Pow'r,
While golden Sunset on its Bosom glows,
While Tuft or Spiry Tree, or Shrub or Flow'r,
Reflected, each, within its Mirror Shows,
Does to this Vale yet more than Stillness lend,
Repose more hush'd, a softer, deeper Calm.
Well, with Reluctance, listless may I bend
My Footsteps hence; for sure the sacred Balm,
Sweet Influence on my Heart of Heav'n's own Peace,
To sooth me, ling'ring here, can never cease.

Fonthill Aug 4 1800[28]

The best way to see the Alpine Garden was to cross the lake on a boat from the west side to a place called the New Landing on the east side, which is marked by four stone urns on pedestals today. Britton identifies the variety of scenes as the visitor took the tour of the area, including the 'Fairies Lawn', surrounded 'by rising ground and rocky cliffs, clothed with hanging woods; the bottom enlivened with the gay vegitation of shrubs and flowers'; 'a large wild quarry' of 'uncouth ground'; 'a root-house with a bowling-green in front, encircled with lofty firs, intermingled with lilac, woodbine and laurel'. There were also various scenic 'points of view' which would become a trademark of the Fonthill Abbey landscape. Leaving the root-house area and passing through an open grove, visitors caught a 'confined view of the lake' before reaching the head of the quarry, where they beheld 'a vast extent of sylvan scenery, displaying broad masses, principally the foliage of oak and pine, waving over numerous hills'. The next view in the walk was a 'distant perspective of the mansion … through a narrow rocky vale'. Thereafter, 'striking down a savage path, screened on either side by thick, dark, and almost impenetrable wood', walkers came upon 'a smooth level of green turf, on the top of a rock, where an urn or sarcophagus [was] to be placed, dedicated to the memory of Alexander Cozens'. In a short distance from this site, on the highest point in the quarry, Beckford had erected a rustic rotunda, called the Paliaro. It was 'thatched with straw, like the huts of Calabrian shepherds; and supported by six rude unbarked firs as columns'.[29]

The idea of developing the Alpine Garden in the 'savage manner' could have been influenced by Beckford's maternal great-uncle Charles Hamilton. Hamilton was considered one of the great landscape gardeners in the century. His garden at Painshill was considered a masterpiece of 'savage gardening', which Horace Walpole characterised as that 'kind of alpine scene composed almost wholly of pines and firs, a few birch, and such trees as assimilate with a savage and mountainous country'.[30] During a tour of England in 1779, Beckford visited Hamilton who was then living in Bath and at the age of eighty still busy with landscaping ten acres of land there. Redding noted later that the sight of Hamilton's landscaping accomplishments 'strengthened that love of rural economy and gardening which was afterwards so marked a trait in Mr. Beckford's history'.[31] It is not known whether Beckford ever saw Painshill, but it is important to note that he hired Josiah Lane, a native of Tisbury, to construct a romantic grotto at Fonthill in imitation of the one his father Joseph Lane had made at Painshill.[32]

Lane appears to have been at work on the lakeside grotto project as early as the fall of 1784, as evident from a letter Beckford wrote to Henley in October: 'Mr. Lane is rockifying, not on the high places, but in a snug copse by the river side, where I spend many an hour'.[33] The finished work, on the eastern shore of the lake not far from the area of the Alpine Garden, was called 'one of the most striking beauties upon the old part of the demesne', and described years later in *The Times*:

> The grotto … lying against, or rather cut into, the belly of the hill … consists of two divisions, the one above the other. In the upper department, amidst a labyrinth of small caves and passages, a rude basin of rock, surrounded by crags, and overhung with lofty trees, receives the drizzlings of a tiny stream, called the 'Petrifying Spring'; the range of cave below is divided into three arched chambers; and, from the centre vaults of these there is an opening to the lake, which flows up in a miniature creek, half way into the apartment. There is something, in fine weather, very delightful about the place. The vaulted roof of this last centre cavern we mentioned runs low towards the front that opens upon the water, so that the stranger's prospect (standing erect) scarcely reaches across the lake; the basis or little creek in the mouth of the apartment is as clear to the bottom as a Fonthill vase of crystal; and the trout which lie concealed among the roots about its margin shoot away with the speed of lightning at the approach of a human figure.[34]

In his description of Fonthill in 1801, Brittton observed that the grotto, 'a work of the well known Lane', was 'ornamented within by grotesque petrifactions, stalactites, madrepores, &c. aquatic plants and flowers shooting from the crevices. Its large interior space resounds with perennial springs trickling from various parts, and through channels here visible, and there unseen, hurrying along till lost in the waters of the lake'.[35]

A remarkably close description of this grotto appeared in Elizabeth Hervey's *Melissa and Marcia*, which Beckford incorporated in *Modern Novel Writing* as one of the features of Lord Mahogany's country estate:

> The paths became more numerous and intricate, till they brought you to some irregular steps cut in a rock; the light insensibly stole upon you as you descended; and at the foot of the steps you found the entrance of a spacious cave. All here was hushed and silent,

save that the trickling drops of a purling rill struck your ear, while it softly bent its way toward the parent stream. A broken arch opened to your view the broad clear expanse of the lake, covered with numerous aquatic fowl, and weeping willows adorning its banks.

Round this cave no gaudy flowers were ever permitted to bloom; this spot was sacred to pale lilies and violets. An outlet, at first scarcely perceived in the cave, carried you through a winding passage to an immense amphitheatre, formed by a multitude of irregular rocks; some bold and abrupt, others covered with ivy, periwinkles, and wall-flowers. One of these grottos was destined for a bath, and ornamented with branches of coral, brilliant spars, and curious shells. A lucid spring filled a marble bason in the centre, and then losing itself for a moment underground, came dashing and sparkling forth at the extremity of the cave, and took its course over some shining pebbles to the lake below (pp. 131-2).

Hervey published *Melissa and Marcia* in 1788 which fits the time frame supplied by the available documentation.

Beckford also engaged Lane to construct another series of caves on higher ground above the lakeside grotto on the same side of the lake. While it is difficult to provide a precise date for when this work began, Beckford referred to this activity in a letter to James Wildman of 5 August 1790 in which he wrote: 'my works at Fonthill, buildings, planting etc. are going on very briskly. I have been raising towers and digging Grottoes'.[36] This is an important statement since Mowl has described Lane's 'rockifying' as a superficial makeover carried out in grottoes that Beckford's father had already constructed.[37] Beckford's explicit description here that he was 'digging grottoes' reveals that he was doing much more by bringing new grottoes into existence. Redding also confirmed that Beckford constructed grottoes at Fonthill. When discussing Beckford's love of extreme contrast in building and landscape design, Redding observed that 'The effect of breaking out of a gloomy passage into the sun's utmost glare was a favourite stratagem of his own in constructing grottoes or galleries ... '.[38] In addition, there is a tablet carved in the stone of one of these caves which displays the inscription 'J. L. 1794', which Lane may have placed there himself.[39] We also know that the grotto was finished by this time since Henri Meister, a French visitor to Fonthill in 1793, while describing his walk along the banks of the lake, referred to a temple dedicated to Hercules 'built on a small eminence almost disjoined from the other hills'.[40] Meister's description derived from the existence of a large statue of Hercules inside the grotto. The broken remains of a muscular statue can still be seen in this grotto today.

While evidence exists that Beckford directed the development of grottoes on the east bank of the lake, the artificial constructions of a hermitage and a tunnel under the public road on the west side cannot be attributed to him. The hermitage itself was originally constructed as an evocative feature along the lakeside in the style of mid-eighteenth-century gardens and consisted of a dark cave with two openings. The cave in its early stage was occupied by a statue of a hermit, presumably in lieu of hiring a hermit as Charles Hamilton had done at Painshill.[41] Not far from the hermitage were the remains of a monolith which Rutter identified as a 'Cromlech'.[42] Nearby also was a grotto-like tunnel underneath the public road to Semley which may have been the work of Josiah's father Joseph. Rutter described it as 'hewn in the rock' formed with great boldness of 'very considerable dimensions, and possessing all that gloom and mystery' that gave it the character of 'romantic magnificence'. [43] While these features were in accord with Beckford's taste, there is nothing to preclude the possibility that they were done after Alderman Beckford had ordered the construction of a vaulted boat house at the northern end of the lake. In other words, they could have been designed as elements of the picturesque scenery to be indulged during a boat ride along the west side of the lake.

It has long been believed that Beckford's interest in landscape gardening was so strong that he also carried out extensive landscaping activities during is year of residency at Monserrate beginning the summer of 1794, and that much of his landscaping there served as preliminary design work which he then carried over to Fonthill. In a comprehensive study, *The English Garden Abroad*, published in 1992, Charles Quest-Ritson posited that Monserrate played an important role in the history of English gardening primarily because Beckford conducted landscape improvements there.[44] Quest-Ritson also pointed out that Beckford rebuilt a chapel that was destroyed in the earthquake of 1755 in the shape of a ruin and moved it to a visibly prominent location as an evocative feature that dominated the view of the forest from the house. He believed that the creation of this ruin was done during the same period of time when Beckford was contemplating constructing a similar feature at Fonthill. Quest-Ritson also claimed that Monseratte had a 'Cromlech, not unlike the stone folly Beckford built at Fonthll'. Jose Cornelio da Silva and Gerald Luckhurst in their book on Sintra also attributed the construction of a cromlech at Monserrate and a circle of stones to Beckford,[45] noting that the latter feature was recorded by Thomas Cargill in 1870:

> Above the Poet's stone, a winding way
> Few paces thence removed doth pleasant veer,
> Leading the Pilgrim to a circle grey
> Of ancient stones, meet resting-places here,
> In the far Mata for his weary feet;
> A waving Cork-tree guards this cool retreat … .
>
> Memorial this of Vathek's taste and love
> For Beauty wheresoever her devious steps may rove![46]

Cargill also attributed to Beckford a dramatic element in the landscape scene, consisting of a large arch constructed of massive boulders set in a romantic bower covered by laurel, identifying it as 'Vathek's Rocky Bouldered Arch', a feature which still exists today:

> This choicest spot doth end, I ween,
> In a deep-sheltered cool retreat,
> Shadowed all o'er by Laurels green….

Here Vathek sat, and he did use,
Oft in the sultry noon to muse
In this fastidious bowery-wove
Of circling rock, and leafy grove,
His own creation: mortals now
Spread oft their rural banquets here
And pour libations free their vow
To Bacchus, and to Ceres, cheer
Grateful in summer's thirst! Oh! green
Retreat, all Laurel-canopied
Sun-shielded, charméd circle wide,
To mirth devote![47]

Beckford's most important improvement, however, was said to be the 'rock cascade where a stream bursts out over a great cataract and then races down a dark ravine, breaking and turning over boulders in a succession of different movements',[48] reminiscent of Charles Hamilton's cascade at Bowood that Josiah Lane was involved in creating.

New research has now thrown all of these earlier attributions of Beckford's landscaping activities at Monserrate into question. A legal document, drawn up in 1791, reveals that de Visme himself was heavily involved with gardening activities at Montserrate. In this document, de Visme explains how he was 'dignifying the quinta with as large house, ample roads, pathways, water reservoirs, fountains, and everything that art can provide to make the place agreeable and delicious… '.[49] Furthermore, an anonymous article from the *European Magazine and London Review* of 1818, uncovered by Luckhurst, and signed tantalisingly 'your humble servant B'., delineates landscaping activities, including the creation of the cascade before Beckford took ownership:

The sides of the hill were tastefully laid out in shrubberies and gardens, orchards, and vinyards, and embellished with every object that could delight the eye or gratify the taste. Shrubs, plants, and flowers of every country and form, were scattered in wild profusion along the mossy banks and borders of the crystal brooks. The orange groves loaded the gale with their perfume, and invited thousands of nightingales and other feathered songsters to take up their abode among the branches. A limped stream gushing from a neighbouring rock, enabled M. De V. to form a fine reservoir of water for the purpose of a cascade. In short, the beauties of the place began to open and wear an enchanting aspect, but, as all of the charms of this world seem to consist more in perspective than possession, after expending upwards of £23,000. M. De V. in a fit of disgust, abandoned the whole, came to England and never saw it more.

This place afterwards became the property of Mr. Beckford, and I understand has since fallen into the possession of the original owner of the land.[50]

While it is now clear that de Visme directed many of the landscape features, it is still true that Beckford carried out extensive landscaping work at Monserrate. During his residence there, he wrote to Sir William Hamilton in August 1795 of 'my proceedings here in building, gardening, etc.' and in September of having 'built houses'.[51] The question now is how much did he do to develop this estate and what specific features did he contribute to the plan. The fact that he continued to engage in such activities while abroad remains a testimony to his commitment to landscaping that he then would bring to fruition at Fonthill.

More important, the experiments Beckford carried forward on the Fonthill Splendens estate prior to the development of a more grandiose scheme on the Fonthill Abbey estate constitute a clear commitment to the English or natural style of gardening at the time. As a prologue to his later work, these early activities were significant because they exhibited the same taste for irregular beauty and concern for topography, the same love of contrast and sense of composition that were to become the hallmarks of the new Fonthill.

From an Ornamental Convent in Ruins to the Celebrated Abbey: 1790–1800

The idea of designing a landscape garden that would bear the stamp of his own imagination and one that would be constructed as a work of art separate and distinct from Old Fonthill did not receive Beckford's earnest consideration until the early 1790s. It began in rudimentary form with a proposed building project, the erection of a solitary tower on the summit of the highest hill on the estate, called Stop's Beacon, in an area west of Splendens. The triangular foundation had been laid already by his father after the design of Alfred Tower at Stourhead, and Beckford felt that he should complete what had been started.[1] The earliest reference to this project appears in a letter he wrote to Lady Craven in January 1790. Here he explains that an unexpected windfall from one of his Jamaican estates would be put to this use. 'I am growing rich', he wrote, 'and mean to build Towers and sing hymns to the powers of Heaven on their summits'.[2] Shortly thereafter, he called upon James Wyatt, who had achieved some acclaim for his work in the neo-Gothic style at Lee Priory in Kent and the restoration of a number of Gothic cathedrals in England, to provide him with some possible designs by the summer of 1791. Wyatt, who had a reputation for being dilatory, neglected to give this task his proper attention and the delay frustrated Beckford, forcing him to follow up with a letter to Wyatt in October just before a planned trip on the continent. 'Dear Sir', he wrote, 'I have been waiting for you the *whole* summer: if my plans would allow me to wait the *whole* winter also, I might perhaps still afford a month or two's patience; but in a fortnight I have agreed to move, and therefore, should you still retain any idea of coming again to Fonthill, let me beg and intreat you to give me an opportunity *within the ten days of the present date* of assuring you that, notwithstanding the disappointment it has been your pleasure to afflict me with, I am ever, dear Sir, your faithful and obedient Servant, William Beckford'.[3] It appears that Wyatt did not respond in time, and Beckford left on his trip in November and remained abroad until May 1793. It was during this period of time, however, that Beckford began to conceive of a work on a larger scale of which a tower would be an essential part.

The new scheme was marked upon his return by ordering the construction of a seven-mile wall, twelve feet high, to enclose 519 acres of the area surrounding Stop's Beacon, which provided the outlying acorn-shape form of the new estate. It was built of 'hewn stone', gathered from the area, and 'finished with a strong painted paling, inclined outwards, as a *chevaux de frize*'.⁴ He told Cyrus Redding that building the wall was prompted by the number of hunters he found trespassing on his land in the summer of 1793. But he also explained to Lady Craven shortly after the wall was completed a year-and-a-half later, that he planned to spend some time in his new enclosure. 'In process of time', he explained, 'when my Hills are completely blackened with Fir, I shall retreat into the centre of this gloomy circle like a spider into the midst of his web. There will I build my tower and deposit my books and my writings and brood over them till it please Heaven to … open the doors of a pleasanter existence'.⁵

After contracting to have the wall constructed, Beckford left for a trip to Lisbon in November 1793. A month later, he displayed his own talent for architectural design by outlining a plan for a house in Lisbon that contained many of the features of the future Fonthill Abbey. The drawing, dated 28 December 1793, showed an uninterrupted vista through a series of rooms, a central octagon, a sanctuary devoted to St Anthony of Padua, and even a fountain court outside the building.⁶ He sent the Lisbon plan to Wyatt in April 1794 for his advice, explaining that 'my appetite for humouring St. Anthony … is still so keen that I cannot live without a little tid-bit of a sanctuary'. He then went on to explain what he was planning for the Lisbon house: 'I want a new oratory, a sort of tabernacle with curtains and lamps and two candelabra and 6 altar candlesticks. All these holy implements may be made in Portugal at a very trifling expense—the lamps of bronze with the candelabra of wood—provided you will settle the proportion and design. As I have some beautiful straw-coloured silk ready, I have thought of hanging round the whole room with curtains of these materials. The recess, I rather think, should be of another colour, perhaps lilac; but upon this also I beg your advice'.⁷ At this stage, these features were restricted to the planned Lisbon house, but it was only a matter of time before they would become essential elements in the designs being crafted by Wyatt at home for Fonthill.

While the record of Wyatt's efforts to put Beckford's ideas down on paper is sketchy, it is clear from the same letter that another project was in the works and that Beckford had already received from the architect a 'magnificent plan' for a 'chapel upon Stop's Beacon', which he hoped Providence and his financial situation would allow him to carry into execution.⁸ No additional description of the new structure is provided. However, Beckford ended the letter by saying that 'we may still live to erect the buildings both grecian and gothic you designed for Fonthill'.⁹ John Rutter, in his own description of the origin of Fonthill Abbey in 1823, described this chapel, in perhaps a slightly more advanced stage, as a 'convent' which would be a striking decorative feature in a garden scene made picturesque by being partly in ruin. It was to contain a suite of rooms large enough to make possible 'the enjoyment of a day, whether of sunshine or of shower'. According to Rutter, the final drawing showed the 'chapel, the parlour, the dormitory, and one small cloister alone' as having survived the ravages of time, while the 'refectory, the kitchen, and every other part of the edifice' were buried in 'one common ruin'.¹⁰ Beckford felt it was a 'magnificent plan' but it was never carried into execution; instead it served as the germinal design, melded with the plans for the Lisbon house, for a larger structure, the future Fonthill Abbey, to be built on the ridge north-east of Stop's Beacon, called Hinkley Hill.

In the meantime, the construction of a separate tower on Stop's Beacon remained a viable element in the design as late as February 1797.[11] Joseph Farington provided a sketch of it in July 1796, based on his conversation with Wyatt. The drawing, at that time, showed a tower which was seventy-five feet square at its base and elevating in three stories to a height of 175 feet.[12] There was a living storey on the second level containing dressing rooms, bed chambers, and a gallery. The upper storey was to be a single room lighted by a lanthorn at the top. Farington went on to explain that Beckford directed that he be buried 'at the top of the lanthorn'. A slightly different description of the tower appeared in the *Gentleman's Magazine* in September 1796:

> William Beckford, Esq., of Fonthill is collecting the materials for a building of wonderful grandeur and utility. It is to consist of a tower to be erected on Stops' Beacon, near Fonthill, the loftiest scite in the neighbourhood; it is to have a square of 80 feet clear, within the walls, at the base, and to be 280 feet high, with a lantern at the top, so that it will command a view of near 80 miles every way, and the lantern to be seen by night at a greater distance. It is to be furnished as an observatory, and notwithstanding its immense height, is to be so constructed as that a coach & six may be driven with ease and safety from the base to the top, and down again. This stupendous work will probably employ hundreds of the neighbouring poor for near ten years.[13]

It is difficult to determine precisely when the plan of the 'convent' became the plan of the Abbey with the separate tower scheme merging with a larger conventual structure, but Britton believed that a foundation was laid in the fall of 1795. While this is possible, it could not have represented at that point in time the final design of the building since Wyatt continued to make modifications at Beckford's behest. We do know that building and planting projects began to accelerate following his return to England in June 1796. In a letter of 5 October 1796 he indicated that the 'Convent advances'[14] and seven days later wrote: 'Wyatt has been doing wonders according to custom, and he has given the great Hall another push 20 feet or so; we shall reach Knoyle before we have done. You will see Wyatt and converse with him upon all subjects, and arrange by all means some plan of getting forwards with the Convent more rapidly. The windows should be put into the painters hands without delay'.[15] The 'great Hall' was the western wing of the building which Beckford originally conceived of as a dining hall or refectory. In November he wrote to his mother that 'I have extended the front of the Abbey in the Woods from the dimensions you saw us working upon, to near two hundred feet, and a good part of the building has already reached the first floor'.[16] He also added that he was attending to the grounds: 'The Conservatory and flower Garden, which are to surround it, are begun. My Walk, which you will recollect is, according to the Plan, to be carried out considerably more than twenty Miles thro' and round the Woods (to which I have just made an addition of ground by the completion of a new purchase) has already proceeded to nearly the length of nine Miles. The Season proves admirable for my planting, and, if it continues as open till Christmas, I think Vincent will by that time, with all the hands allowed, have got above a million of Trees into the Ground for this Year's work'.

By February 1797, furthermore, work had proceeded rapidly enough for Beckford to report that the 'pleasure building in the shape of an abbey' was '*already half finished*'. 'It contains appartments', he added, 'in the most gorgeous Gothic style with windows of painted glass, a chapel for blessed St. Anthony—66 ft. diameter & 72 high—a gallery 185 in length, & a tower 145 feet high'.[17] These dimensions correspond to the report in *The European Magazine* with the chapel of St Anthony being located in the unfinished octagon room.[18] Rutter recorded that during the winter of 1796–97 Wyatt was completing a series of designs, 'comprising the grand octagon of the present structure, and the whole of the buildings to the south and west of it' that represented the basic form of the structure minus the north and east wings, or as they became known in time, King Edward's Gallery and the Eastern Transept. Rutter wrote about these early architectural plans in 1823 that the 'style and archetype' of the original plan was built upon but never lost sight of in the various and progressive additions. 'The general arrangement of the plan in these designs', he explained, 'is therefore nearly the same as we now find it in the Abbey, though a few of the apartments may have changed their destination and some others their names. The Western Yellow Drawing Room and Gothic Cabinet were then the chamber and dressing room of the proprietor; the Great Octagon was a chapel, and the Western Entrance a dining hall, having no communication with the Octagon, except that a tribune or gallery overlooked it, from whence it might be presumed the lectures were to be delivered, as was usual during meals in all monastic establishments'.[19]

Some of the extant early designs of the Abbey tower, however, differ significantly from the final design.[20] One shows a squat tower and spire emanating from the centre of the structure. A pen and wash sketch by Wyatt exhibiting this feature is currently in the collection of the Royal Institute of British Architects. There is also a watercolour perspective from the south-west by Turner in the Bolton Museum and Art Gallery. This work shows the same squat tower configuration and appears to be made from Wyatt's design modelled after the monastery of Batalha. Wyatt was familiar with the Batalha design even before 1795 and adapted it for the tower he constructed at Lee Priory in Kent in the 1780s. J. C. Murphy's book on the Batalha architectural designs was also published in 1795 and Beckford was one of the subscribers. It may well be, as has already been suggested, that the squat design was the first tower under construction for the Abbey and the version that Wyatt exhibited at the Royal Academy in the summer of 1797.[21] It appears that the taller tower came into play by the end of the summer of 1797. At that time, Farington reports seeing 'designs for Beckfords Gothic building—which is now much enlarged', and then in November described the change as a spire 300 feet high.[22] What prompted the shift in design might have been a collapse of a part of the tower as it was under construction.

Rutter reported that the first tower was run up too quickly before the base was sufficiently secure to support it. Consequently, one day in the winter or spring of 1797, a strong wind caught a large flag which had been attached to a scaffold pole on the tower and the force of it brought this structure down.[23] The manuscript of Redding's memoirs provides a description of this event with additional details, including Beckford's reaction to what had occurred:

This first edifice was hurried on by day and night through Mr. Beckford's uncontrollable impatience. A tower was erected, but in so hurried a manner and with such slight materials, that on loading its summit with a lofty staff and flag it fell to the ground. Mr. Beckford only regretted he did not happen to be present that he might have witnessed the crash. The superintendant alarmed at what Mr. Beckford would say absented himself fearing his employer's furious outbreaks of passion in consequence. But he said, 'O he is very wrong to stay away upon the account. I had the pleasure of seeing it once after it was completed and I never expected to see it a second time'. He then ordered it to be reconstructed in a better manner exclaiming 'what a jaw that must be which can sustain the loss of such a tooth!'[24]

This was the turning point in Redding's mind, the moment that Fonthill Abbey as a residence was born. 'Thus', he wrote, 'out of the once ornamental ruin of a convent, sprung up the celebrated Abbey'.

Beckford thereafter gave the orders to resume construction, but this time with a more expanded design and a taller spire.[25] The RIBA collection includes a second-stage drawing, a west view, showing a higher octagonal tower and a spire rising from it.[26] This elevation appears to have served as the basis for the watercolour often attributed to Turner, now in the Yale Center for British Art, showing a view from the north-west with an elongated tower rising triumphantly from the octagon with a flight of stairs at the end of the northern wing projecting west. A contemporary label on the verso of the painting makes it clear that this is the composition that Wyatt exhibited at the Royal Academy in the summer of 1798, matching as it does the title of exhibit no. 955: 'North West view of a building / Erecting at Fonthill at Wiltshire / the Seat of Wm. Beckford Esq / in the Style of a Gothic Abbey / James Wyatt R.A.'[27]

Wyatt also drew a third-stage sketch elevation, a north-west view, whose spire was even taller than the second-stage design and for the first time he included all four legs of the final cruciform plan. This latter design was likely the one Wyatt exhibited at the Royal Academy in 1799, entitled 'View of a building now erecting at Fonthill, in Wiltshire, the seat of William Beckford Esq. in the style of a Gothic abbey' (no. 1016).[28] Beckford liked this painting well enough to hang it on the wall of the Dutchess of Hamilton's Chamber in the Abbey. It ultimately sold as lot 724 in the furniture segment of the Fonthill sale of 1823. While the catalogue described this lot in sparse terms as 'a fine drawing as originally planned for *Fonthill Abbey*', a report in the *Morning Chronicle* about the sale provided a detailed description which makes the identification possible.[29] This report described the drawing as a 'watercolour' by Wyatt. It then proceeded to consider the substantive differences between this design and the final one: 'The edifice, as it at present stands, is in some respects materially different from the original design, particularly in the eastern wing, where the two towers that terminate the Baron's Hall were intended to be balanced by two others of similar dimensions to the west. The northern wing is also different, as the Lancaster turret was designed to project, and to have an external flight of steps, which is not the case at present. There are several other minor discrepancies, but the principal distinction is, that in the drawing the great tower is surmounted by a lofty spire'. This description matches a design by Wyatt in the RIBA collection showing an even taller tower than the second-stage design with a flight of stairs this time facing south. The *Morning Chronicle* description of the dimensions of this new design differ from Farington by defining the height of the spire itself as 124 feet and then describing 'the whole altitude from the ground' as 400 feet, 'or about 60 feet higher than St. Paul's Cathedral'. At this height, the spire would have matched Salisbury Cathedral's altitude from the surface. There also exists in the Victoria and Albert Museum another watercolour rendering of the Abbey with a sky-kissing spire by the artist Charles Wild after Wyatt's third-stage design.

The construction continued to advance in stages as ideas flowered in Beckford's mind. By November 1797, he considered the possibility of demolishing Splendens and transforming the Abbey into his home. As Farington recorded: 'Beckford yesterday told Wyatt that He had an intention of taking down *Fonthill House,* which is badly situated—and in that case enlarge the Gothic building now erecting to be His Mansion House'.[30] He began to think of his new home as a repository for his books, expensive furniture, and a place that could display great works of art, particularly by Englishmen, setting himself up to become a patron of the arts in the tradition of other wealthy land owners of his time. One of his first steps was to hire Joseph Nollekens, John Flaxman, J. C. F. Rossi and Richard Westmacott to carve four Gothic statues for the place. Before long, Beckford provided commissions to Benjamin West, William Hamilton, Henry Tresham, Ozias Humphrey, and Turner to contribute original works to the enterprise. Farington noted this celebratory role for the Abbey in his diary entry of 16 November 1798:

> The Abbey to be endowed, & Cathedral Service to be performed in the most splendid manner that the Protestant religion will admit—A gallery leading from the top of the Church to be decorated with paintings by the works of English Artists. Beckfords *own tomb* to be placed at the end of this gallery—as having been an encourager of Art.[31]

Farington seems to limit the encouragement of art to 'paintings' by English artists, but Beckford actually had a grander scheme in mind, one that would incorporate within the walls of his new structure many other forms of art that were not as widely appreciated by his contemporaries. In time, the Abbey would become a repository for examples of art that tended to be devalued in favour of sculpture and painting, the traditional higher forms of art. In other words, Beckford took a more liberal approach to the arts than was characteristic of other owners of great estates in his day by including outstanding examples of craftsmanship in furniture, china, glassware, carvings and other objects of virtu. Abbé Macquin touched upon this rationale for Fonthill to promote a democratisation of the arts in an essay published in the *Literary Gazette* in 1822. He emphasised that as a museum Fonthill Abbey provided an 'enlarged view' of the state of the fine arts from the fifteenth to the early part of the nineteenth centuries than had been traditionally the case:

> We here see how the talents of great Artists were often employed. In our times pictures and statues only are deemed deserving of the hand of Genius. A modern *Artist* would

probably throw a teacup or a nautilus-shell at his patron's head, or at least let them fall (in astonishment) and break at his feet, if he were asked to exercise his ingenuity in painting them: In fact, such productions have been degraded from their station; and the successors of the famous chasers, designers, carvers, embossers, of former times, have sunk into a mechanical class. Under such a change, it is not a little striking to contemplate the minute and painful labours of those worthies whose fortunes flourished and whose immortality was achieved on the handles of vases and the embellishments of tankards. A multitude of their most remarkable performances are comprised in the collection at Fonthill, and may be very advantageously studied as works of fertile invention, high fancy, rich taste, and extraordinary execution.[32]

Beckford, himself, provided an additional motive for the Fonthill project in a letter to his mother, dated 29 November 1796, in which he explained that he intended to realise a humanitarian goal as a major employer for the poor and the needy in the adjacent villages. 'I have the satisfaction', he wrote, 'of giving constant Employment to some hundreds of People in one way or another'. This use of his wealth, he believed, was more meaningful than to devote his time to 'bumpering port and Madeira with Country Squires, in running for the Sweepstakes at Salisbury Races, figuring at a Country Ball, or a Mayor's Feast'.[33]

Another rationale for Beckford's decision to choose a grander design for his Gothic abbey was identified in *The European Magazine* in February 1797. The editor explained that Beckford's father during the period of his ownership ordered the demolition of a medieval church, dedicated to St Nicholas, because it was located too close to the principal mansion. This church contained monuments to the Mervyn family, one of the original owners of the Fonthill estate and ancestors of the Beckford family. The Lord Mayor had a new church built—this one in a square, classical style with a domed cupola—further removed from his mansion at a more convenient site on the Hindon–Tisbury road. But the monuments in the original church, which were examples of expert sixteenth-century workmanship, became 'exposed to the open air' and 'neglected till their ornaments became mutilated and their inscriptions effaced'. The construction of Fonthill Abbey, then, would be an opportunity to redress a debt of the past while paying homage to his ancestors: 'Mr. Beckford has designed his Gothic Abbey as a memorial tribute … to this ancient family. Their Arms, in regular series, and with their different Quarterings, are to be painted on the windows of this edifice, and the names and dates of each successive member of the family inscribed on mural tablets, in the galleries and cloysters of the Abbey'.[34] To accomplish this task, Beckford hired Sir Isaac Heard, the Garter King at Arms, who was already busily engaged in January 1797 in preparing 'Armorial Sketches for the Windows etc'., but, as he wrote to Beckford, '[I] have not yet been able to complete the proofs of all the descents'.[35]

The new structure finally received its name as 'Fonthill Abbey' by July 1798.[36] The scope of the operating plan for the building at this point in time can be gleaned from the list of dimensions published in the 24 December 1798 issue of the *Salisbury & Winchester Journal*:

To the top of the great spire	450 feet
The Octagon tower	225 feet
The spires of the eight octagon towers	264 feet
The great Octagon within	120 feet
Ditto wide	66 feet
Choir	140 feet long
	56 feet high
	28 feet wide
Length of long gallery	308 feet
From the West Door to the end of the Choir	284 feet[37]

These dimensions correspond to Wyatt's third-stage design with the spire now being fifty feet higher than the 400 feet reported by the *Morning Chronicle*. The height of this spire would now reach beyond Salisbury Cathedral and St Peter's at Rome (at 437 feet). While making allowances for the reliability of a second-hand report, these dimensions do reflect the final cruciform design of the Abbey. The 'long gallery' of 308 feet approximates the final exact length of the north and south galleries combined. The mention of a 'Choir' is the first reference to the east wing, whose dimensions cited here in combination with the west wing came to within twelve feet of the final measurement from the door of the west wing to the end of the east wing. The use of the word 'Choir' may explain why Farington wrote that the Abbey would be 'endowed, & Cathedral services to be performed in the most splendid manner that the Protestant religion will admit'.

It was on the second level, above the choir or chapel that Beckford was planning a gallery to display the works of English artists, his own tomb, and the Revelation Chamber, containing paintings from the Apocalypse by Benjamin West. In a conversation with Wyatt in December 1798, Farington recorded additional details about this gallery:

> Wyatt told me that Mr. Beckfords Gallery which is to lead to the *Revelation Chamber*, in the Abbey now building, is to be 125 feet long and 12 feet wide. It is to be wainscotted with Ebony, and in compartments are to be Historical Pictures by English artists.… Tresham is to paint four pictures for one of the Compartments. The largest of them 4 feet 3 Inches wide—The Revelation Chamber is to have walls 5 feet thick in which are to be recesses to admit coffins. Beckfords Coffin is to be placed opposite to the door. The room is not to be entered by strangers, to be viewed through wire gratings. The floor is to be Jasper. This Gallery and room are to be over the Chapel. West is to paint all the pictures for this room, and is now limited to £1000 a year while He is proceeding with the pictures.[38]

We have suggested that the idea of a Revelation chamber was inspired by the mausoleum at Batalha, but it was also reinforced by Beckford's association with Benjamin West and the artist's taste for apocalyptic subject matter in his paintings. West was a prestigious figure at this time. He was not only President of the Royal Academy, but he had ready access to George III, who had appointed him as his history painter. West's interest in portraying dramatic scenes from the Bible in his 'Dread Manner' coincided with the sombre religious character of the Abbey, and Beckford was impressed by the first picture West did for him entitled *Michael Casteth out the Dragon and his Angels*, which was exhibited in the spring of 1797. What followed was a series of paintings depicting scenes from the *Book of Revelation*, three of which were done for Beckford in 1797, before any mention of a Revelation Chamber in the Abbey, suggesting the possibility that the room was set up to accommodate West's works.[39] West's paintings would set the right tone for a room where the body of Beckford as an encourager of the arts would be entombed and forever memorialised. Beckford ultimately abandoned such an elaborately oppressive scheme but reserved a small apartment for West's paintings which was called the Revelation Chamber. Eventually, West did seventeen paintings for Beckford, including six works after scenes in the *Book of Revelation*.

Paintings displaying historical and religious subjects were in keeping with the character of a Gothic abbey and would dominate the rooms of the structure. In a letter to the bookseller, Robert Bowyer, on 5 July 1798, Beckford rejected an offer of two paintings by Jacques de Loutherbourg as too modern and not in keeping with character of the place. 'Subjects of a grave, religious Cast', he explained, 'will in general best suit the solemnity of its character, & except for the Decoration of Windows and of certain Scenes of a peculiar Sort in the Abbey, modern Painting will not answer my views & I shall be obliged chiefly to turn my Researches toward the old School of Italy'.[40]

An important part of the interior of the Abbey were the stained glass windows. Beckford turned to highly skilled artists to accomplish this work. The first was James Pearson (d. 1837) who had introduced an improvement in the colouring by painting in enamels on sheets of plain glass before firing, which allowed him to hide divisions of lead and iron. One of his best examples of this technique was *Brazen Serpent in the Wilderness*, after a design by John Hamilton Mortimer, for the east window of Salisbury Cathedral. Pearson, who often worked with his wife Margaret, was under consideration to copy some of West's works, but he was too expensive and seems to have been limited to one work by West, the painting entitled *St. Thomas à Becket*. However, local newspapers reported that Pearson was hired to copy eight of West's cartoons for the Abbey for which he would receive 4,000 guineas.[41] Furthermore, the Revd James Dallaway in an historical essay on stained glass in England published in 1817, in which he praised the work of Pearson and his wife, suggested that they made additional contributions to Fonthill, pointing out that 'they have been much employed for bordures and mosaics at Fonthill Abbey for Mr. Beckford, and usually selected subjects from the best Italian masters'.[42] James Storer indicated in 1812 that the armorial bearings of the Mervyn and Latimer families in the window of what became the Oak Library were 'beautifully executed by Pierson [*sic*]'.[43] In a letter to Isaac Heard on 3 July 1798, Beckford asked Heard to speak to Wyatt about ten shields 'intended for the great window to be painted by Pearson with the Effigies of our Lady, the Holy Virgin, St. John the Evangelist, St. Michael the Arch Angel, blessed St. William, blessed St. Nicholas & the glorious Martyr St. Thomas of Canterbury'.[44]

The rest of the glass in the Abbey was done by Francis Eginton (1737–1805) and his son William Raphael Eginton (1778–1834).[45] Francis revived the art of glass painting in

England in the 1780s and was hailed for his work in St George's Chapel, Windsor and for his contributions to a number of windows in Salisbury Cathedral. The article on him in the *Dictionary of National Biography* indicates that he did thirty-two windows at Fonthill for which Beckford paid him £12,000. Since most of the glass in the Abbey is gone, it is difficult to assess the accuracy of these figures. Among the Beckford Papers, however, is a copy of a bill from Eginton, dated 24 April 1799, indicating the total cost of the glass 'finished' as £954 4s with a description of where the glass was located:

8 Windows for South Front	210	
6 Large Windows for the Great Hall	312	18
4 Coats Arms for the Windows that are alike in the Gallery	25	4
2 Coats of Arms for Windows over the Chimney	12	12
3 d[itt]o for what was called the Revelation Window	18	18
2 large Crests for d[itt]o, d[itt]o, d[itt]o	8	8
8 Large Figures for the great Window in the Library	210	
Rich Ornamental Window for the Slip	84	
Mr. Jordans Bill for small Frames for 6 of the Arms	3	3
Messrs. Keir [?] Co. for Iron Frames	63	4
Mr. Smiths d[itt]o for packing Cases	5	17[46]

It has also been pointed out that Beckford collected ancient glass which he also had incorporated into the windows of the Abbey.[47]

The most reliable information which exists on the design and the progress of the building by the end of 1799 can be found in the detailed sketchbooks of Turner, now in Tate Britain.[48] The sketchbooks contain various perspectives of the Abbey under construction and were made in preparation for a set of watercolours of the building in its setting commissioned by Beckford. Turner spent three weeks on the estate at the end of summer in 1799[49] and exhibited five finished watercolours at the Royal Academy in the following summer. The original sketches Turner made show the upper structure of the octagon tower in the process of completion, along with the west and south wings. It is not yet evident from these views that the spire design had given way to the final great central tower plan. Turner's drawings clearly display the fragility of the tower at this stage, with the interlacing timbers rising above the rest of the building in a ghost-like filigree. Meanwhile, Lettice wrote in September 1799 that he had visited the Abbey 'three times' and that the tower had reached the height of 200 feet: 'I went up to the top and was much delighted and was much impressed with the fine and extensive views that present themselves all around.'[50]

It is not known with certainty how high the tower rose in the Wiltshire sky at this time, but *The Times* reported that it was '120 feet above the stone work'.[51] Furthermore, the *Morning Chronicle* explained years later that the lofty spire that was under construction was made 'entirely of wood' and therefore subject to an early fate.[52] The result was that on 17 May 1800, a strong gale wind brought the upper storey with boards, beams, and scaffold poles falling inside the tower with a loud crash, constituting a second collapse of the tower. This time the newspapers reported the mishap, with *The Times* taking the lead in a report on 20 May:

> On Friday a heavy gale of wind came on from the S.W. which ere the dawn of Saturday morning had increased to a tempest: the tower of the famous Gothic Abbey, just erected at Fonthill, stood exposed to all its fury, and at three o'clock a considerable portion of this famed building came down with such a tremendous crash as to alarm the country for a considerable distance around. Thus, in a moment, perished the labour of hundreds of feeble mortals bestowed for years on this once favourite object, and the expence of very many thousands.[53]

A week later, after receiving additional information, *The Times* published a correction indicating that they overstated the amount of destruction. It was a costly event, but the rest of the building escaped damage:

> Fonthill Abbey has not been injured by the late storm to the extent reported. The damage has been confined to the timber frame which had been erected about 120 feet above the stone work; but no other part of this stupendous building has sustained the least injury[54]

It was the *Morning Chronicle* report on the event, however, that had an impact on Beckford and remained in his mind as he described to others what happened. They first reported the damage in the issue of 22 May, explaining that the 'Tower of Fonthill-abbey, a capricious building which Mr. Beckford has been erecting on the summit of a hill at an enormous expence, was blown down by the high wind on Monday last'.[55] They then followed up with a more humorous report: 'The *damage* done by the late high wind to the *tower* of *Fonthill Abbey* is greatly to its advantage. It now looks like what it was intended to be, and more resembles an *ancient Gothic* edifice than ever!'[56]

Beckford was furious, blaming Wyatt for the shoddy work and failure to be on the job providing close supervision. 'Determined to sink no longer from disappointment to disappointment', he wrote to the architect, 'I give you this plain and decided warning. If you take it as it is meant I shall soon see you at Fonthill. If not—the whole shall be stopped, every workmen discharged, the reasons which have compelled me to adopt so violent a measure stated at large in the [*Morning Chronicle*] and every other Chron. Morn. Or Eve. which appears in London'.[57] These were strong words that seem to have had an effect on Wyatt because a great stir of building activity followed. Beckford, it seems, was determined as ever to move forward. It may have been this occasion that led him to decide to forego the spire design. 'We shall rise more gloriously than ever', he wrote to Heard, 'provided the sublime Wyatt will graciously deign to bestow a little more commonplace Attention upon what is supposed his favourite Structure. The Crash and the Loss sound magnificently in the Newspaper, I neither heard the one, nor feel the other'.[58] More than a year later, the tower was still not secure and never would be.[59]

Work on the building and grounds continued throughout the remaining months of 1800 but reached a fever pitch by winter time in preparation for an elaborate reception Beckford held in honour of Lord Nelson in late December. Nelson arrived on the 20th with Sir William Hamilton and Emma Hamilton. Benjamin West was present, along with John Walcot, Henry Tresham, Wyatt and an assortment of ladies and gentleman. Tresham wrote an account of the event in the *Gentleman's Magazine*.[60] The *pièce de résistance* of the festivities was a visit to the Abbey, a memorable event for Nelson and all of the guests. Beckford had designed a series of lighting effects with lamps in the trees along the path through the woods with the slow-moving carriages lit by flambeaus. The lighting was heightened by the sounds of drums placed at different points among the surrounding hills and by music echoing through the dark woods. The grand display was the Abbey standing in the darkness but illuminated by the blaze of lights for dramatic visual effect, revealing sections of the walls, battlements, turrets and the great tower vanishing into the gloom above it. Tresham provided a description of the interior of the Abbey as well which constitutes a record of the way it looked at this stage of its development:

The parties, alighting in orderly succession from their carriages, entered a groined Gothic hall through a double line of soldiers. From thence they were received into the great saloon, called the Cardinal's parlour, furnished with rich tapestries, long curtains of purple damask before the arched windows, ebony tables and chairs studded with ivory, of various but antique fashion; the whole room in the noblest style of monastic ornament, and illuminated by lights on silver sconces. At the moment of entrance they sat down at a long table, occupying nearly the whole length of the room (53 feet), to a superb dinner, served in one long line of enormous sliver dishes, in the substantial *costume* of the antient abbeys, unmixed with the refinements of modern cookery. The table and side-boards glittering with piles of plate and a profusion of candle-lights, not to mention a blazing Christmas fire of cedar and the cones of pine, united to increase the splendour and to improve the *coup-d'oeil* of the room. It is needless to say the highest satisfaction and good-humour prevailed, mingled with sentiment of admiration at the grandeur and originality of the entertainment. It should not be omitted, that many of the artists whose works have contributed to the embellishment of the abbey, with Mr. Wyatt and the President of the Royal Academy at their head, formed a part of the company. These gentlemen, with the distinguished musical party before mentioned, and some prominent characters of the literary world, formed altogether a combination of talents and genius not often meeting at the same place.

Dinner being ended, the company removed up stairs to the other finished apartments of the abbey. The stair-case was lighted by certain mysterious living figures at different intervals, dressed in hooded gowns, and standing with large wax-torches in their hands. A magnificent rooms hung with yellow damask, and decorated with cabinets of the most precious japan, received the assembly. It was impossible not to be struck, among other objects, with its credences, (or antique buffets) exhibiting much treasure of wrought plate, cups, vases, and ewers of solid gold. It was from this room they passed into the

Library, fitted up with the same appropriate taste. The Library opens by a large Gothic screen into the gallery; which I described to you in a former letter. This room, which when finished will be more than 270 feet long, is to half that length completely fitted up, and furnished in the most impressively monastic stile. A superb shrine, with a beautiful statue of St. Anthony in marble and alabaster, the work of Rossi, placed upon it, with reliquaries studded with brilliants of immense value, the whole illuminated by a grand display of wax-lights on candlesticks and candelabras of massive silver gilt, exhibited a scene at once strikingly splendid and awfully magnificent. The long series of lights on either side of the room, resting on stands of ebony enriched with gold, and those on the shrine all multiplied and reflected in the great oriel opposite, from its spacious squares of plate-glass, while the whole reflection narrowed into an endless prospective as it receded from the eye, produced a singular and magic effect.

As the company entered the gallery a solemn music struck the ear from some invisible quarter, as if from behind the screen of scarlet curtains which backed the shrine, or from its canopy above, and suggested ideas of a religious service; ideas which, associated as they were with so many appropriate objects addressed to the eye, recalled the grand chapel scenes and ceremonies of our antient Catholic times. After the scenic representation a collation was presented in the library, consisting of various sorts of confectionary served in gold baskets, with spiced wines, &c. whilst rows of chairs were chairs were placed in the great room beyond, which had first received the company above stairs.

Shortly after the event, West expressed his admiration for the imposing edifice and its creator and the impact the whole event had on him: 'When I reflect on the progress, which the combination of arts have made, directed by true taste, since I first rode on the ground on which the Abbey stands—I am lost in admiration—and feel that I have seen a place raised more by majick, or inspiration, than the labours of the human hand: this is the sensation which the examination of that elegant edifice produced on my feelings; and when the part which remains to be finished, is accomplished, must raise a climax of excellence without an example in the European world—and to give an immortality to the man whose elegant mind has conceived so vast a combination of all that is refined in Painting, Sculpture, and Architecture'.[61]

The Art of
the Fonthill Abbey Landscape

While the construction of Fonthill Abbey was an enormous undertaking, complicated by structural problems and costly delays, the laying out of the grounds surrounding the building was as challenging in scope and central to Beckford's total artistic scheme. From the outset, Beckford planned a landscape garden in which the Abbey would be a central feature. Begun as a convent in ruins, graduating thereafter to a neo-Gothic museum of the arts and then to a residence, the building was always seen within the context of a landscape composition in the tradition of the English garden. Beckford's landscape would not be in the formal style that had been characteristic of some of the great estates that preceded Fonthill. This landscape garden would bear the mark of his own particular artistic taste and reflect the 'new' aesthetics of the picturesque as expounded by such theorists as Uvedale Price and William Gilpin. Consistent with their theory, the picturesque landscape garden represented an attempt to apply the principles of landscape painting to the laying out of grounds surrounding an architectural focal point. The accent was on the visual aspects of the garden scene presented as part of a whole composition. Various points of view were incorporated in the design to facilitate appreciation of the landscape scene as one would appreciate a landscape by Salvator Rosa or Gaspar Poussin in the gallery of a museum.

That Fonthill was recognised early in its development as more than a neo-Gothic structure is apparent from Humphry Repton's interest in playing a role in the development of the grounds surrounding it. One of the most famous landscape architects of the day, Repton offered to contribute to its design in 1799. Beckford was flattered, but he preferred to play that role himself. 'It is impossible not to be flattered with an offer to contribute to the Ornament of my place from an Artist of your Eminence and Celebrity', he wrote to Repton, 'but Nature has been liberal to Fonthill, and some Embellishment it has received from Art, has fortunately gained so much the Approbation of my friends that my Partiality to it in its present state will not perhaps be thought altogether inexcusable. I am, nevertheless, much honoured and obliged in your having thought Fonthill considerable enough to merit your attention'.[1]

The major landscaping projects at Fonthill were begun in the early part of 1795, when the barrier wall was receiving its finishing touches. Between this date and February 1797, they reached a fever pitch. During this period, Beckford purchased an additional 1,700 acres of land and hired over a hundred persons to work on the ground improvements alone with astonishing results.[2] Under the direction of his gardener James Vincent, a conservatory and flower garden were begun, nine miles of a twenty-seven mile ride were completed and more than one million trees planted. Furthermore, a variety of walks and avenues were formed, each of considerable length and width and all laid in smooth turf, the most impressive of which was a broad straight walk, later called the Great Western Avenue. This stretched from the entrance of the Abbey to the barrier wall, where it connected by 'means of a bridge over a road, with a bold terrace, four miles and a half in length'.[3]

It was evident from the initial improvements that Beckford was striving for naturalistic effects in his garden plan. Laying out the small walks and pathways, for example, he made every attempt to avoid strict regularity. He generally made their lines winding in gentle curves through various sections of the woods to avoid the sharp turns which had become so common in the formal gardens of the eighteenth century. When he did make the walkways straight, he broke the formality of their lines by planting flowers, shrubs, and trees close to the edges. According to John Rutter, they all appeared to be 'ordinary features of woodland landscape'.[4] As for the newly planted trees, Beckford avoided the kind of obvious clumping that had become an artificial characteristic of gardens in the style of Capability Brown. 'The ornamented grounds of Fonthill', wrote Rutter, 'though unequalled in extent, contain very few objects that will admit of individual description. The great principle upon which this labyrinth of groves has been constructed is that of exhibiting an union of the wildest and the most ornamented scenery, the picturesque and the beautiful, in close society. The utmost profusion of expence has been bestowed not to amaze the senses by some rich and magical effect of art, but to keep the mind in a perpetual enjoyment of the most striking beauties, and richest decorations of nature'. Citing a passage from Tasso, Rutter added: 'No where appear'd the arte which all this wroughte'.[5]

The most obvious illustration of Beckford's avoidance of the straight line could be seen in the construction of the Great Western Avenue, the central approach to the Abbey. Approximately one hundred feet broad and almost a mile in length, it was made along the top of a high wooded ridge, which declined on both sides into deep valleys, the sides of which were covered with fir trees that contributed to the impression of an Alpine scene. Unlike a formal planner who would have been satisfied with a broad formal avenue leading up to a central residence, Beckford made a deep depression about half way along the avenue to vary the surface and to give it a natural effect. He also gave the avenue an air of informality by bounding its sides with a variety of trees and undergrowth, planting them at irregular intervals. Finally, he carpeted the avenue with a fine, close turf thereby avoiding the formal character of the gravel surface.

The use of turf as a replacement for gravel in the laying out of his central avenue was a masterstroke in informal design, a solution to a problem of composition that was plaguing the major picturesque gardening theorists. Brown had banished all avenues from the landscape in his severe reaction against the formalism of the geometric garden. Knight, Price, and Repton brought them back in their attempts to modify Brown's extremism, but they did so with some reluctance. Repton believed, for example, that the 'great mischief of an avenue' was that it divided the park into separate parts and destroyed 'that unity of lawn or wood which is necessary to please in every composition'.[6] Price felt that although 'a broad dry walk near the house is indispensable to the comfort of every gentleman's habitation', the pared formal edges of a gravel walk produced a poor effect in the foreground.[7] Beckford solved the problem with turf and by planting approaches 'composed of a thick elastic body of various kinds of evergreen moss, low ground-fern … wild thyme, and numerous sweet-smelling ground-flowers; the whole matted and interlaced together by a network of wild strawberries', which blended well with a lawn and eliminated the necessity for the 'horror' of the straight line.[8]

Beckford also understood that a smooth relationship between building and grounds was important for a unified design. He recognised that a structure of the size he was contemplating would serve as a focal point of interest to which everything else was related. Ordinary builders too often disregarded the role of the *l'architecto-pittore* and prepared their structures without regard for the general landscape, but Beckford took steps to ensure that the Abbey was integrated into the garden scene. He did so by allowing formal treatment close to the building. In doing so, he agreed in principle with such garden theorists as Chambers, Walpole, Repton, and Price, who argued that 'a house is an artificial object, and, to a certain distance around the house, art may be avowed'.[9]

Although in the vicinity of the Abbey the area appeared clear in contemporary illustrations, J. C. Loudon. the landscape garden historian and encyclopaedist, noted during his visit in 1807 that there was in one angle, formed by two projections of the building, a small flower-garden, a sun-dial and fountain.[10] Not far off was the herb garden and a range of exposed workmen sheds, Beckford's carriage shed, and stables for ponies. The formal features here were limited in number, but they combined with a wide, smooth, and almost unbroken lawn, which encircled the house for some distance, as accompaniments of art. The graded lawn then melted by degrees into the forest to serve as an appropriate bridge between the Abbey and the wilds. Without this transitional element, a shift from art to unadorned nature would have been too sudden, the design would have lacked that 'gradation and congruity', which Price felt was 'so necessary in all that was to please the eye and mind'.[11]

Besides the formal areas close to the house, there were other ways the Abbey as a central feature was integrated into the landscape scheme. Its Gothic style of architecture, considered in Beckford's day as an important element of picturesque requirements, reflected, with its sudden breaks, variations of form, and enrichments of surface, the irregular patterns of the outlying grounds. For this setting, Gothic was more appropriate than Grecian because it was more rugged in appearance and more picturesque. A Grecian structure would have been too symmetrical; its surfaces would have been too smooth and even. 'Mr. Beckford', wrote an anonymous author in *The Gazette of Fashion*, 'has judiciously chosen the Gothic style of architecture, which harmonises delightfully with the surrounding scenery of rock, river, and wood; the severe beauty of the classic Greek models, or even the more redundant grandeur which characterised the Roman temple, would not so well accord with English landscapes as the Gothic Abbey'.[12] 'Gothic architecture', Price observed in terms relevant to Fonthill, is generally considered as more picturesque, though less beautiful, than Grecian; and, upon the same principle that a ruin is more so than a new edifice.... In Gothic buildings, the outline of the summit presents such a variety of forms, of turrets and pinnacles, some open, some fretted and variously enriched, that even where there is an exact correspondence of parts, it is often disguised by an appearance of splendid confusion and irregularity.... Every person must be struck with the extreme richness and intricacy of some of the principle windows of our cathedrals and ruined abbeys. In these last is displayed the triumph of the picturesque; and its charms to a painter's eye are often so great as to rival those of beauty itself.[13]

Beckford appreciated Grecian architecture as a classical form of beauty, but, as he once explained to Cyrus Redding, 'his associations were with the North and the country to which himself and his father belonged'. The models for Fonthill, Redding further explained, were the examples Beckford 'found in our ruined abbeys and existing cathedrals'.[14] It was in keeping with this interest in authenticity that Beckford set aside a special library on the second floor of the Abbey called the 'Board of Works', (Oak Library) where the artists and craftsmen employed in the building designs of the Abbey could consult an authoritative collection of books and plates in the fine arts as they attempted to recreate some of the characteristics of the traditional style of Gothic architecture.

That Fonthill was to be his personal creation was evident in the extent to which he participated in the landscape projects and exercised oversight of the entire scheme. 'All these splendid works', noted the editor of *The European Magazine* in 1797, 'are not merely effected in consequence of Mr. Beckford's orders, and by means of his fortune; but his own genius, whose comprehension and activity appear equal to any undertaking, has been the informing spirit of the whole; every one of the ... projects, whether of use or ornament, having originated from himself, and their plans, of whatever kind, having been assisted or corrected by his own pure and classic taste. One of his principal amusements at Fonthill consists in attending and frequently directing the superior workmen in the execution of his schemes; and such is the ardour with which he is carrying forward his favourite building, the Abbey, that the frost and snow of the present winter were never suffered to stop any part of the work, which could still go on, nor to prevent his own daily excursions to the spot'.[15]

By the winter of 1800-1801, in time for Lord Nelson's visit, Beckford completed one of the most important single elements in his scheme, a winding fifteen-mile drive, composed of the Nine Miles Walk and a six-mile carriage ride, both located within the boundary walls and both made of turf. It was this feature which provided a vantage point to almost every interesting view of the Abbey and the surrounding landscape which could be commanded within the estate.

A study of the Nine Miles Walk, as it looked later,[16] shows how essential the elements of variety and contrast were to the design. Along its entire length, within the barrier wall, were planned a sequence of pictures which led a person from a bright open view to the contemplative dark, covered woods. If a visitor crossed the southern lawn near the Abbey, he was presented, at the very beginning of the walk, with a striking landscape scene. Here the closely shaved lawn, bordered by plantations of oak, fir and hawthorn, and the reflective waters of Bitham Lake, combined with the wood of the middle distance and the terrace of Wardour Castle rising along the distant horizon, to form a beautifully balanced scene. Following the walk from this point as it proceeded in a north-easterly direction around Hinkley Hill, the scene shifted from this open view to a closed, heavily wooded path. For approximately two miles, 'an impervious fence of oak, elm, beech, hazel, almost completely shut out the distant landscape', giving it the quality of 'perfect seclusion'.[17] Such a long stretch of walk ordinarily risked the possibility of monotony, but Beckford managed to maintain interest by undulating its surface at various intervals along the way and by carpeting the walk with moss of varied tints and colours. This kind of variety was also heightened by the different character of the trees as the 'sparkling and feathery birch' succeeded the 'dark and solemn pine', or as the humble hawthorn followed the lofty ash. Not until the end of this first arm of the walk, in the area of one of eight gates on the Abbey estate, called the Lower Street Gate, did the eye so long imprisoned in the thickly planted avenue, range freely over the distant hills beyond Chilmark.

The second arm of the walk, which extended south-west from the Lower Street Gate to the summit of the Great Western Avenue, was designed, in contrast to the first, to be more open. A thinner tree line now afforded occasional glimpses of the Abbey, which served to stimulate curiosity until an open area brought it suddenly into view. Rutter noted, after passing beyond the Lower North Terrace, that a beautiful view of the south-western side of the Abbey was presented at the intersection of the Nine Miles Walk and a long 'natural' avenue called the Clerk's Walk.[18]

From the Clerk's Walk the drive pursued a winding course through an enclosure of pine and Scotch fir until it reached the western extremity of the Great Western Avenue, the beginning of the third arm, where, upon turning east, the Abbey burst into view in 'all the huge splendour of exalted height and magnificence'.[19] Proceeding in an easterly direction towards the Abbey, the walk followed the Great Western Avenue until it was intersected by an avenue which ascended south to the top of Beacon Hill, where the original tower was to be erected. It was here that Beckford created a terrace that cut across the whole breadth of the garden, a distance of approximately two and a half miles, providing striking views of the Abbey in its setting as well as the surrounding countryside. Beacon Terrace, as it was called, contributed to the unity of the total design by being 'bounded in an irregular line by every variety of forest tree and garden shrub' in keeping with the other walkways and avenues on the estate.[20] As a finished work in 1814, Beckford thought it was superior to the formal terrace at Stourhead: 'Believe me, the terrace at Stourton is no longer comparable to that at Fonthill: the lines too straight, the ground not undulating, a repetition of pyramids, larches planted regularly everywhere like the *fleur-de-lis* on the royal robe which used to be at St. Denis. I don't like it, I can't admire it'.[21]

The next striking view of the Abbey could be seen as one descended eastward from Beacon Hill along the final section of the walk. Over a long measure of ground, 'varied by gentle undulations and studded with clumps of trees, displaying a rich assemblage of glowing and luxuriant tints', the Abbey appeared, 'forming a grand mass of embattled towers, surmounted by the lofty octagon' and backed 'by an elevated woodland of a sombre aspect, which by contrast heightens the striking and brilliant effect of the edifice'.[22] As one proceeded down the hill, the focus of interest shifted to a series of alternating scenes designed to keep the eye stimulated. The uneven pine lawn on the right opposed in texture and colour the rolling turf on the left, while the tall stately wood of White Mead Woods which followed gave emphasis to the depth of Bittern Vale, a few steps beyond. Passing through the open light of valley, the scene again shifted to the broken lights and shadows of the trees and thickets surrounding Bitham Lake.

Bitham Lake, one of the finest landscape features on the Fonthill estate, was a testimony to the principles of picturesque landscaping. While the creation of it through damming pre-dated Beckford, he did capitalise on its potential for strong visual effects.[23] This was most evident in the way in which the deliberate arrangement of coves and inlets of various sizes and the heavy planting along the edges concealed any lines of definition and broke the uniformity of the banks reminiscent of the treatment of the lake in Old Park. Here the 'luxuriance of the shrubs and trees', wrote John Britton, 'the wildness of some spots contrasted with the smoothness and softness of others', and the 'shape and undefined borders of the lake' rendered the entire scene attractive, particularly to the 'artist and botanist'.[24] James Storer felt that it looked like 'the crater of an ancient volcano', whose shape was such that its 'stretching and meandering' contributed to the illusion of a greater size than it really possessed.[25] In some places, moss-covered stones and knotted tree-roots were allowed to remain exposed because they mixed well with the different coloured soils and the tints of vegetation, while the overhanging trees, shrubbery, and sky reflected in the water enhanced the quality of the scene. From its southern side, the lake and its surroundings formed a perfect foreground in a picture which presented the Abbey to great advantage. J. Sidney Taylor (1795–1841), the correspondent who was assigned to provide reports on Fonthill in 1823 for the *Morning Chronicle*, recorded the palpable effect of this vantage point on an occasion when the Abbey was bathed in the soft radiance of a moonlit night:

At night I had an opportunity of seeing the effect of a serene and beautiful moonlight sky upon the Abbey and the surrounding scenery … where there is a better combination of circumstances for a well composed picture of this kind than any I have yet seen. The mellow lustre and broad shadows which fall upon the majestic towers, the rugged battlements, the shafted oriels, and arched recesses of the Abbey, destroy all the detail of those parts which, in the broad-day, appear confusedly heaped together, and force upon the spectator the idea of disproportion and incongruity. The antique form of the edifice takes its full effect both on the eye and the imagination. The newness of its colour is not then at variance with the ancient character which its formation assumes. It does not seem to be an usurper upon the realms of antiquity, but a legitimate inheritor of the honours that are paid her. Entrenched in gloomy grandeur in its woody heights, tinged with the silvery flickering lights, which give a deeper tone to its solitude, and reflecting its broad masses in the calm transparency of the lake below, on which sometimes the wild bird raises his lonely cry; it seems the throne of ancient superstition, which has stood amid the storms of ages, and overlooked the revolutions of time … [26]

As for the tone of this section of the garden, it was in keeping with the general character of the place, 'tranquil and secluded'. For Beckford it was a *tour de force* in naturalistic design. 'The lake looks as if God had made it, it is so natural, without the least trace of art; I don't say it is marvellous, for its banks are too flat, but it spreads itself grandiosely and the swans look as if they are in Paradise'.[27] The beauty of the lake was enhanced in 1810 by the completion of an American garden on the northern end of the lake, the last major landscape feature as the visitor walked up a steep incline to the southern lawn where the nine-mile excursion finally ended.[28]

The carriage drive within the Abbey estate extended approximately six miles, starting from the eastern side of the building, running down through the southern portion of the grounds, and skirting north around Beacon Hill to the Stone Gate, located at the beginning of the Great Western Avenue. We know this drive was finished in 1801 because Beckford used it to show Lord Nelson the estate in a horse-drawn phaeton. As the story goes, Beckford pursued the drive at such a spanking pace that Nelson became nervously agitated and asked him to stop, saying 'this is too much for me—you must set me down'. They then walked the rest of the way with Beckford later expressing amazement that the brave hero of the Nile could be so emotionally fragile.[29] Actually, this carriage drive was part of a longer ride, connecting with it at Stone Gate, which traced the outer boundaries of the entire Fonthill domain, a distance of almost twenty-two miles.

The design of the section inside the Abbey grounds was similar to that of the Nine Miles Walk. The first mile was bounded and shut in by a thick plantation of pine, fir, and larch, with wild underwood and flowering shrubs filling the spaces between trees so that the extent of their thickness could not be judged. With the exception of an unexpected opening about a quarter of the way along its length, this first stretch moved in a winding course almost entirely through deep and solemn shadows. At any one time, it was not possible to see more than a hundred yards ahead until a point was reached near the Eastern Gate where the drive turned abruptly to the right and passed through an irregular line of more open woods.

To maintain interest along the ride remaining inside the barrier wall, its course was planned to curve by the southern bank of Bitham Lake to take advantage of the special view of the Abbey that Storer liked so well. A rough lawn was added farther south to oppose the darkness of Whitemead Wood on the hill to the north of the drive. The drive then curved north past the Norwegian Lawn on the left where Beckford had constructed a Norwegian Hut, a log house in keeping with the Alpine character of the trees growing in this area and on the slopes of Beacon Hill. It then proceeded almost directly north past the Laurel Walk on the left before reaching its terminal point inside the Abbey grounds at Stone Gate.

The prevailing characteristic of the design of the carriage drive was once again naturalistic: another example of the planned informality of the grounds. It was like reading a page from Price's *Essay on the Picturesque*: 'The banks [were] sometimes broken and abrupt; sometimes smooth, and gently but not uniformly sloping; now wildly overhung with thickets of trees and bushes; now loosely skirted with wood; no regular verge of grass, no cut edges, no distinct lines of separation; all is mixed and blended together, and the border of the road itself, shaped by the mere tread of passengers and animals, as unconstrained as the footsteps that formed it: even the tracks of the wheels ... contributed to the picturesque effect of the whole'.[30] As in the case of the Nine Miles Walk, the carriage drive seemed not to be the consequence of artful design but cut through the woods by the forces of nature, so that it was possible to appreciate its design in accordance with Price's theory for 'not from what *had*, but from what had *not* been done'.[31]

After the completion of the fifteen-mile walk and drive in 1800, Beckford concerned himself with additional improvements on the estate. 'I love building, planting, gardening', he told Cyrus Redding later, 'whatever will keep me employed in the open air. I like to be among workmen'.[32] Macquin reported that even the royal works of St George's Chapel, Windsor were set aside during the time that Wyatt was serving as Surveyor-General to allow four hundred and sixty men to be employed at Fonthill, working in shifts by day and by lamp at night and on weekends as well, regardless of weather conditions, to expedite the work, whether on the grounds or the building.[33] Beckford at this time, Macquin reported, was on constant watch 'surveying the work thus expedited, the busy levy of masons, the high and giddy dancing of the lights, and the strange effects produced upon the architecture and woods below ... wasting the coldest hours of December darkness in feasting his sense with this display of almost superhuman power'. He then added that 'these singular traits of character will not surprise those who have made mankind their study.... The minds most nearly allied to genius are the most apt to plunge into these extremes: a Beckford builds a Babel by torchlight, a Byron writes a Cain with exultation; and Eratastrus burns the Temple of Diana to gain an immortal though infamous celebrity'.

With this kind of activity much was accomplished in creating the setting for the Abbey in the years that followed: the extension of the twenty-two mile drive around the entire domain outside the Abbey estate's barrier wall, the completion of the American Garden in 1810 and Beacon Terrace across the breadth of the Abbey estate in 1814. The problem of handling the transition between the Abbey and the immediately surrounding grounds was solved, and the horticultural work carried out almost automatically every year. The construction of the Abbey with its inherent structural problems was costly but the creation of the surrounding grounds and the ongoing tasks to maintain so vast an area was formidable and were a constant drain on Beckford's financial resources.

One of the few visitors to gain access to the estate during this period of development was William Cobbett, whose keen interest in horticulture motivated the visit. He examined the grounds in August of 1808 and was impressed with what he saw:

Well, we saw Fonthill, but even if I had the talent to do justice to it in a written description, ten such sheets as this would not suffice for the purpose. When I see you, I will at times give you an hour's account of it. After that sight, all sights become mean until that be out of the mind. We both thought Wardour the finest place we had ever seen, but Wardour makes but a single glade in Beckford's immense grounds and plantations. The grass walks at Fonthill, fifteen feet wide, if stretched out in a right line, would reach from there to London, upwards of ninety miles; there are sixty-five men and ten horses constantly employed in the pleasure-grounds, a thousand acres of which, being the interior and more private part, are enclosed within a wall of squared stone from ten to twelve feet high, with an oak palisade at top pointed with iron. Scarcely any soul is permitted to enter here, and, from what we had heard, we had not the least expectation of it.… But not to see the house, which no one as yet has seen the inside of. The outside we approached very near, and, like the rest, it sets description at defiance.[34]

Three years later, after being committed to Newgate prison for his criticism of the military, Cobbett wrote to Beckford to obtain seeds for his own estate at Botley:

Colonel Johnston, who has I understand, lately been at Fonthill, has, by what he has told me of your disposition to oblige me in the *planting way*, emboldened me to give you this trouble. He did, indeed, bring me a message from you, that you should have pleasure in directing your gardener to furnish me with anything that I might want that you had to spare.…

To you, who know so much about planting, and who have, of course, so often experienced the disappointments, arising from seeds got from those most faithless people the Nurseryman (I mean *false*, for they may have as much *belief* as the rest of this most believing nation); to you I need not describe the vexations that I have suffered from the same cause. The fact is, that I have lost so much time and labour from this cause, beside what I have suffered in the way of vexation, that I have almost made a vow never to trust to a Nurseryman's seeds again. It is a principle with me, that, when a man begins to beget children, he ought if possible, to begin to plant, or sow, trees. I did so the moment I had a foot of land for the purpose; and the greatest pleasure I have in the way of occupation (next after giving good hard blows to despotic rulers) is in raising trees of all sorts, but particularly timber-trees. This is but a poor apology for plaiging you, but it is the best I have to offer.

What I would beg leave to ask of you is this: that you would have the goodness to direct your gardener whom, I believe I saw in 1808, and who appeared to be a very clever man, to cause to be collected for me, at the proper time, the following things

12 Bushels of Larch Cones
12 Bushels of Spruce fir cones
12 Bushels of Scotch fir Cones
6 Bushels of Weymouth Pine Cones
2 Bushels, or any *Smaller Quantity*, of any other sort of fir Cones, and as many sorts as he can
3 Bushels of *Sycamore Seeds*
A Gallon of Acacia Seed

A Gallon of Laburnum Seed

2 Bushels of Horse Chestnuts

and a small quantity of any other *Tree* Seed that it may be convenient for him to collect ... .[35]

Beckford responded to Cobbett by indicating that because of a recent thinning of the woods around the Abbey that it would take 'some years to come at least to produce any quantity of seeds worthy your acceptance'.

Among the changes at this time, the horticultural work on the estate deserves some special attention. The role of plants in the Fonthill landscape design rank in importance with some of its other features. As early as 1803, Lady Anne Hamilton was impressed by the plants during her visit, noting that a 'finer feast for the botanist than this Noble place is, cannot be'.[36] It is noteworthy that the Fonthill landscape restored the status of the individual plant in the garden scene which in the extreme formal garden of the eighteenth century had been almost totally neglected. For years the individual plant had been an insignificant element in a mathematical scheme, one that was shaped, cut, or treated at the architect's whim. For a similar reason, flowers had been rarely used because they tended to grow in a free, unrestrained manner without regard to artificial form. But Beckford recognised their importance for colouring, contrast, and variety and incorporated them eagerly into his plan. He often sought new varieties of plants and took special care to avoid the excesses of botanical exhibits.

The horticultural experiments for Fonthill were performed on a portion of an eight-acre kitchen and flower garden, belonging to the old estate, approximately a mile and a half north of the Lower Street Gate. This extensive project, hidden by a row of lofty pines, was completed before February 1797, when a detailed description of it appeared in the *European Magazine* article. 'Mr. Beckford's next undertaking', the editor wrote, 'was the formation of a new Kitchen and Flower Garden, contiguous to each other, in a more convenient scite, under a warmer aspect, and upon a scale four times larger than the old one. The Hot Walls, Pineries, Conservatories, quantity of glazed Frame-work, the Gardener's House, importation of soil for this extensive spot of many acres, with its plantation and nurseries, and an extensive inclosure of handsome brick-wall round the whole, have altogether concurred to render this work almost as unrivalled in magnitude and convenience, as it must have been in matter of expence'.[37] Within the vicinity of the Abbey, Beckford would later add a small hot-house for Piero, his dwarf-servant, and an herb garden, 'containing such plants as we may suppose the monks might have cultivated to use in medicine'.[38] Near the end of the Nine Miles Walk, he half-concealed a Chinese garden, surrounded by a light iron fence and 'particularly appropriated to the culture of the rarest flower'.[39] J. C. Loudon recorded in 1807 the existence of a 'rose-ground' and 'thornery' treated in a naturalistic manner so as not to appear as obvious contrivances,[40] while Storer described in 1812 a mile-long path next to the Clerk's Walk that presented during the spring and summer a 'fascinating display of flowers of spontaneous growth, of luxuriant shrubs and variegated hollies'.[41]

It is evident that Beckford seems to have been well aware of the problem of clumping plants as displays foreign to the landscape and totally without connection to the layout as a whole. The way he used exotic flowers as by-scenes in the woods to curb this problem has already been mentioned, but the American garden at Fonthill, created on the northern margin of Bitham Lake by Beckford with the help of his head-gardener Mr. Milne may serve as another example. It consisted of a great variety of American flowers and shrubs. Its winding paths led the visitor through rhododendrons, some places fifteen feet high. In his description of it, Rutter wrote that the 'deep pink flowers shed an universal glow over an extensive declivity—here and there the beautiful magnolia displayed the exquisite whiteness of its large blossoms—while clusters of azaleas mingled with these loftier exotics in the richest harmony of colour and fragrance; the Carolina rose profusely studded the walks with its gorgeous blossoms—the allspice of the same region shed its exquisite perfume over the whole extent of these gardens—and the arbutus luxuriated in groups as lofty and as branching as the Portugal laurel'.[42] The whole display added considerable colour to the scene and provided a dramatic contrast to the monochromatic character of the Gothic Abbey and the dense, gloomy woodland.

The American plantation also created in Beckford's words, a 'great effect' because of its 'unusual arrangement'.[43] The flowers and shrubs were so carefully 'disposed in groups and thickets that it appeared that they had sprung up naturally'.[44] To ensure coherence of design every step was taken to make the foreign plants seem native to their setting. 'In this spot', wrote a visitor, 'the formality of gardening is absolutely lost. These enormous exotic plants mingle with the oak, the beech, and the pine, so naturally that they would delight a landscape painter'.[45] Here, as throughout the Abbey estate, the usual natives of the forest, the heath and the garden, wrote another visitor in 1823, 'meet together in one spot, and form one beautiful and happy family; and all flourish and bloom together, by mutual consent. Roses blush from out the bosom of the heath furze; rhododendrons filling their gorgeous flowers at random among ferns and forest shrubs; the frail woodbine hangs its dependent clusters upon the everlasting laurel; and on the ground all sorts of rich (so called) *garden* flowers group themselves with those gentle families of the earth which we … have chosen to banish from our presence into the fields and hedges'.[46]

It is clear that, whether laying out drives, avenues, and walkways, or planting woods, shrubs, and flowers, Beckford made every effort to avoid the artificial extravagances of the architectural garden, favouring instead a freer design based on the irregularity of natural landscape. Following the tradition of the late eighteenth-century naturalistic designers, he incorporated variety and asymmetry into his garden plan. As J. S. Taylor reported in the *Morning Chronicle*, Beckford was eminently successful in this regard:

How little and contemptible is the taste displayed in the vaunted gardens of Versailles compared with that which has formed these beautiful grounds, where the only ambition of art has been to follow nature. Here no absurd artifices remind us of the geometrical gardener, with his compasses and his diagram, binding and torturing native charms in one chain of ostentatious formality. Nature has not here by barbarous refinement been dislocated out of her proper graces; she did not appear tight-laced and in a hoop petticoat, without the merit of simplicity, or the fascination of true elegance. In the grounds of Fonthill all beauty has been cultivated on so just a principle, that it seemed the spontaneous effect of natural fertility. From the lighter sprinkling of verdure, to the deepest gloom of almost impervious foliage, all partakes of the freedom of untrained production, and whether 'by hill or valley, fountain or fresh shade', the votary of nature may feel himself under the influence of her acknowledged supremacy. The diversity of situation and circumstance is also very great. Here are extent, repose, and majesty for the pencil of Claude; the rugged grandeur that would attract R[u]ysdael, and the deep and savage wildness which suited the genius of Salvator. Here might Collins indulge in the dreams of fanciful enchantment, Gray soar upon the eagle wing of an ardent ambition, and the classic Thomson 'lie at large, and sing the glories of the circling year'.[47]

Taylor went on to explain that the Abbey's style was middle Gothic and its 'external gives the impression that it was never originally contemplated as a whole, but made up of parts combined without much reference to general proportions and symmetry'. For this reason, it could not compare with the workmanship of Westminster Abbey or Salisbury Cathedral. 'But it is the charm of the grounds', he wrote, 'and the embellishments of its interior, which are its real and exquisite sources of attraction. The former are at least equal to any kind which I have seen; the latter surpasses all I could have conceived'....

'The Gewgaws of Luxury':
The Fonthill Splendens Sale of 1801

It was soon after Nelson's visit that Beckford decided to make the Abbey more suitable as his permanent residence. The idea then of maintaining two mansions on the same estate became insupportable due to serious financial issues he had to face. The increasing financial drain of building the Abbey and the outlay involved in the design and construction of its grounds was just one of the factors that led to the ultimate demise of Splendens. The loss of several sugar plantations in Jamaica in 1799, following a long-contested and expensive Chancery suit, suddenly reduced the income generated from Beckford's plantations by twenty-five per cent, a dramatic cutback at a time when his expenditure was so high. To complicate matters, since 1782 Beckford's financial agents had continuously engaged in underhand activities that increased his debts and financial insecurity.[1] Rumours about the state of his financial affairs were already in circulation, but dismantling a major portion of such an impressive building provided visible evidence that 'England's Wealthiest Son' needed to retrench. Beckford took the first step by beginning to dismantle part of his father's mansion in the summer of 1801, thereby precipitating the sale of the contents of the mansion in August. Eyebrows were raised when the papers announced his forthcoming sale:

PART of the SUPERLATIVELY ELEGANT and MAGNIFICENT HOUSEHOLD FURNITURE, *French Plate* PIER and CHIMNEY GLASSES of signal magnitude and perfection, CHANDELIERS AND LUSTRES; a superbe ORGAN (*in the Ha*ll) built by Crang; Gobelin Tapestry in *fine Preservation*; MARBLE BUSTS and GROUPS, ANTIQUE BRONZES, PICTURES, Granite and Tessellated Slabs, mounted in Or-molu, as CONSOLES AND PIER TABLES, *Antique* CABINETS, enriched by valuable *Gems* and fine *Specimens* of the ARTS, superbe DRAWING ROOM SUITES *in rich and beautiful Silk Damasks and Satins*; CURTAINS, Sophas and Chairs to correspond; a STATE BED, enriched by *Crimson Velvet Hanging*s, and rich Ornaments; the SPLENDID and SUMPTUOUS SUITE OF SATIN HANGINGS and FURNITURE, trimmed with BULLION and Silk FRINGE, designed with singular Taste and fitted *a la Turque*, and a Variety of Rare, Curious and Valuable Effects, the Genuine Property of

WILLIAM BECKFORD, ESQ.OF FONTHILL, Wilts.

The Assemblage of DOMESTIC FURNITURE is of a *superior Description*, and elegant Satin Wood BOOKCASES, COMMODES, PIER, CARD, DINING, PEMBROKE AND DRESSING TABLES, formed of choice WOODS; *Suites* of CHAIRS, covered with *Damask, Morocco, Satin and Cotton*; large and excellent SOFAS, CHAISE LONGE, FAUTEIULS, and BERGIERS; AXMINSTER, TURKEY, BRUSSELS and NEEDLEWORK CARPETS, of large Dimensions; Sets of Window Curtains, *elegant* TRIPODS,CANDELABRAS and GIRANDOLES; *highly polished Steel* REGISTER STOVES; capital *Four-post and Field* BEDSTEADS, with rich COTTON and DIMITY Hangings, and Window Curtains en suite; *prime* GOOSE and DOWN BEDS, and *excellent* BEDDING; WARDROBES, Chests of Drawers, and the usual Assortment of Chamber Furniture—*The whole of which is formed with Taste and expensively finished.*

One of the first reactions to this announcement came from *The Times*: 'The sale of part of MR. BECKFORD'S fine furniture at Fonthill has caused much surprise to many people, more especially as he is still laying out so much money at that place. We are assured, however, that the works are still going on as usual, and that it is intended to re-furnish the greatest part of the house in another stile'.[2] Beckford appears to have attempted to lay the rumours to rest by providing information through his agents to the *Morning Post*. This paper reported shortly after the sale that 'when one considers that Mr. Beckford possesses above one hundred and thirty thousand a year income, it is idle to suppose that a diminution of £6000 a year would drive him from his home, and compel him to sell his furniture and the materials of his house. We are well assured by those in the confidence of Mr. Beckford, that no decree in the West Indies, or elsewhere, to deprive him of part of his income, ever did exist'.[3]

It has long been believed that Beckford had only one auction at Fonthill in 1801, but he actually held two.[4] There was a second sale on 7 October and the following two days which consisted of building materials, furniture and eight fine marble chimney-pieces. While it has been overlooked, it is referred to in a letter to Beckford in Paris from his general agent Nicholas Williams, dated 11 September 1801, in which he explains that he intended to 'return to Fonthill before the Sale for the Materials of the Wings, which is to take place the first Week in October'.[5] A catalogue for this sale was issued and sold for two shillings.[6] Some idea of the contents of this sale can be gleaned from the auctioneer Harry Phillips's announcement in various public venues:

THE valuable BUILDING MATERIALS of the two Wings and Offices of FONTHILL MANSION, Wilts, the Property of WM. BECKFORD, Esq. Comprising the copper and lead coverings, sashes, doors, wainscotting, flooring, pavements, stone stairs-cases, iron balustrades, 40 solid stone columns and pilastres, and the stone which form the colonades; stout mahogany doors, formed of choice and beautiful wood; magnificent statuary chimney-pieces, enriched by statuary figures, 4 and 5 feet high, supporting the mantles, of exquisite sculpture and classically designed; together with the Furniture of two suits of rooms, comprising two large pier and chimney glasses, a few pictures, register and Bath stoves, chairs, tables, bedding, and miscellaneous articles of utility.[7]

The impact of the building materials sale was to leave the east and west wings of Splendens standing for the most parts as empty shells.[8] The final decision over the fate of Splendens would not be made for another six years.

While two copies of the building materials sale catalogues have survived, they do not contain information about the buyers or prices. However, the catalogue copy of the principal sale in August, now in the Wallace Collection, belonged to Phillips himself with names of buyers, prices paid, and various notations throughout making it possible to reconstruct the event.[9] It even includes a final accounting of the proceeds of the sale, Phillips's total expenses incurred and a note of his five per cent commission of £358 8s. Beckford's legal representative for the sale is also identified as the firm of Foxhall & Fryer, furniture makers and upholsterers, of Old Cavendish Street, London.

The first sale generated a great deal of public attention over the four days it was held from the 19th to the 22nd of August. With the public view beginning on the 10th of August, the roads to the estate were clogged with people and carriages and for a radius of fifteen miles it was practically impossible to find overnight accommodations. The *Morning Chronicle* reported that from 'Salisbury, Andover, Bath, Weymouth, &c. all the subordinate towns, the villas, and even the hamlets in their respective vicinities, the roads swarmed all the morning with shoals of the young and the gay, slaving as they could to this splendid exhibition'.[10]

Fonthill Splendens naturally attracted the attention of English society when the sale was announced. Beckford's acknowledged reputation as a connoisseur, the prominence of his family and the public scandal involving his relationship with William Courtenay undoubtedly had something to do with the fact that the public flocked to the estate for the principal sale. On the first day of the auction and three following days at 11:00 a.m., every room in the mansion and the adjacent park swelled with people, the court- and stable-yard were crowded with carriages, and all the gates, doors, and passages with 'lackies and beggars'.[11]

At the outset, *The Times* scoffed at the importance of the sale, noting that the 'principal competition is expected among the Farmers. Though it is said some of the best speculators despise *or-moulú* and *tessellated slabs second-hand*'.[12] The report continued to make light of the forthcoming event: 'The price of grain will be accurately known by that of tripods and candelabras, and many a Miller's wife is toasting to "wheat £50 a load", or else no bullion-fringe and satin-hangings. The *Landed-interest* must surely exult at the taste and spirit which thus disperses gems, antiques, and specimens of the arts amongst their tenants. For our part, we confess we would rather at any time have the Farmer's *collection* than the "Squires"'. As it turned out, all ranks of society were in attendance, and many of the bidders on the scene were prominent members of the landed gentry and nobility. A correspondent, who attended the third day of the sale, had a different assessment of the offerings: 'There never was in this part of the country, or perhaps in the world, a collection of finer or more superb furniture, in proportion to its quantity. So very ill founded has been the foolish surmise that nothing was meant to be sold but old-fashioned and worn-out articles. The books and a very few of the best paintings only have been kept back'.[13]

Based on the layout of the catalogue, the auction appears to have taken place in the east wing on the first day, then moved to the west wing on the second, ending up on the last two days in the Great Entrance Hall of the main building. The weight of some of the lots and their appeal in being seen in their original location would have encouraged the sale of the items *in situ* rather than moving each one by hand to the Great Hall. For Phillips, who stood at the podium to open the event, it was an important sale. After working with James Christie, he had been on his own as London auctioneer since 1796, but he now began an association with Beckford that later culminated in his handling of the famous thirty-seven day Fonthill Abbey auction of 1823, a sale that enhanced the reputation of the New Bond Street firm.

The first day offerings consisted of the furnishings of the east wing, including stoves, couches, chairs, carpets, bedsteads, chests and window hangings. Henry Thomas Fox-Strangeways (1747–1802), 2nd Earl of Ilchester, bought the most expensive items of the day: lot 33, a four-posted bedstead from the East Corner Bedchamber, described as having 'carved and fluted mahogany feet posts, japanned cornice, 6 feet wide, with a handsome chintz cotton furniture, lined throughout and fringed'; and lot 72, a high mahogany guarderobe, measuring eight by eight and a half, containing sliding shelves and four drawers in the central part flanked by two wings lined with green baize. Both lots sold for £27 6s each. One of the most active buyers was the Revd John Savile Ogle of Kirkley (1786–1853), son of Dr Newton Ogle, Dean of Winchester, and brother-in-law of Richard Brinsley Sheridan, who took in eleven lots on the opening day.[14] Some locals also bid. Mr 'Bracher Tisbury', who bought a mahogany oval dining table, was undoubtedly a member of the Bracher family which occupied land over a long period of time in Tisbury, a short distance from Fonthill. Other local bidders were the Revd Thomas Prevost, Vicar of Tisbury, and Dr Lambert, a Hindon surgeon and apothecary (whose colleague, Dr Ames, shows up as a buyer on the second day).[15] Another local bidder, identified as 'Andrews Knoyle', was likely James Andrews, Beckford's deputy gamekeeper.[16]

The name 'Westmacott' appears among the successful bidders on the first day. This was in all probability Richard Westmacott (1775–1856), an associate of Beckford's architect James Wyatt, who was on hand all four days supervising the sale. Two years earlier, Westmacott had completed a statue for Beckford called *La Madonna della Gloria*. Other notable buyers included John Francis Gwyn, owner of Ford Abbey, near Axminster, Devon, Lady Stafford (1745–1805), third wife of Granville Leveson-Gower, and Lady Shaftesbury (1773–1865), also known as Lady Spencer, daughter of the 3rd Duke of Marlborough. One of the most intriguing bidders on this and subsequent days was William Evill, the upholsterer and auctioneer of 18 Milson Street, Bath, who was representing William Wyatt Dimond (1750–1812), the joint proprietor of the Theatre Royal in Bath. Evill bought lot 90, which, according to a tantalising note written in the printed catalogue, was 'a picture of ruins'.[17]

The furnishings in the second day's sale came from the west wing. The catalogue's description of individual lots is sparse, creating problems in any attempt to trace the provenance of important pieces once owned by Beckford or his family. A case in point is lot 5, which Phillips lists simply as 'a harpsichord'. Beckford was known as a masterly player of this instrument. 'When he touches the Harpsichord', observed a visitor to Fonthill in 1793, 'you fancy you hear Piccini, Gluck or Orpheus himself playing on it'.[18] Dedicated to music, he would always insist on playing on the finest instrument. In 1781, while in Augsburg, he bought a harpsichord for Fonthill,[19] and since the great harpsichord and organ maker in Augsburg at the time was Johann Andreas Stein (1728–1792), there is a possibility that lot 5 was made by him.[20] Ironically, it was knocked down for £8 8s to Mr Sawney of Salisbury, but according to a note Phillips included in his final accounting of the proceeds, he never paid for it. Two other musical instruments were sold: both pianofortes by John Broadwood (1732–1812), of Great Pulteney Street, London, known for the high quality of his craftsmanship. Lot 16, on the third day, was a pianoforte with a mahogany case inlaid with satin and other woods, probably an early square or rectangular model.[21] A more elegant Broadwood, 'a fine-toned GRAND PIANO FORTE' (lot 186) sold for £63 on the fourth day.

A pier table (lot 62, second day), bought by Henry Stephens of Chevenage House, Gloucestershire, may be identified with the help of a contemporary account of the sale. The sale catalogue lists this as 'An *elegant* mahogany *pier table*, richly inlaid and ornamented with metal work'. This may well be one of the tables the *Morning Chronicle* referred to when observing that 'Two Library Tables, also of the most elegant construction and exquisite workmanship, hardly brought one half of what was expected of them'.[22] It is known that back-to-back writing and dressing commodes were sold at this sale, but they appear to have been separated, as was often the case with this type of furniture instead of being placed together to form a large centre-table. The companion piece to lot 62 may have been lot 14, on the second day, bought by Penleaze [23] for fifteen guineas ('An *elegant* mahogany PIER TABLE, richly ornamented with ormolu'). Little was known of their whereabouts after the sale, until one of them was sold in Phillips's rooms by Sir George Holford in 1928; its companion then surfaced in London in 1956 and was purchased by the Victoria and Albert Museum.[24] The two most expensive lots of the second day were the bedsteads in the north-East corner Bed Room and the south-west corner Bed Room. The first of these, lot 7, bought by Groves for £36 15s, was described as 'An *elegant* 4 feet 6 *four-post* BEDSTEAD, neatly japanned and gilt, lined with tester and cornices, japanned, to match bedstead, with chintz cotton furniture, lined with pink lutestring and full valence [*sic*], fringed, 4½ feet wide'. Edward Seymour, 11th Duke of Somerset (1775–1855), and brother-in-law to the Duke of Hamilton, bought the second, more ornate one for £32 11s. It was portrayed as 'A *capital* four-post wainscot double-screwed lath bottom bedstead, 6 feet 2 inches wide, with carved feet posts, japanned and gilt, with a *chintz cotton furniture*, lined and fringed, with a sweep top cornice, japanned'. Mrs Wyndham of Marshwood House, Dinton, bought lot 13, the mahogany lady's dressing table with a folding top.[25] Most of the expensive mirror glass for which Splendens was famous and which gave the interiors of the mansion the effect of extended space was bought in by Scott. The three exceptions were the gilt framed pier mirror in the middle Bed Room secured by William Davis (lot 54) and the gilt framed chimney mirrors in the south-east corner Bed Room (lot 38) and middle Bed Room (lot 55) bought by Joseph Vidler, the Salisbury upholsterer and cabinet maker.[26]

On the third day, the scene shifted to the contents of Mansion House itself where some of the most expensive furnishings were found, stimulating great interest and sometimes very high prices. The auction was held in the Great Entrance Hall, a massive square room almost eighty-six feet high and thirty-eight and a half feet square. Supported by enormous piers of solid stone, the floor was made of polished Italian marble. There, visitors upon entering saw the magnificent Crang organ which someone was hired to play until the auction began. The power of its rising sounds filling the room contributed to an atmosphere of elegance.

The press drew particular attention to the Turkish Room, on the west side of the Egyptian Hall on the ground level below. As one reporter observed, the 'richness of the hangings, all silk or satin, of superlative quality—the brilliant French plates of glass which decorated and enlivened every side in the room—the sofas formed in the most sumptuous stile of Oriental magnificence—the chairs and stools, all gilt with burnished gold, attracted every eye'.[27] It was a superb example of Beckford's taste for oriental décor, a room that he personally designed and furnished during his proprietorship of Splendens. John Britton has provided the most vivid account of how this room looked at the time, which he said was 'as splendid and sumptuous as those magical recesses of enchanted palaces we read of in the Arabian Nights Entertainments:'

The ground of the vaulted ceiling is entirely gold, upon which the most beautiful arabesques and wreaths of flowers are delineated, in the vivid colours of nature, by the pencil of those distinguished French artists, Boileau and Feuglet. The whole room is hung round with ample curtains of the richest orange satin, with deep fringes of silk and gold. Between the folds of this drapery, mirrors of uncommon size appear as openings leading to other apartments. The carpet, of a reddish Etruscan brown, contrasts admirably with the tints of the hangings. The windows are screened by blinds of orange silk, admitting a warm glow of summer light. Opposite to these apertures, an altar of the finest verde-antique contains the fire-place, secured by a grate-work of gilt bronze. On each side are two cabinets, of an elegant and novel form, sculptured and gilt in a very magnificent style. The upper panels, painted by Smirke, are very inferior to the generality of this artist's productions; but the drawers, by Hamilton, in imitation of antique cameos, are designed with the utmost grace, and executed with spirit and correctness. Candelabra, vases of japan, cassolets, and piles of cushions, are distributed about the apartment, which combines more splendor, singularity, and effect, than any room of its size in the kingdom. The space is not large, not above twenty-six by twenty-three; but the whole is so managed, by the aid of mirrors, as to appear boundless, and to seize most powerfully upon the imagination.[28]

When Phillips took the podium on the third day, he opened with a eulogy, claiming that the lots were 'the most splendid and transcendant he ever had the honour of bringing to the hammer'. There was not 'an item in this day's sale', he added hyperbolically, 'which might not, both for value and magnificence, suit any Palace in Europe'.[29] The buyer of the first lot, identified as 'Greville Hon.', was in all likelihood Charles F. Greville (1749–1809), the horticulturalist, son of the first Earl of Warwick and nephew of Beckford's friend Sir William Hamilton. Among the other bidders were Henry Stephens who bought lot 18, consisting of 205 yards of 'Barre' satin hangings fringed with gold from the Turkish Room for £110 5s and lot 21, the 'six STOOLS, *gilt in burnished gold*', which could have been the ones Edward Foxhall, Beckford's upholsterer, made after designs by James Wyatt.[30] Lord Digby (1773–1856), whose country seat was Sherborne Castle, Dorset, managed to buy the French plate glass mirror over the chimney in the Turkish Room for £105. A new significant bidder was Sir Christopher Bethell Codrington (1764–1843) of Dodington Park, Gloucestershire, who was represented at the sale by an agent named Barker. Codrington had engaged Wyatt to build a neo-classical country house for him at the same time the architect was building Fonthill Abbey. He was with Wyatt when the architect was killed in a carriage accident in 1813. Codrington bought the Turkish style tripods designed by J. J. Boileau (lot 22), but his most expensive purchases were the French pier and chimney glass (lots 66 and 67), the brilliant cut glass chandelier of 'ten lights' in the Tapestry Room (lot 79), and a gold framed mirror from the Great Dining Room (lot 92), for which he paid a total of £402. At the Fonthill Splendens sale six years later, Codrington would buy the main staircase of Splendens, ultimately incorporating its wrought ironwork at Dodington Park.[31] It would not be a surprise to find that some of the plate glass from the 1801 sale was also incorporated at Dodington, but none has yet been identified.

The massive organ built (lot 46) built by John Crang (died *c*. 1792) was described as in a high state of preservation with a mahogany front, the '*pipes richly gilt, the outside elaborately carved with trophies of music and surmounted by a figure of* FAME, painted dead white, about 26 feet high and 15 wide'. Cyrus Redding recorded that its original cost was £2,000,[32] but it realised only £304 10s at this sale. It has been described recently as 'one of the important organs of its type and period'.[33] The catalogue indicates that the buyer was George, Prince of Wales, but, oddly enough it never transferred to him since it reappeared as lot 338 in the Fonthill sale of August 1807. To complicate matters, the press reported that Revd Ogle was the final bidder in the 1801 sale.[34]

A set of six settees (lots 47-49, third day), has been identified recently as possibly the work of John Soane.[35] Four of these went to the Revd Ogle and the other two to Henry Stephens. Innocuously described as having fluted legs and rails, with carved backs and crimson cushions, they sold for £7 7s a pair.[36] The name Southey appears as a buyer for lots 150 and 151 on the fourth day of the auction, but Phillips adds a note that this bidder was a resident of Warminster. There was a John William Southey living there who married Elizabeth Massey in Warminster in May 1801.[37] It is not clear that there is any relationship to the poet: Southey did have an uncle named John, but he was a lawyer in Taunton.

The Revd Richard Warner, who visited Splendens in September 1800, took special notice of the statues of Apollo and Venus, which were sold as lots 50 and 51. He felt they enhanced the Great Entrance Hall with their singular beauty, both made of white marble mounted on veined marble pedestals.[38] Although he did not mention the name of the artist, they were the work of Joseph Wilton (1722–1803), sculptor and Keeper of the Royal Academy of Arts. Records reveal that he did a *Venus de Medici* for Lord Charlemont and a *Venus and Apollo* for Lord Pembroke.[39] He was a friend of the architect William Chambers and the decorative painter G. B. Cipriani, two men who played a significant role in Beckford's past. When a young woman placed herself inadvertently next to Wilton's statue of Venus at the point when it went under the hammer, a wag from the audience asked which of the two was meant. Phillips, seized the opportunity to please the audience, replying with modest aplomb that 'the one was above all price, and he was authorised only to dispose of the other'.[40] This seems to have had an impact since the Apollo sold for £29 8s but the Venus went for £43 1s.

Among the notables at the auction was Thomas Hope (1769–1831), the art collector, furniture designer and future author of *Anastasius*, who turns up on the list of buyers on the third day. There are many interesting intellectual and artistic parallels between Hope and Beckford; both were important collectors, men of wealth and authors of famous Eastern tales and the two men became friends. Hope's presence at this sale was in part due to his purchase and remodelling of a mansion in Duchess Street, Portland Place, London, in 1799.[41] It is worth noting that the final designs for the interior rooms wove together classical and Eastern motifs. One of the first things visitors saw when they entered the Duchess Street mansion was a large portrait of Hope dressed in Turkish clothing—a symbolic statement of his combined cultural interests. One might expect that he would have bought objects from Beckford's Turkish Room but, instead, Hope carried away the two porphyry busts of Pompey and Vitellius (lots 56 and 57) that flanked the Crang Organ in the Great Hall.

A total of forty-four paintings were sold during the four-day auction. These included works by Robert Smirke, G. Duhamel, J. J. Boileau, Feuglet, and Andrea Casali. The most important works offered included the four ceiling paintings in the Turkish Room by Boileau and Feuglet (lot 29, third day), which went to 'Phillips by P. C.', the initials presumably standing for 'private commission', equivalent today to an anonymous absentee bid. In addition, twenty-one paintings by Casali were offered for sale and attracted a number of prominent buyers, among them Samuel Cox, owner of a considerable estate in Beaminster, Dorset,[42] who bought eight works by Casali during the final two days. Two unidentified historical pictures, lots 60 and 100, third day, one located over the chimney in the Grand Entrance Hall and the other over the chimney in the Great Dining Room went to him. He bought Casali's *Pigmalion* (lot 199, fourth day) and the five historical paintings (lot 99, third day) on the ceiling of the Great Dining Room. Recent research has established that Cox installed one of these five paintings, *The Banquet of the Gods*, in his Manor House and stored the remaining four, which depicted respectively the figures of Pan, Ceres, Mercury, and Pomona. After he died, his son, Samuel Jr, decided to sell the four in storage which were purchased in 1823 by Hastings Elwin for the Bath Royal Literary and Scientific Institution and incorporated in the ceiling of the Pink Room on the first floor where they can be seen today.[43]

The remaining works by Casali were sold on the fourth day. Lot 164* was added by Phillips after the catalogue was printed; it is described as a 'Picture in the Great Hall cieling [sic]', which must be the allegorical painting *Apollo in Grand Concert with the Muses*.[44] This is the painting that Britton found so distasteful—a 'proof of the wretched state of the arts about forty years ago'.[45] Harris bought it for £13 2s 6d, but failed to follow through on the payment, probably due to the expense of removing it, so it remained to be sold at a later date. The dealer Jeffrey bought two large paintings by Casali from the Picture Gallery, *K. Edgar, Elfrida and Athelwold* (lot 197) for £24 3s and *Gonaldi* for £21 (lot 198), both eight and a half by seven feet square. Michael Tijou, carver, gilder and looking glass maker, of 22 Greek Street, London, took in *Alexander and his Mistress* (lot 200) and two other unidentified Casali's (lot 202) for £28 7s. The painting *Diana* on the ceiling of the State Dressing Room (lot 115*) went to Dimond, as did *Susanna and the two elders* and *Cleopatra* (lot 201) and the five historical paintings on the ceiling of the Picture Gallery (lot 196). The latter paintings depicted the Arts and Sciences which Dimond incorporated in the ceiling of a new Theatre Royal constructed in Bath a few years later. They were purchased in 1845 by William Blathwayt (1797–1871) for Dyrham Park and all five of them can be seen there today. Three of the smaller panels *Personifications of Architecture and Astronomy*, *Personification of History Writing on the Back of Time*, and *Personifications of Music and Painting* were installed in the ceiling of the Great Hall of Dyrham Park.[46] One of the interesting features of the personification of Architecture is that she is seen in the painting as holding up a drawing of the façade of Splendens.

Among the most elegant works in the sale were two pieces of Gobelins tapestry that covered the walls in a small drawing room in Splendens called appropriately the Tapestry Room. Commissioned by Beckford's father, they measured twelve by eleven feet four inches and were in superb condition. The Revd Warner identified them as the work of Neilson and said they represented 'Esther dressing for her interview with Ahasuerus; the other her acceptance by him as his queen'.[47] The workshop of Jacques Neilson (1714–1788) at the royal Gobelins manufactory in Paris was renown for weaving sumptuous tapestries of highest quality at the time. These two pieces together with the ninety-three feet of rich gilt moulding that surrounded them (lots 68-9, third day) went to James Randall, clothier and carpet manufacturer in Wilton, for £189.[48]

On the fourth and final day of the auction, two thousand people attended, and bidding intensified for some of the most sought-after items from Splendens. The first was the sumptuous state bed designed by Soane. A tribute to the monumental Greek style, it had a canopied superstructure topped by a finial inspired by the Choragic Monument of Lysicrates in Athens. Commissioned in 1788, this elaborately carved bed bore the marks of Beckford's personal involvement in the design that Soane carried out.[49] Indicative of Beckford's effort to establish that the bloodlines of his family were blue, it was hung appropriately with crimson and scarlet fabrics with a heraldic symbol embossed in the headboard. Phillips describes this lot as 'A *magnificent* STATE BEDSTEAD, the *feet posts* richly carved and gilt, crimson velvet furniture, the inside and outside of tester and valance, richly ornamented with carved and gilt ornaments'. William Evill bought the bed for Dimond for £52 10s. Dimond must have been interested in securing it for a stage set because two months later it appeared in a performance of Othello at the Theatre Royal, Bath. The play-bill announced that 'Desdemona would be exhibited on the very sumptuous state bed, which was sold at MR. BECKFORD'S sale at Fonthill'.[50] The use of it as a prop, particularly if it continued to appear on stage, may explain why this bed is untraced today.

Newspapers mistakenly reported that the bed was designed originally for Lord Melcombe and cost £1,500. They also supplied a story that Lord Pembroke of Wilton once borrowed the bed for King George III to sleep in during a visit. But the most interesting anecdote came to light after Dimond purchased the bed. During the process of working on the bed, an upholsterer discovered a manuscript in a drawer concealed in the dome. This document contained the following statement recorded by a hired London wood monger and bed-joiner by the name of Thomas Linfoot:

This canopy was dellianiated by Thomas Linfoot, Bedjoyner in general, and performed by him partly, and entirely under his direction in the months of August, September and October in the year of our Lord and saviour JESUS CHRIST 1768 and in the Reigne of George the 3rd. N. B. The above sade Thos. Linfoot was borne at a village called Waten on the Yorkshire Woulds, in the East Riding of the County, served his time or Apprenticeship to a Cart and plough Wright at Butten Crumbe near Yorke. Cound not draw a Lease of any sorte at 30 years of age nor ever went to larne but did it by mere dint of Industry October 13th. 1768 514 Cross Lane Long Acre. London.

> Kind reader whome so ere thou be
> As thou art now so once was I
> But time that Eats uup all shall Tell
> Tho I dont hear thy passing Bell
> That thou wile dy as well as me
> Yet I hope we Both shall rise and see
> A glorious Eternity amen Thos. Linfoot.[51]

In spite of the splendour of the Soane bed, it was the French plate glass mirrors, known for their brilliant clarity, that were the prize items of the day. The most expensive lots in the entire sale were the two matching pier mirrors that hung in the Great Saloon (lots 140 and 141), each measuring 119 by 64 inches, set in richly carved gilt frames. Codrington bought both for £420 and £400 respectively as well as the chimney mirror, measuring 107 by 56 inches, from the State Bed Chamber for £273 (lot 123). Morell, Lord Ilchester, and Shute also bought French plate glass on the fourth day.[52]

In addition, there were some striking pieces of furniture. For £63, Lord Ilchester bought the satin wood bookcase, eight by eight and a half feet, that stood in the State Bed Chamber.

It was ornamented with gilt beads and ormolu moulding with four panelled doors in the lower section and four plate glass doors in the upper (lot 127). Vidler bought a similar bookcase, located in the Cabinet Anti Room [sic], but with folding doors and recesses (lot 156). From the same room were two magnificent cabinets: lot 157 was made of satin wood with a marble top which contained fifteen drawers and two folding doors, the whole ornamented with ormolu (bought by Shute for £60 18s); and lot 158, a cabinet with a satin wood and leather top inlaid with tulipwood and flowers painted by Feuglet., was acquired by Maxse, a bidder from Bristol, for £43 1s. One of the final notable pieces of furniture was lot 213, a satinwood commode, banded with tulipwood and ormolu mouldings, containing five drawers and four folding doors with figures painted by William Hamilton. William Moody, very likely an alderman of the Salisbury Corporation, obtained this piece for £44 2s.[53]

In a letter shortly after the sale, Nicholas Williams informed Beckford that the total amount received was £8,000, far short of what was expected. The actual amount Beckford realised was considerably less. The Wallace Collection catalogue includes a complete account in Phillips's hand of the various costs levied against the gross tally of the sale (£7,165 5s). After deducting the cost of producing the catalogue, Phillips's travel, lodging, commission and other expenses, the amount Beckford received was £6,386 19s, not a figure that would provide a great deal of financial relief for the prodigal of Fonthill.

The newspaper reports commented on the fact that many objects sold much less than their value and speculated on how this collection of finery would be in stylistic accord 'with any other Household of ordinary excellence'. The Morning Chronicle chose to conclude with a critical observation that was repeated in other newspapers, including The Times: 'The fact is this extraordinary Auction has drawn forth all the false taste and superfluous gaiety of the county. It has pampered the vanity of the old, and fired the passions of the young with the tinsel of fashion and the gewgaws of luxury. We trust that the audible murmurs and the significant criticisms of the company, during the exhibition, will have a salutary effect, however, upon their minds, and teach them that he only can expect to sit down happy in the enjoyment of what he buys, who is governed in his purchases by moderation and simplicity'.[54] These comments prefigured a similar assessment from William Hazlitt, Beckford's most venomous contemporary critic. Twenty-one years later, Hazlitt, would strike the same moral chord in his commentary about the contents of Fonthill Abbey: 'What soul', he asked, 'can you look for in a gilded cabinet or a marble slab?'[55]

The Demise of 'The Old Palace of Tertian Fevers' in 1807

While the stage was set for making the Abbey more habitable, a new financial blow occurred in December 1801 with the loss of Beckford's richest West Indian property, the Esher plantation, which had been in his family for sixty years.[1] A dispute over the title had been going on for years, but the property was finally removed from his ownership by a decree of the Court of Chancery. He then lost Catherine Hall, another rich estate, in 1807. Furthermore, the price of sugar had by now declined to a point below the profit level placing the entire West Indian enterprise in jeopardy. So dire was his financial situation at this point that Beckford had to borrow £40,000 from his new Jamaican agent John Pedley to address the persistent lawsuits. Then there were the mounting debts he accrued for the cost of building the Abbey, which had by now reached the staggering sum of almost £90,000, or the equivalent of £6,800,000 in today's value. Two unpublished letters from Dr Lettice in the Redding manuscript provide an insider's view of the crisis that Beckford was facing at this time. The financial situation had worsened to the point that Lettice became concerned that his salary for his position as tutor to Beckford's daughters would have to be curtailed:

> I hear the new manager [John Pedley] is come from Jamaica where he advanced £40,000 (wherever it came from!) to stop a threatened lawsuit for some estates there. Keep this to yourself. But added to all the other embarrassments and the humour of Abbey building still all alive etc., it makes even my ordinary claims precarious. I fear 'tis all rotten ground that may give way within no long time to others as well as to me. (August 1802)

Four month's later, Lettice's anxiety intensified:

> I am a present under serious apprehensions of a diminution of my own income from Mr. Beckford unless some representations I have made him, should avert [?] his present intentions and I have not much hope of their success, though nothing can be stronger than my pretentions to his utmost considerations. (8 December 1802)

After citing these letters, Redding added that in the month of June 1803 Lettice 'made a complaint that his salary had actually been curtailed, and in July 1803 complained further that a payment of his income for the education of the Miss Beckford's had been suffered to get into arrears'.[2] The heavy financial drain had to be faced, and so to prevent further bleeding Beckford decided to cease all work on the Abbey for a period of three years.

Beckford then proceeded to engage Christie's to conduct a sale of paintings in February 1802, followed by second auction of pictures 'Consigned from Paris' the following month. The retrenchment continued later with a Sotheby's auction of 316 book lots in May 1804, followed by another auction at Christie's, disposing this time a valuable collection of John R. Cozens's drawings in April 1805.

In the meantime, Lady Anne Hamilton, daughter of the ninth Duke of Hamilton and a guardian of Beckford's daughters, visited Fonthill in September 1803 and provided an invaluable record in her unpublished diary of the state of construction of the Abbey building at this time.[3] Based on the information she left behind, it is evident that many of the interior rooms were now fitted up for residence. Among these, for example, was the 'Abbot's Parlour' on the ground floor of the south wing, later called the Brown Parlour or the Oak Parlour because of its dark oak wainscoting. This would serve as Beckford's dining room and contained a full-length portrait of Peter Beckford, Beckford's great grandfather, the man responsible for accumulating the great wealth in Jamaica that supported the Beckford family lifestyle. Lady Anne described the dimensions of this room as fifty-four feet long by twenty feet wide with a height of thirteen feet. She noted that it was adorned with scarlet and purple curtains (the latter bordered with the royal tressure of Scotland) and observed that the views through the windows of the near and surrounding countryside provided an 'admirable Effect'. The upper section of the windows were filled with stained glass paintings of kings and knights (the work of Eginton after drawings by William Hamilton), representing some of the distinguished persons purported to be of Beckford's ancestry. Beckford would fill this room with Dresden and Sèvres china, decorative gilt plate from various periods and a striking pair of silver candlesticks that he designed. Visitors to this room in 1823 also saw two impressive salvers bearing the initials of William and Mary, two ewers and two tazzas designed by Jean-Guillaume Moitte and Henri Auguste and an engraved cup dated 1624 from the Margravine of Anspach collection[4] Lady Anne also described the southern wing as 136 feet long ending with an altar and a statue of St Anthony of Padua holding a child 'surrounded by 36 wax lights in Gold Branches and Candlesticks'. This corroborates other reports placing the chapel at this stage of the Abbey's development in the Octagon room. Her diary also included dimensions of the Great Western Hall with the entrance door described as thirty feet high and the height of the Great Hall Entrance as sixty-two feet. She recorded that the Octagon Hall was 145 feet high and that the Great Tower rose at this time to a height of 250 feet, though this latter figure is lined out and 300 feet written in next to it by what appears to be another hand. She identified the proposed north wing as the 'Picture Gallery' and noted that combined with the south wing and 'Octagon Hall' it would produce a vista of 312 feet in length. Recognising that the tower may not have reached its final height, Lady Anne's figures are very close to the final dimensions of the Abbey as identified by Rutter in 1823.

Work on the Abbey resumed in 1805 but proceeded slowly in light of the continuing economies. The construction of the tower continued to pose a major problem when it was discovered that a new experimental product called compo-cement that Wyatt had used was now crumbling rapidly and threatened to bring the whole structure down again. This resulted in hiring a number of workmen from London in the summer of 1805 to dismantle a great part of the tower and rebuild it in stone adding considerably to the building costs and causing another long delay. The workers were still engaged in making this repair in December 1806, as an anonymous letter in the *Gentleman's Magazine* reported:

> To the instances of failure of *compocementing*, noticed by An Architect in p. 1005 [of the *Gentleman's Magazine*], the disgusting appearance of the handsome elegant tower of Fonthill abbey, in this neighbourhood, might have been added. It is the property of William Beckford, esq. M.P. and an entirely modern structure, on which a number of workmen from London have been employed during the summer in taking down a great part of it, from the decay of the cement, and still remain to prepare the materials for restoring it with stone, at an immense expence, though seven years have not yet elapsed since its completion.[5]

A major economy move was made by November 1806 with a decision to demolish most of the rest of the family mansion, leaving only the western pavilion, probably for use as a guest house. It was an inevitable move and much of the stone from Splendens could be used to construct additional wings for the Abbey. This precipitated two more Fonthill sales, the household furnishings sale in August 1807 and the subsequent demolition sale of the mansion in the following month.

Sir Richard Colt Hoare, the historian of Wiltshire, believed that the household auction in 1807 was the most important of the early group of sales at Splendens. He rated this sale highly because it included the famous Crang organ, an impressive array of important paintings, magnificent furnishings, fine porcelain and some outstanding French plate glass.[6] While it did not rival the attention of the two Fonthill Abbey events which followed in the 1820s, this sale did generate its own public notoriety over its seven-day period from the 17 to 24 August (Sunday excluded). With the public access beginning on 27 July, the roads to the estate were burdened with people and carriages, many eager to witness the opulent offerings put up for sale and perhaps catch a glimpse of its elusive owner, one of the most famous men in England. Newspapers reported that the sale was 'attended throughout by all of the rank and opulence of the adjacent counties' and 'displayed every day an assemblage of the most beautiful females, each seeming to vie with the other in the display of their taste in dress'. The crowds were so large and overnight accommodations in the vicinity so difficult to find that even cottagers were successful in renting 'their hovels for one and two guineas a night'.[7] For the seven-day period of the sale, the park and the lake provided an 'enchanting scene' with people in groups combing the 'verdant hills' and enjoying 'cold collations' while barges on the lake sought shady retreats along the banks, the nearby quarry and the woods. This would also be the last time to see one of the England's most distinguished mansions, a source of lament for *The Times* as it compared this loss to the fate of other splendid edifices in the country, such as Bubb Dodington's mansion, Eastbury, the Duke of Chandos's house at Cannons and Sir Gregory Page's residence at Blackheath.[8]

In a move that foreshadowed the private sale of Fonthill Abbey to John Farquhar in 1822, Beckford actually attempted to sell the mansion and its contents to Edward Foxhall (d. 1815), the London furniture maker and upholder of Old Cavendish Street, before the sale but after the public distribution of the descriptive sale catalogue. A copy of the agreement among the Beckford Papers in the Bodleian Library, dated 31 July 1807, reveals that Beckford offered Foxhall all of the effects listed in the catalogue and the mansion itself with the exception of the west wing for £16,000. According to the document, Foxhall would be allowed until 29 September 1810 to dismantle Splendens; otherwise whatever remained on the grounds would revert to Beckford. Foxhall was also to pick up the costs already incurred for mounting both sales in 1807. It is evident that the deal fell apart because Phillips was still looking for a buyer of Splendens as late as 16 September, the first day of the building demolition sale.[9]

While a limited number of catalogues of the household effects exist for this sale, no annotated copy with buyers' names and prices is known to have survived. Information gleaned from news reports, the auction catalogue, and subsequent research on the current location of lots sold in 1807 help to reconstruct the event and shed light on the quality and diversity of the items that were sold at this time.

Splendens was known for its array of exquisitely carved chimney-pieces by some of the masters of the day, including John Flaxman (1755–1826), John Bacon (1740–1799), Thomas Banks (1735–1805), and John Francis Moore (d. 1809). Four of the nineteen marble chimney-pieces that sold over the seven-day period came up on the first day, one of which (lot 113) stood in the room adjacent to the dining parlour of the basement storey was identified as by Flaxman. By this time, Flaxman had acquired international status as a leading neo-classical sculptor. Phillips provided very little information about this work other than calling it a 'handsome statuary' marble chimney piece. It is quite possibly the work Beckford commissioned Flaxman to carve around 1787, when the artist was under the employ of Josiah Wedgwood and just before he left to supervise the Wedgwood Studio in Rome.[10]

The works of three other celebrated sculptors, Bacon, Banks, and Moore also figured prominently in the sale. In a journal entry dated 6 July 1787, Beckford wrote that 'Bacon and Banks are making chimneypieces for me'.[11] The Bacon work located in the Satin Drawing Room, described as a richly sculpted 'modern statuary' chimney-piece (lot 301) was one of these. Records reveal that Bacon supplied Beckford with a chimney-piece in 1790.[12] The catalogue provides more detail about the chimney-piece in the Great Dining Room (lot 319), which was supported by 'two pastoral figures' with a tablet in the centre of the mantle of Diana and Apollo.[13] Phillips failed to identify the sculptor but it was by Moore, who did the well-known statue in 1767 of Beckford's father as the Lord Mayor of London, now on display in the Ironmongers' Company. Moore also executed a 'white marble fountain representing the four elements' in the same room, which does not appear in the sale catalogue,[14] and lot 336 in the Grand Entrance Hall, which Phillips scantily describes as a marble chimney-piece 'elaborately sculptured, with 2 emblematic figures of Music and correspondent entablature'.[15] Beckford's half-sister Elizabeth Marsh, writing in 1768, confirmed the existence of Moore's chimney-pieces in both rooms. She describes the one in the Great Dining Room as bearing a tablet that depicted 'a conversation between Apollo and Diana; [with] the supporters [being] Daphne and Arethusa'.[16] For the chimney-piece in the Entrance Hall, she provides more detail, noting that it contained Apollo and the Muses in the mantle tablet accompanied by a frieze with Mercury, Amphion on the one side and Orpheus on the other, 'who has allured by his ravishing Musick the wild beasts and trees to gather round him to listen to his sweet harmony' and with two large figures of the Muses as supporting statuary.[17]

Contemporary reports indicate that Mr Abbott bought the Moore chimney-piece in the Great Dining Room (lot 319) for 130 guineas.[18] Abbott was bidding at the sale as an agent for Thomas Johnes (1748–1816) of Hafod. Johnes was a major buyer due to the unfortunate circumstance of a fire at Hafod that destroyed almost the entire interior of his house in March 1807. Eager to rebuild, Johnes seized upon the opportunity at Fonthill to find replacements for his lost items. He also took in the impressive chimney-piece (lot 425) in the Drawing Room 'formed of *statuary* and *sienna*' in highly polished state with pastoral figures in high relief on the mantle for 230 guineas[19] and a magnificent fireplace (lot 477) by Banks from the State Bed Chamber: 'An *elegant statuary marble* CHIMNEY-PIECE, with enriched tablet (opening 3 feet 9 wide, by 3 feet 4 high, and veined hearth'. The side supports of this work actually contained full-length figures of Pan and Iris, 'worthy of Canova', with Penelope and Ulysses in the centre tablet.[20] Bidding for the Banks chimney-piece must have been spirited because it sold for the extraordinary amount of 1,400 guineas, certainly evidence of Johnes's desire to own it.[21]

Moore's chimney-piece from the Grand Entrance Hall ended up in Clumber Park, Nottinghamshire. Henry Pelham, the 4th Duke of Newcastle (1785–1851) bought Hafod in 1833 and, when he sold it in 1845, decided to take some of the elaborate mantle-pieces with him to Clumber, including the one by Moore. It was then sold at the Clumber sale in 1937.[22] Beckford was interested in the Hafod sale, commenting that Johnes had 'bought considerably' at the Fonthill House sale', but restricted his interest to the Hafod library. 'The library', Beckford wrote, 'I always understood contained some extremely fine Italian books', and then he added a comment about Johnes's taste for imbibing, 'and the cellar no doubt some equally precious specimens in this line, for Mr. Jones [*sic*] was to the full as convivial as the D[uke] of Roxburg'.[23]

Besides the chimney-pieces, Johnes bought lots 408-10, three exquisite French mirrors from the Grand Saloon, which he believed were among the finest in Europe, each in a carved burnished gold frame, for a total of 1,225 guineas.[24] Each one measured over nine feet wide and five feet high. The French mirrors in the sale were said to realise almost £5,000.[25] He also bought the celebrated seven foot statue of Bacchus (lot 623), once owned by Beckford's great uncle Charles Hamilton (1704-1786) of Painshill, for the incredibly low price of 210 guineas.[26] Hamilton supposedly paid £2,000 for it in Rome in 1727; Beckford bought it in 1797 for £400.[27] Farington reported that only the trunk and the head of the figure were original, while Joseph Nollekens (1737–1823), who sculpted his own statue of Bacchus in 1761, said he would not have given ninety guineas for it.[28] Seeing it in the Great Dining Room, John Britton described it as a noble statue whose 'arms, and part of the torso, are restored; the head is of the finest Greek sculpture … placed in a spacious niche, lined with dove-coloured marble very highly polished, [which] gives an aid of dignity to the apartment'.[29] After it left Hafod, the statue was considered lost for years until it was discovered in 2001 at Anglesey Abbey. The plan is now to return it to Painshill Park after restoration work is completed on the Temple of Bacchus where it is to be placed.[30].

One of the featured items, a 'Capital ORGAN, built by CRANG' came under the hammer on the third day (lot 338) for the second time in its history. This massive instrument was located in the Grand Entrance Hall, an imposing room almost eighty-six feet high and thirty-nine feet square with a floor of polished Italian marble. It made an earlier appearance as lot 46 in the 1801 sale and realised only £304 10s. This time, the Earl of Pomfret bought it for the bargain price of 150 guineas[31] and then presented it to St Lawrence's Church, Towcester, in 1817 where it remained until 1977 when a fire in the church caused some damage to the organ and led to the decision to present it to the Victoria and Albert Museum in 1980.[32] Beckford's father evidently had a taste for very expensive organs. Richard Pococke, visiting the earlier Fonthill mansion in 1754, singled out for attention 'a very fine large organ in the hall, which playes [sic] thirty tunes without a hand'.[33] The *Gentleman's Magazine*, noting that it cost £5,000, said that it had been destroyed in the fire of 1755 that put an end to the mansion that Splendens replaced.[34]

An impressive collection of paintings was offered on the sixth day. Fortunately, the press notices provided more information about the names of the buyers and the prices paid for these lots. One of the most active buyers was Henry Jeffrey, who must stand as a remarkable example of a professional eclectic. He was a chemist and druggist by trade, known for selling medicines, wines, spices and glass in his place of business in Market Place, Salisbury, but who simultaneously ran an art gallery on the same site where he regularly marketed original works by ancient and modern masters .Visiting his gallery, one could find works hanging on the walls ascribed to Leonardo da Vinci, Nicolas Poussin, Teniers, and Rembrandt.[35] Jeffrey, along with William Dell, an auctioneer from High Street, Southampton, and Edward Imber of Hatton-Garden, London eagerly sought commissions to represent buyers at the sale by placing prominent notices in the *Salisbury and Winchester Journal*.[36]

Jeffrey's attendance on all seven days paid off since he walked away with some treasures. The *Gentleman's Magazine* identified him as the buyer of Hendrik de Cort's views of Salisbury Cathedral (lot 573) and the Cathedral of Exeter (lot 574) for eighty guineas and twenty guineas respectively. Towards the end of the day, he managed to take in Nicolas Poussin's *Woman taken in Adultery*, in perfect condition, (lot 621) for 130 guineas and a companion piece by Poussin *The Magdalen washing our Saviour's feet* (lot 622) for 210 guineas. In addition, he was successful in bidding for lot 617, *The Geese, Birds*, by the Dutch master, Melchior d'Hondecoeter, considered to be the 'Raphael of bird painters'.[37]

One of Jeffrey's most important purchases was Turner's celebrated *The Fifth Plague of Egypt* (lot 581), which he secured for 155 guineas. This painting, which actually depicted the seventh plague with Moses overseeing thunder, hail and fire on the Pharaoh and the people, was exhibited in the Royal Academy in 1800 to considerable public acclaim. Now in the Indianapolis Museum of Art, this work with its dark, brooding character set in an atmosphere of environmental turbulence, marked the emergence of Turner's distinctive style and his movement towards full-blown Romanticism.

Equally distinguished was Romney's *The Gypsy* [Indian Woman] from Shakespeare's *Midsummer Night's Dream* (lot 582), which Jeffrey took in for 200 guineas. Phillips called it the '*chef d'œuvre* of that distinguished artist'. Painted in 1793 and bought by Beckford in 1797 for 300 guineas,[38] this work was inspired by Titania's lines about her favourite page in Shakespeare's play:

> His mother was a vot'ress of my order,
> And in the spiced Indian air, by night,
> Full often has she gossip'd by my side,
> And with me on Neptune's yellow sands,
> Marking th' embarked traders on the flood,
> When we have laugh'd to see the sails conceive
> And grow big-bellied with the wanton wind;
> Which she with pretty and with swimming gait
> Following, her womb then rich with my young squire,
>
> Would imitate and sail upon the land
> To fetch me trifles, and return again,
> As from a voyage, rich with merchandise.
> But she, being mortal, of that boy did die;
> And for her sake do I rear up her boy,
> And for her sake I will not part with him. (Act II, sc 1)

Britton described this painting in highly complementary terms in 1801 after his visit to the estate: 'The design, colouring, and execution of this piece, are all admirable. The effect it produces, as reflected in the large glass opposite, is quite magical. We seem to behold the glowing atmosphere of an exotic climate, and to enjoy in imagination, "the spiced Indian air".[39] This painting was considered lost for many years, but it came to light in a private collection and was exhibited for the first time in 2002 in the Walker Art Gallery in Liverpool.

Among the notables at the sale was the architect John Soane (1753–1837), who was commissioned by Beckford in 1786 to convert a corridor on the attic floor, measuring sixty-nine feet long by seven-foot wide and eleven-and-a-half feet high into a picture gallery that was to be filled with light by a series of overhead glass domes. Soane was also commissioned to design chimney-pieces for Splendens, two niches for the Tapestry Room and the sumptuous state bed, which sold at Fonthill in 1801 to W. W. Dimond. While Soane's designs for the top-lit gallery exist, the construction of it never took place. It was in the existing gallery that Beckford hung views of early mansions on the Fonthill estate, various designs of the new Fonthill Abbey by Wyatt and Turner, and Hogarth's *Rakes Progress*, which Soane acquired in 1802 for 580 guineas.[40] The corresponding set of Hogarth's *Harlot's Progress* was destroyed by the fire in 1755. Obviously familiar with Beckford's collection because of the early commissions, Soane showed up for this sale and bought for 150 guineas Canaletto's *View of Venice* (lot 605), which Beckford had obtained from the Charles-Alexander de Calonne collection in 1795. Hanging today in the Soane Museum, this work is now considered to be one of Canaletto's finest paintings.

A room adjacent to the proposed gallery of Splendens was decorated with a splendid collection of prints after Raphael of his Vatican *Loggie* frescoes called 'grotesques' (*grotteschi*), hand coloured by Francesco Pannini. Beckford was so proud of these prints that he had planned to display them in all their magnificence at the beginning of Soane's top-lit gallery.[41] Phillips describes this set (lot 596) as unique, 'comprising forty-two impressions … esteemed the finest and most precious extant; the colouring *equal in execution to the most exquisite miniature, and the varied tints vivid and unfaded, heightened by gold embossments and pencilling* by F. Panini, and in high preservation, *sumptuously framed*, and glazed with *plate glass*'. Mr Paul bought this astonishing collection for 630 guineas, which may have been the highest price for art sold on the sixth day.

Hastings Elwin, Sr (1742–1833), London barrister and distinguished collector, also attended the sale.[42] Elwin held his own sale of old masters that attracted the *beau monde* in May 1806. *The Times* said it surpassed 'every exhibition we have yet seen exposed to sale'. It was during this auction that Elwin sold *An Old Lady by Candle-light* by Rubens, which Sotheby's sold in 2004 for £2,469,600. It was his son, Hastings Elwin, Jr (1777–1852), who founded the Bath Literary and Scientific Institution in 1823. It was Elwin, Jr, as previously noted, who purchased four Andrea Casali (1720–1783) paintings that had come from the Fonthill sale of 1801. At the 1807 sale, Elwin, Sr acquired Leonardo's *The Infant Saviour and Saint John*, for 290 guineas (lot 613),[43] which the catalogue indicates came originally from the Aldobrandini collection: 'in a high state of preservation; possessing all the beauty, energy, and characteristic perfections of this great master'. Elwin may have sold this painting soon after since a work by the same title showed up in Jeffrey's gallery and was offered for sale in his catalogue of 1 May 1809.[44] The Revd Richard Warner, who visited Splendens in September 1800, described this painting as 'Two Boys kissing each other' and remarked that it was in an 'exquisitely finished' state.[47] This painting seems to have disappeared after it left Beckford's hands, though a painting under the name of Leonardo with the title *Infant Saviour embracing the little St John* appeared later in the Ashburton collection.[46] A painting that was sold at a London auction in 1978 called the *Holy Children*, showing the two figures in a kissing embrace became the subject of a television documentary in 2006 entitled *Da Vinci's Lost Code*. Its attribution as a legitimate Leonardo painting has become the subject of considerable controversy in the art world. However, with all of the investigation conducted thus far to determine the legitimacy of this work as genuine Leonardo painting, one of the findings in the film is that there seems to be no 'chain of attribution' linking Beckford's painting to the picture bought in London.

Warner also mentioned another painting from the Aldobrandini collection offered at the Splendens sale, said to be Lodovico Carraci's *The Nativity* (lot 614) which was knocked down for 350 guineas. 'The most perfect cabinet picture', Phillips wrote, 'in which composition, light and shade, colouring and design, vie with each other for pre-eminence, and receive additional dignity from the exquisite expression that pervades every figure in the group'. About this painting, Warner reacted in similar terms: 'The chief beauty of this picture is the management of the light, which emanates from the new-born infant, and illuminates the enraptured beholders in a manner surprisingly artful'.[47] Unfortunately, the buyer's name remains a mystery. Farington reported that Elwin also bought two paintings by Claude-Joseph Vernet, lot 618: 'A CALM, *with shipping and figures*' and lot 619: A STORM, [with shipping and figures] for a total of 550 guineas.[48] Phillips noted that these two pictures '*were presented by this celebrated painter to his patron* WATTELET, at whose sale they were purchased by the DUKE DE PR[A]SLIN'.

The only other person known to have bought paintings at this sale was Walsh Porter (d. 1809). Porter was an art dealer, collector and decorator and well known for designing elaborate Egyptian and Gothic interiors in Craven Cottage, his house in Fulham. He was a friend of the Prince of Wales, often served as an advisor for the Prince's art purchases and helped with the redecoration of Carlton House in 1802. It was reported that he paid 105 guineas for two Raphael works set in a single frame called *Charity and Nymph*.[49] They came originally from the Borghese as *Charity and Dancing Figure*.[50] Warner refers to them as 'two small allegorical figures' entitled 'Charity and Pleasure'.[51] Phillips presents these works as 'undoubted original'. 'Charity' surfaced in 2012 at a Sotheby auction in New York and sold for $28,125 as a work from the circle of Raphael.

Beckford offered twenty-one paintings by Andrea Casali in the 1801 household sale. Three were then listed in the building materials sale of 1801,[52] and eighteen more were offered in this sale bringing the total Casali paintings to forty-two installed in the mansion, lending credence to Beckford's complaint that Splendens was marked by too many 'dauberies à la Casali'.[53] Two of these works worthy of notice (lots 594 and 595) in this auction consisted of the ceiling painting in the Grand Saloon presided over by Aurora, the goddess of dawn and the second identified as *The Muses* from the ceiling of the Grand Entrance Hall. Casali's allegorical painting *Apollo in Grand Concert with the Muses* that occupied this ceiling supposedly sold in 1801 as lot 164*, a manuscript entry by Phillips after the catalogue for that sale was printed. At that time, Phillips listed Harris as the buyer, but, as we have noted, he never paid for it. Instead, it resurfaced in the 1801 building materials sale but it failed to sell.[54] When it came up in this new household sale, it appeared to be sold, but, once again, it did not pass to the high bidder because it showed up in the building materials sale in the following month as lot *526 with a description that fits the more elaborate character of what had to be a massive work: 'The MUSES an elaborate Painting, by Cassali, on the Cieling [*sic*], of the Grand Hall; not cleared by the late Purchaser'. This time it was hammered down for £26 5s, almost twice the hammer price in the 1801 sale.[55]

Featured in this collection were also six lots that displayed the work of the distinguished French artist Jean-Jacques Boileau. One of the most unusual items in the sale was an enclosure for a fireplace (lot 161) in the Tartarian Room that when not in use converted into a pier table with four carved and gilt doors in front, bearing paintings by Boileau.

The front doors were divided by carved quivers of arrows with doors at each end hiding eight drawers which made the whole look like an elegant cabinet enriched by   ormolu and surmounted with a granite top. Lots 162 and 163 were companion pieces occupying the same room, whose panels were exquisitely painted by Boileau. The first was a china press that continued the quivers-with-arrows motif and bore satinwood panels that served as the base for the paintings; the next was an impressive pier commode with oval panels painted by Boileau with a granite slab top and open ends to display ornamental china. Jeffrey bought all three of these elegant pieces and offered them for sale in his 1809 exhibition catalogue.[56] Boileau also designed a pair of tripods (lot 439) *'richly carved and gilt in burnished gold'* located in the Drawing Room. This set matched another that surfaced in the 1801 sale, (fourth day, lot 113) situated in the State Dressing Room, for which Thomas Atkinson, a builder from Salisbury, paid £117. There were also two Boileau paintings over the niches in the Satin Drawing Room (lot 315) and a third in chiaroscuro entitled *Apollo and Muses* (lot 578).

A pair of 'SUPERBE CABINETS' (lot 438) with paintings by William Hamilton (1751–1801) escaped the attention of the press at this sale. Phillips described them as 'composed of purple, satin, and other choice woods, enriched with carved and burnished columns and mouldings gilt, and paintings by the celebrated *Hamilton*, black and gold marble tops and shelf'. These pieces were reminiscent of the commode that sold in 1801, lot 213, fourth day, and the two cabinets with paintings by Hamilton that Britton saw in the Tapestry Room in 1801, which were located in the two niches designed by Soane.[57] Farington identified the buyer of this lot as 'Mr. Oakley'. This could possibly be George Oakley, a London upholder and cabinet-maker, who had a shop on the south side of St Paul's Church in 1807.[58]

Two other interesting items that received no notice in the press were one of Hubert Robert's (1733–1808) evocative paintings of ruins (lot 580) for which he had achieved renown and a statue of Hebe by Jean-Guillaume Moitte (1746–1810), 'a beautiful specimen of sculpture' (lot 624).[59] It is surprising that Beckford disposed of the Robert painting since the subject of the painting, combined with Robert's reputation for picturesque garden design, would seem to have earned a place for him in Fonthill Abbey.

On the seventh and final day, the porcelain was sold, consisting of 'Jars, Cisterns, Vases, Urns, and Cabinet Gems; Dinner, Dessert and Tea Services' and a collection of 'Old Gold Japan, Bronzes, Carvings in Ivory'. Illustrative of the quality of these lots, a part of a dinner service from the Royal Sèvres manufactory, including eighty-four plates, ten dishes, four tureens, covers and stands, sold for 120 guineas.[60]

At the conclusion of the sale, the newspapers complimented Phillips on his handling of the auction and for obtaining the best prices for the lots: 'On the whole, Mr. Phillips had certainly no reason to complain that his oratory was ineffectual, as we understand the total produce of the sale very far exceeded the appraisement'.[61] While there is no definitive record of the final tally, *The Times* said that the bidding was spirited and that the 'amount must exceed £20,000'.[62] With all of the interior furnishings and opulent accessories removed, only the shell of this distinguished edifice remained awaiting its demolition in September when the building materials were scheduled to be sold.

'A Fine Prudent Act':
The Demolition of Fonthill Splendens

In July 1807, William Beckford wrote to his future son-in-law, Alexander Hamilton- Douglas, then Marquis of Douglas and from 1819 the 10th Duke of Hamilton, that he would be in an 'ecstasy of enthusiasm' when he saw the soaring tower of Fonthill Abbey.[1] He was trying to be reassuring since Douglas had already expressed concern that this architectural venture could only be accomplished by sacrificing the existing residence on the estate. Douglas wanted Beckford to save the family mansion, but at this stage of his life Beckford explained to Douglas that he could not afford to maintain two residences. The taxes and constant repairs would be ruinous, he told Douglas. Furthermore, he needed the materials from the old mansion to help complete his new structure. Despite the urgent plea, Beckford, 'amidst all the fracas and dust of demolition on the one hand and building on the other', pronounced the death knell of the house in which he grew up: 'You will forget the old palace of tertian fevers with all its false Greek and false Egyptian, its small doors and mean casements ... its ridiculous chimney-pieces and its wooden chalk-coloured columns, without grace, nobility or harmony. No, my dear Douglas, I cannot honestly regret this mass of very ordinary taste, and in my actual circumstances I believe I have performed a fine prudent act'[2]

It is also evident from a letter Beckford wrote in November 1806 that he now had a model in his possession of Fonthill Abbey in its final form. 'If you could see the model of the entire Abbey', he wrote to Douglas a few months later, 'and were asked—will you, for the sake of a good common House in an uncommonly bad situation—renounce the execution of such a plan—I think you w[oul]d give way and join with me and Wyatt in full accord'.[3] This card model, which has survived,[4] shows the tower without a spire, an extended northern wing to balance the southern extension and an imposing eastern transept completing a total asymmetrical design. If Douglas could see it, his fears, Beckford hoped, would be ameliorated.

This was not the only model of the Abbey created during Beckford's lifetime. Another contemporary model of the Abbey was constructed by a travelling showman named John Bellamy (1808–1893), who toured England between 1837 and 1893 in a caravan of a British Model Gallery, consisting of a collection of cork and card models of historic British buildings. He visited the Abbey ruins in 1834 and, after twelve months of work, with the aid of published designs, created a model of Fonthill Abbey on a scale of 'one tenth of an inch to one foot'. An advertisement in the *Cheltenham Free Press* stated the Abbey model was 'inspected by Sir Geoffrey [Jeffrey] Wyattville and Mr. Nash, Architects to the Royal Family', and pronounced by them and other scientific gentlemen to be a 'most accurate' and beautiful specimen of the original building.[5]

Harry Phillips presided over his fourth Fonthill sale which began on 16 September 1807. His copy of the published catalogue dealing with the demolition of Splendens, which included the names of the buyers, prices paid for the lots sold and various annotations throughout auction, has survived and is now in the Wallace Collection.[6] The existence of this document provides the opportunity to examine for the first time the materials sold and the identity of some of the buyers and agents who were involved.

Phillips's copy of the catalogue makes it clear that many lots did not sell on the scheduled days they were offered. The problem may have been due to the challenge and cost of the removal of some of the materials. According to the conditions of the sale, the purchaser of the lot had to take down the material and remove it from the premises without damaging anything associated with it. Furthermore, if the buyer failed to do this work in a timely way, then the 'vendor' would order its removal at the '*expence of the purchaser*'. Phillips allowed four months from the date of the sale to remove all interior furnishings and eighteen months for the removal of the roof and the stone work, thereby establishing a completion date for the elimination of the entire structure by March or April of 1809, a target date that would not be met. Indeed, the removal of all of the building materials from the site would turn out to be a more formidable task than anticipated. As late as May 1808 and November 1809, John Gerrard and Co., a Salisbury auction firm, was hired to conduct sales on the premises of the building materials that still had not been removed, including stone, chimneypieces, iron gates, doors, panels, water closets, Venetian windows, sky-lights, and a 'handsome dove marble niche'[7].

Phillips provided the surnames of the buyers in his copy, but they are not easily identifiable with the first names missing. One of the known bidders, however, was once again Henry Jeffrey who was an active buyer in the earlier Fonthill household sales. Jeffrey was likely serving as an agent in this sale for he eagerly sought commissions to represent buyers by placing prominent notices in the *Salisbury and Winchester Journal*.[8]

The catalogue lists a range of materials with Jeffrey's name as the successful bidder. For example, on the first day he bought four panelled doors from the Purple Gallery and two Ionic columns from the Alcove Pink Room. Later, he was successful in buying the 'carved trusses, cornices, and pilaster to the double doors' at both ends of the Long Gallery and the carved base moulding in the Great Dining Room and the State Bedroom. He also took in the Corinthian columns from both the Drawing Room and the Grand Entrance Hall, but, perhaps, his most ambitious purchase was the entire black and white Italian marble floor of the Grand Entrance Hall, measuring '1160 feet', for which he paid £207 16s 8d. He also bought lot 303, which consisted of 257½ feet of 'veined and marble squares' associated with the Best Staircase on the ground floor.

While most of the individuals in attendance were tradesmen interested in salvage materials, the names of some notable figures do appear in the catalogue. One such individual was 'Sr J. Keane', likely to be Sir John Keane, who had just been returned by election on 28 July, as MP for Youghal. He bought the oak batten dowelled floors from the 'Sattin' Drawing Room, the Drawing Room and Music Room, presumably for Cappoquin House, his eighteenth-century Georgian mansion in Waterford, Ireland.[9] 'Sr. W. Middleton' was another recorded bidder, in all probability Sir William Middleton, the former MP for Ipswich who took in the large window in the Grand Saloon with its mahogany and oak fittings along with the 'carved ovolo', 'pannel shutters' with 'boxing, soffits, and carved architraves and swing bar fastenings', which could well have ended up in his palatial house in Shrubland Park. Finally, Henry Ford ('Ford of Wilton'), who served as the estate agent for the Earl of Pembroke from 1810 to 1840, bought the oak floor in the Grand Saloon for £70 16s.[10]

Almost all of the lots offered fell in the category of building materials, but one distinctive item was a colossal circular lantern 'with sashes, the glass bent circular, with curb and cornice … 12 feet diameter, 6 feet 3 high' (lot 456). This fixture appears to be an exterior lamp that hung in the central portico above the landing of the grand staircase on the north front of the house since it is identified in conjunction with the exterior 'coppering' sold separately in lot 454 that had been installed 'over [the] grand staircase and lantern'.[11] A similarly imposing hexagonal ormolu lantern hung on a gilt chain from the ceiling of the Grand Entrance Hall. The buyer of the portico lamp is listed as 'Green', very likely the London goldsmith and jeweller of the firm Green, Ward, and Green, 1 Ludgate Street. Beckford hired Green to supply the golden lamp that suspended from the ceiling of the Oratory in Fonthill Abbey.

Phillips kept a fairly detailed account of the bidding during the first three days, but commencing with lot 427, which initiated the sale of copper coverings on the exterior of the building, the names or prices begin to thin out. With lots 458 through *526, involving roof rafters, ceiling beams, framed flooring, mahogany doors and a painting, only three identifiable surnames are recorded: 'Rowe of Salt Ash' bought lot 459, 'three circular metal skylights and glass' for £9 9s, 'Spencer' took in lot 513, the framed flooring of what once had been the library located on the ground floor for £10 12s 6d, and the third was lot *526, a painting on the ceiling of the Grand Entrance Hall by Andrea Casali.

This painting known today as *Apollo and the Muses in Grand Concert* had been offered at the three previous Splendens sales, as we have noted, but failed to clear or receive an offer. It was put up again at this auction and sold to a person named 'Dennys' for £26 5s, but its current whereabouts is not known or if it even survived the challenge of removing such a massive work from the ceiling.

The sections in the catalogue devoted to the exterior stone work of the mansion (lots 516-603), including the internal staircases, are almost entirely blank. One major exception is lot 549, the grand staircase consisting of Portland stone steps and landing with rich scroll iron-work and a mahogany-moulded cross banded hand rail. Wyatt is listed as the buyer representing Codrington of Dodington Park, Gloucestershire at this sale. Codrington had engaged James Wyatt to build a neo-classical country house for him at the same time the architect was building Fonthill Abbey. He bought this staircase, ultimately incorporating the wrought ironwork connected with it at Dodington Park. The total hammer price is not clear from the catalogue, but Phillips placed the figure £105 in the 'At per' column of his ledger.

The Wyatt name appears in the margin of two other lots: 594 and 596, the first involving 1,520 feet of Portland paving stone from the south front and the second 725 feet of the same from the north front. No bids are recorded, but Phillips wrote 'To Morlidge or Wyatt by P.C.' in the margin of each lot. John Morlidge was the clerk of the works at Longleat House, Wiltshire, working from 1807 to 1813 under Jeffry Wyatt (later Wyattville), the nephew of James Wyatt. In this case, 'Wyatt' could refer to Jeffry. Thomas Thynne, the 2nd Marquess of Bath, had commissioned Jeffry to design some improvements for Longleat, with the actual work beginning in 1806.[12] Morlidge also bought 2,704 feet of paving connected with the Grecian Hall and the 'clean deal batten' floors from seven rooms in Splendens for a total outlay of £318 0s 3d.

Demolition of such a large building was usually accomplished by contractual arrangement between the landowner and a local builder. Private deals are likely to have occurred in this case as an efficient way of disposing the heavy stone work of Splendens, thus explaining the existence of so many blank pages. One of the manuscript notes Phillips left in the margin reveals that Beckford himself bought back some of the stone undoubtedly to be used in the ongoing construction of the Abbey: 'The newly erected Stone of the East Area is Sold to Mr. Beckford—the Value to be ascertained by Mr. Hayter & The Bevis's'. Here Phillips is referring to Beckford's clerk of the works George Hayter and to Thomas and James Bevis, stone masons from Tisbury. Another manuscript note indicates that these stone masons bought some of the stone work by private contract and resold it during the sale. Below the description of lot 295, the Corinthian columns in the Grand Entrance Hall, Phillips wrote: 'Sold by Bevis & Co. by P.C. to Jeffrey'.

That the Bevis family played a major role in the dismantling the stone is also apparent in an advertisement that appeared in the *Salisbury and Winchester Journal*, a month before the scheduled building materials sale. This notice also includes another name, that of Richard Beckett, a stone mason from Hindon:

> To Stone-Masons
> EIGHT OR Ten STONE-MASONS may meet
> With Employment and good Wages, by applying
> To Thomas Bevis of Tisbury, or Richard Beckett, of
> Hindon; either to cut or set—It is a large job.[13]

Beckett turned out to be the person responsible for taking down the 'Grand Stone Staircase' that ultimately found its way to Dodington. Records at Dodington show that Beckett received payment for conducting the dismantling work on 20 October 1810, three years after the sale.[14]

Sir Richard Colt Hoare reported that the final tally for the Fonthill salvage sale was £9,000.[15] It is not clear how Hoare obtained this figure. Phillips's catalogue shows considerably less for the lots that were sold during the auction. The final amount for the lots sold was £2,580 0s 3d. The total for the 'bought in' column totalled £816 14s 7d. If he disposed of these lots at the end of the sale for the bought-in price, the total realised would be only £3,396 14s 10d. However, since many lots, particularly on the third day, appear in the catalogue without prices or the names of bidders, the amount received for the disposal of these lots could well have reached the total Hoare indicated. But even Hoare's figure must have been a considerable disappointment to Beckford in view of the fact that Splendens cost £150,000 to build.

Beckford never seemed to express regret at being responsible for the demise of his father's house despite its grandeur and that it was the residence where he spent a good portion of his life. Even though it took at least three years to clear completely the site where Splendens stood, few public elegies followed and no sketches or engravings of the building in ruins have survived. While there were laments in the press over the loss of Splendens as a distinguished work of architecture, a visitor to Fonthill Abbey in 1823, upon spying Hendrik de Cort's impressive painting of Splendens in the billiard room of Lancaster Tower, took a more critical position: 'once, on the borders of that beautiful lake in the outer park, stood the model of a mansion;—and yet *enough* remains to memorialise the folly and fickleness of that taste which would consent to its downfall and dilapidation. Its few inconveniences were more than compensated by its many comforts, and are very far from being redeemed by the mere splendours of the 'tall' 'fragile' 'bully', for which it was made the sacrifice'.[16]

The Magic of Optics:
The Interior of the Abbey

Beckford finally moved into the Abbey in the summer of 1807. Interior finishing work would continue for years particularly with the plans for additional wings. The interior walls of the great Octagon Hall were not completed until September 1808, followed by the incorporation of windows and fan   vaulting.[1] Eight large columns, ninety feet high, were installed in the Octagon to provide support. The tower, itself, remained a web of scaffolding until the fall of 1809.[2] We learn from a letter to Franchi in June 1810 that the carpet for the 'ante-sanctuary' had not yet been laid—the first indication that the sanctuary would be relocated to the end of King Edward's Gallery.[3] While there is no record of when it happened, the west wing appears to have received its final conversion from a banquet hall to grand entrance during the period 1809–10 with the addition of a massive flight of stairs leading up to the Octagon Hall. Disguised as a labourer, William Bankes gained access to the grounds in 1811 and reported seeing the finished stone stairs and the great entrance hall looking 'very much like those of some large Colleges, with windows on both sides & a rich Oak roof very much gilt'.[4] Construction of the north wing, King Edward's Gallery, named after King Edward III, began in 1808 and was sufficiently finished to be included in James Storer's published description of the Abbey in 1812. Storer's book on the Abbey constitutes an important record of the way the interiors of the Abbey looked prior to the later accounts of Britton and Rutter.

In this account, Storer also refers to the planned eastern wing: 'We are told it is the intention of Mr. Beckford to build a superb chapel, directly opposite to the great hall'.[5] Beckford's correspondence for this period indicates that the foundation for this new venture, the Eastern Transept, was laid in August 1812.[6] The influx of new money from the sale of another property, Witham Friary and its 2,300 acres near Frome in October 1811, spurred him to move ahead with this project in spite of urgings from his lawyer to economise. Modelled after the entrance gateway to St Augustine's monastery at Canterbury, with its imposing octagonal towers, the construction of the Eastern Transept was a major undertaking and, in the end, never completed. Beckford's compulsion to build could not be controlled even when the additional expense would add to a growing burden of debt. As he wrote in August 1812: 'Some people drink to forget their unhappiness. I do not drink, I build. And it ruins me. It would be cheaper to find another distraction… '.[7]

The outer walls went up at a furious pace with Wyatt on hand to supervise the work, but in September of the following year the architect died in a carriage accident, leaving the major portion of the supervisory work in Beckford's hands with the assistance of George Hayter, the Clerk of the Works at Fonthill, and the occasional assistance from Wyatt's nephew Jeffry. The instability of the structure as a consequence of Wyatt's careless work continued to be a major concern and the hired labourers devoted almost two years to rebuild with stone various parts of the Abbey to forestall another major collapse. Some days as many as forty cart loads of stone were carried to site to complete the work on the new building. Franchi provided some specific information on the state of affairs at Fonthill in 1814 in a letter to Beckford's son-in-law:

> You ask me for details about the Abbey. I would like to give you satisfactory ones, but that is impossible if I tell you the truth. Almost all that the villainous Bagasse [Wyatt] built has been dismantled (to forestall finding ourselves buried in its rotten ruins); all the walls in the in the Fountain Court have been very solidly rebuilt in stone; the chimney-flues have been changed, together with a thousand other errors which sooner or later would have damaged the edifice—this is the work upon which we have been engaged for the last two years. The kitchen has been finished, and with its adjoining offices it is the finest bit in the Abbey.[8]

In 1815 the roof and the turrets of the two towers were added to the Eastern Transept. Some of the financing for the ongoing construction work was handled by selling timber on the estate where the pine that had now grown to a height in some places of ninety feet. In addition to the pine, the workers were also felling oak to be used in the construction. A measure of the extent of the continuing work is apparent from the consumption of massive amounts of wood to complete various projects. The quantity of pine alone used for joists, roofs, partitions and stairs exceeded 360 tons. 'You can judge of the work that is being done', Beckford wrote in October 1817, 'by the following: "since last Friday a hundred tons of wood have been used and 30,000 laths!" Since the beginning of this new and total ruin 482 tons have disappeared, besides the dry pine and the oak … '[9]

The interiors of some rooms were finished on the first floor of the Eastern Transept in 1817–18, namely the Great Dining Room, the Crimson Drawing Room and the Grand Drawing Room. Beckford's enthusiasm for completing the rest of the wing began to wane in the absence of Wyatt and as structural problems multiplied. The Eastern Transept would have to remain unfinished, and he now began to consider seriously the possibility of giving up the entire venture. 'My resolution to abandon the theatre of so much useless labour', he wrote in October 1817, 'is fortified every hour that I stay here, experiencing blasts of wind, blasts of cold, blasts of rheum and financials blasts in this uninhabitable place'.[10] Indeed, the 'financial blasts' led him to dispose of more personal property in the London auction rooms. He engaged Sotheby's to sell 321 lots of books and prints on 9–11 June 1808 and then 323 lots of books and drawings on 6–8 May 1817, followed by a sale of pictures, drawings and furniture (468 lots) at Christie's a few days later. The latter sale included the elegant and useful furnishings of his London house at 6 Upper Harley Street which he was forced to give up in the face of his financial crisis. He also sold by separate arrangement in 1808 two of his most famous paintings known as the Altieri Claudes, *The Landing of Aeneas* and *A Sacrifice to Apollo*, painted by Claude Lorraine in 1675 for which he received 10,000 guineas.

By 1818, the final design of Fonthill Abbey took the shape of a huge cross, 312 feet long from north to south and 270 feet from east to west, in the centre of which rose the great, octagonal tower, which was said to be 276 feet high.[11] The whole building, Redding wrote, 'covered as much ground as the far famed York Minster'.[12] H. A. N. Brockman concluded in his study of the Abbey that by 'planning in cruciform, with West and East as comparatively short and stubborn buttressing elements and with North and South galleries to afford length (seen from almost any angle), which helped the building "lie" gracefully, Wyatt had, for his share in this partnership, undoubtedly achieved one of his finest architectural massings'.[13] The result was the formation of a well-balanced architectural grouping which echoed the balanced irregularity of the basic garden plan. This was especially evident from Stop's Beacon, looking towards the south-west side of the building, where the display of 'a variety of forms and members, of studied dissimilarity', as Britton observed, combined successfully to constitute a pleasingly picturesque whole.[14] This was not true of every perspective of the Abbey. The south-east view, for example, suffered from the disproportionate size of the Eastern transept with its massive walls ninety-five feet high and twin octagonal towers, each 120 feet high, which tended to diminish the loftiness of the central tower and dwarf the size of the southern and northern wings of the Abbey. Britton noted the 'want of combination and harmony' here, but believed that Beckford had planned to counteract the imperfection. 'This part of the building was to have been enclosed by an embattled wall', Britton explained, 'with a tower gateway, and other architectural appendages: these were to have extended from the mansion to the north, where a mass of coach houses, stables, and other buildings were also to have been erected in a style corresponding with, and apparently forming part of the Abbey'.[15]

The interior of the Abbey also tended to blend harmoniously with the external landscape to create one of the most important examples of the picturesque interior for this period. The long corridor-like galleries created by the cruciform plan reproduced the landscape effect of a tree-lined avenue. This was particularly evident in St Michael's Gallery, the south wing of the Abbey. It was a long fan-vaulted chamber, extending for 112 feet with a width of over thirteen feet, and a height of fifteen feet.[16] The first half of this gallery from the Octagon was lit by five arched windows on the west side, four of which had plate glass in the lower section and stained glass in the upper. The fifth was a copy of one of the windows in the transept of York Cathedral. The second half of the gallery had three oriels on the east side, two of which were filled entirely with stained glass, so that throughout the day the direct light alternated with the more subdued, producing a soft contrast similar to that which could be found as one walked through some of the winding paths of the estate.

From the angel corbels on both walls of St Michael's Gallery, the mouldings rose in succession and expanded into intricate fan-tracery over the entire length of the ceiling, creating the effect of interlacing trees on forest avenues. This internal landscape was then united with the external grounds at the southern extremity of the gallery, where a large oriel window provided a magnificent view of the lawns and rising forests. As a final touch to the landscape effects in this wing of the building, an uninterrupted vista of 307 feet was provided from the south oriel looking up the aisle to the Octagon through which the perspective was continued to the Oratory at the very end of the northern wing of the Abbey. The long perspective, in Brockman's view, provided another link to the Gothic past. As he explained: 'These long, corridor-like galleries were the cheapest and quickest means of attaining the internal "landscape" effect of an avenue of trees which Beckford was undoubtedly echoing by this attenuated inward projection. The "bare ruin'd choirs" of Shakespeare and, indeed, in the minds of many who still thought that the origins of Gothic were to be found in the interlacing trees of forest avenues, were there reflected.'[17]

The gradations of red tones throughout this room also contributed to its impressive visual effects while simultaneously serving the purpose of emphasising the blue-blood lines of Beckford's ancestry. The floor was covered with a crimson carpet marked with white heraldic cinquefoils in recognition of his Hamiltonian background. The walls were pink in tone, and throughout the gallery the windows contained stained glass by Eginton that displayed Beckford's ancestral bearings, royal crests and the effigies of historical and religious figures—all dominated by red and purple colouring. Where there were no window openings, the walls were lined with recessed bookshelves and marble-topped ebony cabinets concealed partly by long double drapes. The colour of the outer curtain for the recessed areas and the windows was purple (though it appears dark blue in the coloured engravings of the interior) with gold trim in contrast to the prevailing colour of crimson in the gallery. The inner curtains were scarlet. It was a colour scheme designed to cultivate a sense of repose as the eye contemplated the rich décor that served as the setting for the furniture, candle stands, and tables made of carved ebony, along with the dazzling metalware, ewers, vases, silver candlesticks by Henri Auguste, Mazarine cisterns and other art treasures on display in the gallery.

One of the striking pieces, a large amber cabinet, sat prominently in front of the south oriel. Set against natural light, it offered a mesmerising display of all the various hues of the amber as it filtered the changing light of the day. As Storer described this characteristic, 'in some parts the palest yellow is suddenly succeeded by the richest orange; in others the tint increases to a garnet red, and again declines to a purity almost white; its sides are adorned with medallions likewise in amber'. This cabinet, said to have been owned previously by the Queen of Bohemia, daughter of James the First, stood upon 'a table of ebony, with torsel feet, which formerly belonged to Cardinal Wolsey'.[18] To the left of this cabinet on the chimneypiece was a medieval Limoges enamelled reliquary which Christie described as a Greek shrine of metal, for containing relics' bearing compartments with a crucifix, figures of saints with drapery of coloured enamel 'brought by St. Louis from Palestine [which] had been deposited at St. Denys, whence it was taken during the French Revolution'.[19]

There were two domestic rooms off the west end of St Michael's Gallery worth noting since this area contained one of the most celebrated pieces of furniture Beckford owned. In one of these rooms, known respectively as the Eastern and Western Yellow Drawing Rooms due to their yellow damask hangings, stood one of the touted features of the Fonthill sale, the 'Holbein' Cabinet. Christie in his 1822 catalogue described the provenance of this piece as from the Palace of Whitehall executed from designs prepared by Hans Holbein for Henry VIII. Beckford believed this to be the case, but now in the collection of the Victoria and Albert Museum the cabinet has been determined to be of German origin by an unknown artist made around 1560 with the stand dating about 1800. Even with the distinguished provenance set aside, the cabinet is considered to be one of the finest examples of its kind, made of quartered oak with finely detailed boxwood carvings applied to the front of a series of drawers with the inner compartments lined with arabesque marquetry or ash veneer. Thomas Dibdin upon examining this work in 1822 believed it to be an appropriate inner sanctum to hold and then display such precious curiosities as rare coins whose beauty would be enhanced by their association with such an exquisite work of art.

The chamber which composed the second half of this long perspective, King Edward's Gallery, extended for a distance of 127 feet, with a width of nearly seventeen feet, and a height of almost eighteen feet.[20] It consisted of a main chamber and three compartments opening out of each other, known as the Vaulted Corridor, the Sanctuary, and the Oratory respectively. Looking up the gallery, Rutter described the view as 'another of those picturesque effects, for which Fonthill Abbey is so justly remarkable'. Like St Michael's Gallery, it was designed to promote heavy visual accents in a composition of colour and contrast. 'As in an excellent picture', Rutter added, 'the light and shade, the composition and the colouring, have been carefully and successfully studied. The powerful aid of association has been called in, and the united influence of the excitement of the mind and of the imagination is fully felt'.[21]

Beckford's appreciation for colour and its effects was well known among his close associates. This was particularly evident in his use of the draperies in this room. To control the strong light emitted through the large windows, the inner scarlet curtains would be drawn causing a 'general magical tint' to be projected throughout the gallery—a warm harmonious light that Beckford liked so well. Redding wrote about Beckford that he studied the theory of colour as he studied music and 'felt the art of pleasing the ear and eye with true judgement'[22] Well before the creation of Fonthill, Beckford spoke of the powerful role of drapery in creating a picturesque effect. 'I have often wondered', he wrote in 1787, '[why] architects and fitters-up of apartments have not availed themselves of the powers of drapery. There is no ornament I like so well or that admits of more variety'.[23]

For sixty-eight feet of its length, the ceiling of King Edward's Gallery appeared to be quite different from that in St Michael's Gallery, being flat and of oak. Yet the two galleries were thematically linked in their spatial unity and in the continuation of the dominance of the crimson colouring, contrasted by the purple and gold accents, and by the repetition of the religious and genealogical motifs. The ceiling of this gallery was laid out in square panels containing the Latimer Cross, an allusion to Beckford's claimed descent from the first Lord Latimer. Below it for further enrichment ran a cornice of oak whose frieze contained quatrefoils with emblazoned shields of seventy-two knights of the Garter whom Beckford considered to be ancestors. A flowered red damask covered the walls, while a crimson carpet with flower prints covered the floor. As in the case of St Michael's Gallery, purple and scarlet curtains adorned the windows. In the middle of the eastern wall, there was an alabaster chimney-piece flanked on either side by three recessed bookcases, all of which continued the horizontal emphasis of the ceiling. Above the bookcases were six portraits: John of Montfort, Alphonsus V, John of Gaunt, Edward IV, Henry VII, and the Duke of Montmorenci. A large portrait of Edward III by Matthew Cotes Wyatt, James's son, occupied a central position directly over the chimney piece, as the founder of the Knights of the Garter that this gallery was designed to commemorate. To avoid the mathematicarol repetition of identical patterns, however, Beckford applied the same pictorial principle he used in laying out the grounds: the principle of occult balance. Preferring to give added unity to the scene by means of balanced irregularity, he made certain that the horizontal lines of the chimney piece and the six bookcases were offset in the opposite wall by seven tall pointed windows whose linearity was markedly vertical. These lofty windows combined with the long narrow curtains, which hung on each side from the ceiling to the floor, and with a row of single candles, which rested conspicuously on high slender stands, to furnish a vertical emphasis sufficient to give the scene visual equilibrium and relieve the formal and flat effect that otherwise would have existed.

In the middle of this sparsely furnished room, beneath the portrait of Edward III, stood the imposing 'inlaid table of pietra commesse', nine feet. long and four feet six inches wide, said to have been formerly in the Borghese Palace and considered today to be one of the most important pieces of *pietre dure* tables in existence. This magnificent table is now at Charlecote Park. Beckford bought the top of the table and designed the base to support it. Clive Wainwright described the top as weighing 'several tons' and concluded that the 'elaborate oak base fits in so well with the iconography of King Edward's Gallery—with Beckford's beloved Latimer cross appearing on the ceiling panels and on the cabinets beside the fireplace as well as on the base itself—that it must have been designed especially for the room'[24] Rutter's book on Fonthill provided a coloured plate of King Edward's Gallery with this table prominently featured along with three of Beckford's finest pieces of ivory carvings removed from another room for the occasion. These included an ivory cup and cover believed at the time to be by Magnus Berg, now in the Royal Collection, flanked by two ivory vases, now in the British Museum, both with mounts by the silversmith David Willaume and ivory sleeves considered today to have been carved by a member of the circle of Giovanni Battista Pozzo.

In Britton's view of the same table in King Edward's Gallery, he featured a very large nautilus mounted on an ivory plinth mistakenly identified as carved by Cellini but so arresting as a work of art that Rutter also displayed it as a centre piece in a vignette entitled 'Rarest Articles of Virtu' in his Fonthill book. This piece received appropriate attention because Beckford was known as a major collector of superbly-mounted nautilus shells with finely engraved ornaments, butterflies, insects and other naturalistic designs often the work of Cornelius van Bellekin. He was drawn to them for their natural beauty and skillful carving.

Not far off in the same gallery was the Mazarin Chest named after its previous owner Cardinal Mazarin. It later came into the possession of the Duc de Bouillon and then was bought by Beckford in 1800. The Victorian and Albert Museum purchased it in 1882 when it became available at the Hamilton sale. It is considered today to be one of the most outstanding pieces of Japanese lacquer dating from the seventeenth century. This striking chest was painted in black, gold and silver lacquer, inlaid with gold, silver and mother-of-pearl shell, depicting on the front and sides various scenes of buildings and landscapes and other designs of exceptionally high quality workmanship.

Moving beyond the gallery proper, through folding plate-glass doors, the wing narrowed suddenly to a width of fourteen feet by means of internal false walls, whereupon the scene shifted from light to dark. Finished in oak with gilt mouldings, the Vaulted Corridor was without windows, but there were on each side three pointed doorways with perforated bronze doors which allowed dim light to filter through from the narrow windows of clear glass in the outer walls, modelled after Henry the Seventh's Chapel in Westminster Abbey. This dim corridor, designed to be an appropriate prelude to the solemn mood of the Oratory, was then succeeded by a square Sanctuary, elevated by a single step. The ceiling here was done in oak, with gilt mouldings and bosses 'covered with a reticulation of lozenge work', in contrast to the vertical ribbing of the Vaulted Corridor.[25] The walls were covered with crimson damask, but the absence of oak ribbing allowed a stronger indirect light to pervade the room, providing another contrast along the way. The wing terminated finally in the Oratory, a five-sided apse, each angle of which contained a slender gilt column, from whose capital rose a 'fan-work reticulation of burnished gold, spreading upward over a ground of deep crimson'.[26] At the intersection of the mouldings was a gilt boss from which was suspended a golden lamp created for Beckford by goldsmiths Green and Ward of Ludgate Hill.[27] At the east end was the altar spread with a Persian tapestry of patterned silk, on which stood a marble statue of Beckford's patron saint, St Anthony of Padua, executed by sculptor John Charles Felix Rossi. For lighting effects in this room, silver candelabra, containing giant tapers, were placed on either side of the altar, the golden lamp provided a subdued light, and two small lancet windows filled with stained glass emitted a glimmering and multicoloured illumination which alternately threw touches of light and shadow on the carved projections and recesses of the statue, and along the face of the gilt mouldings, all designed to produce the effect of repose and harmony.[28]

Turning around at this point to look down the long architectural vista from the north end back to the oriel window at the southern end presented, in Rutter's words, an astonishing scene:

> To reach us, the distant light of the southern oriel has to traverse the Vaulted Corridor, King Edward's Gallery, the Grand Saloon, and the Gallery of St. Michael, every receding step of which is marked by some splendid architectural feature, by some brilliant meuble, by a burst of light, a breadth of shade, or a glow of colour, in varied and almost infinite succession. It is from this point, that the mind of the spectator receives its deepest

impressions of the grand conception, the successful execution, the poetic taste, and the commanding wealth of the possessor of Fonthill.[29]

Missing was the cold stone walls of the typical English cathedral. 'Everything was rich and warm and glorious', Redding wrote,

> … it looked like a palace of enchantment … .books, pictures, statues, vases, cabinets, mirrors, candelabra … in one blaze of gorgeous array.[30]

Since the interior of the Eastern Transept was never completed, it is difficult to discuss its aesthetic relevance to the Fonthill plan as a whole. It was originally designed as a chapel and then evolved on the second floor into a Baronial hall to commemorate the Barons who had signed the Magna Carta from whom Beckford claimed he was descended. Internal architectural effects were almost totally absent in this wing, as Rutter noted, even as late as 1822, when the estate was sold.[31] There were three finished rooms on the first floor, however, that deserve notice. The first was the imposing Great Dining Room with its massive overhead beams and crimson hangings. This room contained two of Beckford's most important French furniture—a pair of Boulle armoires, ten feet high by five feet wide, made of ebony with tortoiseshell, brass marquetry and gilt bronze mounts. They were supposedly made for Louis XIV after the designs of André-Charles Boulle, which later became part of the Duc d'Aumont's collection and are now in the Louvre. This room also contained George Romney's full-length portrait of Beckford and Thomas Phillips's portrait of the Duchess of Hamilton. In a recessed area on the east side was a eight-foot high ebony cabinet with representations on its folding doors of Curtius on Horseback leaping into flames and the young Roman Mutius Scaevola burning off his right hand after attempting to kill an enemy king. In this cabinet Beckford kept one of his most precious hardstones, the exceptional 'Rubens vase'. Carved from a single piece of agate by a Byzantine artist dating from *c.* 400, this extraordinary work passed through a number of prominent collections before being purchased by the Flemish painter Peter Rubens; whereupon it later obtained its current name. Rutter described it in 1822 as a hollowed out sardonyx vessel, oval in shape with a surface of exquisitely executed leaves, bearing sculptured heads of satyrs at the handles on each side. Britton displayed it on the title-page of his Fonthill book in 1823, and Beckford felt it was important enough never to have sold it during his lifetime. Today it is owned by The Walters Art Museum.

The Crimson Drawing Room that followed continued the same crimson and ebony colour scheme. It displayed six ebony chairs with silver castors from the palace of Esher that once belonged to Cardinal Wolsey and a Japanese lacquer box given to Maria Van Diemen that was once owned by Madame de Pompadour. There was also an assortment of fine ebony cabinets, commodes, and a jewelled cabinet, most notably one set with rubies and emeralds with decorative figures by Edme Bouchardon after the models created by him for his famous public fountain in Paris called the Fountain of the Four Seasons. Among the valuable paintings in Beckford's extensive collection, this room included

Salvator Rosa's *The Interview between Job and His Friends* (now in the Uffizi, Florence), Leonardo's *The Infant Saviour*, Berghem's *L'embarquement des Vivres*, Mieris's *A Lady Feeding a Parrot*, Carracci's *Sibylla Lybica*, Bellini's *Doge Leonardo Loredan* (now in the National Gallery, London), and Gerard Dow's *The Poulterer's Shop*, among the twenty-four works hanging on display in this room.

The third apartment, The Grand Drawing Room, shifted in style from the preceding two rooms by being more decorative as evident by the overhead beams ending with carved and gilt corbels and the hangings in 'garter-blue' silk damask lined with gold mouldings. Some important paintings occupied this room by Watteau, Teniers, Dow, West, Rubens and Rembrandt, but the emphasis tended to be on striking pieces of furniture and art objects. In the centre of the room stood a large table with a marble slab mounted on three bronze dolphins. The slab was said to have been brought from Egypt by Napoleon and given as a gift to the Empress Josephine. On it sat a jewelled hookah of carved jad once owned by Tippoo Sahib, the ruler of the kingdom of Mysore. On the right side of the room was the famous desk by Riesener made for the Comte d' Orsay. There were four Boulle candelabras with designs by Cellini, the ivory cup and cover said to be by 'Magnus Berg', and the previously mentioned two vases of ivory which Beckford believed to have been carved by Fiamingo. Surrounding at least two sides of the room were chairs in the symmetrical and orderly classical style in contrast to the rest of the Abbey and to the Gothic altarpiece, designed by Wyatt, that occupied the centre section of one of the walls.

One of the most impressive features of the Abbey was the Great Western Hall. Begun originally as a banquet hall, it was converted in 1809–10 into the principal state entrance when its enormous size precluded the possibility of adequate heating. The Tribune, originally conceived as a elevated gallery to give readings during meals in the manner of early monastic establishments, and an enormous fireplace, both of which separated the hall from the Octagon, were removed to provide direct access to the centre of the building.

The common entrance was on the rear eastern side of the Abbey which was surprisingly modest in view of the grandeur of the rest of the building and the state entrance. Rutter felt that the planned gradual approach through more modestly decorated rooms to the remarkable beauties that were eventually to be seen was consonant with rules of art which 'apply as well to architecture as to poetry and painting'. 'By this route', he explained, 'we avoid astonishing the spectator, by a too sudden display of the colossal dimensions and unparalleled magnificence of the Abbey; a precaution, the neglect of which might produce a sensation of comparative indifference with regard to the minor beauties of the place; and something like dissatisfaction with the succeeding objects of ordinary magnificence'. 'The great attractions of the edifice are now judiciously husbanded', he added, 'till many of the other apartments have been passed; inferior indeed to those unequalled portions, upon which the fame of the Abbey must mainly rest, but quite beautiful and brilliant enough to satisfy abundantly the ardour of a first curiosity'[32]

The entry to the hall from the outside was by way of massive double-doors thirty-five feet high, hung upon four hinges which were supposed to have weighed more than a ton and cost £1,500.[33] The hinges were designed in a way that they could facilitate easily the opening and closing of these doors. As an illustration of Beckford's love of 'extreme contrast', Redding claimed that Pierrot, the dwarf servant, would be required to open these massive doors upon the arrival of distinguished guests thereby creating an astonishing effect.[34]

The hall itself was sixty-eight feet long by twenty-eight feet wide. Above the entrance was a roofed niche, surmounted by a cross, which contained a statue by Joseph Theakston of St Anthony of Padua. Crossing the threshold, the dimensions of this grand portal and the extreme height of the archways inside must have been felt with surprise and astonishment. Seventy-eight feet from the floor was a hammer-beam roof painted in imitation of old oak, which displayed a frieze moulded and arranged into ornamental forms. Above the entrance was a Minstrels's Gallery or Music Loft. The walls of the hall were finished to look like stone, with oak wainscoting on each side to a height of eleven feet. On the south side were three arched windows, and on the north were three recesses in the same form filled with crimson curtains. In the centre recess stood J. F. Moore's full-length marble statue of Beckford's father in his robes as Lord Mayor of London depicted in the act of making his famous reply to the King. It held a prominent place in a special niche in a large gallery created for it in Splendens after Moore had conveyed it to Fonthill in 1767 by way of a wagon that could support its weight of 7,000 lbs. A wide flight of twenty-nine stairs led to the higher level of the Octagon floor, making the Octagon Hall or saloon the focal point of the whole building where all four wings could be seen.

As in the case of the other principal wings of Fonthill Abbey, visitors to the Great Western Hall found the carefully planned effects of light and shade to be particularly masterful. Rutter felt that the 'the atmosphere of the coloured light, and the solemn brilliancy of the windows' produced an effect closely associated with the contemporary theory of the sublime and combined with the dark colour of the roof, the massive piers of the great portal, and the general contour of the noble archway to contrast powerfully with the 'light, the freshness, and the depth of the 'marble air', and the delicate colouring and simple outline of the external scene'.[35] It was another example of Beckford's taste for visual opposition, producing a dramatic appeal to the senses that compared in like manner to his love for passing from 'noise into the profoundest silence' and 'from company into solitude'.

The centrepiece for all four divisions of the Abbey was the Octagon Hall which ultimately became known as the Grand Saloon. Measuring thirty-five feet in diameter, it rose to the height of 132 feet where a sixteen-sided lantern hung from a vaulted roof—'high enough for the Nelson column at Charing Cross to stand in'.[36] In each of the eight walls was a pointed arch eighty feet high. In four of them were purple curtains which hung from the top of the arch to the floor and gave access to the four wings of the Abbey. The other four contained curtains fifty feet high, above which were stained glass windows of purple, crimson, and yellow, modelled after windows in the Batalha monastery in Portugal. Three of them contained a pattern of crimson Lancastrian roses with yellow centres, each surrounded by a quatrefoil of mazarine blue bordered with gold. James Storer observed in 1812 that the 'light emitted through the painted windows of the octagon presents a most enchanting play of colours, and the effect produced by the sombre hue of twilight, contrasted with the vivid appearance at different hours of the day, is indescribably pleasing and grand'.[37] A correspondent from *The New Monthly Magazine* reported the visual effects of the Grand Saloon during various times of day as unrivalled in his experienced. 'For ourselves', he wrote, 'we have experienced its effects under every variety of circumstance; in the stillness of the fresh morning, when the sun was visiting it with his first rays—in the glare of mid-day, when gazing crowds were pacing it, looking upward and around in empty admiration, and not daring to speak, lest they should put to flight the superb silence that seems to be the presiding Genius of the place—in the gloaming of evening, when the receding light seems reluctantly to leave its gorgeous windows, majestic arches, and mysterious recesses—and finally, in the still darkness of midnight, by the guiding ray of one glimmering lamp, we have wandered through its "visible darkness", and explored the dim vestibules and vaulted corridors, and winding turrets, that adjoin to it, till the spirit of old Romance young again within us, and we have yearned to act over again *The Mysteries of Udolpho!*'[38]

Above the arches was an open gallery, called the Nunneries or Nun's Walk, which connected with a series of apartments. Above this gallery was the fan vaulting that rose to support the great lantern. The dramatic effect of this room was its upward thrust creating a sense of awe particularly in visitors who entered from the lower northern and southern galleries. Rutter noted that the colossal height of this room emulated the length of the horizontal views elsewhere in the Abbey and that it was constructed on a design executed from a sketch by Beckford himself. Wyatt's taste, in Rutter's mind, would not have produced such a bold effect. 'The colossal height of is dimensions', Rutter wrote, 'the defiance of all common-place or ordinary arrangement, and the daring originality of its design, were probably far beyond the range of his professional architect, whose *forte* lay in the production of the elegant, rather than the sublime'.[39]

The Grand Saloon also supplied a final scenic effect that should be noted. From the top of the side stairs looking down through the entrance hall, as an anonymous visitor described it in 1823, one became aware of the way in which the romantic interior of Fonthill Abbey blended with the exterior grounds to create a totally unified scene: 'Instead of looking along a level, as in the preceding views, the eye, immediately on reaching the extremity of the octagon, or saloon, descends down a spacious staircase, which terminates in a grand entrance-hall, built in the old baronial style; which hall opens of the Great Western Avenue, or lawn, by a pair of arched gothic doors, more than thirty feet in height.... The effect of the view through this door, up what is called the Great Western Avenue, is highly characteristic and impressive; and it is imagined in fine taste—blending together, as it does, the outer domain with the inner, and forming them into one stately and magnificent whole'.[40]

These then were the principal interior arrangements of the wings of the cruciform, planned in keeping with the style of the whole Fonthill scheme as it evolved over time. While what has been described could fall in the category of the public sections of the Abbey, there was also a suite of rooms on the second floor designed for Beckford's private use and intimate arrangements. One of the important rooms was the 'Board of Works', previously mentioned, designed as a working library for Wyatt and other artists working on the Abbey who could consult and be inspired by artistic designs and architectural examples of the past in the fine collection of books and prints that Beckford had amassed. To continue the theme of royal ancestry the room was dressed in crimson damask. It had four bays overlooking the Fountain Court with windows on each side bearing the Mervyn and Latimer shields executed by Pearson. A striking scarlet and black carpet occupied this room and extended to other rooms in the area as a connecting feature. A massive library table covered with purple velvet stood in the recess area of the window with two cabinets dressed with bronzes by Vulliamy and a portrait of the Duke d'Alençon by Clouet, now at the Brodrick Castle, Scotland hanging on the wall. A large mirror was placed in the western wall panel with a Buhl cabinet beneath it. In a small apartment off this room Beckford kept drawings of the buildings that were part of his personal family history, including various drawings of Splendens, two views of the Fonthill Mansion that burnt down in 1755, a view of the first Fonthill mansion as it appeared in 1566, an early design for Fonthill Abbey and another for the Beacon tower. Appropriately, as an early inspiration for undertaking the construction of the Abbey, hung a view of Hollar's *The Grand Chartreuse* done in 1649.

To the right of the mirror on the west side of the Oak Library was a concealed door that led into an octagonal room inside the turret called the Cedar Boudoir which was designed for total seclusion or 'immurement', the need for which Beckford once discussed with Cozens. Its walls were lined with books while the casings and ceiling were made of cedar that filled the room with the pervasive fragrance of this wood. The mouldings were also of cedar and bore gilt designs of the Hamiltonian cinquefoils; two small windows look out upon the end of the Great Western Avenue and at a great distance could be seen Colt-Hoare's Stourhead estate.

On the east side there was a connection to the Vaulted Library which ran above St Michael's Gallery. It was forty-four feet long with a vaulted ceiling, the walls lined once again with bookcases and oak armoires between a series of miniature windows. A mirror was placed at the end to give the impression of an extended vista. At the north end of this library was the Chintz Boudoir, a small twelve by ten foot room for Beckford's private use. The walls were covered with yellow chintz of a damask pattern and displayed Van Eyck's *Virgin and Child*, Lodovico Caracci's *St Francis in Ecstasy* and West's *Two Subjects of the Apocalypse*. Here could also be found two bronze vases said to be from the Borghese palace and a pair of candlesticks after the designs of Cellini.

All of these rooms constituting Beckford's private place were designed to have a strong sensory impact. So important was sensory appeal and visual richness in the decorative context created inside the Abbey, namely the theatrical effects of light and colour throughout the rooms augmented by the beauty of the fine and applied art, the sumptuous bindings of the rare books on display, the dominant religious and ancestral symbols in the stained glass and elsewhere, that even domestic comfort was sacrificed. Thus, the dining room, called the Brown Parlour, located in the south-west corner of the Abbey, was the farthest apartment from the kitchen, which lay below the Octagon Hall on the ground floor. The offices on the same floor were cold, poorly lighted and without means for baking, washing, or brewing. Equally impractical were the eighteen bedrooms about the Abbey, thirteen of which were not readily accessible and lacked light and ventilation. The other five had no dressing room. Beckford's own bedroom, the Gallery Cabinet, on the second floor, was nothing but an unheated cell with one small window and a narrow bed without hangings, certainly a dramatic contrast to the sumptuousness of the rest of the Abbey and another piece of evidence to show that at Fonthill function and comfort gave way to pictorial effect.

The death of Hayter, who had been supervising the building repair and interior work of the Abbey, in December 1818 caused Beckford great concern and had dire consequences for the future of Fonthill. A new Clerk of the Works was appointed almost immediately, but the inevitable end was in sight. By January 1819 Beckford was beginning to consider with great reluctance the sale of his beloved Fonthill properties. The steady erosion of sugar prices in England over the years had continued to reduce his income from his West Indian estates. Annual interest on the mortgages on his Fonthill properties and an accrued indebtedness that reached £145,000 finally forced Beckford's hand.[41]

The total cost of the Abbey remains something of a mystery. Beckford told Cyrus Redding years later that the total outlay was £273,000, but Macquin, who was in a position to know, said in 1822 that it was £400,000, the equivalent of approximately £37,000,000 today. Beckford made a desperate attempt to recoup by suggesting to his son-in-law, the Duke of Hamilton, that he liquidate a large portion of the debt in return for the guaranteed inheritance of the Fonthill estate and all of his possessions.[42] Hamilton, however, was unwilling to become entangled in Beckford's financial affairs, and so the inevitable result was that Fonthill was to be sold by auction in the fall of 1822, including all its buildings, land, and most of the valuable contents of the Abbey. The announcement of such a sale would come as a shock to a society that had come to believe that Beckford, as Byron had dubbed him, was indeed 'England's wealthiest son'. As one contemporary writer reflected: 'The vast wealth which he expended here, one would have thought, was a stream from an exhaustless source; but the golden tide has had its ebb; the uncalculated treasure, which in its effects rivalled the power of enchantment, is dissolved like Cleopatra's pearl'.[43]

The Sale of Beckford's 'Holy Sepulchre' in 1822

While the Abbey grew in size and expense, rumours about Beckford's financial difficulties continued to be a topic of discussion in the drawing rooms of England. Benjamin West, who was close to the situation, was the source of some of them, having shared them in detail with Joseph Farington. We learn from Farington's diary, for example, that Wyatt's poor work habits and use of shoddy materials had cost Beckford an unnecessary £30,000. Farington also noted that the Jamaican estates continued to lose money and that Beckford was forced to dispose of property he owned in Bedfordshire and St Pancras. 'Nothing now remains to Him', Farington wrote, 'but His unproductive Jamaica estates, & the Fonthill estate which is reckoned at £10,000 a year: more might be made of it were the extensive park & grounds turned to greater advantage'. Farington then continued:

> [Beckford's] carriages & Horses have been sent away for sale, & Coachmen, Grooms & attendants discharged. He also desired West to assist Him in disposing of His valuable collection of pictures and drawings, saying at the same time He would feel much at parting with them as they never could be recovered by Him.[1]

As the weight of debt continued to mount, Beckford's first thought was to dispose of all of his treasures in the Abbey, with the exception of his books, then build a cottage somewhere on the grounds, and let the Abbey go to ruin. He said he could live there in 'perfect tranquillity for four thousand per annum'. It was the kind of escapist statement he would make from time to time in the face of increasing pressure. 'Let's make a cottage in the midst of a shrubbery of myrtles and laurustinus', he wrote to Franchi, 'there we will live on fish, mutton, Fonthill pheasants etc'.[2] But after judging this first idea unworkable, he made up his mind to sell all with the exception of the 'larger part of his books' some pictures and certain articles of virtu. This time he was firm. 'The building and its contents', he told Redding, 'have cost me best part of a million. I must leave it: I had better do it at once. I cannot tenant a structure that now costs me an expenditure of thirty thousand annually. The world will say that I have squandered my large fortune. I am prepared for the world's ideas as the subject all to me is a matter of perfect indifference'.[3] Upon hearing this statement, Redding observed that Beckford 'felt deeply at the necessity of parting with such a matchless property, but he was too proud to let the world see it'.

To assist in the disposal of the Fonthill property and its magnificent contents, Beckford chose Christie's. Notices began appearing in the press throughout the land that this major auction would take place in September 1822:

MR. CHRISTIE has the Honor very respectfully to inform the Nobility and Publick (the Connoisseurs and the Lovers of Virtú in particular), that on TUESDAY the 17th of September, and nine following Days (Sunday excepted), he will SELL by AUCTION, at FONTHILL ABBEY—The MAGNIFICENT ORNAMENTAL CONTENTS of that distinguished Mansion: including the Collection of PICTURES, ancient and curious GOLD and SILVER PLATE, CABINETS, JAPAN, AGATE, PORCELAIN, and a multitude of costly and precious ARTICLES, no less remarkable for their intrinsic value than for the fine taste with which the whole have been selected.

The Pall Mall firm, headed up at this time by James Christie, the younger, had handled four earlier sales for Beckford with the most recent being in 1817, a sale of pictures, drawings and furniture, but this auction was a coup for the firm because it contained some of Beckford's most valuable possessions. An enthusiastic Christie highlighted some of the most important contents to be sold in the preface to the catalogue he issued, beginning with the pictures:

… *The Laughing Boy* by L. Da Vinci, which was long preserved and admired in the Cabinet of the famous Earl of Arundel; the *Sibylla Lybica* by Lod. Carraci, formerly in the Lansdown Collection; (*Job and his Friends*, the famous Santa Croce Masterpiece of Sal. Rosa;) the *Poulterer's Shop* by G. Dow, and several precious Gems by Berghem, Mieris, V. Huysum and other Masters, from the Choiseuil and Praslin Cabinets.…

The Assemblage of *Porcelain* … are of the finest Oriental, and of the old Seve, and other European Manufacturers: that of the old Japan Lacquer upon wood is without rival in this or any other Country. It will exhibit unexpected examples of the Ingenuity and Taste of the Japanese … especially a Coffer of Japan, incrusted with animals of solid Gold and Silver, formerly the property of Cardinal Mazarin, and a casket of extreme beauty, which formed a principal ornament of the collection of Madame Pompadour.

The *Sculptured Vessels* of Topaz, Sardonyx, Agate, and Crystal, are numerous. One of them, in particular, is presumed to be from the tool of some Asiatic Greek Artist of the times of Classic Antiquity—others are Sculptured by Benevento Cellini, or mounted with exquisite Jewellry and Chasings.

Among the Ivory Carvings will be found undoubted Specimens by Fiamingo, Magnus Berg, Strous, and other great Artists in that line.

The *Armoires* contain a sumptuous display of ancient Silver-Gilt Vessels, such as Sideboard Dishes, Ewers and Salvers, one of which belonged to K. Charles I.; others are of Moorish and Persian Chasing, a great number of rich and massive Silver-Gilt Candlesticks were designed by Moette, and executed by Auguste.

The *Furniture* comprises Cabinets of Buhl, and Ebony with the finest Florentine Mosaic, of Japan, and other costly Materials, including one very beautiful, designed by

Bernini, and another by Holbein from the Palace at Whitehall; as also, a Set of Ebony Chairs, from Esher, which belonged to Cardinal Wolsey; and above all, a Magnificent Table of Florentine Mosaic, of extraordinary dimensions, inlaid with Marbles, of the Time of the Medici, formerly preserved in the Borghese Palace: the finest in Europe for Size and the disposition of its valuable materials.[4]

Copies of the catalogue were made available for purchase in London and elsewhere in England, and since in Christie's mind this auction had international interest, as well as in bookshops in Amsterdam, Brussels, and Paris.

In accord with Beckford's wishes, the 'contents' of this sale did not include the library, though there were in excess of 30,000 volumes on the shelves in the Abbey at the time. While he was willing to forego some remarkable paintings, furniture and *objets d'art*, Beckford's attachment to his books was too strong to separate from them easily. It was an exceptional library that in many respects diverged from the more typical collection of Greek and Roman classics. It also bore his personal imprimatur since many of the volumes were arrayed in his armorial bindings and contained pencil notes he was in the habit of writing in the flyleaves.[5] He was not yet ready to make this supreme sacrifice—financial problems notwithstanding. It was for this reason that when Christie issued the pink wrapper catalogue in July the books were conspicuously absent.

For the first time in its history, the sealed precinct of Fonthill Abbey was open to the public. The admission tickets issued with the catalogue for a guinea granted multitudes access to the building and the grounds and hopefully a glimpse of one of the most renowned recluses in England. Once the gates were open for visitors on 1 July 1822, a pilgrimage to the Abbey became a major social event, and the reaction to the experience was often described in hyperbolic terms. 'Since the days of Henry the Eighth', announced the *Morning Herald*, 'there has been nothing in England that might be compared with the scenes to which the opening of this edifice has given rise'.[6] 'It is impossible', explained another report on the event in *The Gazette of Fashion*, 'to do justice to the extraordinary beauty and splendor of Fonthill:

> … so long jealously secluded from the world's gaze, it now bursts upon the public eye like a region of enchantment. We behold all the wonders of nature and of art, the richest and most precious materials, decorated with still more costly workmanship; wealth that would prove the ransom of an emperor, added to the laborious occupation of the longest span of life. The painter, the sculptor, and the architect, have exhausted the treasures of their genius; and the bodily strength of the mechanic, the sweat of the brow, and the waste of the limb, have been called forth to aid the designs of the most exquisite talent. We have here the work of ages past, and the touch of yesterday; and we require the recollection, that dust is all that is left of many of the sublime artists whose resplendent contributions form a miracle and a wonder, to prevent us from exalting human beings to a level with the gods, when we behold the perfection of beauty, the gorgeousness and the elegance which the hand of man assembled at Fonthill'.[7]

Beckford, himself, fully enjoyed the public attention. 'The Holy Sepulchre', he wrote, 'has at last become one of the most animated spots in England. People go to it as to the waters; they admire it, they devour it with their eyes, they vanish into its thickets, doubtless regretting not yet being able to *retire* behind West's great dauberies. Yesterday seventy waggons, each drawn by several horses, followed by innumerable gigs, deposited at the foot of the Great Portal several dozen insipid personages of that diversity of persuasions in which we glory in this blessed Isle'.[8]

Captivated by Beckford's acknowledged reputation as a wealthy connoisseur and by the impenetrable secrecy of his pleasure dome, the public found itself afflicted by the 'Fonthill Fever', as Thomas Dibdin characterised it in a series of six articles about the event which he published in *The Museum* under the pseudonym Cuthbert Tonstall. 'The FEVER raged without control', he wrote. 'The whole country seemed to feel, in a *social* degree, what the earth would, in a *physical* degree, if a slight shock of an earthquake had agitated it. Across the country, in all directions, for some 50 miles, parties were in a perpetual state of locomotion'.[9]

Symptomatic of the rage to participate in the 'view', letters and essays about the Abbey and the grounds appeared in numerous newspapers and magazines throughout the country. The excitement surrounding the event also spawned a number of entrepreneurial ventures. One of the earliest of these was hatched by John Rutter, who hastily produced a guidebook to Fonthill that ran through six editions before the end of the year. George B. Whittaker joined in with his descriptive account to capitalise on the event, while James Easton chose this opportune time to reissue his Salisbury guide with an expanded section on Fonthill Abbey. Since these guides borrowed from James Storer's book on Fonthill, Storer himself decided to reissue it with eight engravings in a royal octavo and a large quarto format.[10] Many artists seized the opportunity to produce original drawings which were then engraved to accompany the written accounts that were published at the time.[11] Some individuals reacted by writing poems celebrating Fonthill as an astonishing artistic creation. One example appeared in the *Literary Chronicle and Weekly Review*:

FONTHILL: A SONNET

Upraised as by a wizard's powerful spell,
Or like the fitful scenery of a dream,
Far on the eye the towers of Fonthill gleam,
While memory wakes the ancient minstrel's shell.
Borne on the breeze now choral anthems swell,
Now fancy scenes of long past years will frame,
Scenes swept away by Time's devouring stream,
Which crush'd the monkish fane and hermit's cell.
Yes, they have vanish'd; but this gothic pile,
With magic power, the mental eye inspires
To trace long trains, amid the vaulted aisle,

Of holy monks and red-cross knights and friars;
To raise the spirit of those days of yore
When steel-clad warriors strove on Judah's shore.[12]

The written accounts which appeared in 1822 and the following year serve as testimony
to the keen interest in and popularity of Fonthill and remain of significant value in
forming an estimate of its impact on the consciousness of its time and its architectural
achievement.

As soon as the gates were opened in July, the roads leading to the estate were once again
crowded with people from all levels of society. The press fuelled the intensity of the event
by printing the names of prominent citizens who came to pay homage.[13] The Duke of
Gloucester, the King's brother-in-law, spent a night at the Beckford Arms on the estate to
have sufficient time to examine the contents of the Abbey and was impressed by what he
saw. He was followed by the Duke of Wellington who after his visit declared that nothing
could be compared to Fonthill anywhere in Europe. The Dukes of Buckingham, Beaufort,
and Devonshire also came as did an array of lesser-titled individuals. The newsheets noted
that Romeo Coates, the actor, spent three nights at the Lamb Inn in Hindon to indulge
himself in the experience, living up to his motto 'While I live, I'll crow'. Many visitors
came in private coaches, others on horseback, and still others on foot to see first hand
what had only been the stuff of rumour or daydreams. Kendell and Richardson's public
coach service ran three days a week to carry passengers from Salisbury to the Abbey on
the road that became the main thoroughfare to the Abbey. Once at the Abbey, the *Morning
Herald* noted, 'there is no idea of rank. A Marquis's equipage is obliged to wait until a
tax-cart full of the farmer, his wife, his grown-up daughters, and his whole nursery, have
passed in'.[14] On one day, more than 700 people inhabited the Abbey at one time. By 14
September nearly '15,000 guineas' were received for tickets of admission to the grounds
and the Abbey.[15]

Rooms in nearby Hindon, Tisbury, Mere and the surrounding towns were impossible
to come by and the source of inevitable frustration. 'He is fortunate', *The Times* reported,
'who finds a vacant chair within twenty miles of Fonthill.... Falstaff himself could not
take his ease at this moment.... The beds throughout the county are literally doing double
duty—people who came in from a distance during the night must wait to go to bed until
others get up in the morning'.[16] Every week the numbers swelled until a total of more than
7,200 people were admitted to the grounds.

Fonthill became an attraction that even drew people from beyond the borders of
England, as *The Times* noted: 'The languages of France, of Holland, and of Germany; the
peculiarities in tongue, of Scotland and Ireland, the broad dialect of Somersetshire, the
tinkling accent of Wales, and the more polished tones of metropolitan residents, are all,
at the same moment, heard clashing and contending together'.[17] Author and publisher
Charles Knight would later recall that in the year 1822, 'the world went mad about Mr.
Beckford's wonders. No profane eyes had ever looked upon his towers and pinnacles—
his domes and galleries. There was mystery, then, to combine with what was really worth

seeing at Fonthill. Its exhibition and its auction produced as much excitement as a Crystal Palace upon a small scale.'[18]

Throughout the acclaim, Beckford was elated. He relished the attention and knew that in the end this mania would facilitate the sale and his financial interests. He could hardly contain himself in a letter to his son-in-law the Duke of Hamilton:

> The rage is at its height. They dream only of the Abbey, they talk only of it. I doubt whether since the beginning of printing they have ever uttered such extravagances. Semiramis, Babylon, Persepolis no longer count for anything: they proclaim that Vathek and his tower have surpassed them.... In short, it is a veritable Rage, and buyers present themselves from all sides.
>
> ... Before the most attractive object in the whole world (according to the frenzied impression of the day) is for ever lost to us, come and glance at it, try to glide one fine Sunday up to the demonstrator of the magic lantern, our faithful and wellbeloved Franchi. He will tell you what is passing, what has passed. He will relate a thousand anecdotes which would make a fortune if one cared to print them—for the avidity with which they swallow everything which people choose to scribble about Fonthill is unexampled.
>
> The strange things which are passing in my affairs do not cast me down. The Saint who inspired me with the Abbey will also arm me with supernatural courage to do without it, and perhaps even to erect yet another monument to his glory. It will not be for a modest sum, you may be very sure, that I will deprive myself of the fruit of so much labour and so much trouble, in fact of an object which all England beholds agape. It seems that they believe in Fonthill as blindly as in pious times they believed in the most inconceivable legends.
>
> If by any chance the *Literary Gazette,* the *London Museum,* the *Gazette of Fashion,* the *Observer, Morning Herald, Chronicle* etc. etc come into your hands, read them and you will hear only once voice and one acclamation, and that voice the most sonorous and that acclamation the most deafening that was ever raised. And all this only costs me the trouble of reading the most ridiculous declamations and the most highflown phrases, for neither I nor any of my satellites have paid a sou for puffing. On reading them I have cried a hundred times 'The dog star rages, Bedlam is let loose'. And so will you ... [19]

It is evident from his letter that Beckford was angling for a private arrangement that would allow him to dispose of the entire estate at an attractive price. In the end, the Christie sale became the bait to attract the right buyer. The Duke of Somerset, the brother-in-law of the Duke of Hamilton, was interested as was Harriet Mellon the actress and recent widow of the wealthy banker Thomas Coutts. Others, like Earl Grosvenor, flirted with the idea but were unwilling to pay the £300,000 Beckford wanted to close the deal.

The puffery in the press was more than Beckford anticipated, but he nevertheless continued to spin his own web behind the scene to extricate himself from a difficult financial situation. He was aided initially by a member of his inner circle, Abbé Ange Denis Macquin, who contributed to the promotional effort by providing a series of four articles, an original drawing and a poem celebrating Fonthill and its creator in the August

and September issues of William Jerdan's *Literary Gazette*. The poem concluded with lines
that undoubtedly helped to nourish Beckford's rising celebrity status:

> Through the blazoned halls,
> The storied galleries and princely rooms,
> A bright galaxy of heraldic stars,
> Long lines of noblest ancestry, declare
> Who planned, who raised the splendid mansion, where
> Above the puny jarrings of the world,
> Above the strife for glory and power,
> Wrapt in his cloak of learning and of wit,—
> A mind of fire, a deeply feeling heart,—
> A founder stands aloft—a stranger to our sphere![20]

Macquin was a miscellaneous writer and a professor of rhetoric and belle-lettres in
France before coming to England in 1792. A frequent resident of the Abbey, he assisted
Beckford as librarian for the Fonthill collection and as an occasional genealogist.
Beckford's entrepreneurial instincts had to play a role in Macquin's descriptions of the
Abbey and its contents in the articles published. Macquin would also have shown
the manuscript to Beckford for any last-minute changes to insure accuracy in the
details, thus making these articles important authoritative sources of information on
Fonthill.

   If the celebratory nature of Macquin's pieces were not enough, Beckford approached
Macquin in August and proposed that Sir George Beltz, the Lancaster Herald, prepare
an informative article on the armorial bearings in the Abbey which led to the lengthy
work that appeared in several issues of the *Gentleman's Magazine* in the autumn of 1822.[21]
Beckford understood the importance of timing and the role the 'rage' would ultimately
play in serving his personal interest as he made clear to Macquin: 'Now is the moment. I
think the public will gladly swallow it up, for they are beginning to busy themselves with
the Abbey, and they even seem disposed to panegyrise everything about it'.[22]

   The original date for the auction was set for 17 September but then postponed to
1 October and then delayed again until 8 October. No cause for the delay was given to
the public. Most assumed that it was due to the constant stream of people to the estate
which seemed to increase on a weekly basis rather than diminish. What was not known
was that negotiations were taking place behind the scene to sell the entire estate to the
wealthy merchant John Farquhar. Farquhar, who was represented in the negotiations by
the auctioneer Harry Phillips, was a native of Aberdeen, Scotland. He had made a great
deal of money by manufacturing gun powder and selling it to the Government. He
was also a partner in the London agency house of Basset, Farquhar & Co. and a major
shareholder of Whitbread's brewery. He was known to have a weakness for speculation
and found Phillips's argument compelling that the purchase of Fonthill would elevate his
social position instantly as owner of one of the great estates in England.

The deliberations remained a secret until an agreement was reached on 5 October 1822, three days before the auction was to begin. James Fownes, Beckford's solicitor from the London firm of Fownes and White, drafted a memorandum of agreement entitled 'Argument for the Sale & Purchase of the Fonthill Abbey Estate & Effects'.[23] Various maps, plans, and surveys were supplied by James Still, Beckford's land steward. James Christie was now out of the picture, but his catalogue was a document of record in the agreement. Beckford identified certain lots in the catalogue that he wanted set aside for himself.[24] Farquhar, a serious book collector in his own right, wanted the library to be included among the effects. This was a sore point for Beckford, but he ultimately relented after negotiating the retention of one-third, or approximately 10,000 volumes of 'bound Books, Works in letter press, Manuscripts, Books of Prints, Prints and Drawings' and incorporating a carefully written arrangement in the agreement to govern the selection process, which read: 'the said William Beckford or his Nominee, having the first choice, and the said John Farquhar, or his Nominee, the second and third choice (each choice to apply to the full extent of each individual Work so chosen) and so on till the whole shall be divided as aforesaid'.[25] Beckford also excepted the unbound books, all of the articles in his bedroom, the wines and plate not in the catalogue, the useful china in the custody of the kitchen maid, the family portraits, the Japan and other objects within the closet of the Yellow Room, along with a portrait of a woman in a striped dress and a carved ebony chair, the statue of St Anthony from the Oratory, two green China jars in the 'new Book Room', and all of his writings, private papers, and account books. He also set aside two riding horses and for his devoted secretary at Fonthill Franchi 'one Horse and Gig'. In the end, Beckford agreed to accept the sum of £275,000 for the estate and an additional £25,000 for all remaining effects, the equivalent today of approximately £33,000,000.

So secret were these negotiations that not even Christie was informed that they were taking place. While notices of the cancellation of the sale were posted in towns near Fonthill on 6 October, it was only when he arrived at the Abbey on Monday, 7 October, that he learned that he would not preside over the scheduled auction. Dismayed and undoubtedly feeling undercut by his competitor Harry Phillips, Christie dashed off a letter to the *Salisbury and Winchester Journal* in which he made it clear that he was not a party to these deliberations:

As the Advertisements for the Sale of Effects at Fonthill Abbey were sent by me to your Journal, and have appeared under my name, I consider it due to the many respectable individuals who have quitted their homes to attend this sale, the greater number of whom I conclude are at this time readers of your Journal, that through the same medium I express my concern at the disappointment they must have experienced, a disappointment in which I in some degree partake, and to which I have been unintentionally (if) instrumental.

I arrived at the Abbey on Monday at one o'clock, to undertake the sale, in consequence of the latest notices I had been directed to publish up to the time of my departure from London on Saturday—It was then only that I was informed of orders that had been received, forbidding further proceedings and the admission of company.

I am sensible that in every transaction of business I have a duty to fulfill to the public, as well as to my employer, and the discharge of my public duties is never unmixed in the present instance, that I have been allowed such imperfect means of performing the first of these, and that the last, as far as the public are concerned, is to me extremely painful. I feel persuaded, however, that the very unexpected and sudden disposal of the whole Estate has alone induced the Proprietor to determine on a measure, which involved so much disappointment to the public, and to avoid which, he had formerly rejected an offer made to him for the private purchase of the whole of the articles contained in the catalogue of sale.

I am, Sirs, Your very obedient humble servant,

JAMES CHRISTIE
    Amesbury, Tuesday, Oct. 8, 1822[26]

Christie was obviously worried about a negative public reaction to him and his auction house and seemed to hint at an earlier offer he had made to buy the contents of his catalogue *en bloc* which was rejected.

The general public's reaction was one of dismay—a 'Grand Disappointment', as the *Morning Post* characterised it.[27] 'Humbug Fonthill Abbey' another dubbed it. Some dealers and connoisseurs felt duped by what they ultimately perceived to be a great marketing scheme. Reports also followed in the press about the possibility of some legal actions initiated by individuals to recoup the expenses incurred from travelling great distances to the Abbey. Another spurious account indicated that Beckford was so financially embarrassed that the Sheriff had actually taken entire control of the contents of the Abbey, disguising his own officers as servants during the view, to ensure liquidation of the indebtedness.[28] But rumours and strident complaints faded quickly as winter approached and as the Fonthill rage abated.

Meanwhile, Beckford expressed great relief that he was finally free from his debts. 'Let me announce a great piece of news', he wrote at the time, 'Fonthill is sold very advantageously. I am rid of the Holy Sepulchre, which no longer interested me since its profanation; I am delivered of a burden and of a long string of insupportable expenses. At present I have only to distribute my funds prudently and await the outcome of events. For twenty years I have not found myself so rich, so independent or so tranquil'.[29]

Tranquil, Beckford was not for very long. The selection clause involving the identification of the property to be divided between Beckford and Farquhar proved to be contentious, causing an extended delay of the legal transfer and the final payment from Farquhar. Beckford's book agent William Clarke and Chevalier Franchi participated in these negotiations as Beckford's representatives. Farquhar hired the bookseller George Lawford to provide assistance with the division of the books and prints. The wrangling was almost inevitable.

By December, with these matters not resolved, Beckford was beginning to have second thoughts about the entire contract with 'old Filthyman', as he dubbed Farquhar. In advance of a scheduled meeting to obtain agreement, Beckford urged Fownes to find a way to cancel the contract. 'They ought not to quit the Cabinet', he wrote, 'without a signed paper authorising the specific offer required for the annihilation of the agreement in all its branches. This would give me more heartfelt joy than all the 100,000s in the miserable old Reptile's Den'. The loss of Fonthill was troublesome—'a place I can never forget'—but the loss of his library that he spent years collecting was particularly galling. 'All the collective importance of the Library', he lamented, 'is destroyed. The gaps in every class are so wide that the repurchase of 10,000 volumes would hardly fill them. O that the galling contract was dissolved & my books restored! … How cheerfully would I pay all incurred expences & square matters so as to exist upon capital till the sale of effects, gutting of the Abbey, disposal of Hatch & of Jamaica the 1ˢᵗ favourable moment, came to my assistance. God send the miserly old Man one ray of intelligence. What a dreadful load would he take off his own shoulders & what a burden of eternal regret from mine'.[30]

It was too late to turn back. The negotiations at that meeting must have been successful because a report surfaced in the press in January that a final agreement had been reached which was 'either agreeable to the original contract, or in consequence of subsequent purchase'.[31] The same report made clear that that the 'purchase money' had not yet been paid because of title complications involving the 'houses and land in Hindon and the neighbourhood, together with a moiety of the Representation of the Borough'. Furthermore, it was stated that Farquhar had already 'resolved to bring the whole of the furniture to sale in August next; previous to which the Abbey and effects will be shown by tickets, as before, and with far less reserve'. At this stage, Farquhar may not have made up his mind as to what would constitute the 'furniture' of the Abbey, but it soon also included paintings, drawings, china, a stunning array of works of art and an extraordinary collection of books and prints. It was a decision that ensured that the rage of Fonthill fever would revive again in the months that followed.

As it turned out, the final settlement of the Fonthill sale did not take place until after 25 March when Beckford sent a letter to Farquhar expressing relief that the protracted negotiations were 'upon the eve of final settlement' and offering him as a present the 'fine works of plate [which] still remained at Fonthill Abbey'.[32]

The conclusion of the Fonthill proceedings enabled Beckford to establish permanent residence in Bath by the purchase of houses in Lansdown Crescent in the summer of 1823 where before long he would build another tower amidst a landscape garden on a much smaller scale than Fonthill. The loss of two-thirds of his library would remain a permanent source of discontent, and he spent the rest of his life buying back 'Fonthills', as he called the books he lost in the sale, and when he could not afford to take them in, he would have his bookseller run up the price at an auction to 'teach them the immense value of the worst books from the F[onthill] Library'.[33]

The other loss he lamented was the role he played as the major employer of the poor and needy in the population surrounding Fonthill. Despite the rumours about his imperious manner, he was known to have been a generous landlord. To alleviate the stress of poverty, he established a House of Industry in 1800 at his own expense near Fonthill to feed, clothe and employ sixty children who would learn how to spin wool under the care of resident teachers. There were also frequent notices in the press acknowledging Beckford's contributions as a major employer of the poor in his neighbourhood, as in the case of a correspondent of the *Morning Chronicle*, who characterised the expenditure of monies on Fonthill as a patriotic act:

> This interesting sale, which will take place in a very few days, has given occasion to a great variety of remarks in the public prints, and to some animadversion on the large sums that have been expended by the Proprietor in extravagant projects. It should, however, be considered, that the judicious employment of a princely fortune is a happy art which few have able to attain. In cases where an income may exceed what is necessary for the individual happiness of the owner, the most fastidious objector must surely admit, that calling forth the genius of the architect and the artist, and the labour of the artisan and the husbandman—that constructing a palace where not a shepherd's hut stood before— that clothing with woods a heath or a sheep down, and distributing a large portion of this wealth among the many who co-operate in such works,—is true patriotism There are some persons who have attained more than a competence by partaking of the sums so expended in this instance, and hundreds are thereby now enjoying a livelihood in comfort.[34]

The absence of Beckford's proprietorship as the area's principal employer would be keenly felt before long. Eight years later, Hindon, Tisbury and the other towns surrounding Fonthill experienced extreme poverty due to scarcity of work and plummeting wages. Thrashers were forced to work for seven shillings as week, the mill at Fonthill became unoccupied and only a handful of people worked the grounds. A correspondent from Salisbury reported in *The Times* that the whole area 'seems fast sinking into ruin'. The lands in the vicinity were no longer as well cultivated as they once had been and that a common scene was cottages in a state of decay with their windows frequently broken—all signs of a dire change of lifestyle from the 'once prosperous and happy peasantry of Mr. Beckford'.[35]

In a letter Beckford wrote in January 1823 to John Still the Rector of Fonthill Gifford, he asked that a man caught stealing wood on the estate be released from responsibility. 'This perhaps may be the last opportunity I may have in my power to lessen the sum of misery in my former neighbourhood', he wrote. 'I shudder to think of the distress which is impending over it'.[36] This was one of Beckford's last acts as proprietor of Fonthill. His reign had come to an end. It was Sir Richard Colt Hoare, long captivated by the Abbey and its owner, who wrote the epitaph for the *Gentleman's Magazine*:

> The pleasing vision is now past, and the noise of the Auctioneer's hammer will not be heard—silence pervades the long-drawn ailes—the lofty portal is closed—and the Abbot is returned to his Cloysters, with thanks to his Patron Saint, St. Anthony, for the numerous Pilgrims who have been attracted to his shrine. But with a farewell look he will shortly bid adieu to his cloistered walls, and extensive solitudes, which are now doomed to greet a second Abbott.[37]

'The Gay Haunt of Eager Curiosity': The Fonthill Sale of 1823

The reason given for Farquhar's decision to dispose of Beckford's collections, according to newspaper accounts, was he felt that the contents were unsuited to the Gothic character of the Abbey. He was 'resolved to furnish it according to his own taste in a solid and substantial style of magnificence'.[1] Having unshakable confidence in his own artistic interests, Beckford undoubtedly reacted to this revelation with amusement. But Farquhar's taste tended towards a more traditional style of interior décor, one marked by simplicity and formal grandeur and more characteristic of the other great estates in England. One correspondent explained that

> the various articles with which Mr. Beckford furnished the Abbey in so elaborate a style, never accorded with Mr. Farquhar's taste. The latter is said to admire the bold and substantial, rather than the delicate and ornamental, in all works where the force of original genius is called into action; and hence he is not pleased with the numberless minute objects which the former has collected. As toys, he thinks they may amuse for a moment, but as decorations for a Gothic edifice he regards them as alike offensive to common sense and good taste.[2]

It was also rumoured that Farquhar was inclined to promote a national interest in the Abbey by making it an English *Louvre*, open to the public certain times of the year as a museum set up to display splendid specimens of the fine arts.[3] If this indeed was a plan that Farquhar ever contemplated, he never moved to carry it into execution.

Phillips, as a reward for assisting Farquhar in the original purchase of Fonthill, was hired to preside over the sale of the 'effects' scheduled to begin on 9 September 1823. Providing public access to the Fonthill estate for the second time within a year was bound to create an even greater stir than Christie's aborted sale. The Christie sale, after all, was much more limited in scope than the sale of 1823, as was evident from its scheduled run of ten days. The Christie catalogue included pictures, gold and silver plate, antique cabinets, rare japan, agate, and porcelain, some furniture, and no books and prints. By comparison, the sale conducted by Phillips on behalf of Farquhar was so much more extensive that it took thirty-seven days to complete.[4]

Both Phillips and Farquhar anticipated an increase in the volume of visitors and planned accordingly. During the Christie view, many of the rooms of the Abbey were closed off to the public. Farquhar, by contrast, ordered the opening of all of the previously closed rooms, including Beckford's bedroom (the Gallery Cabinet), the Anti-Room, the Vaulted Library, the Grand Drawing Room, the miniature cabinet in the south-east tower, Beckett's Passage, and the Great Northern Passage. These changes allowed the visitor to complete a tour of the building without retracing any steps as was not possible in 1822.

In the previous year, the Beckford Arms, Lamb, Swan, and Crown Inns nearby were filled to capacity, much to the disgruntlement of the crowds looking for overnight accommodations. For the 1823 sale some of the pressure on the local inns was relieved by fitting up the remaining pavilion of Fonthill Splendens under the direction of Thomas Harrington, proprietor of the Black Horse Inn in Salisbury. Accommodation included bedrooms offered at a reasonable rate, a large common coffee room and private sitting rooms. William Dore of the White Lion Hotel in Bath provided spirits and food all day long in the Fountain Court on the west side of St Michael's Gallery as another hospitable gesture to those individuals who arrived from great distances.

The unfinished Eastern Transept was set up under the direction of the architect Stedman Whitwell as the site of the auction to provide ample room to display to advantage the objects of virtu, paintings, furniture and books for sale. The walls were covered with a tapestry, while the rafters and joists above were cloaked with a false ceiling made of striped muslin. The auction rostrum stood in the middle of the floor surrounded by a range of wooden benches which rose from the floor in amphitheatre effect to the upper sections of the walls. The Oak Parlour, the Crimson and Yellow Drawing Rooms were also set aside as auction sites for some of the paintings and other items.

Tickets for visiting the Abbey on any two days sold for a guinea each; tickets with sale catalogues, which admitted three persons every day, except Sundays, during the viewing and sale went for 5 guineas each. The ticket required for entrance was an impressive design by Whitwell, displaying the great tower from the perspective of the rear façade of the Eastern Transept. At the bottom of this card were two ornamented sections. One would be detached for the first visit; the second removed upon return. All tickets were checked at a single entrance gate at the barrier wall. In lieu of a guard house that was used for the previous viewing, Farquhar had a rustic lodge in the form of a 'moss clad shed' constructed at the gate which John Rutter depicted in a vignette that appeared in the title-page of his 1823 guide book, *A New Descriptive Guide to Fonthill Abbey and Demesne*.

Once visitors reached the Abbey, there were two entrances: one for viewing the Abbey and the other to enter the saleroom. The first was normally the servants entrance through the door of the Eastern Postern Tower, described as 'a little low portal, latticed, and opening to a small passage' leading to the Oak Parlour.[5] The *Morning Post* described the other entrance in what appears to be in the north side of the Eastern Transept: 'Just before entering the great quadrangle on the south of the Abbey, a carriage-road branches off to the right, and soon after turning to the left, by a new cut, sweeps, on a kind of natural terrace, in front of the lofty façade of the eastern transept. In the centre of this, and necessarily at

Above left: William Beckford, oil on canvas by John Hoppner, *c.* 1800. (*City of Salford Art Gallery, Salford, England*).

Above right: Lord Mayor Beckford, mezzotint by unknown artist, published by Sayer and Smith, *c.* 1769. (© *The Trustees of the British Museum*).

Above left: Maria Hamilton Beckford, Beckford's mother, oil on canvas by Benjamin West, 1799. (*National Gallery of Art, Washington, Andrew Mellon Collection*).

Above right: G. B. Piranesi, pen and brown ink drawing by Pier Leone Ghezzi, 1749. (© *The Trustees of the British Museum*).

Fonthill House in 1566, drawn and engraved by J. & H. S. Storer, published by Sherwood & Co., 1822.

Fonthill House Before the Fire in 1755, drawn and engraved by J. & H. S. Storer, published by Sherwood & Co., 1822.

Opposite above: Old House, Fonthill, 1740, copy of George Lambert painting as Fonthill House appeared when purchased in 1745, watercolour and graphite on wove paper by unknown artist, between 1800 and 1810. (*Yale Center for British Art, Paul Mellon Collection*).

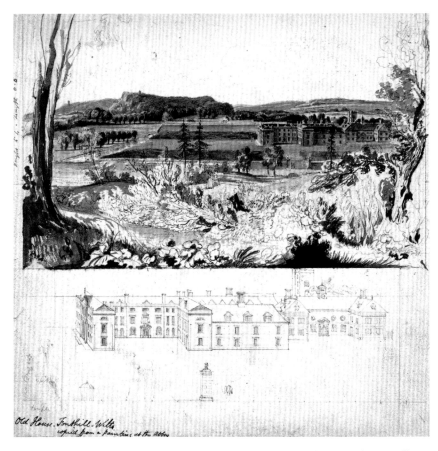

Old House. Fonthill. Wilts
copied from a painting at the abbey

Below: View of the Entrance to the Grand Chartreuse, etching and aquatint by J. F. Albanis Beaumont, *c.* 1787. (© The Trustees of the British Museum).

Above left: Batalha Cathedral Interior with Tomb of Don John, etching by William Wallis after James Holland, 1849. (© The Trustees of the British Museum).

Above right: William Chambers, R.A., mezzotint by Richard Houston after Francis Cotes, 1772. (© The Trustees of the British Museum).

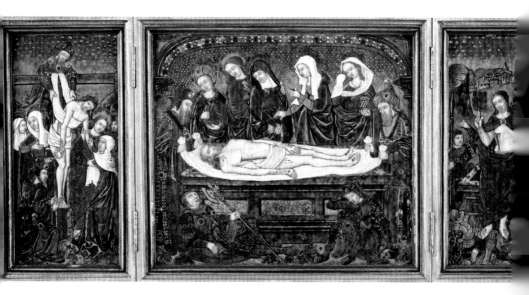

The Deposition; the Entombment; the Resurrection, triptych attributed to Nardon Penicaud, enamel and gold on copper, *c.* 1510. (© The Trustees of the British Museum).

Aedes Fonthillianae, landscape scene of Fonthill House, lithograph by W. Byrne after a painting by Hendrik de Cort, published by Edward Foxhall, Cavendish Street, London, 1793.

A View of Fonthill House from the North, watercolour by John Buckler, 1806. (*Wiltshire Heritage Museum and Library, Devizes*).

Left: Fonthill Estate Gateway, (photograph by author).

Below: Landscape Plan for Old Park, drawing by James Wyatt, *c.* 1781. (*Bodleian Library, University* of *Oxford,* MS Beckford, c. 84, f. 110).

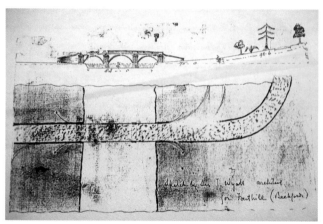

Left: Alternate Three-Arched Stone Bridge for Old Park, sketch by James Wyatt, *c.* 1781. (*Beinecke Rare Book and Manuscript Library, Yale University,* Beckford Collection, box 6, f.111).

A Scene in Alpine Gardens, vignette engraved by W. Hughes after a drawing by Stedman Whitwell, 1823. (*John Rutter, Delineations of Fonthill and its Abbey*).

A View of Mr. De Visme's Country Seat at Montserat, Portugal, engraved by Wells after a drawing by Noel Bulwer, 1795.

James Wyatt, R.A., engraved by Joseph Singleton after Ozias Humphry, 1793. (© The Trustees of the British Museum).

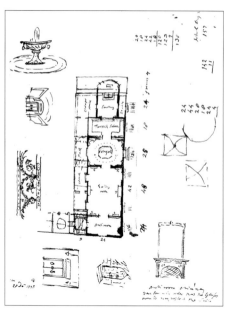

Left: *Architectural Design for the Lisbon House*, drawing by William Beckford, 28 December 1793. (*Bodleian Library, University of Oxford*, MS Beckford, c. 84, f. 107).

Middle: *The Fonthill Convent in Ruins*, vignette engraved by Thomas Higham, 1823. (*John Rutter, Delineations of Fonthill and its Abbey*).

Below: *Map of the Fonthill Domain*, engraved by B. R. Baker and printed by J. Boosey & Co., 1823. (*John Rutter, Delineations of Fonthill and its Abbey*).

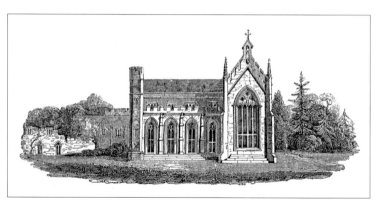

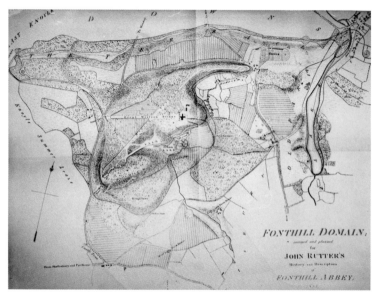

FONTHILL DOMAIN,
surveyed and planned
for
JOHN RUTTER'S
History and Description
of
FONTHILL ABBEY.

Perspective View of Fonthill Abbey from the South West, with a squat tower design, watercolour and gouache by J. M. W. Turner, *c.* 1797. (*Bolton Museum and Art Gallery, Bolton MBC*).

Projected Design for Fonthill Abbey, with a spire, watercolour and graphite on wove paper by James Wyatt; attributed also to J. M. W. Turner, 1798. (*Yale Center for British Art, Paul Mellon Collection*).

Alternative Design for Fonthill Abbey, with a taller spire, watercolour by Charles Wild, *c.* 1799. (© Victoria and Albert Museum, London).

Near View of Fonthill Abbey, under construction from the south east, graphite on paper by J. M. W. Turner, 1799. (*Tate Britain*).

South View of the Gothic Abbey, Now Building at Fonthill, 1799, engraved by T. Crostick after a watercolour by J. M. W. Turner, published by John Sharpe, 1828.

Lord Nelson's Reception at Fonthill, plate published by *The Gentleman's Magazine*, April 1801.

View from the End of the Western Avenue, engraved by J. Thompson after a sketch by T. Higham, 1823. (*John Britton, Graphical and Literary Illustrations of Fonthill Abbey*).

Bitham Lake (*Photograph by author*).

Above left: Fonthill Abbey from the American Plantation, engraved and drawn by James Storer. 1812. (*James Storer, A Description of Fonthill Abbey*).

Above right: Fonthill House Sale Catalogue, Second Part, 1801.

View of the Scenery of the American Plantations, engraved by W. Hughes after a drawing by S. Whitwell, 1823. (*John Rutter, Delineations of Fonthill and its Abbey*).

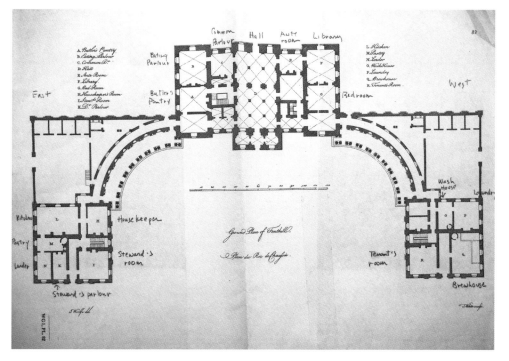

Ground Floor Plan of Fonthill House, engraved by T. White after John Woolfe, 1767. (*Vitruvius Brittanicus*, 1739).

Left: Writing Table and Dressing Commode, closed, attributed to John Channon, mahogany and padouk, inlaid with brass; gilt-bronze mounts, *c.* 1765. (© Victoria and Albert Museum, London).

Right: Writing Table and Dressing Commode, extended.

Left: Crang Organ, by John Crang, early 1760s. (© Victoria and Albert Museum, London).

Above: Pair of George III Double-Chairback Hall Benches, attributed to John Soane, mahogany, late 1780s. (*Courtesy of Dukes of Dorchester, Fine Art Auctioneers*).

The Muses of Painting and Music, ceiling painting by Andrea Casali, *c.* 1760-66. (*Great Hall of Dyrham Park*).

The Fifth Plague of Egypt, engraved by C. Turner, drawn and etched by J. M. W. Turner, published 1808. (© The Trustees of the British Museum).

The Indian Woman, oil on canvas by George Romney, 1793. (*By permission of current owner and courtesy of the Walker Art Gallery, Liverpool*).

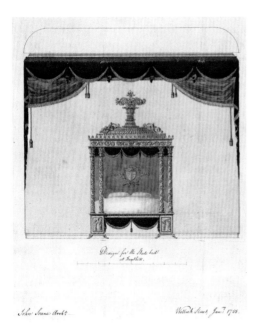

Above left: Design for the State Bed at Fonthill Splendens, pen and watercolour by John Soane, 1788. (*Bodleian Library, University of Oxford*, MS Beckford, b. 8, f. 1).

Above right: Statue of Bacchus, marble in the style of Praxiteles, Anglesey Abbey, Fairhaven Collection, various dates as a pastiche. (*By courtesy of the National Trust/Eric Crichton*).

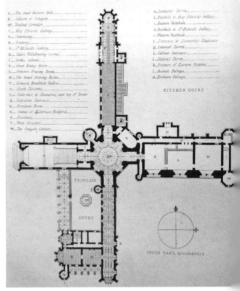

Above left: John Soane, author of 'Designs of Buildings', etching by Daniel Maclise for *Fraser's Magazine*, 1836. (© *The Trustees of the British Museum*).

Above right: Plan of the Principal Story of Fonthill Abbey, engraved by J. Cleghorn after a drawing by J. Rutter, 1823. (*John Rutter, Delineations of Fonthill and its Abbey*).

The Riva degli Schiavoni, looking West, oil on canvas by Giovanni Antonio Canaletto, 1736. (*Courtesy of the Trustees of Sir John Soane's Museum*).

Remains of Fonthill House after demolition, brush drawing in grey wash over graphite, drawn by T. Higham after Philip Crocker, 1828. (© The Trustees of the British Museum).

Fonthill Abbey in 1812 without the Eastern Transept, drawn and engraved by James Storer, 1812. (*James Storer*, A Description of Fonthill Abbey, Wiltshire).

The 'Studied Dissimilarity' of the Abbey in its Setting, engraved by S. Rawle after a drawing by C. V. Fielding, from a sketch by J. Britton, 1819. (*John Britton*, The Beauties of Wiltshire).

Above left: The Beckford Coat of Arms, thirty quarterings registered at the College of Arms in 1808. (© The College of Arms, London, MS Norfolk 2, p. 176).

Above right: Window in St. Michael's Gallery, engraved by Havell & Son, drawn & etched by H. Shaw from a sketch by G. Cattermole, 1823. (*John Britton, Illustrations, Graphical & Literary, of Fonthill Abbey*).

Right: Medieval Limoges Reliquary, copper, engraved, chiselled, stippled, and gilt, *c.* 1180-90. (*The Metropolitan Museum of Art, Gift of J. Pierpont Morgan, 1917*).

Left: The 'Holbein' Cabinet, quartered oak, with ash-lined drawers, boxwood carvings and inlay of various woods, artist unknown, South Germany, 1550-80; stand possibly made in Britain, 1800-20. (© Victoria and Albert Museum, London).

Interior of St Michael's Gallery, engraved
by J. Cleghorn after a drawing by W. Finley,
aquatinted by D. Wolstenholme, 1823. (*John
Rutter, Delineations of Fonthill and its Abbey*).

S. End of St. Michael's Gallery,
engraved by M. Dubourg after
a drawing by G. Cattermole,
1823. (*John Britton, Illustrations,
Graphical & Literary, of Fonthill
Abbey*).

*Interior of King Edward's
Gallery*, engraved by Havell &
Son, etched by J. Cleghorn after
a drawing by C. F. Porden, 1823.
(*John Rutter, Delineations of
Fonthill and its Abbey*).

Above left: The 'Magnus Berg' Cup and Cover, ivory, silver gilt, emeralds, rubies, turquoises, attributed to Johann Gottfried Frisch, *c.* 1700 with later additions. (*The Royal Collection © Her Majesty Queen Elizabeth II 2014*).

Above right: Ivory Vase, silver-gilt mounts by David Willaume, carved ivory sleeve attributed to circle of Giovanni Battista Pozzo, early 1700s. (© The Trustees of the British Museum).

Left: Buhl Armoire, tortoiseshell and brass on oak, gilt bronze mounts, ten feet by five feet wide, by André Charles Boulle, *c.* 1630s. (*Hamilton Catalogue of the Collection of Pictures, Works of Art, and Decorative Objects*, 1882).

Above: The 'Rubens Vase', agate and gold, *c.* 400 by a Byzantine artist with the gold rim added in France 1809-19. (*The Walters Art Museum, Baltimore*).

Britton's Display of Art Objects on the 'Borghese Table' in King Edward's Gallery, engraved by J. Le Keux after sketches by G. Cattermole, H. Shaw etc., 1823. (*John Britton, Illustrations, Graphical & Literary, of Fonthill Abbey*).

A Group of the Rarest Articles of Virtu, vignette, engraved by W. Hughes after a drawing by T. Higham, 1823. (*John Rutter, Delineations of Fonthill and its Abbey*).

Below: The Van Diemen Box, Japanese lacquerware, 1636-1639. (© Victoria and Albert Museum, *London*).

Above: The Mazarin Chest, flat-topped Japanese lacquer chest with hinged lid, *c.* 1640. (©Victoria and Albert Museum, London).

Right: St Anthony in the Oratory, drawn and engraved by J. & H. S. Storer, published by Sherwood & Co., 1822.

Below: The Grand Drawing Room, engraved by John Cleghorn after a drawing by Stedman Whitwell, 1823. (*John Rutter, Delineations of Fonthill and its Abbey*).

Riesener Roll-Top Desk, oak, marquetry of holly, walnut, ebony, box, sycamore, amaranth, gilt bronze, by J. H. Riesener, *c*. 1770. (*The Wallace Collection, London*).

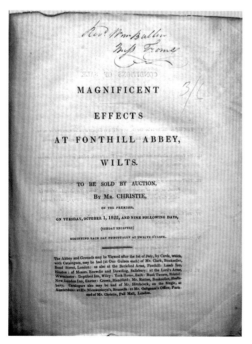

Above left: Magnificent Effects at Fonthill Abbey, Wilts. To be Sold by Auction by James Christie, Christie Sale Catalogue, October 1, 1822 and nine following days.

Above right: John Farquhar, Esq., engraved by W. T. Fry, published by T. Boys, 1823. (© The Trustees of the British Museum).

Interior of the Great Western Hall, engraved by J. C. Varrall after a drawing by G. Cattermole, 1823. (*John Rutter, Delineations of Fonthill and its Abbey*).

Fonthill Abbey S. E. View, engraved by W. Tombleson, sketched by T. Higham, drawn by S. Rayner, 1823. (*John Britton, Illustrations, Graphical & Literary, of Fonthill Abbey*).

Left: Octagon, or Grand
Saloon, 1823. (*John Britton,
Illustrations, Graphical &
Literary, of Fonthill Abbey*).

*Below: South West View
of Fonthill Abbey*, with the
addition of the Eastern Transept,
brush drawing in grey wash
by John Britton, 1821. (© The
Trustees of the British Museum).

Right: Hall from the Octagon, blending the interior with the exterior grounds, engraved by R. Sands, drawn by H. Gastineau from a sketch by G. Cattermole, 1823. (*John Britton, Illustrations, Graphical & Literary, of Fonthill Abbey*).

Below: Fonthill Abbey in Its Setting, view from the south, engraved by R. Havell & Son after a sketch by T. Higham, published by Robert Havell, *A Series of Picturesque Views of Noblemen's and Gentlemen's Seats*, 1823.

The Pavilion (used as Dormitory for the Visitors) and the Lake in the Old Park, engraved by J. Cleghorn, drawn by W. Finley, 1823. (*Rudolph Ackermann*, Repository of the Arts).

View of the Fountain Court within the Western Cloister, set up as a public refectory, engraved by J. Boosey and Co., drawn by Stedman Whitwell, 1823.

Above: Fonthill Abbey from the Barrier Gate, engraved and drawn by T. Higham, 1823. (*John Rutter, A New Descriptive Guide to Fonthill Abbey and Demesne*).

Right: The Controversial 'Cellini Cup', smoky rock crystal ewer with enamel, gold, and diamonds, now attributed to the workshop of Ferdinand Eusebio Miseroni, *c.* 1680. (*The Metropolitan Museum of Art. The Jack and Belle Linsky Collection, 1982*).

Below: Ruins of Fonthill Abbey, The Tower fell 21 December 1825. 'And thus this unsubstantial Fabrick falling left a sad wreck behind!', lithograph, drawn on stone by W. Westall after a drawing by J. Buckler, 1825. (© The Trustees of the British Museum).

Above left: A Sketch from the Ruins of Fonthill, caricature of John Farquhar, etching published by G. Humphrey, October, 1826.

Above right: Fonthill Ceramic Souvenir, Clews Blue Historical Staffordshire Tureen, *c.* 1825.

Above left: William Hazlitt, wood engraving after a drawing by William Bewick, *c.* 1825. (© The Trustees of the British Museum).

Above right: A Poulterer's Shop, oil on oak, by Gerrit Dou, *c.* 1670. (*The National Picture Gallery Library, London*).

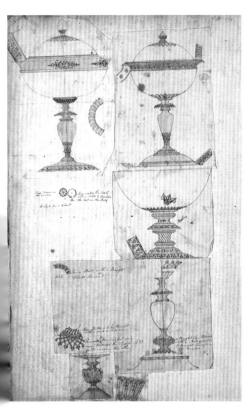

Left: Design for Mounted Cup, pen and ink and wash, drawing by Gregorio Franchi, from an album assembled by James Aldridge, *c.* 1815-20. (© Victoria and Albert Museum, London).

Above: Cup and Cover, agate with chalcedony knops set with rubies in silver mounts, designed by Gregorio Franchi, commissioned by Beckford, maker's mark of James Aldridge, 1815-16. (© *Victoria and Albert Museum, London*).

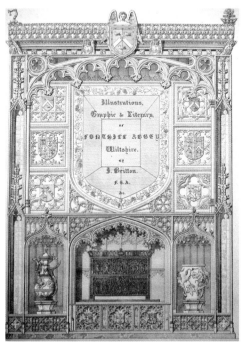

Above left: John Britton, Esq. F.S.A., stipple and etching on chine collé, engraved by James Thompson after a painting by John Wood, 1828. (© The Trustees of the British Museum).

Above right: Architectural and Heraldical Title Page, with a niche of a medieval chasse surrounded by the Gaignières ewer and the Rubens vase, designed by J. Britton, engraved by J. Le Keux after J. Rayner, 1823. (*John Britton, Illustrations, Graphical & Literary, of Fonthill Abbey*).

Above left: George Cattermole, black chalk on blue paper, self-portrait by George Cattermole, *c.* 1820 (© The Trustees of the British Museum).

Above right: St Stephen's Hall, Westminster, platinum print mounted on a card, by Benjamin Stone 1897. (*Victoria and Albert Museum, transferred from the British Museum*).

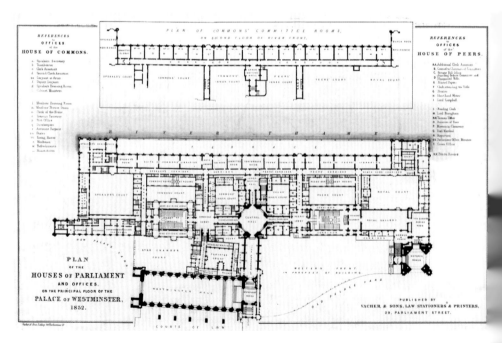

Plan of the Principal Floor of the New Houses of Parliament, Palace of Westminster, showing central octagon with radiating wings, lithograph, 1852, published by Vacher & Son.

a great height from the ground, owing to the great excavation beneath, an opening has been made, to which a broad and commodious covered bridge, with two flights of stairs, gives an easy and safe access'.[6] Upon entering the building, the visitor came upon a double staircase with the right side leading to the saleroom; the left side of the stairs was used for the purpose of exiting the building. Following the right staircase, the visitor passed through an anteroom that then led to the saleroom at the level where the highest seats were located in the constructed amphitheatre.

Public inspection of the estate began on 16 June. Heavy rains marked the weather for the two months preceding the auction, but the public was undeterred. They continued to travel for hundreds of miles from all parts of the country to obtain a first-hand look at Beckford's palace and its lavish contents. By 8 August newspaper reports indicated that over 5,000 people had visited the estate.

Farquhar himself increased the numbers dramatically by reserving Sunday, 7 September for all the inhabitants of neighbouring towns and villages to attend the viewing free of charge. Over 1,500 people descended upon the estate in that single day. The visit was orderly despite the great numbers wandering the grounds and gaping at the treasures on display inside the Abbey. But a crisis occurred when the ceremony was to end at 3:00 o'clock in the afternoon. A gong was sounded to inform everyone it was time to leave when suddenly another very large group of 'Hindonians' and 'Tisburinians' arrived who were not aware that the view would be closing at that time. It was quickly determined for the purpose of maintaining order that the newcomers should be accommodated, but as soon as those leaving detected what was happening, they too crowded the entrance door and forced their way in for a second tour. As the *Morning Post* reported: 'Again they paraded the superb galleries, and praised and stared, and pointed at the treasures which they contain. They remained thus occupied for an hour and a half, when the gong again bade them 'part in peace'. Highly gratified by the indulgence extended to them by the present Proprietor, they obeyed the signal, and retreated in excellent order'.[7]

It must have been unsettling to the owners of other great estates in Wiltshire that the ex-residence and collections of the most celebrated pariah in England was receiving so much attention. Perhaps to placate them, the *Salisbury and Winchester Journal* tried to promote other attractions in the Wiltshire area:

> The admirers of architecture will delight in the splendid remains of Malmsbury and in the simple magnificence of the Cathedral at Salisbury, which, as a perfect and unmixed example of the early English or pointed style, stands unrivalled.—Longford Castle (the seat of the Earl of Radnor) with its inestimable Claudes—Wilton, and its superb cloister, erected by the Earl of Pembroke, to contain his rare and extensive collection of busts, statues, &c.—the fine mansion, chapel, and ruins of Wardour Castle, the property of Lord Arundel—the Marquis of Lansdowne's picturesque seat at Bowood—Longleat, the princely residence of the Marquis of Bath—Sir Richard Hoare's house in the romantic grounds of Stourhead—and Corsham, the seat of Paul Methuen, Esq. will all furnish forth an ample feast for the lover of taste and the amateur of paintings. The geological

treasures of the county are not uninteresting; and the antiquarian will be gratified by an inspection of the mysterious Stonehenge, and will find abundant materials for reflection in the antiquities of its surrounding plains. In short, there are few counties which can boast of superior attractions either to the man of science or of pleasure, especially when, to all the beauties enumerated above, is added the immense and costly assemblage of the world's rarities which is to be found within the classic walls of Fonthill.[8]

In view of the abrupt cancellation of the Christie auction, there was a great deal of anxiety and suspicion about the likelihood of the second sale meeting the same fate. In 1822 some dealers and connoisseurs felt duped by what they ultimately perceived to be a shrewd marketing scheme that Beckford had engineered. The cynicism that developed at this time continued to be strong as Farquhar's sale approached. To alleviate such fears, frequent reassurances in the press were made that this sale would take place and, indeed, this time no postponement occurred. It began as announced on 9 September at 1:00 o'clock in the afternoon.

Public cynicism also extended to the contents of the forthcoming auction. Undoubtedly as a consequence of the division of property that occurred as part of the sale contract between Beckford and Farquhar, rumours began to circulate in public that many of the most valuable books and articles present in the previous 'view' of the Abbey, were not going to be available for purchase this time. A letter published in the *Morning Herald* on 29 August suggested that there was a grand deception afoot that needed to be addressed in the interest of truth:

> Sir,—There are a number of reports as to the abstraction of curious books and valuable articles from Fonthill, since last year. They are to my knowledge, at present exceedingly rife among 'the trade' in London; and I imagine that you will agree that it would be only doing justice to all parties to afford a timely opportunity of proving falsehood of such injurious assertions, by at once making them public, and thus preventing the enchantment of Fonthill from being whispered away by interested individuals. Allow me, therefore, to state, that among other things, it is rumoured, Mr. Farquhar's house on the New Road, has been lined in some places, 'thick and threefold', since last year, with the best and most valuable pictures which he purchased from Mr. Beckford. It is also said, particularly in this part of town, that a selection from the rest of the late proprietor's property has been disposed of either in a like or a different manner; and it is added, by way of climax, that previous to the opening of Fonthill for public inspection this year, the vacancies created by the above abstractions, were filled to overthrowing by no less than eighteen wagon-loads of articles, most of which have been already proved to be well adapted for the hammer! Reports of this sort, however absurd in themselves, assuredly require contradiction, which those who intend to become purchasers may, I suppose, easily accomplish, in some degree at least, by obtaining one of last year's catalogues of the sale then intended, and comparing it with the catalogue now published. To the public at large it would, perhaps, be acceptable, if some less troublesome and more direct means were taken of letting them know the truth. I am, Mr. Editor, Your Constant Reader [9]

Dibdin returned to the Abbey for a second visit about the same time the above article appeared and added fuel to the fire with a letter he sent to the *Morning Chronicle* signed with the pseudonym 'Isaac Littlebury'. Joined by his colleague Joseph Haslewood, collector and a founder of the Roxburghe Club, Dibdin complained that many of the rare books they had previously seen a year earlier were now missing: 'Guess the surprise and horror, of my friend, when hoping to fold within his arms, the magnificent volume of *Chinese Idols*, a frightful porcelain Mandarin figure obtruded itself upon his sight—where is *Breydenbach?*—where is *Rauwolf?*—where is *Torfous?*—all disappeared! and the precious manuscripts too!!!' Dibdin concluded his letter by asking the editor to 'untwist' the mystery.[10] A rejoinder followed in the *Morning Herald*. A correspondent signed 'TRUTH' affirmed that not 'an *item* of any class has been sold or removed from the Abbey since the purchase' with the exception of only those books and miscellaneous objects 'which were, by previous arrangement ceded to Mr. Beckford' in accordance with the contract of sale.[11] Dibdin also published another letter as Isaac Littlebury in the *Morning Chronicle* complaining about the books in the Abbey being behind wire mesh and inaccessible. 'During the autumn of last year', he wrote, 'I visited Fonthill Abbey; my *compagnon de voyage*, a learned Orientalist, entertained me on the journey with some extraordinary anecdotes respecting the owner, connected with his splendid library. My imagination revelled in graphic and typographic luxury; and curiosity was at the highest pitch, by the expected perusal of the numerous manuscript criticisms, and remarks, with which the collection is said to have enriched almost every volume in his library: these are of so piquant a nature, that the dullest tomes sparkle with intelligence—the plastic hand of the master "maketh the foul stone precious". Judge of the mortification we endured, on our arrival, at beholding the magnificent volumes within imprisoned bars. Sad and sickened to the heart to be constrained to confine our adoration to their exterior, we had recourse to our tablets, in order to be gratified when the happy period of their thraldom should cease'.[12]

As was the case in 1822, a pilgrimage to the Abbey achieved the status of a major social event stimulated by extensive press coverage. The mania became so intense that the *New Monthly Magazine* announced at one point that the 'world may just at present be divided into two classes; those who have seen Fonthill Abbey, and those who have not'.[13] The press monitored the crowds as they arrived and reported whenever possible their rank, attire, and occasionally their reaction to the experience. One account on the day before the auction observed that 'numberless visiters continued to arrive from an early hour in rapid succession, and at one o'clock the beautiful vista opposite the grand portal of the Abbey displayed various groups in every part, all attired in light costume, and occasionally selecting the most favourable views of the splendid edifice as they passed along the "velvet turf"'. The different apartments in the interior were equally crowded; and, among the personages of distinction who seemed to admire the countless objects of rare curiosity which presented themselves to the eye, were Lord Arundel, Lord Ellenborough, Lord Northwick, with several others of the Nobility and Gentry. The ladies were very numerous, and nothing appeared to escape their notice'.[14]

That this event brought about a mingling of the various levels of society became a source of fascination and amusement. One reporter attempted to distinguish between the ranks of society by describing a situation in which 'native vulgarity' was in full display:

> This day brought with it a succession of visiters from an early hour. Among them were many of the bourgeois, but there were also some personages of higher note, who sported splendid equipages. They all occasionally promenaded the grounds, and inspected the interior of the Abbey. The prevailing dress among the ladies was pink, blue, and violet-coloured sarsnet, with hats or bonnets to correspond; and I must observe, however ungallant may be the assertion, that there were several of them to whom it was no difficult matter to discern the stout and sturdy daughter of the yeoman from the 'gentle maid' of higher lineage, though both were equally attired in the gay robes of fashion. The former could not pass through any of the apartments without handling every object of curiosity that came in her way, gazing at it at the same time with a vacant stare, and always stumbling on a misnomer in her attempt to guess the proper designation. The latter was never observed to touch any thing, and appeared content to receive her information from those who were more experienced than herself, asking only such occasional questions as good taste and propriety suggested. In the course of the day this distinction was forcibly exemplified by the conduct of two lumpish-looking sisters with fat florid faces, prominent teeth, and large globular eyes; a pair of damsels whom Nature would seem to have formed only to stand as a marked exception to every thing wild and amiable to the sex. They had scarcely waddled into the grand saloon, when turning up the whites of their eyes in wild amazement at the splendour of the scene, they both burst forth into exclamations which provoked the laughter of all who heard them.[15]

Some of the most privileged and well connected were invited to stay overnight at the Abbey. Among them were the Marquess and Marchioness of Lansdowne, with their son Lord Petty, the Dowager Lady Roden, Mr Pares, the business partner of the Lord Mayor of London, Douglas Kinnaird, Byron's London banker and literary agent, and the Bishop of Winchester, who ended up incurring an injury to his leg after falling on the stone stairs in the Great Western Hall.

The newspapers were also eager to note the presence of Beckford's son-in-law, the man Beckford once rejected as an unsuitable husband for his daughter. In one report, General Orde, who came with his daughters, is described as a

> ... fine-looking man, about fifty years of age, with an air and manner strongly indicative of his profession, but he appears exceedingly depressed in spirits, nor indeed is it to be wondered at, considering the close relation in which he stands towards the late proprietor of Fonthill. He now sees the magnificent mansion of his father-in-law—a palace worth of an Eastern Prince, denuded from day to day, of all its rare and gorgeous embellishments, while the structure itself, with the vast tracts of which it formed so proud an ornament, must, no longer, be regarded as the enviable inheritance of the Beckford family. All has

passed into the hands of strangers! The General was accompanied by two fine little girls, his daughters, and the grand-children of Mr. Beckford. He evinced the tenderest paternal affection towards them, leading them by the hand through the different rooms, and directing their attention to such objects as he thought likely to gratify their curiosity.[16]

The press enjoyed noting the differences in rank all brought together in one place. But understandably they concentrated on the higher echelons of British society and identified them by name whenever possible. Almost every newspaper article on Fonthill published in 1823 included a list of the most prominent visitors who travelled to the estate. The *Morning Post* even revealed the existence of a book that all visitors signed upon entering the Abbey. Their correspondent used it on one occasion to transcribe the names of those who signed it and then published the list in the issue of 13 October.[17] The whereabouts of this record is not known and unfortunately may well be lost forever. It would have provided a valuable record of those who passed through the Fonthill portals. In the absence of this document, the only sources of information are the auction catalogues of 1823, containing the names of successful bidders, and the list of prominent figures reported by the press. A compilation provided in Appendix I attempts to fill this gap and is based on the numerous press notices that recorded the names of prominent citizens, both native and foreign, who made an excursion to the estate during the four-month period of public access.

These included the land-owning aristocracy, representing families of wealth, blood and title, members of Parliament and other persons who held high positions in government, officials of the Anglican Church, military figures—in short, those individuals who collectively constituted the cultural establishment of the country. The irony of their presence at Fonthill could not have been lost on Beckford whose secluded life there was to a great extent due to his ostracism from the very social groups who were now eager to see his residence and its trappings. Having been a place of peace and privacy, Fonthill was now transformed into a watering place, the 'scene of crowded resort', the 'gay haunt of eager curiosity'.[18] Under Beckford's ownership, there had been an air of mystery and solitude about this forbidden place which now yielded to 'business, pleasure, fashion, and popular wonder' as variegated groups of people revelled in the delights that Beckford had at one time reserved for himself. For so long a symbol of isolation and security, Fonthill had now become a poignant object of loss and transiency with its treasures about to be dispersed throughout the world. Two years later, its fate would be further reinforced as a symbol of mutability when its proud and lofty tower came crashing down to earth.

Sic Transit Gloria Fonthill:
'The Gem and the Wonder of Earth'

The first ten days devoted to the sale of a portion of the books were surprisingly uneventful with attendance being lower than expected. On the opening day of the auction, Phillips made it clear that there would be no reserve on any of the lots offered for sale. The first lot *Memoirs of the Rev. Alexander Geddes* sold for twelve shillings. Any books containing Beckford's notes in the flyleaves drew great interest and were quoted extensively in the press much to the enjoyment of the readers. One of the volumes which received the most attention was Walpole's *Life of the Late Charles James Fox*, containing Beckford's notes about Fox that were reproduced in detail in the published accounts. Before long, a caustic anonymous response to these remarks followed in *The Times*: 'Several papers have published a heap of loose memoranda from a manuscript by Mr. Beckford, of Fonthill, abusive of the character of the late Mr. Fox. We suppose that few persons care to know what Mr. Beckford thinks of Mr. Fox: if Mr. Fox had ever thought it worthwhile to express an opinion concerning Mr. Beckford, that, indeed, might be a matter of interest and curiosity'.[1]

The prominent London booksellers Rodd, Lawford, Triphook, and Longman were among the heaviest buyers. John Upham, a bookseller from Bath, outspent many bidders. Clarke was present as Beckford's representative doing his master's bidding and took in thirty lots the first day of the sale. But many of the books were knocked down to private individuals, including Sir John Wrottesley, William Miles, son of a Bristol merchant and banker, and the Earl of Arundel. The ubiquitous Richard Heber was there, taking in items at his usual rate. Members of the nobility and other prominent members of society could also be seen on the grounds or examining the treasures inside the Abbey.[2] Lord and Lady Lansdowne spent the night entertained by the strains of Mr Goodall, the organist to the Earl of Arundel, who played by candlelight in the Grand Saloon and elicited the admiration of the listeners with a piece called 'The Storm', and the 'music of the witches' scene in *Macbeth*. Lord F. Leveson Gower was at the sale as was Sir James Mackintosh. Sir Henry Wilson made the most ostentatious entrance by arriving in a coach drawn by six horses.

It was not long into the sale before a controversy broke out accusing Phillips of adding books and paintings that were never owned by Beckford. The strongest onslaught came from the *Leeds Intelligencer*. Following a comparison of the paintings listed in Christie's catalogue with Phillips's a year later, the *Leeds Intelligencer* noted that while Christie had listed 115 paintings, Phillips's catalogue included 415 pictures. Where Christie had one work by Teniers for sale, Phillips offered 22 by this artist. This published report also went on to argue that a man of Beckford's taste would not have owned some of the books listed in Phillips's sale catalogue:

> We should deserve to be scorched to a cinder by the terrible eye of the Caliph Vathek, if we could bring ourselves to believe for a single moment that Mr. Beckford, of Fonthill, who spared neither pains nor expense in the collection of his books, could ever have been prevailed upon to admit within the precincts of his splendid library, 'A Dictionary of Painters, bound in sheep, to imitate morocco!' or triplicate copies of such publications as the following, which we notice among a vast many more of the same quality in Mr. Phillips' Catalogue:—
>
> Watt's Views of the Seats of the Nobility and Gentry, 3 copies!
> Angus's Views of the Seats of the Nobility, 3 copies!
> Rogers's Imitations of the Old Masters, 3 copies!
>
> These copies, the triplicates of which are, as may be supposed, introduced at respectable distances from each other, are all of precisely the same quality and appearance. Of the last book each copy is differently designated—a system which is pursued in numerous other instances throughout the catalogue. The object of thus varying the titles 'cannot be mistaken'. That the *genuine* Fonthill library should have comprised three sets, none of them proofs, of such common trashy Auction Mart works as the above, is perfectly incredible; and almost equally so, that it should ever have contained duplicate and triplicate copies of such rubbish as
>
> Beaumont's Travels through the Leopontine Alps.
> Smith's London and its Environs, folio.
> Deuchais' Etchings, folio.
> Marchant's Gems (one of the sets *framed* and *glazed*.)
>
> There are a vast many other items hardly more worthy of preservation, which it would be an insult to common sense to consider as a part of the collection of Mr. Beckford.[3]

Some of the booksellers present at the sale labelled the added books 'foists', believing that the sale was 'made up' from rakings from the stalls of London. Another accusation claimed that the prices Beckford recorded on the inside cover or flyleaf for each book he bought had been altered in an effort to push up the prices artificially. The *Literary Gazette* provided further fuel to the controversy by hinting that the bookseller Lawford was involved in the scam and identified the libraries from which many of the books supposedly came.[4] Lawford responded with a letter to *The Times* in which attacked the *Literary Gazette* and defended himself:

> Availing myself of the liberal offer with which you prefaced an article appearing in your journal of the 22d inst., purporting to be copied from an obscure publication, called the *Literary Gazette*, (although I should not have considered it worthy of notice, had it remained in its narrowed limits), but being copied in so respectable a channel, I feel it due to my character, to give it that refutation which it deserves, by broadly asserting it a falsehood; and allow me, Sir, through your medium, to assure such noblemen and gentlemen who have favoured me with their commissions, that in defiance to such invidious calumny, I shall be found to discharge my duties to them with that integrity that I hope shall entitle me to their future patronage....

Seville-passage, Sept 25   G. Lawford[5]

Needless to say, these reports caused tongues to wag and led to reprintings of the accusatory article throughout England, including an appearance in *The Times*. Alaric Watts, who was the editor of the *Leeds Intelligencer* at this time, recaptured the controversy his own newspaper created in a lengthy poem 'The Sale at Fonthill A Fragment', published in the November issue of the *Literary Museum*:

Fonthill Sale A Parody

Who has not heard of the Sale at Fonthill,
With its *bijoux* the brightest that earth ever gave;
Its pictures and books—and its knights of the quill,
Who of all its 'attractions' so ceaselessly rave....

When gems, bronzes and paintings, are gleaming half shewn,
(Mr. Beckford's we mean—t'other half would not please Sir)
From tables of ebony—rosewood—and one
Which they tell us belonged to the Prince de Borghese, Sir;
But *geese* we should be all we hear thus to hug,
Since we know many come from the Prince of HUMBUG!

Then to see all the China from Nankin and Dresden,
The 'rare Oriental' and 'famed Japanese',
Mixed with all kinds of trumpery, but recently pressed in,
Our judgements to dupe and our pockets to ease!
With bronzes and boxes—*chef d'oeuvres* of skill,—
Made 'to order' they say, for the sale at Fonthill!

Here the music of bidding grows loud and more loud;—
Here the *sweetener* is conning his hints for the day;
And here by the rostrum, apart from the crowd,
Billy Tims and his brethren are scribbling away
(Striving who shall bedaub Mr. Phillips the most)
Their puffs for the *Chronicle, Herald* and *Post*!
Let us pause ere we blame, for 'tis well understood,
Though some things are so so, Harry's dinners are good,
And since paying and feeding the piper's no jest,
Sure they ought to play for him the tune he likes best.

Here a blackletter hero, with ratsmelling air,
Tipping winks full of meaning, squats down in his chair,
The veteran of many a Bookauction is he,
And he'll not be bamboozled, we think, Mr. P.!
If the item is genuine, away goes his nod,
And if cheap, is knocked down with "tis yours, Mr. Rodd',
If a '*foist*' and his glance of contempt is enough,
Why, he dives for his snuffbox and only takes snuff!…[6]

Copies of the Leeds article circulated freely at the sale and in the local inns to the dismay of Phillips who protested his innocence from the podium, chastised Thomas Barnes, the editor of *The Times*, for reprinting the damning piece and attempted to shift blame to Longman by pointing out that he was the proprietor of both the *Leeds Intelligencer* and the *Literary Gazette*. He did allow that Farquhar had added some furniture and valuable effects from the Marshal Bessières estate in Paris, but he believed that this was the prerogative of the new owner of Fonthill. Thomas Adams, a Shaftesbury bookseller who attended the sale, characterised the atmosphere that had evolved, claiming that he 'never was at a Sale where so much suspicion and jealousy reigns'.[7]

The sale of books continued, nevertheless, with the finest items being readily identifiable by the knowledgeable buyer. But just when the dust had settled, a new, more dramatic flap occurred involving one of the most highly touted works of art in the collection. This was lot 1567, described as a topaz cup with a dragon handle of enamelled gold, set with diamonds and mounted on a tripod stand, and said to have been made by Benvenuto Cellini as a wedding present for Catherine Cornaro. Phillips offered it for bidding on 23 October, the 32nd day of the sale whereupon its authenticity was immediately challenged by Kensington Lewis, a London silversmith and antiquities dealer. The Salisbury and Winchester Journal reported the dramatic details:

A singular scene took place in the sale-room at Fonthill Abbey on Wednesday last. The magnificent Topaz Cup, which has been so long considered as one of the chief objects of curiosity in the Abbey, and on which Benvenuto Cellini lavished all his skill, was put up for sale. A Mr. Lewis, a London silversmith, declared it was not a topaz, but a crystal! This assertion, so unhesitatingly made, seemed to startle the company who were assembled to witness the disposal of this celebrated gem. Mr. Phillips expressed his astonishment at the boldness of the assertion, and declared that he would not only undertake to sell it as a topaz, but would realise his description of it. The cup, he said, had been for many months submitted to public view, during which time it had been seen by many scientific men, none of whom had ever ventured to express a doubt upon it. Mr. Beckford, whose refined taste and judgement were so well known, and so infinitely superior to Mr. Lewis's, never entertained any other opinion than that it was a topaz; and he (Mr. Phillips) thought Mr. Lewis presumed too far, in declaring it to be a crystal, considering the very limited acquaintance he had with the article. He desired Mr. Lewis to understand that long before he was born, it was his (Mr. Phillips's) practice to sell nothing under a false description, and that if his sense of honesty did not prompt him to do this, his conditions of sale would bind him to do so. (Applause)[8]

While managing to sway the crowd in the room, Phillips was still anxious about being undercut in a way that would deflate the hammer price of the item. He then appealed to Robert Hume, Beckford's London agent who was on the scene, and Hume declared that Beckford had always considered it to be a topaz. A heated argument followed wherein Phillips suggested that Lewis's motive was to try to buy the cup himself at a depreciated price and threatened to secure redress if the 'cup should be injured by his unjustifiable attack upon it'. The cup was finally put up for sale at 300 guineas and sold for £630, a sum that was considered far below its value. Still agitated, Phillips cited William Buckland, chair of mineralogy at Oxford, as an authority who had examined the cup earlier and declared it to be his conviction that it was formed of a block of genuine Hungarian topaz. The report in the *Salisbury and Winchester Journal* concluded that the 'highest credit is due to Mr. Phillips for the great coolness and spirit with which he conducted himself, and we do not envy the reproof which Mr. Lewis received'.

The Times, keeping an ever watchful eye on activities at the Fonthill sale, republished a great portion of the article from the *Salisbury and Winchester Journal* on 28 October, which drew a detailed response from Lewis a few days later in which he defended himself and continued to question Phillips's integrity on the conduct of the sale.[9] Notably, he pointed to the fourth condition published in Phillips's catalogue: 'The lots to be cleared away, with all faults and errors of description, at the purchasers' expence, without reference to the identity of subject or master'. Lewis found this clause too obviously self protective. 'Surely', he continued, 'if Mr. Phillips never sells under "false descriptions", or, as his duty demands, without first satisfying himself as the to "identity of subject or master", this condition must have been unnecessary, and I am quite satisfied would not have been included by any other auctioneer.... As to his threat of legal proceedings against me, he may be assured that I shall meet him in Westminster-hall, where, perhaps, I may have an opportunity of exhibiting a little more of his "practices, sense of honesty, and manner of doing business"'. This was a strong personal attack against Phillips which might have been dismissed as intemperate, but then Lewis provided some provenance of the cup that continued to cast a shadow over its authenticity:

And now, Sir, for the history of this topaz (which I have taken some time and trouble to ascertain)—I have traced it originally to have been in the possession of Mr. Stanley, of Bond-street, who offered it twice for sale by auction for about £300, but was unable to obtain that bidding, and ultimately sold if for considerably less. I have Mr. Stanley's authority for stating, that the vase was in his possession for a year and a half at that price; and that during that time he repeatedly offered it to the trade, including Mr. Farmer, of Tavistock-street, and Mr. Foster, who are well-known dealers in articles of vertu, without being able to obtain a purchaser. It ultimately got into the hands of Mr. Baldock, of Hanway-street, who sold it to Mr. Beckford for less than £300.

Lastly, Sir, permit me to repeat my opinion, that the vase is not a topaz; and to state that my judgment has been since supported by some of the most experienced jewellers, and dealers in articles of vertu, in London; including Mr. Hawley, of the Strand; Mr. Jarman, of St James's-street; and of Mr. Farmer and Mr. Foster, whose names I have already mentioned.[10]

Lewis's history of the ewer appears to be credible, based as it was on his own familiarity with the principle dealers and auctioneers in the trade. Beckford did, in fact, buy the ewer in 1819 from Edward Holmes Baldock, a prominent antique dealer of 7 Hanway Street, London. There is a document among the Beckford Papers entitled 'Description of Vase of Topaz of Saxony—Work of the Celebrated Benvenuto Cellini', which Beckford received from Baldock when he purchased it. The document outlines its spurious history from the time it was executed as a wedding present when Georgio Cornaro married Elizabeth Morosini and then from the Cornaro family to the ducal family of Gonzaga of Mantua and then to London sometime in the eighteenth century.[11] It eventually ended up in Lord Rothschild's collection where it remained until it was sold to Jack and Belle Linsky of New York. From the Linsky collection it went to the Metropolitan Museum where it remains today.

Lewis's mineralogical assessment that it was rock crystal instead of topaz also turned out to be correct. In fact, another article appeared in the *Salisbury and Winchester Journal* on 17 November 1823, testifying that by then several 'eminent mineralogists' had examined the cup and even dismounted it to determine its specific gravity. They concluded that it was indeed quartz, but the report want on to cite René Just Haüy, founder of the science of crystallography, whose book *Mineralogical Treatise* was published in Paris in 1822. Haüy explained that quartz had different names depending upon its colour. If yellow in colour, it was called smoky or Indian topaz, brown crystal, oriental or Bohemian topaz, violet in colour was amethyst. The writer advanced the view that 'the article in question, we believe, was smuggled into England within a rough block of marble, in which it was carefully imbedded, and the two pieces of the block ingeniously cemented together'.[12] The most recent evidence indicates that the rock crystal bowl was probably carved in Prague in the seventeenth century, while the mounts appear to date from the early nineteenth century.[13]

There is no record of Beckford's reaction to Lewis's charge, but he was aware of the possibility that it was not an authentic Cellini and was attempting to investigate its provenance. As he wrote to Chevalier Franchi in 1819, 'You may admire the Zenobia [a sardonyx gem portrait] as much as prejudice permits; for my part I prefer the Cornaro—if it is the Cornaro. I've searched in vain so far for any information about this real marvel in the writings of Benvenuto Cellini. In his treatise on the goldsmith's art he talks a good deal about enamelling, but I can't see that he ever quotes this vase as an example'.[14] So it is evident that Beckford was not deceived into believing that it was an authentic Cellini work. He bought it as a beautiful work of art: 'I'll return to this research another day, though it matters little whether or not I find the answer—the object in itself deserves the most wholehearted eulogy'. He admired its craftsmanship and rich beauty, calling it a 'sublime *objet d'art*' and noting that its 'diamonds, topaz and enamel—everything glitters in a magical way'.[15]

Phillips's reaction did appear in *The Times*. In his response he distanced himself from any responsibility by noting that he relied on the Christie catalogue for the description which was 'precisely that which was given Mr. Farquhar when he purchased it'. 'If', he added, 'contrary to my expectations and the deliberate judgment of many eminent mineralogists, it should prove to be any thing but an Hungarian Topaz, it will be returned to Mr. Beckford, as not answering the description he gave of it when he sold it'. He then concluded with the following defence:

> The assertion which I made respecting Professor Buckland's opinion of it, whether true or false, could have no possible influence on the sale of it, as it was not made till *after* the Cup was knocked down, when it was communicated to me for the first time, by authority which I could not doubt....
>
> Some allusion has been made to one of my conditions of sale; I have only to remark, in reply, that it is a condition which I have used for many years, and which is to be found, in effect, in every catalogue that ever was published, and is in many instances much more summary and decisive, being frequently summed up in these very comprehensive words—'The lots to be taken away with *all faults*'.
>
> My conduct and character have been long before the world; and the large share of its favour which I have gratefully received, seems to render any defence of them unnecessary; but I think the explanation I have given is due to those friends and patrons with whose confidence I have been honoured.[16]

The Topaz cup incident stirred up such controversy in the press that it found its way to the London theatre in a Christmas pantomime at the Theatre Royal, Drury Lane in December 1823, entitled *Harlequin and the Flying Chest; or, Malek and the Princess Schirine*. Arranged and produced under the direction of William Barrymore, it included a series of dioramic views painted by Clarkson Stanfield.[17] The diorama featured a series of moving scenes of the Plymouth breakwater in the process of construction and a striking view of 'Fonthill Abbey and a Village' by David Roberts—a picture of the surrounding grounds and an interior view of King Edward's Gallery in the Abbey.[18] But the highlight of the play was a pantomime by Mr Paulo. In the pantomime, Paulo donned a black coat and hat in imitation of Harry Phillips at the Fonthill sale to recreate the scene of selling the Cellini ewer as a great hoax. *The Times* reported the crowd's reaction: 'The happiest part of Paulo's performance last night was, where, as an auctioneer, he knocks down a celebrated topaz vase, and afterwards a picture by a great artist of "Finchley", at the Fonthill sale. The pantomime went off with much éclat, and was announced for repetition amidst cheers of the audience'.[19]

The controversy over the authenticity of the Cellini ewer faded as the sale continued for thirty-seven days. There were, after all, many spectacular works of art to consume the interest of the insatiable collector or his representative. Among the furniture, for example, there were the chairs that once belonged to Cardinal Wolsey from his palace at Esher; the ebony state bed of Henry VII with its crimson damask hangings and purple quilt worked with gold; the massive table inlaid with marble, jaspers, and oriental onyx from the Borghese Palace; the 'Holbein' cabinet that Beckford thought was designed for Henry VIII; the celebrated 'Bernini' cabinet encrusted with agates, jaspers and other striking jewels, a large Japanese lacquer chest once owned by Cardinal Mazarin; Japanese cabinets from the Duc de Bouillon's collection; and the desk made by J. H. Riesener for Comte d'Orsay. There were silver plate of various designs, a Miessen dinner service of 363 pieces made for the Prince of Orange, the Rubens vase, the Limoges's enamel reliquary, and the Japanese lacquer Van Diemen Box. There were also 424 paintings which took four days to sell, including works by Rubens, Rembrandt, Teniers, Dürer, Da Vinci, Dow, Van Eyck, and Gainsborough, among others. In short, the Fonthill sale offered a dazzling array of rarities that makes it difficult to accept William Hazlitt's judgement that Beckford's taste was meretricious and the Abbey a 'desart of magnificence, a glittering waste of laborious idleness, a cathedral turned into a toy-shop, an immense museum of all that is most curious and costly, and at the same time, most worthless, in the productions of art and nature'.[20]

The fact is that for many of Beckford's contemporaries Fonthill lived up to its mythical reputation. Now its wonders and glories were dispersed in a thousand directions 'scattered and parcelled out at the fall of the salesman's hammer'. As one author lamented: 'Fonthill, as connected with Mr. Beckford, is no more! and the great rival of Wiltshire's other wonder, Stonehenge, will hereafter lose half of its interest and its glory since it can no longer be associated with the author of *Vathek*'.[21]

The attention in the press, whether positive or not, inspired interest in the event and made participating in the actual 'view' of Fonthill even more irresistible. The sale of the books and prints, which occupied twenty days, had the lightest turn out with reports estimating approximately fifty people in attendance each day. The numbers swelled to sometimes 200 a day for the paintings, furniture and other works of art. Beckford did not personally attend, but his agent William Clarke bought over 640 lots in the book portion of the sale. In the end, Farquhar realised £43,869 14*s* from the sale. Phillips also conducted a separate sale of the choice and valuable wines and liqueurs in the Abbey cellars on 15 November, but the total amount realised from these proceedings is not known.

Throughout the period of the sale, the press was naturally focused on the Abbey and its contents, but there were other articles that appeared about Beckford himself, generally anecdotal in character and designed to satisfy the public appetite for specific information about the mysterious and singular figure who stood behind the scene. One of the most curious pieces about Beckford had to do with the supposed origin of *Vathek* set forth in a lengthy essay that appeared in the *Morning Chronicle*. The author, J. Sidney Taylor, discovered a pencilled note by Beckford in the flyleaf of a book that came up during the sale entitled *Le Histoire de Bretagne composée sur les titrés et les auteurs originaux par Dom Guy Alexis Lobineau prestre religieux Bénédictins de la Congregation de St.Maur*. Based on the content of the note, Taylor believed that he had discovered the origin of *Vathek*. The note made a reference to Gilles de Rais, the Marshal of France in 1429. A highly touted military figure and a companion-in-arms of Joan of Arc, he became a man of great wealth but then wasted it away on an excessive lifestyle and extravagant projects. What caught Taylor's eye was that the story of Gilles de Rais portrayed him as a pedophile who was said to be responsible for the death of hundreds of children and who ultimately was condemn to death by hanging in 1440. Beckford's note made reference to the brutality, cruelty, extravagance and untold horrors of Gilles. In the article, Taylor provided an extended description of de Rais's life in which he found discernible aspects of the Caliph Vathek. While Beckford's tale was disguised by the trappings of Eastern fiction, Taylor was convinced that it derived from the story of 'Laval de Raiz' and provided his reasons for believing it.[22]

Statements followed in the press that *Vathek* was not entirely original but derived, as Taylor wrote, from the dissolute life of Gilles de Rais, 'one of the most atrocious beings in the shape of human that was ever suffered to disgrace society, and we should rejoice to find that our "Savants" were utterly mistaken in their discoveries'.[23] When Beckford read the *Morning Chronicle* article, he sent a note almost immediately through an agent to Taylor assuring him 'upon his honour' that he was not familiar with the Gilles de Rais story when he wrote *Vathek*: 'He acknowledges that the points of coincidence are very strong, and as he said, made out with an ingenuity that would lead most to believe it; but he was anxious that I should understand the book was not in his possession at the time'. Needless to say, the story caused considerable stir. Heber was overheard talking about it in the Fonthill sale room, and the subject was debated extensively at Pyt House, John Bennett's estate adjacent to Fonthill, and all of those present found it convincing and sided with Taylor.[24]

In one of his final acts before the closing of the sale on 29 October, Farquhar ordered the illumination of the Abbey at night and invited the public to the spectacle. The event took place on the evening of 22 October, with a large crowd in attendance. On hand for the event were Sir Henry and Lady Onslow, Sir Alexander Malet, Wadham Wyndham and family, Richard Heber, and the poet Thomas Moore and his wife, among other prominent figures. For the occasion, all of the heavy curtains were pulled aside in the Abbey to expose candle-light flickering its incandescent glow in every room. Light poured out through the windows radiating the colours of the stained glass portraits and the array of rich heraldic symbols. The lantern in the tower streamed its radiance against the dark sky to the silent amazement of those stationed outside on the lawn who, as Taylor of the *Morning Chronicle* observed, 'gazed as intensely as Leander when he looked up to the turret of Hero for the signal-torch which was to guide him to the possession of happiness'.[25]

The doors of the Abbey were then thrown open to the on-lookers who passed through the rooms to indulge more intimately the fully illuminated spectacle inside. To enhance the visual effects, the grand organ filled the air with its 'high and holy harmony'. The visual effect of the play of light inside the Grand Saloon Taylor found particularly impressive: 'The light playing along the shafted arches which lead off to various parts of the structure, and flickering upon the enriched work of the interior of the tower, the height and symmetry of the poetic architecture—the splendour of the lanthorn—all whose stained windows were in a blaze of coloured radiance—the clear brightness of the circular windows beneath, and the deep relief of draperies of solemn richness, all produce the effect of a magical illusion'. Looking up and down St Michael's and King Edward's galleries was an equally imposing sight. 'The lengthened streams of light, along which the eye had an indistinct vision of glittering and accumulated ornaments which yet decorate the walls, gave the impression of a place where genii held their fanciful dominions, or reminded one of those depositories of the treasures of Eastern Caliphs, in which gold and jewels are surrounded by spells, mystery, and enchantment'. It was a fitting farewell for this palace of enchantment, a Keatsian event with a sensory appeal that Beckford himself would have appreciated and indulged.

The villagers of Hindon and Tisbury expressed their own farewell to Beckford as the landlord of Fonthill on 29 September, when they celebrated his birthday. A band played throughout the day in Hindon, bells rang, and the air was rent with exclamations of 'Beckford forever', 'good luck to Beckford', and 'may he last forever *till the world is without end*'. Guns were fired in his honour, while revellers who were voters proclaimed that they would never vote for anyone but him or for the candidate he supported.[26] Contrary to various reports that appeared in the press from time to time that Beckford mistreated those he employed, this occasion was indicative of the good will and gratitude they felt towards him as a generous benefactor, feelings that continued throughout the years that followed. Beckford expressed his own gratitude to the workers on the Fonthill estate by continuing to pay the annual bounty to them in 1823, long after he had any obligation to do so.

As the second Fonthill sale came to a close, the woods and pathways of the estate once again fell quiet and the new Abbot proceeded to settle down to refurnish the Abbey to reflect his own taste and interests. It was not long thereafter, however, that Farquhar received word that the structural weakness of the Abbey was a threat to its survival and a danger to the inhabitants. The information came from Beckford who had been summoned to the death bed of Wyatt's Clerk of the Works and learned from him that, although money had been supplied, he failed to provide an adequate foundation for the octagon tower according to the established specifications. Consequently, the tower was unsafe. Beckford felt it was his duty to report this incident to Farquhar who accepted the information with a cool indifference, saying that he felt the tower would last a lifetime.

Farquhar might, in fact, have known about this possibility after living in the Abbey for awhile. Whenever a strong wind was up, it creaked, groaned, and whistled which once led Beckford to say that because of his own awareness of the situation that he feared that someday he would be crushed like a lobster in his shell. He also complained in 1815 that the Abbey was unsafe and that in a storm he felt blown about 'like bodies (and not holy ones) hanging from a gibbet'. 'I must tell you', he wrote to Franchi, 'this place makes your flesh creep as soon as night falls. Yesterday I thought everything was coming down. My tower swayed so that at three o'clock in the morning the dwarf awoke with a terrific "God-damn!" ... flew down the staircase and ran for safety'.[27]

Charles Knight was in residence one night in 1823, along with Stedman Whitwell and the artist George Cattermole, and reported an alarming experience during a storm that drove the guests who were lodged in the dormitories of the tower to seek safety on the main floor of the building. 'The wind rose', he recollected, 'the storm grew louder and louder; the frail structure rocked, as Gulliver's cage rocked in the eagle's beak. The terrified guests rushed down the broad stairs, and sat directly in the dark saloon till the daybreak gave them assurance of safety'.[28] Well before the sale of Fonthill there was also public awareness that Wyatt had created a perilous situation through his failure to provide a solid foundation for the tower. For example, a writer in the *Gentleman's Magazine* observed in December 1821 that 'the tower is acknowledged to be a weak and dangerous structure, and so tottering are the eight surmounting pinnacles, that they are held on their bases by strong iron bars, to the no less disparagement of the building than of the builder'.[29]

The English historian John Allen Giles, during his visit to the Abbey as a young man, described in detail his experience of climbing to the upper reaches of the great tower by way of a winding staircase to discover that it was not simply the foundation that was insufficient to support the tower. After ascending through 'a round tower attached to the great tower', he reached the level of the hall roof, and then continued his ascent to an even higher level by way of a series of stairs winding round the internal section of the tower. What he observed in the process of this climb was a 'series of circular chambers, which were lighted by windows in the thin lath and plaster wall which separated them from the winding staircase that went round them'. After making the climb five times during the same day, he became aware of the construction of the tower and was surprised to discover that the exterior wall at the upper stage was only '7 or 8 inches thick'. An inner lath and plaster concentric wall and the floors that separated each one of the vertical chambers provided additional support, but Giles became alarmed that the tower was so inherently fragile that it might cave in while they were in it.[30]

Many had hoped that the tower would remain as one of England's finest monuments, raised proudly on its eminence and reaching high into the 'silent fields of air'. But, as feared, the tower did collapse on 21 December 1825, at three o'clock in the afternoon, falling into the fountain court, destroying the octagon and a great portion of St Michael's and King Edward's galleries and the Great Western Hall. Intact were the great organ in its established place and the statue of Alderman Beckford in its niche, 'as if it remained to point to the ruins of his son's ambition'. Sir Richard Colt Hoare published a farewell to the passing of Fonthill in the *Gentleman's Magazine* a few months later—'Sic transit gloria Fonthill'—and arranged to have John Buckler do a dramatic picture of the Abbey in ruins as an historical record of the event.[31] Fortunately, no one was hurt.

The most detailed account of what happened appeared in the *Gardener's Magazine* ten years later.[32] According to an eye witness, Farquhar, who was in ill health at the time, was wheeled out in a chair in the front of the building to examine the deep cracks in the tower which was already tilting off centre towards the south-west. Once again, he dismissed the possibility of it coming down, but just after being taken inside, it toppled causing an immense rubble below as it fell upon other sections of the building. Oddly, neither the servants working in the kitchen nor Farquhar heard the crash, though the dust cloud it created could be seen as far away as Wardour Castle. The witness described the fall as very beautiful as the weakened tower descended in slow motion before his eyes: 'it first sank perpendicularly and slowly, and then burst and spread over the roofs of the adjoining wings on every side, but rather more on the south-west than on the others. The cloud of dust which arose was enormous and such as completely to darken the air for a considerable distance around for several minutes. Such was the concussion in the interior of the building, that one man was forced along a passage, as if he had been in an air-gun, to the distance of 30 ft., among dust so thick as to be felt'.

Once Farquhar realised what had occurred, he observed in his usual cool manner that he was glad it fell, for now the house would not be too large for him to live in. Beckford was supposed to have responded with equal aplomb when he learned of the incident, noting that the tower had made a bow to Farquhar that it had never made to him. From that time on, according to Redding, the relationship between Beckford and Farquhar grew stronger to the point where Farquhar considered bequeathing Fonthill back to Beckford, 'for he frequently observed he had a great inclination to do so'. When Beckford was asked whether he would have liked this legacy, he replied, 'Good heavens, yes, I should have been in an extacy at it, for it would have falsified the old proverb, 'You can't eat your cake and have it too'.[33]

In the end, Farquhar did not follow through on what would have assuredly embellished the Fonthill legend. Plagued by ill health and disinterested in restoring the Abbey, he moved instead to sell the Abbey remains and the land within the enclosure, including land in the parish of Fonthill Gifford and Tisbury, the total amounting to 2,975 acres, to John Bennett of Pyt House, MP for Wiltshire. A second portion, which consisted of 1,400 acres, was to go to Henry King of nearby Chilmark.[34] No sale price was agreed upon for these properties before Farquhar died of apoplexy in July 1826 at his house in London. Since he left no will, the final terms of these sales were not decided until 1838. Farquhar's nephew, George Mortimer, acquired in a transfer that was disputed later, the lower grounds with the remaining wing of the old mansion and 1,200 acres of adjoining land, the value of which was established in court to be £19,700. He proceeded in 1827, in a triumph of utilitarianism over aesthetics, to build a cloth factory at the end of the lake in the lower park. During the same year, Farquhar's library was disposed of by auction at Sotheby's.[35] Mortimer then on 29 October 1829, divided this property into three lots which he sold by auction through George Robins. The first portion, including the pavilion and the park, consisting of 1,000 acres, was knocked down for 40,500 guineas; the second portion, involving the cloth mill, 24 cottages and 39 acres went for £12,000. Legal complications over the estate, however, prevented transfer. These two lots eventually went by private treaty to James Morrison. The third lot, which included Lawn Farm and 107 acres of land, sold for £4,900 and shortly thereafter was sold to John Bennett for £5,000. Again the deeds of purchase because of family legal squabbles involving a Chancery suit, were not signed until 1838.

Oddly enough, Fonthill Abbey remained in ruins throughout Beckford's lifetime. The rubble was finally removed in 1844, the year of his death, after Earl Grosvenor, later Marquess of Westminster, contracted with Bennett to buy the estate. Only a small section of King Edward's Gallery was left after everything was removed from the site. It remains standing today, consisting of the Lancaster Tower and the Oratory, Sanctuary, and Vaulted Corridor on the main floor, the Lancaster State bedroom on the next floor above it, and on the second floor of the tower, the Upper Lancaster Room, which was used as a billiard room in Beckford's day.

Few individuals sought entry to the Fonthill estate in the years that followed the ruin of the Abbey. One on record was Thomas Adams. Jr., the bookseller from Shaftesbury, who wrote an evocation of the Abbey in ruins that was published in the *Gentleman's Magazine* in 1826:

> To the pensive mind there is there is a melancholy interest still lingering about the *Abbey of Fonthill*. A natural sigh is drawn on viewing the great tower prostrate—the total destruction of the octagon—the oratory 'shorn of its beams'—the annihilation of the Third Edward's and St. Michael's galleries—and the architectural and armorial embellishments which lie scattered about in sad confusion
>
> 'SPIRIT OF THE PLACE!' where are the thousands that erst have thronged its portals, and with audible accents of admiration, paced with increased astonishment and delight the princely apartments of this mystically-raised edifice?
>
> … And in them heraldic emblazonings shone, that denoted high alliances and noble descents from ancestors who had fought in Palestine, bled on the field of Arragon, or formed the invincible phalanx of sturdy Barons who compelled John to sign the ever-memorable Charta.
>
> In the plenitude of its attraction, as illusion possessed the mind, that future ages would look with wonder on the fabric, adorned as it was, with an assemblage of all that was matchless and costly; at the same time that the mind reflected with awe, that the convulsions of a neighbouring kingdom alone could have empowered the projector to amass the rare and exquisite decorations which he concentrated here.
>
> The well-known lines of our immortal Avonian Bard, might with singular propriety be applied to this once magnificent structure.[36]

But Beckford himself returned on at least one occasion that is certain. It was on 19 July 1835 that he decided to ride his horse from Bath to Fonthill after being away for twelve years. In a draft to an unidentified person, he recorded the experience, revealing the sense of distance he now felt from the Fonthill phase of his life: 'T'other day I rode all over Fonthill. The woods are still magnificent & on point[?] of the ruins—sublime. Mephistopheles could not have contemplated the whole scene more impartially or with greater composure'.[37] Alfred Morrison, son of James, claimed that one day in 1843, as he was out walking on the estate, he was surprised to discover an old gentleman—'sitting on a small grey cob, motionless and absorbed'—contemplating the ruins. 'It was William Beckford', according to Morrison, 'come over from Bath … to have a last look at the remains of that stupendous folly that he had built'—one year before he died.[38]

Another very important record and the most complete account of the ruins was left by the Bath artist Henry Venn Lansdown, who visited the remains on 28 October 1844, after Beckford's death and before the broken structure was dismantled and hauled away.[39] Upon gaining access to the grounds, he walked to the site and stood in awe before the extensive assemblage of ruins. There stood the Eastern Transept still imposing with its twin towers rising 120 feet into the air but now roofless and completely open to the elements. The remains of the Great Western Hall were now covered with briars and brambles. The lofty painted windows, the heraldic symbols, and the heavy thirty-foot doors were gone. Theakston's statue of St Anthony was in its place still holding out his right hand 'as if to protect the sylvan and mute inhabitants of these groves', but tottering in the wind and soon to be a victim of time.[40] Reaching the octagon, Lansdown observed that two sides remained. As he looked above, he could still see two windows of the four nunneries. 'And what is more wonderful than all', he wrote, 'the noble organ screen, designed by 'Vathek' himself, has still survived; its gilded lattices though exposed for twenty years to the "pelting of the pitiless storm", yet glitter in the last rays of the setting sun'. The only room that seemed to survive the desolation was the Brown Parlour. The eight windows remained intact with William Hamilton's designs of thirty-two figures of kings and knights from whom Beckford was supposedly descended. But even this room, the site of elegant dinners amidst the glowing light of the silver candelabra, was showing the effects of an insecure roof with the floor now covered in a pool of water. Despite the battering over time, King Edward's Gallery revealed something of its former glory. Lansdown commented that the ceilings of the consecutive rooms were still beautiful and as fresh as if just painted with the cornice still preserved and its three gilded mouldings. But the seventy-two emblazoned shields that were a part of the frieze had been torn off by vandals as were other ornaments throughout the remains that they could carry away. The oratory still gleamed with purple, scarlet and gold as if recently painted, but the elegant golden lamp was missing and the floor in the southern end of the gallery had been removed exposing unsightly beams. Looking back down King Edward's Gallery, Lansdown observed that the alabaster chimney piece was still in place but suffering a deep crack in the centre. The recesses for the books with sliding shelves were still there; on the opposite side, however, the window frames and glass windows had been removed exposing the interior to the harsh elements. Finally, Lansdown climbed the circular staircase in the octagon, entered a remaining apartment, ultimately reaching the balcony that overlooked the great octagon where he could view the whole desolate scene at once. 'How deep were my feelings of regret at the destruction of the loftiest apartment in the world', he wrote, 'twenty years ago this glorious place was in all its splendour. High in the air are still seen two round windows that once lighted the highest bedrooms in the world'. He then walked away from the building lamenting the loss of the 'gem and the wonder of earth'.

The Contemporary Assessment of Fonthill

Any assessment of Fonthill today must rely to a great extent on the early nineteenth-century published accounts of the estate since the Abbey in its setting no longer exists in its entirety. These contemporary appraisals are of significant historical value because they were based on the first-hand examination of the building and the grounds when the estate was accessible to the public during the views of 1822 and 1823. They also remain an important testimony to the impact Fonthill had on the collective imagination of the age, giving dramatic expression to the new aesthetic currents, including the solipsistic character of its artistic expression, the nostalgia for religion, the taste for the beauty of the irregular line and the celebration of the animating qualities of the picturesque and the sublime. Nikolaus Pevsner's observation that Fonthill Abbey was 'the first neo-Gothic building to create sentiments of amazement, of shock, even of awe' is borne out by the many essays, poems, illustrations, and even ceramic souvenirs that have been left behind in response to the experience of visiting the Abbey in the early nineteenth century.[1]

Since the Abbey was located in one of the highest regions in Wiltshire, its commanding height set it off to particular advantage and contributed to the awe of visitors who saw it rising towards the heavens for the first time. It was an unusual setting for a building of this type as Taylor observed in the *Morning Chronicle*.[2] In England, Abbeys or ruins of Abbeys were usually situated in valleys or plains surrounded by woods. Valle Crucis or Tintern Abbey, for example, had romantic and tranquil settings, but did not hold commanding views. The elevation of Fonthill Abbey set it apart from similar structures, giving it a singular and arresting character. Such a prominent structure standing in the midst of a magnificent wooded setting, communicated a sense of 'seclusion with authority', as Taylor explained, 'and while it seems to withdraw from the surrounding world, as in conscious superiority, looks down upon it. Thus a lofty sternness appears blended with a mysterious retirement, and like as in the character of Becket or Wolsey, the spectator does not know whether to admire most the real ambition or the assumed sanctity'. In a few sentences Taylor touched upon the essential symbolism of Fonthill Abbey and the basis of its appeal to many contemporaries. Mirroring the increasing secular trends of the age, it was a church devoted to human creations rather than to divine. It drew its sanctity not from any religious associations but from the boldness of its conception and the self-asserting authority of its creator.

What particularly impressed those visitors who were familiar with the Abbey property before Beckford began developing it, was the astonishing transformation of the grounds. Some had remembered sections of barren or sparsely planted land, especially along the broad front of the hill where the Abbey was located, which can be seen in Turner's watercolours of the building under construction in 1799. But by the time of the first sale, the entire area was covered with plants and shrubs of all varieties, and towering pine, Scotch fir, and oak. Looking south over the hill from the Abbey tower, an unidentified observer in 1823 stood in awe of what had been accomplished over a thirty-year period. 'Here we stand', he mused, 'on the summit of this far-famed tower, overlooking a spot which, even within the memory of most of us, was a barren heath—an interminable extent of bare *down*, with scarcely a tree upon it; and which now, by means of one man, and under the inspection of one superintending assistant, has become what we now see it—a magnificent domain, including nearly all the natural beauties that can belong to a spot of the kind, and crowned by a building of unrivalled extent and grandeur'.[3]

Its rich and abundant growth amidst the smooth, rolling downs of Wiltshire prompted some visitors to call Fonthill 'a paradise amidst the wild'.[4] Rutter felt that the cultivation of this terrain was an extraordinary achievement for one man to have accomplished. 'We as constantly feel the presence of the creative power and exquisite taste', he wrote, 'in rendering these woods what poetry might depict of the woods of Arcadia; where the kindliest soil and the most genial climate should strew the earth with every sweet, and a garden should bloom in every wilderness. The luxuriant imagination of Milton has painted a part of that scene, which has been almost realised, under the greatest natural disadvantages, by the enterprising spirit of unlimited wealth'.[5] The remarkable metamorphosis of Fonthill explains why so many visitors described it as a fairy land, a place, as Richard Colt Hoare wrote, 'raised more by majick, or inspiration, than the labours of the human hand'.[6] The age of necromancy has not passed away, explained a report on Fonthill in *The Gazette of Fashion*: 'The Genii of the Ring and the Lamp, under the more modern names of Wealth and Taste, can raise structures equalling, in the richness of their architecture, the fairy palace of Aladdin and convert barren heaths to gardens of delight, rivalling in beauty the oriental splendours of the happy valley'.[7]

Equally remarkable was the interior of Fonthill. Visitors were struck by the powerful effect of the *ensemble* of art as they toured the various rooms. It was noticed that care was taken not to display the art objects in the 'monotonous uniformity of a nun's rosary'. Instead, one visitor wrote: 'The genius of combination has here been exerted with the happiest effect; and with such harmony are the most costly treasures disposed that each article, besides its separate lustre and attractions, serves towards some general design. The mind is thus diverted and relieved from the painful repetition of but one action, the exercise of but one faculty. The imagination is thus roused from the individual wonders of the scene to the contemplation of the grand *ensemble*. In this consists the secret of true taste, and of the witchery of Fonthill'.[8] Indeed, it was Fonthill considered as a total aesthetic experience that impressed many individuals who participated in the viewing. In a letter published in the *Morning Chronicle*, a writer explained that wandering through the rooms of Fonthill with their arranged lighting effects, dazzling display of exquisite works of art and vivid interior décor was so awe inspiring that it could best be described as a self-annihilating experience. It constituted an achievement that extended beyond the reach of ordinary mortals, he felt: 'Here is a palace ready-made and worthy of a King. All that is awful in the Cathedral, all that is magnificent in the modern style of architecture, all that is superb in fitting up, and most of what you find interesting in various museums, all is concentred in this place'.[9] The multifaceted sensory impact achieved through the artistic presentation of interior and exterior scenes promoted an immersion, explained another correspondent in the *Morning Chronicle*, that was deeply moving:

> The long galleries, now thronged, now sprinkled with company, display a fantastic moving picture; while the perspective, interspersed in the distance with Lilliputian variegated forms, either retires into solemn gloom, or opens upon the brilliant and gladsome landscape without. Every moment some new object strikes the attention; at every step the feet, the eyes, are entangled in the folds of luxury.... In most collections some one object prevails to the exclusion of every other: here Art wooes us in all her shapes; Taste holds a hundred mirrors, a hundred magic sceptres in her hand, and shews the glittering treasures of the world around her.[10]

For this individual, Fonthill in its entirety constituted an experience unequalled beyond the borders of England: 'There is nothing equal to the interior of Fonthill in Germany, in Italy, or even in *la belle France*; and the grounds, which include nineteen hundred acres, present a greater variety of beautiful landscapes, wood and water, than we ever saw within the same circumference. Every English man that can ought to visit Fonthill'.

Many contemporaries who recorded their reactions to Fonthill viewed the translation of raw nature into a luxuriant landscape scene as a measure of Beckford's artistic inventiveness and credited him for masterminding it. It was one thing, they felt, to improve with success an already existing landscape garden, as was Humphry Repton's forte, but it was quite another to bring one into existence from humble beginnings. The artist Constable, who lived in nearby Gillingham, was among the curious who reacted this way. 'I was at Fonthill yesterday', he explained to his wife, 'to see that extraordinary place ... on the whole it is a strange, ideal, romantic place; quite fairy-land'. Such a model of elegance and taste seemed almost out of place, as he explained in an earlier letter, 'standing alone in these melancholy regions of Wiltshire Downs'.[11] William L. Bowles used the same subject as the theme of his poem, which appeared in the *Gentleman's Magazine*:

> Lines on a First View of Fonthill Abbey
>
> The mighty master wav'd his wand, and lo!
> On the astonish'd eye the glorious show
> Bursts, like a vision; SPIRIT OF THE PLACE,
> Has the Arabian wizard, with his mace

Smitten the barren downs far onward spread,
And bade th' enchanted Palace tower instead?
Bade the dark woods their solemn shades extend?
High to the clouds yon spiry tow'r ascend?
And, starting from th' umbrageous avenue,
Spread the rich pile magnificent to view?
Enter—from this arch'd portal, look again,
Back, on the lessening woods and distant plain.
Ascend the steps—the high and fretted roof
Is woven by some Elfin hand aloof,
Whilst from the painted windows' long array,
A mellow'd light is shed, as not of day.
How gorgeous all! Oh never may the spell
Be broken, that array'd those radiant forms so well.[12]

Amidst all this praise, some of which was no doubt exaggerated, there were dissenting voices, and one in particular William Hazlitt's, was sufficiently influential to have shaped a negative view of Fonthill to the present day. Hazlitt's first account of Fonthill, which was published in the *London Magazine* in November, 1822, denounced the Abbey and its collections as all 'tinsel, and glitter, and embossing'. It was, he felt 'a system of tantalization', and a 'fret-work of imagination' 'There is', he added, 'but scarce one genuine work of art, one solid proof of taste, one lofty relic of sentiment or imagination!'[13] He paid little attention to the exterior of the building, the interior design, or the library. Instead, Hazlitt seemed more intent on characterising Beckford's taste as given to collecting objects that were expensive trifles—prized for their difficulty of attainment and exclusivity. While many of Beckford's contemporaries praised him as a generous patron of the arts, Hazlitt characterised him as 'an industrious *bijoutier*, a prodigious virtuoso, an accomplished patron of unproductive labour, an enthusiastic collector of expensive trifles—the only proof of taste (to our thinking) he has shown in this collection is *his getting rid of it*' (p. 406).

If Hazlitt found no relic of imagination among the *objets d'art*, he was equally relentless in his criticism of the collection of paintings in the Abbey, labelling them 'mere furniture-pictures, remarkable chiefly for their antiquity or painful finishing, without beauty, without interest, and with about the same pretensions to attract the eye or delight the fancy as a well-polished mahogany table or a waxed oak-floor' (p. 405). He complained that there was no painting that made the spirit soar—no 'heir-loom of imagination'. Or, as he explained in another piece on Fonthill a year later: 'It is obviously a first principle with him [Beckford] to exclude whatever has feeling or imagination—to polish the surface, and suppress the soul of art … to reduce all nature and all art, as far as possible, to the texture and level of a China dish—smooth, glittering, cold, and unfeeling!'[14] What hung on the walls of Fonthill, according to Hazlitt, lacked the eminence and imaginative power of some of the old masters, such as Titian's *St Peter Martyr* which received a great deal of attention

in his 1822 essay. Instead, not 'one great work by one great name, scarce one or two of the
worst specimens of the first masters, Leonardo's *Laughing Boy*, or a copy from Raphael
or Correggio, as if to make the thing remote and finical—but heaps of the most elaborate
pieces of the worst of the Dutch masters, Breughel's Sea-horses with coats of mother-
of-pearl, and Rottenhammer's Elements turned into a Flower-piece' (pp. 405-6). Hazlitt
continued in this vein throughout the article, but then in the very last paragraph, almost
as if sensing that he had gone too far, managed to muster praise for some of the works he
met with at Fonthill, including a triple jewelled cabinet with panels of amber, the striking
nautilus shell with a carved ivory plinth attributed to Cellini, the cup said to be by Magnus
Berg, a work by John of Bologna, and the Borghese table in King Edward's Gallery. As
for the pictures, he mustered thinly positive comments about Berghem's sea-port scene,
' a fair specimen', Ludovico Caracci's *Sibylla Libyca*, 'in the grand style of composition',
Gerard Dow's *Poulterer's Shop*, was 'passable' and Parmegiano displayed 'a good copy of
a head'. He then continued with a few off-hand comments about the Abbey: 'the painted
windows in the centre of the Abbey have a surprising effect—the form of the building … is
fantastical, to say the least'. He concluded by noting that the 'grounds, which are extensive
and fine from situation, are laid out with the hand of a master' (p. 410). In another essay
published in the following year, he would describe the grounds in even stronger terms as
an 'an Eden rescued from a desart'.[15]

Beckford reacted strongly to Hazlitt's attack in a correspondence on the subject with
Macquin.[16] While Beckford's letters pertaining to this subject have not come to light,
their content can be inferred from two letters written by Macquin on 8 and 9 November,
1822, shortly after the appearance of Hazlitt's piece. In the letter of 9 November, Macquin
revealed Beckford's feelings on the subject and his desire to fight back by noting: 'You
seem to want to have M[onsieur] H[azlitt] flogged'. The nature of the flogging turned out
to be a well-crafted retaliation in the press by Macquin which Beckford supported with
the proviso that no mention be made of 'either the abbey or its creator'. Macquin felt that
this restriction would tie his hands in any attempt to mount a counter attack. At the same
time, he stood ready to defend his friend, describing Hazlitt's critique as a 'rambling tirade,
insolent in the extreme, which proves that the author combines the grossest ignorance of
works of taste with the impudence of a hack journalist'. But, as to preparing a published
response, Macquin was more circumspect, fearing that it would only provoke further
reactions. 'I am convinced', he wrote to Beckford, 'that the scorching breadth of a critique
as biting as it would be just would have no other effect than that of suddenly hatching
a new race of vipers a hundred times more venomous than their mother'. 'Let us not
allow him to think', he added, 'that he has achieved his aim. He deserves nothing but the
profoundest contempt. Let us not give him the satisfaction of thinking that he has caused
one moment of anxiety to anyone who loves you or that he took up two minutes of the
sublime imagination of the founder of Fonthill Abbey. His arrows will never reach this
extraordinary man'.

Beckford must have recognised the wisdom of these remarks because in the second
letter Macquin repeats one of Beckford's favourite statements of postured indifference

whenever he wished to distance himself from the fray: 'since you assure me that it is all one to you and I believe you', and then he added by way of conclusion: 'whichever way this thing ends, I am confident I will not disappoint you'. Macquin, of course, was being diplomatic in his careful phrasing while clearly signalling to Beckford that a critique of Hazlitt's views would not likely be forthcoming from his pen and none, in fact, ever did appear.

What may have motivated Hazlitt's sweeping diatribe against the Fonthill collection? Part of it may have been a consequence of Hazlitt's personal feelings about Beckford. There was a decidedly moral cast to Hazlitt's assessment which might have influenced his artistic judgement. He clearly viewed the collection as a sybaritic display of self indulgence, a squandering of great wealth for the narrow purpose of tantalising the senses. While he spoke highly of *Vathek* as a 'mastery performance', that work represented a younger Beckford. In Hazlitt's mind, the creator of Fonthill was now a 'volcano burnt-out' whose talent was vitiated on gathering 'frippery and finery'. It is interesting to note that the *New Times*, edited by Hazlitt's ex-brother-in-law John Stoddart, published an anonymous article in September, 1823, attacking Beckford directly on moral grounds, explaining that no person in the rank of a gentleman would enter Fonthill because there was a 'moral impediment' against doing so. Alluding to the 'original criminality' of the Powderham scandal of 1784, the author wrote:

> The question is, whether a person once excluded from society, for imputations never disproved, shall be indirectly sought to be restored to his former eminence—and we say, No: the purity and honour of our social intercourse forbid it. It is essential to the maintenance of our English delicacy, in considerations of this kind, that the leper be *for ever* cast out of the camp—that the disgraced character remain *for ever*
>
> > A fixed figure for the hand of scorn
> > To point his slowly moving finger at.
>
> And the richer, the prouder, the most ostentatious he is, the more inexorably should he be kept in the state of an Indian *Pariah*, the object of general aversion and contempt.[17]

Moral pronouncements about Beckford and his lifestyle were common fare during his day, but what is particularly puzzling about Hazlitt's review of the Fonthill collection is what he left out. Boyd Alexander has already pointed out that Hazlitt skipped over many important works of art in his assessment. In pointing to the contents of the Christie catalogue to make his case, Hazlitt paid too much attention to the items listed in the first two days of the proposed sale, while ignoring the seventh day where the important pictures were listed.[18] He said nothing, for example, about Bellini's *Doge Loredan*, Rembrandt's *Rabbi*, Perugino's *Virgin and Child with St John*, and Cima da Conegliano's '*St Jerome*', among others. Absent also were such treasures as the Rubens vase, the Limoges reliquary, and the many distinguished pieces of fine French furniture. It may be that Beckford's taste was ahead of his time leading to the purchase of items that were unimportant to Hazlitt who was operating with a different set of standards, more in accord with the conventional eighteenth-century man of taste. It is interesting to note that so much research now devoted to works of art once in the collections at Fonthill and in Bath has affirmed the quality of Beckford's connoisseurship, identifying him as one of the outstanding collectors and patron of the arts in the nineteenth century.

Clive Wainwright's studies on the contents of the Fonthill collection, for example, concluded that 'the Abbey as a whole housed one of the most important collections of paintings ever assembled in this country', ranging from modern works commissioned by Beckford to a wide range of old masters.[19] Wainwright believed that Beckford was not modelling his collection after the mid-eighteenth century antiquarian, such as Horace Walpole in search of medieval relics, but rather on late sixteenth and seventeenth-century prototypes that were outside the artistic scale of values of many of his contemporaries, including Hazlitt. 'Beckford bought objects', Wainwright explained, 'primarily as works of art or virtuoso craftsmanship in precious and exotic materials. These objects had naturally often been owned by or created for celebrated historical figures, but for Beckford this was an extra bonus and not the main reason for their acquisition.'[20]

Wainwright's assessment was confirmed dramatically by a major exhibition of a portion of Beckford's collection of works of fine and applied art organised by the Bard Graduate Center in New York, which ran from October 2001 to January 2002, whereupon it travelled to the Dulwich Picture Gallery in London for another showing that ran to April 2002. This exhibition offered a striking display of 175 works from Beckford's collection, consisting of paintings and drawings, English and French furniture, Japanese lacquer, metal works, European and Chinese silver and porcelain. It was accompanied by a sumptuously illustrated catalogue entitled *William Beckford, 1760–1844: An Eye for the Magnificent*, which traces the history of his collecting habits in pursuit of luxurious examples of the fine and decorative arts from the ancient, medieval, and Renaissance periods as well as the seventeenth, eighteenth and nineteenth centuries. A collection of sixteen informative essays by specialists in their respective fields, the volume explores Beckford's eclectic passion for the arts, break-through taste for the unconventional, love of expert craftsmanship and his frequent personal involvement in providing designs for commissioned work. Among other facets of his collecting habits, the exhibition showed Beckford to be a head of his time as a distinctive collector of Asian and Islamic art. As an antidote to Hazlitt's pronouncements on Beckford's taste, the entire event provided an opportunity with the international attention it received for a contemporary assessment of Beckford's place in British cultural history and in the end gave compelling testimony that he was one of the most important and influential collectors of the nineteenth century who shaped the taste and interest of such private collectors as Lord Hertford, Sir Richard Wallace, the Rothschilds, and J. P. Morgan.

It should be noted, furthermore, that on many occasions Beckford established the provenance himself after he purchased the object, which lends support to the view that his primary interest was the artistic quality of the object with the historical association being a secondary matter, as in the case of the controversial Cellini ewer. Beckford's interest in craftsmanship was also evident in the fact that he would create designs based on research in his 'Board of Works Library' and then have Franchi show the design and the original books and prints from which they were derived to the artists executing the work. Franchi would be in constant attendance to the work in progress to ensure that it met the highest standard of quality. Sometimes Franchi would make the drawing himself in collaboration with Beckford modelled after a finely crafted piece of Medieval or Renaissance metalware. A book of design drawings belonging to the goldsmith James Aldridge has survived that includes a page of drawings by Franchi. As the famous wood carver William G. Rogers recorded as a common occurrence with Franchi: 'He would come into the carvers workshop with a volume of Holbein or Aldegraver, select a spoon or handle and have them executed in ivory or ebony as high as he could get talent to bring them, would watch the progress of work day by day, and the question would often be—"if you spent another day on it could you get it finer?"'[21]

All of this effort may have constituted a preciousness of manner and style that Hazlitt could not abide. He was also not prepared to treat objects of utility or decoration as worthy of serious condsideration as art. In the production of historicist works, Beckford was ahead of his time in believing that such finely crafted objects of utility or decoration could rise to the level of a fine art.

Beckford's wealth assuredly played a role in sharpening Hazlitt's criticism of the Fonthill collection. Four years after the sale to Farquhar, he made it clear that in his mind Beckford's expenditures on Fonthill were lavishly excessive. He wrote scathingly in 1826 that 'thirty pampered domestics sat down in the servants' hall at Fonthill Abbey, to dine on Westphalia hams boiled in Maderia wine, and other luxuries of the same stamp, while old age staggered under its load of labour, or sickness fainted for want of a glass of wine or a morsel of bread in the neighbourhood'.[22] The luxury Hazlitt witnessed at Fonthill must have been particularly grating at a time when he himself was in serious financial straits and had suffered the humiliation of being arrested for debt in February, 1822. Furthermore, research by biographer Stanley Jones led to the discovery of more essays on Fonthill by Hazlitt that underscore his financial desperation and which raise additional questions about his professional integrity as an art critic in regard to his treatment of the Fonthill collection.[23]

Harry Phillips, it seems, in an effort to counteract some of the bad publicity surrounding the possibility of adding scourings from London shops in the 1823 sale, approached Hazlitt and offered him fifty guineas to puff the Fonthill property and its contents in the press. The offer was too attractive to be refused, particularly in the face of his indebtedness, so Hazlitt decided to accept the commission from Phillips even though he had already publicly sacked the collection. The artist Benjamin Haydon heard about the arrangement, recounting in a letter of 26 September 1823, that 'Hazlitt was up last week from Fonthill, where Phillips has fixed him to write up for fifty guineas, what he wrote down from his conscience last year'.[24] Needless to say, it was a considerable challenge to the art critic under the circumstances, but he attempted to be true to his artistic principles, while appearing to praise the Fonthill pictures, by being subtly ironic throughout the anonymous article that appeared serially in four succeeding issues of the *Morning Chronicle*.[25] Keeping in mind Hazlitt's aversion for literal detail and high finishing, the double-edged character of the article is apparent at the outset when he says about Karel du Jardin's *A Riding Horse*:

> The trees in the back-ground (if *back-ground* it can be called, where the objects are seen close upon the eye) are exquisitely touched, with every leaf almost detailed, and yet the masses are finely rounded off. You might fancy the air to have stirred their branches just before, but they had stopped while the artist was painting them—so accurately is every thing expressed, at the same time with 'such happiness and pains', that you hold in your breath while looking at it, as if you could hardly examine with sufficient care, nor admire long enough.[26]

In the second article, 'The Science of a Connoisseur', Hazlitt dropped his ironic pose, and, seemingly to assuage some of the discontent he experienced for his duplicity, returned to his more frontal attack of the previous year in a dramatic piece, involving a conversation between a 'friend' and a 'connoisseur', designed to expose a taste for triviality as represented by the Dutch paintings Beckford owned, beginning with specific attention being paid to Metzu's *Woman Cleaning Fish*. The 'Connoisseur' in the skit becomes the exemplar of false taste with the questioning 'friend' expressing Hazlitt's views. As Hazlitt wrote:

> [CONNOISSEUR] There, Sir—a perfect specimen of the art and the master. They talk of their Ostades, their Mieris's, and their Gerard Dows, give men the ease and nature of Metzu. The *pensive Selima*—the expression is in Gray—look at that kitten on the top of the brass pan, watching the operation of scraping the fish—demure, devout, cautious, expressing the very soul of the feline tribe, and looking as if a turn of the brass pan on which she has perched herself might suddenly upset all her speculations—and then the pencilling is actually of fur.
> FRIEND—I don't think it at all like a cat.
> CONNOISSEUR—(*doucement*)—You are fastidious! But what do you say to the face of the woman? Is it not charming?—Such an easy air, such an arch expression, such clearness of tone, such freedom of touch; and then the fish seem absolutely alive! If you observe, all is done here that can be done by the art of man, and it is done without any appearance of labour. Facility of execution is what charms me most in a picture.
> FRIEND—Was it here in Mr. Beckford's time?
> CONNOISSEUR—No, it is one of those lately added; and alone establishes Mr. Phillips's claims as a judge of art....
> FRIEND—Give me your opinion of the Cuyp. Is it not crowded with too many groups of figures?
> CONNOISSEUR—Perhaps it wants simplicity; but the clearness, the sunny effect seems to prove it to be Albert Cuyp's. It is a very glowing brilliant picture.

FRIEND—What do you think it will fetch?

CONNOISSEUR—I cannot speak to that point precisely, but I should think it would go high—or else I had some thoughts of it myself.

FRIEND—You like the Netscher and the Mieris yonder? I have heard it objected   t h a t the flesh in the one looks like parchment, and in the other like china. Does not the child in the *Judgment of Solomon,* for instance, look as if it would break, if the executioner were to let it fall on the glazed pavement?

CONNOISSEUR—We must not attend to all the nonsense we hear; and we may sometimes hear nonsense talked on the subject of the Fine Arts, as well as every other. *Allons.* These pictures undoubtedly rank among some of the choicest in the collection; and Mr. Beckford must be allowed to have been a judge in this style of art.

FRIEND—But did not his taste run too much on merely highfinished and furniture pictures? There are, I grant, a number of capital and indeed firstrate specimens of minute and elaborate workmanship; but are not the productions of the grand historical style of art a very indifferent description—heavy, lumbering, coarse, and uninteresting?…[27]

In an article published in *The Examiner* that Hazlitt also wrote to do Phillips's bidding, he once again donned the ironic mask to assuage some of the humiliation he felt at having to compromise his principles.[28] This time he returned to some of the 'Carvings in Ivory at Fonthill' that he had praised slightly in the *London Magazine* the previous year. While seeming to admire the works mentioned, he effectively ends up damning them. He starts with the 'Cellini' Nautilus cup as one of the 'splendid ornaments' and observes that the ivory figures on the shell are 'true of nature' and that the ivory is 'moulded into all the softness of flesh', which may seem to be a compliment, but this kind of life-like realism is what Hazlitt particularly disliked in works of art. 'Titian's pencil', he adds, 'could not give more yielding flexibility'—a statement that Hazlitt inserted parenthetically because Titian was in his view was an important example of a noble artist whose works were marked by breadth of conception rather than the elaborate craftsmanship of a small decorative piece. When Hazlitt says that he finds no traces of Cellini's 'bold and licentious life' in the 'classic purity of his style', he means this as no compliment since he goes on to say that the 'fiery spirit' of this artist has been 'tamed into a sort of playful ease and tenderness by the difficult materials in which he worked'. Similarly, Hazlitt describes an ivory vase sculptured by Strous of a marine venus with tritons as 'very fine' but then offers a mixed assessment of the work—'the figures are not perfectly proportioned, but they have grace of spirit, and the faces a voluptuous, passionate expression, which redeems very mechanical defect'—leading to a final pronouncement that the work 'is wonderful in so small a compass' which following his previous commentary ends up seeming more disparaging than complimentary.

In his discussion of 'Magnus Berg's' ivory cup, which he identified as the *Hunting Piece*, the satiric mask begins to slip and assumes a more direct tone. It is a 'most curious and elaborate piece of workmanship', Hazlitt says, but he finds it wanting as a work of art. 'The pains taken, the finishing, the spirit, the resemblance to life in the figures, the animals, the landscape, are admirable, but they at the same time excite a feeling of regret that where so much was done and attempted, there should be a want of any thing to crown the success of the artist, and that he should be so near touching the highest point of art, and yet come short of it'. The problem is that Berg did not in Hazlitt's mind display any connection with the great tradition of classical art. The figures displayed in the ivory were 'not nymphs and goddesses', the figure of Diana on the top of the lid was not the 'Goddess of Chace' and the 'Hercules that supports the cup (the Atlas of this little world)' was simply 'old'. The inevitable conclusion for Hazlitt was that 'Magnus Berg had not the *ideal* faculty'—the quintessential criterion for high art in his mind.

Fonthill Abbey would remain in Hazlitt's view a celebrated example of false taste and a waste of wealth on the 'elaborately little'. It was a smouldering irritant that would rise to the surface from time to time, as it did again in 1828 when he wrote: 'This quaint excrescence in architecture, preposterous and ill-contrived as it was, occasioned, I suspect, many a heart-arche and bitter comparison to the throng of fashionable visitants; and I conceive it was the very want of comfort and convenience that enhanced this feeling, by magnifying, as it were from contrast, the expense that had been incurred in realising an idle whim'.[29]

The legacy of Hazlitt's appraisal of Fonthill, particularly in view of his own reputation as a distinguished nineteenth-century critic, cannot be underestimated. It accounts, to a great extent, for the tendency today to treat Fonthill lightly, even contemptuously, as an example of a silly rich man's whim. As Boyd Alexander explained in 1962, 'Hazlitt's vitriolic attack on the art treasures which Fonthill housed and the taste which it displayed has left an uneasy memory of triviality and meretriciousness'.[30]

While Hazlitt was at Fonthill during a second visit in 1823, a close friend of his Peter G. Patmore was also present preparing his own article on the pictures for his series 'British Galleries of Art' in the *New Monthly Magazine*. The two men spent some time together visiting other estates in the area, so it is likely they shared their respective views on Fonthill. Patmore's own analysis seems to have been written with Hazlitt's criticism in mind since he covers some of the same territory and even refers to the excesses of 'Flemish finishing'. But, Patmore's views were not entirely in accord with Hazlitt's. In fact, they seem to be directed at providing an antidote to the art critic's venom. Striving to give a fair impression of the character of the Fonthill collection, he singled out Albrecht Dürer's *Virgin and Child* as a 'rich little gem', a 'perfect specimen of what *finishing* ought to be—of how far it ought to be carried, and at what point it should stop'.[31] Whereas Hazlitt trashed Metzu's *Woman Cleaning Fish*, Patmore pronounced it 'without exception the very best' of the specimens he had seen of the Flemish school of finishing whose object, he explained, was to produce 'natural impressions'. 'The little work before us', he added, 'is the most purely *natural* effort of the pencil that I have ever seen; so much so, as to have required nothing less than *genius* to produce it' (p. 405). Patmore also found at Fonthill other noble specimens of art, citing Ludovico Carracci's *Sibylla Lybica* ('merits to be called the grand style in art'), Teniers's *Temptation of St Anthony* ('a force of conception, a vividness of imagination, and a truth and facility of hand, that have never been united in any other person'), 'Berghem's *L'embarquement des Vivres*, ('the most faultless of the whole collection'). Of the Flemish school of finishing that Hazlitt so deplored, Patmore found some pictures of extraordinary merit, including Mieris's *A Lady Feeding a Parrot*, Dow's *Poulterer's Shop*, and Philip de Champagne's *Adoration of the Shepherds*. Patmore believed that among over four hundred pictures, exhibiting such a great diversity of technique and subject matter, there are bound to be varying levels of quality—some fine and some mediocre—and even some bad canvases. In his view, it was a mistake to try to build a great collection by limiting price rather than the number of paintings. With the space that Fonthll offered and one hundred thousand pounds, one could create a private gallery finer than any in existence. 'The late Mr. Angerstein', he concluded, 'was known all over Europe, and will not soon be forgotten, for no other reason than that he possessed ten of the finest pictures in the world!' (p. 408).

While neither Hazlitt nor Patmore devoted much attention to the artistic qualities of the Abbey as a building or to any extended examination of the landscape design, there were published contemporary accounts that addressed these matters. On occasion, these accounts were written by individuals who brought professional expertise to bear on their critical assessment and who tried to provide some balance between strengths and weaknesses in their accounts. One such work appeared under the title 'Candid Critique on the Architecture of Fonthill Abbey' in the *Gentleman's Magazine*.[32] It was signed with the initials 'W. G.'. This was William Garbett, surveyor to the Dean and Chapter of Winchester Cathedral for twenty-five years and the person who supervised the architectural repairs of this cathedral from 1812 to 1828. John Britton, who knew Garbett well, shared this article in manuscript form with Beckford shortly before publication.[33] His reaction to it is not known, but it is likely that he would have concurred with Garbett's sentiments. Beckford did examine the architectural work of William's son Edward at Theale, Berkshire, considered to be one of the first churches of the Gothic revival designed in the Early English style, and he was quoted as having 'passed the highest encomiums on the taste of the architect, in having selected the purest style of pointed architecture'.[34]

While not a great deal is known about Garbett, he felt strongly enough about his own restoration work that when the more prominent architect John Nash tried to dictate advice about restoration, he published a pamphlet in 1824 entitled *Observations and Correspondence occasioned by the Failure and Renovation of a Principal Pier in Winchester Cathedral* in vigorous defence of his own plans. He is also known as the author of the account of the city of Winchester in Britton's *Picturesque Antiquities of English Cities* (1828-30). The work he carried out at Winchester Cathedral included the reconstruction of two defective piers and the design of the Bishop's throne, among other restorations.

Garbett understood the difficulties any architect faced in an attempt to revive the authentic Gothic style of the medieval period. In the first place, he believed that the original ecclesiastical structures were built without any consensus regarding the underlying principles of construction. He also noted that extant examples of the buildings in England and elsewhere often exhibited the same disparities that critics were fond of pointing out as weaknesses in revival Gothic. His own work in the field led him to believe that the slavish adoption of ancient models would be unsuited to the present age because the 'improved conveniences of modern times' required substantive changes in both structure and design. In his view, any attempt to revive an architectural style could only be accomplished in a evolutionary manner, building upon the stylistic refinement that developed from the actual practice of creating new buildings or modifying old ones. But in the end, as with other ancient architectural styles, the Gothic style had to address the practical needs of the current age and therefore would never be completely recreated. It was a point of view his son Edward continued to support in his own emphasis on the role of functional convenience in architectural design.

In his examination of Fonthill Abbey, Garbett identified structural weakness as the central problem with the building. He attributed this considerable deficiency to the fact that the Abbey was not constructed from a well-planned design but evolved over time as Beckford moved from his original conception of a tower design to a grander conception of a Gothic residence. Looking at the Grand Saloon, Garbett felt that it lacked solidity as a base for the tower, noting that the walls were too thin to provide the necessary support. A greater mass would have permitted the use of staircases without the necessity of turrets, which, 'however they may add to picturesque effect, may be questionable as objects of intrinsic beauty in design'. Expanding the size of the tower base would have the effect of increasing the size and function of the second level of rooms called the 'Nunneries'. With thicker walls, the removal of the turrets, and the addition of flying buttresses, he explained, the 'cloud-capt' spire that Beckford originally conceived would have been possible.

Garbett also believed that Wyatt had sacrificed 'rational symmetry' to 'picturesque effect' in the lack of height and width of King Edward's and St Michael's galleries, the northern and southern wings of the Abbey, 'more particularly in the upper spaces within their roofs, and in the diminutive upper windows'. This became more noticeable when the Eastern Transept was viewed in relationship to the two galleries, since its enormous size tended to emphasise their more diminished character. While recognising that the Eastern Transept was never finished, Garbett further observed that the three large and imposing windows on the south side cried out for the creation of an ancient hall 'appropriated to the hospitable purposes of the banquet', following the model of Hawksmoor's work at All Soul's College, Oxford (p. 493).

In the interest of authenticity and further structural support, Garbett would have added buttresses to both the eastern and western wings. In addition, the lack of ornamental detail on the vast surface of the wall of the Eastern Transept seemed to him to be out of harmony with the rest of the building as were the 'perforated parapets' which were too light in character to harmonise with the 'general tenor of the design' (p. 493). The paucity of decorative detail on the surface of the Abbey was also shared by J. S. Taylor in the *Morning Chronicle* who believed that it was needed to harmonise with the embellishments of the interior which called for a more 'florid style' in the surface of the exterior, 'enriched with the most elaborate decorations of quaint devices and antique imagery'.[35] It was a problem generally with revival Gothic since there were few craftsmen around who could accomplish it.

Proceeding to the interior of the Abbey, Garbett itemised some deficiencies in workmanship, such as the fan vaulting supporting the lantern in the Octagon, which he believed lacked the elegance and grace of other parts of the Abbey's interior but which might have been corrected had Wyatt lived long enough. The Brown or Oak Parlour, a long low room on the ground floor with foreshortened windows, he found out of keeping with the Gothic style as he did the two Yellow rooms above it, but he was highly complimentary about other rooms: 'when we come to the [Great Western] Hall, the Octagon, and the South and East Oriels, we find the style approximate much nearer to ancient models; the Lobbies to the Brown Parlour, the Green Cabinet Room, and the West and South Arcades, approach still nearer to perfection; and finally, the Galleries forming the library, combined with the Sanctuary and Oratory, merit the highest commendation, as well for general effect as for elegance of details' (p. 494).

In other instances, where critics might have issued condemnations as deviations from 'abstract notions of correct and congruous style', Garbett was more liberal, willing to embrace the superiority of aesthetics over rules. Where some might be critical of the extreme height of the western entrance hall, he felt that any diminution of it 'would destroy one of the finest effects produced on this stately edifice, particularly when viewed from the perspective of the Octagon'. If others argued that the arches of the Octagon were too 'acutely pointed' to satisfy the true Gothic style, Garbett answered 'that the piers supporting the Tower, being evidently elevated to the utmost admissible proportion, the acute shape of the arches rising from them will, in the eyes of those who prefer pleasing forms to fancied rules, appear a beauty rather than a defect'. While the cavilling critic might make the charge of an inappropriate mixture of the modern with the Gothic in the absence of mullions and tracery in the windows of the Octagon, Garbett argued that this would have diminished the quality of light infusing this hall and prevented the stained glass from creating the splendid effect of light that was felt and noted by almost every visitor (p. 491). In short, these qualities showed that Wyatt was not insensible to the 'grace surpassing rule and order'.

So, in the end Garbett leaned in favour of the overall aesthetic qualities of Fonthill despite the faults he observed as an experienced architect. He found that the Abbey could not be judged simply as an imitation of an earlier style and according to some perceived rules of old. Indeed, the fusion of elements of the modern with the ancient was not only inevitable but necessary. 'It must therefore be pretty obvious', he concluded, ' that the most fastidious architectural critic of the present age would be as little pleased to inhabit a mansion built after the exact model of one of the fourteenth century, as the most discontented political reformer would be with the precise constitution of the same period. When all these circumstances are duly considered, it must remain for ever questionable, whether any other person would have conducted the same undertaking with greater success than the deceased Architect of Fonthill' (p. 494).

What is instructive about Garbett's analysis is that he ended up in the same place as many of his contemporaries in their assessment. He understood that Fonthill Abbey was not to be judged simply as imitation Gothic. It was not based on any specific existing models. The Gothic style played an inspirational role, and there were some influences, such as the monastery at Batalha, but there was no exact prototype for Fonthill. As a building, the Abbey did not conform, as Garbett elucidated, to any 'abstract notions of correct and congruous style'. Indeed, it was often the deviations from a pre-conceived type that constituted this structure's beauties producing what Garbett described as pleasing 'effects'. In keeping with the artistic currents of the time, the Abbey's visual appeal and emotional impact replaced the authority of imitation as an aesthetic ideal.

Garbett's essay, despite its balanced approach, still reflects the ambiguities of the Gothic revival movement and its fruitless attempts to recreate an architectural style of the past in any pure sense. The religious spirit that produced the Gothic style had long since waned. The impulse behind Fonthill Abbey, on the other hand, was the romantic urge for self-dramatization. It was a secular church reflecting the dynamic trends of an age setting about to embrace earthly concerns.

Even from the point of view of a professional architect of the period, Fonthill had to be recognised as an original work and assessed in terms of its impact on the observer. Garbett was candid when he observed that in the fabric of this magnificent structure there was evidence that picturesque effects superseded the importance of rational symmetry. Fonthill was, after all, aligned with the aesthetics of asymmetry and expressive art. It is not surprising, therefore, that most contemporaries who recorded their reactions to Fonthill almost consistently found that it promoted feelings of awe and amazement. They cared little about its congruence to the Gothic style.

Another important architect, Charles C. Cockerell (1788–1863), known for his work in the 1830s on the University Library, Cambridge, the Ashmolean Museum and Taylor Institution, Oxford, visited Fonthill in August 1823 and recorded his observations in an album entitled *Ichnographica Domestica*, a fascinating record of his visits to English houses in the process of conducting studies of various architectural styles.[36] His analysis of Fonthill Abbey was not as extensive as Garbett's, but significant enough to cite as another example of an assessment by a contemporary practitioner and theorist. Cockerell, undoubtedly influenced by rumours that he had heard, had anticipated a patchwork quilt at Fonthill but, instead, was surprised to find an interior layout that exhibited an overall controlling purpose and orderly design. He was particularly impressed by the way the Octagon Hall served as an axis of communication with the major wings of the Abbey. 'I was agre[e]ably surprised at Fonthill', he noted during his visit, 'not finding it as I had supposed a monstrous caprice. The system of the plan seems to me judicious, as you arrive by the vestibule at once into the centre, which is the means of communication to & from the various apartments of the House, which lies … round it. How much preferable is this to the quadrangle as at Blenheim, Wooburn or even as at Blenheim, Luton (& my Wellington Plan) when there are two small courts as at Kedleston'.

Cockerell's assessment also stressed the Abbey's iconographic character, and unlike some visitors, emphasised a lighter tone in the interior environment rather than the more typical emphasis on the pervading sombre lights and hues of the Abbey in the evening or the magical tints and colours caused by the stained glass in the late afternoon.

Walking through the Abbey on this day, Cockerell observed the daylight quality of the radiating wings. 'In the history of ichnography', he wrote, 'Fonthill ranks as highly interesting example, as novel & excellent in many respects, the considerable plan offering great cheerfulness, light, and greatest possible facilities of communication'. Interestingly, Cockerell focused almost entirely on the structure, believing that there was no apparent relationship between the building and the exterior grounds and prospects. Instead, he tended to view the Abbey as a 'studious abstraction for persons living indoors delighting therefore in that respect'. In his mind, the Abbey was a monument to self sufficiency, lending itself to the cultivation of habits that do not lead to or require the open air. The breathtaking scenes were all within the building—'hence these vistas of 330 feet, this octagon Hall 130 feet high—this bold elevation & vastness'. 'It is evidently the production of a sedentary literary person', he continued, 'a poet & composer of Vathek who proposed to pass his life in the Cloister Gallery of 300 feet & in the contemplation of this vast tower'.

The two major illustrated books by John Britton and John Rutter respectively provided a broader assessment of Fonthill, incorporating the Abbey in a grander artistic scheme by considering it within the aesthetic context of a landscape garden. Both volumes have stood out over time as important written and visual records of Fonthill. As a prescient writer in the *Salisbury and Winchester Journal* noted in 1823, 'Whatever may be the destiny of FONTHILL ABBEY,—whether its lofty head may defy the loud blast of Boreas, and remain an object of admiration to future ages; or like certain edifices renowned in story, it may fall a sacrifice to the raging storm or devouring flame—neither the enterprising genius of its founder, nor the skill of its architect, will be lost to posterity, so long as a faithful description and accurate delineation of the Abbey shall remain in the library of the virtuoso'.[37] Both volumes can also be considered major authoritative works that document the history and conception of Fonthill because of Beckford's willingness to provide assistance as a source of information to both writers. To a significant extent these books can be considered Beckford documents.

Britton was the established antiquarian and topographer among the two writers, having already published the first two volumes of *Beauties in Wiltshire* in 1801, jointly authored with Edward W. Brayley *The Beauties of England and Wales* from 1801 to 1816, and having begun his own fourteen-volume series *The Cathedral Antiquities of England*, the publication of which ran from 1814 to 1835. Britton visited Fonthill Abbey in 1817, and he and his wife Mary Anne were guests there for a month at the height of its celebrity in 1822. During this stay, Britton prepared the notes that would serve as the basis for *Graphical and Literary Illustrations of Fonthill Abbey* which he published by subscription the following year. In addition to his wife, he was also accompanied by George Cattermole, who made many of the drawings for the illustrations in Britton's book. As the leading publicist of the Gothic architectural style after John Carter and collaborating at the time with Augustus Pugin on *Specimens of Gothic Architecture*, Britton naturally wanted to write about Fonthill. Just prior to his visit in late August and early September, he had already published an anonymous piece in *The Museum* in which he referred to the Abbey as a 'unique specimen of the triumph of modern skill and genius over the difficulties of construction presented by the Gothic style'.[38]

Britton was impressed with Beckford and eager to seek his favour. He seemed to be in awe of his strength of mind, the quick wit and breadth of knowledge he exhibited in conversation, and his artistic accomplishments. He told Beckford in 1835 that when he first met him in 1799, he was 'astonished and terrified' by his 'splendours & powers'.[39] Mary Anne Britton's letter of appreciation for being treated so graciously during their stay at Fonthill mirrored her husband's sentiments:

> … All around me seems like the work of enchantment, and I can only gaze and gaze, and wonder how the mind of man should have projected so gigantic a structure and still more, how the mind of man could have so far, almost, outstretched itself, as to have organised and arranged each and every part in such true and perfect order & harmony.
>
> 'Twas for you—and you alone: for your capacious mind and refined taste and judgement to have accomplished a task, which does, and must and ever will be the astonishment of the world. [40]

From the beginning Britton was concerned not only about pleasing his subscribers but Beckford himself. In July 1823, he wrote to Beckford expressing delight that he was willing to look over the proof sheets of the book ('I most cheerfully submit some of them to your keen eye: although I feel much trepidation at the ordeal').[41] Later, he consulted with him about the inclusion of genealogical tables of the Beckford family, a portion of which George Beltz had published in the *Gentleman's Magazine* in the fall of 1822.

It is also a measure of Britton's desire to impress Beckford that he worked so painstakingly on the frontispiece for the volume. For this plate, Britton personally designed an ornate presentation of armorial bearings of Beckford's ancestors. It took the form of an architectural design composed of parts of other ecclesiastical edifices in England in which he saw some stylistic relationship with Fonthill. Thus part of the design was copied from a screen in the nave of Wells Cathedral; the 'arch mouldings, spandrils, and trefoil suspended arches' were drawn from a monument in the north transept in the same church. The six compartments of tracery that enclosed the shields came from Norwich and Winchester Cathedrals, while other elements of the design were copied from specimens in St George's Chapel, Windsor and Exeter Cathedral. It is a remarkably detailed and intricate construction that associates Fonthill Abbey with some of the major examples of Gothic architecture in England while simultaneously paying homage to its creator and to his connection with a revered past through his celebrated lineage. Britton also incorporated in the lower panel of the design two of the most valuable objects from the Fonthill collection, namely a fourteenth century Chinese porcelain decorative piece on the left side, known today as the Gaignières ewer, and a vase on the right that was once owned by Rubens. Britton also intended to incorporate in the centre niche the medieval Limoges chasse from the collection but copied the wrong chasse by mistake.[42] Beckford appears to have noticed the error and brought it to Britton's attention but to no avail. 'I observe that the glaring error in the herald title page', he wrote to Britton, 'remains uncorrected—at least in all the sm[all] paper Copies I have yet seen'.[43]

Britton admitted to having written his Fonthill book hastily, usually after 9:00 o'clock in the evening, after a day of meeting other professional obligations. This may explain, in part, the lengthy preamble that burdens his account, beginning with an address to subscribers, a five-page explanation of the frontispiece, the lengthy description of the plates, a Preface, and then a wordy dedication to John Broadley. Once into the body of the text, Britton presented Fonthill within the context of other great country estates in England and followed the established formula for guide books of his time by dividing his discussion into four major parts: a description of the architectural style of the house, an examination of the grounds and prominent features surrounding it, the details of the building's interior provided on a room-by-room tour followed by the genealogical history of the owner. He also provided some variation of the pattern by interlacing his account with embellishments, such as the description of Lord Nelson's visit in 1800 and a brief review of the reaction of the press and the public during the 'view' of 1822. Beckford also permitted him to publish two of his poems, 'A Prayer' and 'The Last Day'. Britton's most significant departure from the usual guide-book format was exhibited in his tendency to avoid describing the valuable contents and works of art in each room, which may have been a decision resulting from the excess of this kind of coverage in other venues. Instead, he attended to the heraldic shields and armorial bearings that permeated the rooms and stained-glass windows of the Abbey.

Consistent with his interest in the Gothic style of architecture and the ethos that brought it into being, Britton appreciated Fonthill for its nostalgic appeal, specifically the way in which it promoted in the mind of the observer associations with antiquity through the monastic character of its architecture and its commemoration of royal ancestry. 'It is evident', he wrote, 'that Fonthill Abbey is an unique building; that it is large and lofty, of varied forms, styles, and character; that many of its parts are designed more for effect than mere domestic utility; and that externally and internally it presents a succession of scenes which cannot fail to produce powerful impressions on the imagination'.[44] There was also its 'seraphic influence', which Britton described as having experienced in the Abbey, when the play of light and shadow against the walls and gilt mouldings combined with the fragrance of eastern perfume permeating the air and the deep tones of the organ echoing throughout the galleries to produce a total immersion of the senses as if one were transported to another time and place.

It was Fonthill's affective qualities that Britton seized upon because he was well aware that the quality of its construction could not measure up to specimens of Gothic architecture that he had written about and studied. Form could not completely compensate for the functional problems embedded in the heart of the building, but he held Wyatt accountable for this problem. Beckford, he felt, provided the wealth and the grand conceptions. It was up to Wyatt to realise this vision in an edifice that would challenge the vicissitudes of time. Britton believed that Wyatt failed to capitalise on the opportunity that was provided him. 'The architect of Fonthill', he wrote, 'had free and full scope for the exercise of *all* his professional talents: and had these been as considerable as frequently ascribed to him, and had he been impelled by laudable ambition—had he bestowed but common industry on the subject—had he felt that enthusiasm which the occasion demanded, and acted with that inflexible perseverance which his munificent employer had a right to expect, we should then indeed have seen an edifice of surpassing magnitude, beauty, and grandeur; one calculated to prove the fallacy and folly of the common notion, that all excellence and merit in the ecclesiastical species of architecture was extinguished with the dissolution of monasteries'. He then added: 'every incentive and every opportunity appear to have been afforded to the surveyor of Fonthill Abbey; but he was either insensible to their call or incapable of employing them to great and eminent results ... .The present hall has been rebuilt, of nearly double its first dimensions: and the central tower is the third that has been raised! Such things ought not to have occurred'.[45]

William H. Harrison once asked Beckford if Fonthill Abbey was built on his plan. 'No, he answered. 'I have enough sins to answer for, without having that laid to my charge. Wyatt had an opportunity of raising a splendid monument to his fame, but he missed it'.[46] Similar criticism of Wyatt found its way into the press, noting that 'Mr. Beckford's conceptions were not adhered to, and he subsequently often blamed the plan and execution of Mr. Wyatt' which prompted a vigorous response from his son, Benjamin Wyatt. It took the form of a letter in which Benjamin pointed out that Fonthill did not spring from a pre-determined plan nor was modelled after any pre-existing building. Instead, he explained that it evolved from its original conception as a 'Convent' so there could be no original plan to which his father failed to adhere:

> ... When the building now called Fonthill Abbey was first begun, the project was confined *exclusively* (as I can prove by a variety of evidence in my possession), to that small portion of it, which now constitutes the south eastern wing, and which was then denominated by Mr. Beckford 'the Convent'.
>
> I am aware that great efforts have lately been made to suppress the publication of this fact, and thereby to mislead the public as to the merits of my late father as connected with the designs for Fonthill Abbey....
>
> The autograph letters of Mr. Beckford to my late Father, now in my possession, contain, in many parts, expressions of the most enthusiastic admiration of the talents displayed by my father at Fonthill, as well as the most implicit reliance on his skill and experience; avowing, in reiterated instances, on the part of Mr. Beckford, the utter impossibility to proceed without my father's guidance; and, in short, upon the whole, furnishing the most irrefragable truth of feelings and relations, between Mr. Beckford and Mr. Wyatt, as employer and architect....
>
> Mr. Beckford's advocates would do well to leave his reputation to its legitimate merits, instead of attempting to establish for him a spurious distinction, founded on detraction from the fair fame of an eminent professional man, now no longer in this world.[47]

Benjamin made an admirable defence in his father's behalf. He was also accurate in conveying Beckford's admiration for the architect, but the serious issue of the structural integrity of the building was not mentioned despite previous notices in the press about it, and there Wyatt has to assume responsibility as Britton observed.

One of the most valuable aspects of Britton's book were the twelve engraved illustrations he included with the textual material. Here he called upon some of the most eminent topographical artists and engravers of his day to assist him. They included two water-colourists Henry Gastineau and George Cattermole—the latter having worked with Britton on the *Cathedral Antiquities of England*. Cattermole was responsible for the north and south west views of the Abbey for the volume as well as the impressive south end view of the oriel window in St Michael's Gallery, one of the two coloured engravings in the book. Gastineau worked up a more refined drawing of a Cattermole sketch of a striking view, looking down the steps of the Great Hall and out upon the Great Western Avenue. John Martin, considered to be a dramatic and an original historical and landscape painter, provided an impressive distant south-west view of the Abbey in its setting. Among the engravers, the most prominent was Henry Le Keux who had contributed his artistry to Britton's *The Beauties of England and Wales*. Also involved were Thomas Higham and John Thompson, the latter considered to be the most distinguished wood engraver of this time. Then there was Henry Shaw, architectural draftsman, engraver, and a scholar of Gothic architecture in his own right, who did the fine drawing for the coloured engraving of the east window in St Michael's Gallery.

Britton himself was not entirely satisfied with the quality of some of the illustrations, believing that overall they did not measure up to the quality of the plates in his *Cathedral Antiquities*.[48] He was particularly unhappy with some of Cattermole's contributions and conveyed to the artist his dissatisfaction with the drawings of the ground plan and some of the external views. Beckford, on the other hand, found Cattermole's interior drawings to be 'beautiful, correct and full of feeling, particularly his fine perspective of Ed 3rd Gallery and the view from the Hall down the great avenue'.[49] But, so concerned was Britton about a potentially negative reaction from the subscribers to the volume's illustrations that he moved to distance himself from any criticism by declaring at the conclusion of his list of plates that no one could 'feel and lament their imperfections' more than himself and that he hoped the reader 'will not attribute the blame to the author', explaining that the 'author and the publisher of an embellished work is necessarily at the mercy of others: and as all persons have not the same feelings—the same zeal—and the same responsibility, it is not surprising that there be carelessness in one—want of judgment in a second—defective taste in a third—and dishonesty in a fourth' (pp. 13-14). Britton then had seven of the eleven copper plates for the illustrations destroyed to ensure, he said, the perpetual value and integrity of the engravings in the book, but he also added that he took this step because his well established friends and patrons will 'see an inferiority in some of the plates' (p. vii). The fact that five of the seven were based on drawings by Cattermole further underscores his dissatisfaction with the artist. It could not have helped to reduce Britton's distress when Beckford, upon receiving his copy, wrote to Britton that the 'observations you so candidly make on y[ou]r own work, the plates etc., are strictly true & there is nothing so delightful as Truth'.[50]

Underlying Britton's dissatisfaction with Cattermole was a deeper anxiety that began when he learned that Rutter was going to publish a rival work on Fonthill. Britton considered Rutter's move an act of treachery and a direct threat that could only undermine the sale of his own book. He immediately wrote a stinging letter to Rutter, accusing him of being dishonourable as a tradesman for planning this publication when he knew that he already had a volume on the drawing boards. Under the circumstances, Britton felt badly undercut and faced with the potential of financial disaster if he could not recoup the money he had already invested. Things became worse when he discovered that Cattermole and Higham had also been hired to contribute to Rutter's book, which helps to explain some of Britton's bad feelings towards Cattermole and perhaps his dissatisfaction with his work. The correspondence on this matter reveals that Britton resorted to acts of desperation by trying to enlist the aid of others in placing road blocks in Rutter's way. He started with Chevalier Franchi and tried to convince him to prevent the promotion of Rutter's book at the Abbey. Franchi refused but tried to placate Britton with encouraging words regarding Beckford's support. 'I can't prevent the sale at the Abbey of Mr. Rutter's Descriptions & advertisements', Franchi wrote. 'As for plans & views, perhaps he has already stuffing enough for all his purposes. You know how active he is. However his work, I think, will never be sanctioned or encouraged by M[onsieur] Beckford '.[51]

The situation for Britton worsened when Farquhar bought the estate because Rutter was then granted free access to the Abbey. The thought of Rutter being granted this privilege rankled Britton, and he hoped Franchi would come to his aid. But, once again, Franchi reported that he had little control over the matter: 'I have seen several persons here making drawings for Rutter & some very good. Rutter has permission from Mr. Farquhar to do as many as he likes—therefore I could not interpose in any way his progress—he appears very sanguine upon the results'.[52]

Franchi's comment conveying Rutter's optimism about his book must have stung Britton. He went on to express to a number of correspondents his bitterness over Rutter's intrusion into his perceived publishing territory, but not all were sympathetic. Richard Colt Hoare, for example, did not feel that Britton's grumbling was justified. He reminded Britton that the quality of the final work is what really mattered and that he intended to buy both books. 'I think you are not warranted to complain in such bitter terms as I hear you have done', he wrote, 'as to myself, I shall take *both*, & whichever is the *best*, will succeed *best*'.[53]

Britton's book finally appeared at the end of August in 1823 as a limited subscription edition of 806 copies, including six in royal folio, 300 imperial quarto and 500 medium quarto. He offered the six royal folio copies to Beckford, including one with the original drawings bound in. In the end, Britton sold the entire edition but not without leaving some wreckage of personal relationships behind. It is perhaps a mark of the differences between the two rivals that in Rutter's case the artist C. F. Porden and publisher Charles Knight gave Rutter a 'Congratulatory Dinner' at the New London Hotel, Bridge Street, on 22 October 1823, in celebration of the publication of his Fonthill book and 'to express their sense of the liberal manner in which he has acted to all parties'.[54] Britton, on the other hand, issued his own invitation for a celebratory dinner on 19 January 1824 at the same hotel.[55] Cattermole was not on the invitation list. Of the sixteen people who attended, most were booksellers or magazine editors. The artists who contributed to his work either were not invited or did not attend.[56]

While Britton was a well-known figure in England, Rutter was new on the scene, a young upstart of twenty-seven, brought up as a Quaker, who entered the book selling and printing business in Shaftesbury in 1818. It is not known precisely when he met Beckford, but it had to be before he brought out his first guide book for the Christie sale in 1822. He did indicate in the Preface to *Delineations of Fonthill and its Abbey* that 'from the earliest hour that the interesting mansion which is the subject of the following pages, became accessible to the world, the author felt a dawning ambition to prepare a description of it for the public eye' and that he actually visited the estate 'at a time when the rarity of such permissions made it more than an ordinary favour', which suggests the possibility of access earlier than 1822.[57] Because new rooms were opened for the 1823 sale and some rearrangements of the contents made under Farquhar's direction, Rutter brought out a new portable guide book for the occasion that reflected these changes, thereby continuing to demonstrate his entrepreneurial skills and laying additional groundwork for his *magnum opus* on Fonthill.

A question arises regarding Rutter as to how much information in his book was directly from Beckford. Boyd Alexander believed, for example, that the material in Chapter IV, dealing with the description of the grounds within the barrier wall, came from direct contact with Beckford. He felt that Rutter would not otherwise have known the literary quotations from Tasso, Chaucer, and Uvedale Price used in that chapter. Furthermore, Rutter used the same six lines from *Paradise Lost* that Beckford had recited to Henri Meister in 1793.[58] If this is the case, then Rutter's book becomes a very important document as a primary source of evidence for Beckford's original conceptions of Fonthill. Beckford's friend Chevalier Franchi, and particularly the scholarly Abbé Macquin, must have played important roles as additional sources of information as satellite figures for Beckford. It was Macquin, as we have noted, who wrote and published a series of four papers and a long poem on Fonthill in the *Literary Gazette* in 1822. It is also interesting that a Latin epigram on Fonthill that Macquin included in his third paper was quoted by Rutter on the title page of his abbreviated guide books to Fonthill in 1822 and 1823. Beltz provided the genealogical information for the volume. Sir Richard Colt Hoare was the source for the historical material on the manor of Fonthill Gifford, while Farquhar allowed Rutter ready access to the Abbey for observation and study. Just prior to publication, Rutter was also granted access to Wyatt's papers, plans, and memoranda which enabled him to include in Appendix B the important piece on the 'Origin and Progress of Fonthill Abbey'.[59] Rutter's knowledge of architecture was admittedly limited, but here again he sought help by enlisting the aid of Stedman Whitwell who provided the necessary professional assistance. Whitwell was an experienced architect who had designed Brampton Park in the Gothic style for Lady Olivia Sparrow in 1820-21.

Still, Rutter was not without his own capabilities and expertise which were brought to bear on the production of this elegant guide book, particularly in the area of topography in which he had a professional interest. It is noteworthy in this regard that he wrote and published other guide books, including an *Historical and Descriptive Sketch of Wardour Castle and Demesne* in 1822, the *Westonian Guide* in 1828 and *A Guide to Clevedon* and *Delineations of North-West Somersetshire*, both in 1829.

By all accounts, Rutter produced a better book than Britton. Rutter seems to have appreciated the dominance of Fonthill's pictorial impact. He therefore interleaved his descriptive text with thirteen engraved illustrations, three of which were in colour, but then added fifteen wood-cut vignettes illustrating special points of interest inside the Abbey, such as the arranged group of virtu which included the attributed 'Cellini' ewer, the silver lamp in the Oratory, and the corbel of the South Oriel as well the Fountain Court, the American gardens, the entrance gateway to old Fonthill and other architectural elements in the grounds outside the Abbey. Cattermole and Martin, serving no particular master, also made contributions to Rutter's volume, though different perspectives from what appeared in Britton's work. This time Martin provided a dramatic north-west view of the Abbey from the end of the Clerk's Walk, set off by a background of turbulent clouds. Cattermole reversed his perspective of the interior of the Great Western Hall capturing the majestic vertical thrust to the baronial ceiling that visitors experienced as they passed through the massive doors of the entrance. His other work, a distant view of the Abbey from Beacon Terrace, seemed placid in comparison to Martin's more romantic depiction from the same perspective in Britton's *Illustrations of Fonthill*. Rutter employed two lesser-known artists, C. F. Porden and W. Finley, who contributed impressive works that added graphic richness to the volume. In particular, Porden's drawing of the King Edward's Gallery and Finley's interior of St Michael's Gallery, both in colour with the engraving of the one and etching of the other by John Cleghorn, stood out in terms of artistic quality. Among the engravers Rutter utilised, William Hughes was considered to be one of the most prominent wood engravers of the time, having done previous work for *Dibdin's Bibliographical Decameron* (1817) and Ottley's *History of Engraving* (1816). Responsible for most of the vignettes, Hughes was well known for his careful and precise execution. One of the most valuable aspects of Rutter's book, however, was the fold-map of the Fonthill domain surveyed by S. Paull, drawn on stone by B. R. Baker, and printed by T. Boosey of London. Here Rutter provided a detailed display of all of the central features, walks, and rides of Fonthill, leaving an invaluable historical record of the original layout of the entire estate.

The quality of the graphic work was praised by contemporary reviewers and seen as superior to Britton's book in terms of the execution and the subject matter. Britton recognised, though grudgingly, that his own work did not measure up to Rutter's, as he wrote to Beckford: 'I presume you have seen the modest Quaker's book. I cannot doubt but *you readily* perceive its merits & defects. It surpasses my expectations in many points … Though mine shrinks by its side in quality of paper, quantity of Engravings & printing, I hope it will not lose by comparison in matter or manner. Some of its plates are also much better & *all* should have been so had my Artist done his duty'. Beckford's response was very brief, noting that he had seen the 'Quaker's grand Catalogue' and, then in an apparent attempt to muster something negative as a sop to Britton, explained that he found it at times too methodical in its treatment—'in some parts furiously *de raisonné*'.[60]

Unfortunately for Britton, the body of Rutter's work—both in 'matter or manner'—turned out to be more skillfully handled, better organised and more comprehensive in treatment. It was an advantage that Rutter achieved by keeping the reader in mind as he prepared his work. He divided his material into roughly six major parts beginning with a description of the approaches to the estate travelling the roads from London, Bath and Shaftesbury and noting at what points the Abbey could be seen from a great distance. Following the Great Western Road from London, for example, Rutter noted that just outside Salisbury the Abbey could be seen from a distance of almost twenty miles 'as an object of extraordinary height and magnitude, rising out of the side of one of the highest hills on the horizon' (p. 2).

Part two of the book was devoted to a description of the interior of the building. Here Rutter provided a descriptive account of each room in a systematic manner, but separated general commentary from the specific details respecting the architecture, furniture, pictures and heraldic ornaments of each room. It was a novel approach that subdivided the technical, decorative and historical matters under the headings of A (Architecture), F (Furniture), P (Paintings), and H (Heraldry), thereby allowing reader the option of reading the running account of the various rooms without being diverted by genealogical symbols and other specific details. Part three directed the visitor to examine the exterior of the Abbey from different vantage points, both close-up and from distant points on the grounds. Part four consisted of a detailed description of the grounds inside and outside the barrier wall, concluding with the grand ride around the entire domain of Fonthill. Rutter then concluded his account with parts five and six devoted respectively to historical information on the building of the Abbey and the former Fonthill mansions and ended with the inclusion of the genealogical tables based on Beltz's research.

Rutter's treatment of the architectural merits of Fonthill Abbey, derived to a great extent from Whitwell, was more balanced than Britton's by offering criticism from time to time. In his description of the Oak Parlour, for example, he observed that the general impression of it was 'rather unpleasing, from a want of proportionate height in the ceiling and windows; from a deficiency of harmony between the cold pink ground and pale yellow mouldings of the ceiling, compared with the warm and rich colour of the wainscoting of the walls; and from a discrepancy in the style of this wainscoting, and the pointed heads and tracery of the windows' (p. 11). He also made some suggestions for improvement ('if the Tribune were re-opened into the Chintz Boudoir, what still more extraordinary emotions would agitate a spectator entering from the Western Lawn' (p. 62). But then he praised the architectural accomplishment of the Oratory, Great Western Hall, and the Southern Oriel and singled out the Grand Saloon for its incomparable artistic effects: 'In one or two royal palaces in the world, there may be single scenes of greater extent and grandeur, than any one at

Fonthill Abbey; but among them all, has Invention yet produced any thing to be compared with the grand Saloon, its four-fold vistas, its purple light, and superb altitude!' (p. 62).

Aware that some criticism of the interior of the Abbey had indicated that it suffered from too much compositional variety that undermined a unity of effect, Rutter argued that architectural irregularities were inherent in the Gothic style as it developed over time and that 'additions of successive ages in their own characteristic styles are to be found in all of them' (p. 64). Moreover, while admitting that Fonthill was an example of revival Gothic, Rutter did not believe that it should be judged entirely as an imitative work. 'There is', he wrote, 'no sickly affectation of fidelity', or slavish adherence to pre-existing models. So Rutter ended up concurring with Britton that Fonthill was too unique to be judged by common rules: 'The Abbey is no *Frankenstein*, built up of the actual head of one individual, the arms of another, and the body of a third, forming a disgusting and unnatural whole. There is a tower; but it is not the tower, *faithfully copied*, of Canterbury, nor of Gloucester, nor of any tower extant. Its interior is in the ecclesiastical manner, as decidedly as that of any Abbey existing; but where is its exact prototype? Confessionals, and Sanctuaries, and Oratories, have been raised over all Christendom; but when before did genius so temper the light, and conduct the perspective? When did taste so spread the decorations with such inimitable effect! St. Anthony might have had lodgings of larger dimensions at Padua, but he was certainly "enshrined" at Fonthill' (pp. 64-5). Consequently, Rutter placed Fonthill within the context of Romantic aesthetics by believing that as a work of domestic architecture Fonthill was unsurpassed in its originality and that, when contemplated, stimulated emotions 'that have never been excited by any building erected by any private individual in our times' (p. 78).

Moving from a discussion of Fonthill Abbey as an architectural achievement, Rutter once again surpasses Britton's account by emphasising Beckford's view of Fonthill as a landscape garden governed by the principles of England's picturesque movement. Employing with frequency such controlling terms as *picture, composition, balance, breadth of chiaroscuro, light and shade, perspective, middle distance*, and *line of horizon* implied that the rendering of Fonthill was closely allied to the technique of landscape painting. And when he wrote that the most 'picturesque view' of the Abbey was obtained from Beacon Terrace, where 'the great masses from this point, under favourable circumstances of light, have a sufficiently intelligible outline, notwithstanding the excessive intricacy of the detail', and went on to complain that, though the general effect was magnificent, there was 'a want of balance, harmony, and keeping in the great masses; no breadth of chiaroscuro, no repose, but a uniform sparkling of light from the number of facettes into which the surface is cut', he was stressing essentially an assessment of Fonthill as a picture (p. 78).

So closely was Fonthill allied to landscape painting in Rutter's mind that at times his descriptions could easily be applied to a work on a canvas. He wrote, for example, of the Nine Miles Walk: 'The effects of light and shade … give the utmost richness and grace to the broad masses of hanging wood, and the occasional bursts of the distant landscape' (pp. 84-5). In his analysis of the ingredients of the garden plan, furthermore, he continued the connection between the two arts by observing the variations of line in the undulating or rugged surface, the varied tints and textures inherent in the smooth and rough lawns, the long perspective of the avenues leading to a terminal object, and the contrast of tone and verticality in the succession of dark pine and white birch, tall ash and short hawthorn (p. 86).

It was no coincidence, furthermore, when Rutter made references to Price's *Essay on the Picturesque* to illustrate Beckford's work at Fonthill. Beckford was as familiar with Price's work as he was with the works of the major garden theorists of the seventeenth and eighteenth centuries. Parallels between Price's theory and the Fonthill landscape design have already been noted, but Rutter's use of the phrase 'general character of the place' in his survey of the Fonthill grounds is equally significant in light of the evolution of the picturesque gardening movement. By not finding any discrepancy in the general character of Fonthill, he was in effect confirming that Beckford had achieved a unity of design through a careful subordination of parts to a whole—a basic tenet of mature landscape design. This was the implication of his following observations:

The ornamented grounds of Fonthill, though unequalled in extent, contain very few objects that will admit of individual description. The great principle upon which this labyrinth of groves has been constructed, is that of exhibiting an union of the wildest and the most ornamented scenery,—the picturesque and the beautiful, in close society. (p. 83)

The union of garden and the grove is almost universal; and it is impossible to imagine a more charming feature of the place, or one which more clearly indicates the care with which its scenery has been created, and almost matured, by one tasteful possessor (p. 84).

Rutter appeared to be aware that the subordination of detail to a general theme was the key to landscape composition and believed that the Abbey and its adjoining buildings were integral features of the garden plan and in harmony with it. 'In the greater number of walks about Fonthill', he wrote,

... we have felt strongly impressed with the care by which the buildings of the Abbey have been made to harmonise with the general scenery. In this particular, we know no modern erection which deserves such unqalified praise. We too often behold our ordinary builders abandoning the character of *l'architecto pittore*, and preparing their elevations without the slightest notice of their relation to the general landscape. It is not so at Fonthill. The Abbey and its accompanying scenery were produced under the direction of one superintending mind; the building, therefore, and its surrounding woods have an equal character of security and seclusion. We feel, in our romantic moods, that the Abbey is a place dedicated in its grandeur to the most impressive of religions'(pp. 86-7).

It was unity of design that led Rutter to conclude finally that the 'grounds of Fonthill exhibit the true spirit of English gardening carried to its utmost extent of a bold and varied simplicity' (p. 84).

J. C. Loudon visited Fonthill in 1807 and in 1833 to examine the Abbey estate for its merits as a landscape garden. Besides being a landscape gardener himself, he had studied the works of the popular eighteenth-century landscapists and understood the development of the theory of the English informal garden from Sir William Temple and Batty Langley to Repton and Price. His belief that 'the principles of landscape-gardening' were 'derived from nature, as developed by the principles of landscape painting; and, as recognised by a poetic mind, or a mind alive to those general beauties or associations universally felt in civilised society', exhibited their influence.[61] His *Encyclopedia of Gardening*, an invaluable historical record for students in the field, first appeared in 1822. From 1826 to his death in 1842, he published the monthly *Gardener's Magazine*, and in 1842 he edited the *Encyclopedia of Trees and Shrubs* and an edition of Repton's *Sketches and Hints on Landscape-Gardening*.

It was in the September issue of the *Gardener's Magazine* in 1835 that he published his findings on Fonthill. In Loudon's judgement, Fonthill was more than a work of architecture, but a modern example of an English landscape garden that brought together a taste for the picturesque with a taste for the Gothic as a unified composition. 'This place', he began, 'well deserves to be visited by every person who takes an interest respecting, or is desirous of improving himself in, landscape-gardening; because it is the only one in England, in which he will find the most perfect unity of character preserved throughout the grounds'.[62] The term 'character', as he applied Loudon here, was synonymous with a controlling theme or underlying design to which all parts related in order to produce a unified composition. He then proceeded to identify the 'character' of Fonthill as 'belonging to an age long since past in this country, and only now to be found in certain mountainous regions of Catholic countries on the Continent. The chief object of Mr. Beckford seems to have been to impress this character on all the great leading features of Fonthill' (pp. 441-2). Again, as Loudon approached from the open downs on the Hindon side, he observed that 'the occasional glimpses caught of Fonthill … surrounded by woods and without a single human habitation, a fence, or a made road appearing in the landscape, convey to a stranger a correct impression of the character of the place; viz, that of a monastic building in a wild, hilly, and thinly inhabited country, such as we may imagine to have existed three or four centuries ago' (p. 441).

To obtain the best impression of the Abbey and its surrounding scenery, Loudon felt that it was necessary to approach the scene from the Stone Gate at the end of the Great Western Avenue. As he walked up the main avenue leading to the Abbey, he was moved by the 'solemn solitary grandeur of this scene', recalling 'the associations which we have formed of monasteries in alpine countries'. He found the use of turf particularly suitable to the design: 'This avenue is naturally of that fine close turf peculiar to elevated regions and chalky soils; and, in Mr. Beckford's time, it was kept smoothly shaven: the work being always performed during the night, in order that the prevailing character of solitariness might not be interrupted during the day' (p. 442). Near the Abbey, the avenue widened, leaving a broad area in front that was broken by scattered trees so as to appear as 'having been cleared by the founders of the abbey from the native forest'. 'At the distance of a few yards, there was a range of humble sheds, in which workmen of different kinds were employed, hewing and carving for continuous additions of improvements; and this was also quite in character with the scene, as such was often the case with ancient monastic establishments' (p. 443). In short, everywhere Loudon looked throughout the estate—the paths, drives and gardens—he saw evidence of naturalistic design carried out on such a large scale and in such a free manner 'as never once to excite the idea of art or formality'. Loudon continued to make these observations as he walked about the entire estate, until, finally, he concluded: 'We admire in Mr. Beckford his vivid imagination and cultivated mind, and that good taste in landscape-gardening which produced the perfect unity of character which pervades the grounds at Fonthill' (p. 449).

Surviving as a Romantic Icon

Almost fifty years before Fonthill, Horace Walpole set up Strawberry Hill as a model for the Gothic style, but it was tame by comparison to Fonthill, partly because Walpole had an 'Augustan core', as Kenneth Clark noted, while Beckford possessed a greater penchant for risk-taking that enabled him to transcend the classic habit of mind. Beckford himself believed in Fonthill's superiority in the sense of its more dramatic public appeal and immense theatricality, calling Strawberry Hill by comparison a 'miserable child's box—a species of gothic mousetrap—a reflection of Walpole's littleness'.[1] Even Charles Eastlake, at the high point of interest in Victorian ecclesiology and the re-creation of authentic Gothic structures in England, concluded that Fonthill 'for its size, eccentricity of character and bold adaption of Gothic form was unequalled in importance by any which had preceded it'.[2] James Fergusson, fellow of the Royal Institute of British Architects, concluded similarly in 1862 that, despite all its faults, Fonthill Abbey was the 'most successful Gothic building of its day, more Medieval in the picturesque irregularity of its outline, more Gothic in the correctness of its details, than any which had then been erected'.[3]

The appraisals of Fonthill by Eastlake and Fergusson gave it an important place in the history of the revival of medieval design in domestic buildings in nineteenth-century England. But today there is a growing tendency to view Beckford's Fonthill as it was originally conceived—as an artistic *tout ensemble*—more than a work of architecture and more than a landscape garden. The large body of original essays and poems that it inspired during the period of its existence constitute an important historical record of the popularity of Fonthill and the extent and impact of Beckford's artistic achievement. Equally important are the numerous engraved 'views' which appeared in the guide books, periodicals and other descriptive accounts of the period. They provide a visual record of Fonthill and help to account for its persistence as a romantic icon. Examining both the iconographic and written records provides an opportunity for a more objective and holistic assessment of Fonthill as a work of art even though it no longer exists in its original form.

With the contemporary historical record missing, the critical assessment of Fonthill in the first half of the twentieth century has often been limited in perspective, focusing on the exotic character of the Abbey building, while neglecting the contents and the grounds, or on the personal and moral eccentricities of Beckford, without attending to his artistic accomplishment. Since the revival of interest in Beckford in the early 1900s, it has become almost a fashion among modern critics to be dismissive in their treatment of Fonthill. Thus Charles Whibley in the *Pageantry of Life* in 1900 characterised Fonthill as a capital example of 'insensate grandeur' and the 'monstrous Abbey' as 'an orgy of reckless Gothic'.[4] Margaret Jourdain, after quoting Whibley in her essay in *Memorials of Old Wiltshire* in 1906, argued that 'the creation of [Beckford's] extravagance, only too literally the "basic fabric" of a vision, left no trace behind it, and is hence of no more interest to us today than Nonesuch, another "Palace of Delight"'.[5] In *The Drift of Romanticism*, Paul E. More concluded in 1913 that Fonthill was obviously the result of an attempt to satisfy a 'whimsical taste' and a 'disorganised fancy',[6] while Guy Chapman, one of Beckford's biographers, dismissed the Abbey in 1928 as 'one of the more striking monuments to man's vanity and presumption'.[7] These were harsh judgements, to be sure, but perhaps the most severe attack was lodged by John Steegman, who in *The Rule of Taste* in 1936 omitted mention of the Fonthill landscape and condemned the building as an illustration of architectural sterility. 'Fonthill gave birth to nothing', he wrote, 'and … its features passed out of mind'. It was 'an unexpected treasure-trove carried in on the tide of romanticism and crumbling as it struck the shore'.[8]

Typical of another kind of criticism that has contributed to the widespread impression that Fonthill is not worthy of serious consideration as an artistic work, was one voiced in 1954 by a writer who, after a visit to the grounds, made her evaluation with Beckford's moral character clearly in mind:

> As I crossed the wilderness of human wastefulness over which time and nature have drawn a decent pall, I could well believe the astonishing tales I had heard in the village of William Beckford and his palace, stories even more fantastic than appear in the textbooks but none the less likely to be true, and it was with something like relief that I turned away down the long drive and, back again in Tisbury, entered the clean, sweet atmosphere of its noble church.[9]

It is no coincidence that this same article opened with Hazlitt's denunciation of the Abbey and its contents as worthless and trivial. With only traces of the original design left and a fragment of the original structure, Hazlitt's dissenting voice has been and remains strong and influential.

An exception to this tendency to marginalise Fonthill was Kenneth Clark's pioneer book on the Gothic revival which first appeared in 1928. Clark tended to see Fonthill as an important expression of Romanticism in the 1790s and the 'epitome of eighteenth-century Gothic'. His concentration was less on the archaeological purity of the Abbey than on the 'effect' it had on the viewer and, in this sense, he judged it as a major achievement ranking with other important examples of romantic art of the time:

> All that the eighteenth century demanded from Gothic—unimpeded perspectives, immense height, the sublime, in short—was present in Fonthill, and present more

lavishly, perhaps, than in real medieval buildings. Even we, who pride ourselves on classicism, cannot be quite dead to this sudden outburst of romantic rhetoric. We know very well that the plaster tower is mere trumpery, but its sudden vehemence sweeps away our judgement; as Berlioz may suddenly sweep us away from Haydn, and El Greco's nightmare vision of Toledo seduce our eyes from the judicious Poussin.[10]

Clark also understood that Fonthill was influential in the Gothic revival because of the fascination with Beckford the man. In the eyes of the public, Beckford had mythical status and the personal appeal of a romantic outsider. They were interested in him as an aloof, glamorous figure who had committed an unpardonable sin that served, among other things, to illustrate his unconventionality and enhance his appeal. Not surprisingly, there were contemporaries who saw him as the prototype for Byron's Childe Harold. In one of the most candid statements he ever made about the poet, Beckford understood the basis for the comparison but felt that he was more of an outsider than even Byron:

> I really fancy Byron must have taken it into his head to model himself after my gloomy, magnificent Vathek—some perhaps might say after his gloomy parent. There is certainly thorough sarcasm and cynicism enough about both, which might lead some to think the same blood boils in our veins. He delighted in giving defiance to the whole world and God knows I have done by best to defy it also, but I have done better than Byron for I have succeeded to my own satisfaction which he was never able to do.[11]

In Clark's view, Beckford's public persona of a man who stood apart from the world invested Fonthill with its own empowering character, because by 'involving Fonthill in mystery, he made it a brilliant advertisement for the Gothic style'.[12]

Clark's emphasis on the 'scenic effect' of Fonthill and its 'romantic rhetoric' helped to foster a broader view of Beckford's achievement in the twentieth century. One of the first efforts to claim a place for Fonthill in a wider artistic scheme was J. W. Oliver who published a biography of Beckford in 1932. Oliver argued that Fonthill Abbey should be considered as a 'magnificent feature in a magnificently conceived scheme of landscape gardening'.[13] He also placed Fonthill's landscape within the context of the aesthetics of the picturesque, and, while considering it extravagant, defended Beckford's work as the fashion of wealthy men of the age: 'Walpole's Strawberry Hill is an earlier example of the tendency, while Abbotsford is one of the latest, and Beckford should surely not be too severely ridiculed for succumbing to a weakness from which Scott himself, with all his sanity and humour, was not exempt' (p. 231).

H. A. N. Brockman's study of Fonthill, published in 1956 under the title *The Caliph of Fonthill*, helped to provide a more balanced and less defensive assessment for the second half of the twentieth century. Brockman brought his architectural background to bear on his examination of Fonthill. He found that Wyatt was successful in recreating the atmosphere of a medieval monastery and stressed the need to examine the building as part of a romantic landscape ('The jewel in the setting was magnificent') since he recognised that Beckford was devoted to the art of landscape gardening. He believed that the design of the Abbey was also successful as an illustration of revival Gothic with all the appearance of authentic medieval models. It could not be expected to be compared to its models in any true archaeological sense, but it represented for Brockman a break from the classical tradition and, though unsound as an architectural structure, possessed sufficient evocative power to align it with the new aesthetic trends of the Romantic age. As he concluded in his evaluation, 'the curious thing about it is that it really did *sing* as a building; it was frozen music of the most romantic and moving kind; it was, alone of all Wyatt's works, a thing of artistic genius.... Architecturally, it was wicked, but terribly attractive!' (pp. 183-4).

Anthony Dale, in his biography of Wyatt published in the same year as Brockman's work, also discussed the merits of Fonthill. He concluded similarly that its main virtues were scenic and that the Abbey was sufficiently realistic in detail to be the 'greatest Gothic production of the eighteenth century, to shout defiance at [Salisbury Cathedral] its medieval rival'.[14] Dale also noted that as a consequence of Wyatt's work on the Abbey he was able to extend its influence during his lifetime by carrying out commissions at Windsor Castle for George III, the Parliament buildings at Westminster, and Ashridge.

While Wyatt was heavily criticised for his many Gothic restorations during his lifetime, he has now achieved the status of a 'torch-bearer' of the revolution which led to the Gothic revival in England with Fonthill Abbey being considered the greatest of his achievements in the area of domestic Gothic.[15] Other students of the period have found traces of the influence of Fonthill Abbey in Hadlow Castle, Coleorton Hall, Highcliffe Castle, Toddington Manor, Kinfauns Castle, Ravensworth Castle, Childwall, Eastnor, Lowther, and Eaton Hall,[16] all of which demonstrates its architectural longevity and impact. Jeffrey Wyattville demonstrated the influence of Fonthill when he remodelled Windsor Castle, most evident in his design of the Grand Corridor with its striking resemblance to King Edward's Gallery. The entrance hall to the Earl of Shrewsbury's house, Alton Abbey, is another example of the Fonthill influence.

But Fonthill's most significant architectural legacy was in the reconstruction of the new Palace of Westminster following the fire of 1834 that destroyed the Old Palace buildings leaving behind Westminster Hall and the ruins of St Stephen's Chapel. The contemporary architect Charles Barry, with the aid of Augustus Pugin, an authority on the Gothic style, won the commission in 1835 for the construction of the new Palace that led to the creation of one of the world's finest examples of Gothic revival architecture. It is evident from their plan that Barry and Pugin had studied Fonthill Abbey. Its influence is most evident in Westminster's St Stephen's Hall with a flight of steps leading to the Octagonal Central Lobby from which focal point emanates two central corridors, one leading north to the House of Lords and the other south to the House of Commons. A comparison with Fonthill's Great Western Hall leading to the Grand Octagon from which radiated four wings reveals the striking resemblance between the two architectural schemes. The proportions of the Aye and No Lobbies in the Commons are also similar to Fonthill's King Edward's Gallery constituting a further tribute to the indelible impression of Fonthill on its time.[17]

Across the Atlantic, the American actor Edwin Forrest built a castle on the Hudson River in 1852 and called it Fonthill Castle. While not similar in the exterior design, Fonthill Castle did consist of six octagonal towers with the central tower enclosing an octagonal rotunda reminiscent of the central octagonal tower at Fonthill. Forrest owned a copy of Rutter's *Delineations of Fonthill and its Abbey* and used it as a guide for some of the interior design-work. This is evident in the fan vaulting of Forrest's drawing room, modelled after St Michael's Gallery, the oak webbing of the octagonal chamber, a bay window in the west side of the drawing room and in several other details.[18]

Boyd Alexander extended the discussion of Fonthill as a landscape garden in 1962, by illustrating how various aspects of the design of the grounds adhered to the principles of Uvedale Price's theory of the picturesque.[19] This treatment of Fonthill in a broader aesthetic context finally led to the inclusion of Fonthill in a history of gardens by Christopher Thacker in 1979. 'In practice', Thacker wrote, 'William Beckford … went furthest towards achieving a garden landscape which was wholly natural while remaining a garden'.[20] 'It marks the absolute limit of the English landscape garden', he continued, 'and from this point a return to less absolute and less deeply philosophical garden convictions occurs' (p. 222). More recent estimations are beginning to recognise that the formal composition of Fonthill includes three areas of consideration: the Abbey as a neo-Gothic structure, its landscape setting, and the sequence of interior scenic effects as the elements of a calculated artistic totality.[21]

In this study, we have added another dimension stressing that as a landscape Fonthill represented the 'picturesque style' in a deeper, more sophisticated sense than simply the reproduction of scenes from popular landscape paintings of the day. Fonthill was also an important example of the successful application of the technique of landscape painting to the field of landscape gardening because it was based on Beckford's own educated sense of composition and training. The natural elements of its layout were carefully massed and shaped into a harmonious whole according to the basic principles of composition in painting, and there was in the end a definite unity of design to which both Rutter and Loudon gave special attention. Everything contributed to the 'solemn, undisturbed tranquility' of its monastic theme: the high enclosure wall, the density of its woods and groves, the lake, the American plantation, the enclosed walks and drives, and the Abbey itself rising in splendid isolation as the diadem of the scene. The subordination of these details to a single theme was the keynote to the Fonthill composition.

There was also a planned coherence among the various parts of the entire garden scheme. Everywhere the garden melted into the glade, so that all the individual parts could be linked to form a harmonious whole. This was particularly evident, as we have seen, in the connection between the building and the outlying grounds where the wide, smooth, and almost unbroken lawn blended by degrees into the forest beyond. This gradual shift provided the 'insensible transition' so esteemed by the progressive gardening theorists. In addition, the irregular style of its Gothic architecture, the asymmetrical floor plan, and the layout of the interior galleries were all appropriate to the external landscape. The result was a focal point of interest to which all other elements were subordinate, a fine centrepiece in an elaborate landscape setting.

Fonthill as a landscape garden was an original creation personally attended to and conceived by Beckford. He felt it was 'the great work of his life'.[22] He understood the importance of studying the topography of the estate as a prologue to design, a fundamental principle of modern planning. There were other important aspects of the Fonthill design that deserve attention as well: the consistency of naturalistic effect through the careful concealment of art, the restoration of the status of the individual plant to the garden picture, the blending of the different parts of the scheme to form a unified and coherent whole, and the skillful management of such important ingredients as texture, form, colour, light and shade, to enliven the entire setting and provide the force of contrast. In these ways, Beckford's work at Fonthill represented a significant step towards modern design and was in this sense in advance of its age. 'Little had been said by the public about any part of Fonthill but the buildings', Redding wrote, 'yet were the beautiful grounds there nurtured by his taste as superior to the gardens of Versailles as St. James's is inferior to the French palace of that name. The grounds were marvellously fine, no expense being spared in keeping them. They covered nineteen hundred acres within the wall, with three thousand more around it'.[23]

It is unfortunate that Fonthill no longer exists in the original state which made such a powerful impression, imaginatively and aesthetically, on all who wandered within its precincts. But the fact that it did not last is no diminishment of Beckford's accomplishment. Dr Gustav Waagen, Director of the Royal Gallery at Berlin, and one of the most accomplished European art critics of the day, examined Beckford's collections in Bath, and discussed Fonthill with connoisseurs who had been there. When he left Bath, he recorded some very perceptive comments on the nature of the Fonthill experience as a total aesthetic immersion in a multidimensional artistic experience. He wrote:

On the whole, I came away with the conviction that Mr. Beckford unites, in a very rare degree, an immense fortune with a general and refined love of art and a highly cultivated taste. Such a man alone could have produced a creation like Fonthill Abbey, which, from the picture that I am now able to form of it, must have realised the impression of a fairy tale. The extensive Gothic building, with a lofty, very elegant tower, from the views which I have seen of it, must have had, in the highest degree, the grandly fantastic character by which this style of architecture exercises so wonderful a charm. Conceive the interior adorned with ... important works of art, with the most elegant and costly furniture; conceive it surrounded by all that the art of gardening in England can effect by the aid of a picturesquely-varied ground, luxuriant vegetation, and a great mass of natural running water; and you will have a general idea of this magic spot, which so far maintained this character that for a long time no strange foot was permitted to intrude. Accordingly, when Mr. Beckford ... resolved ... to sell it with all its contents, the fashionable and the unfashionable world flocked from all parts of England to wonder at this 'lion', the greatest that had long been exhibited.... Unhappily, Fonthill Abbey has resembled also in its transitory existence the frail creations of the world of enchantment'.[24]

Fonthill in the end was a 'frail creation of the world of enchantment', but interestingly its legacy has transcended the physical character of the Abbey, its magnificent setting, and the works of art within its walls. Despite all of the efforts to diminish its importance and to discredit it as a work of art, Fonthill has remained a fixed image in the minds of students of the Romantic period. It was a fantasy that became as real and as memorable as the works of Gothic fiction writers and the likes of such prominent Romantics as Coleridge, DeQuincey, and Edgar Allan Poe. Why this is so has something to do with the fascination with William Beckford the man, who possessed the allure of other great figures of wealth and singularity in history. In addition, Fonthill was bolder as an artistic totality, more adventurous than any similar work that preceded it. As an expression of Beckford's artistic taste, it was transgressive and rose to a higher order of aesthetic interest. It represented the new Romantic aesthetics that had its roots in Milton's own powerful inversion that gave rise to the beauty of outlaw daring and free expression. It had the appeal of a work that broke through boundaries. In the manner of Piranesi and John Martin, Beckford created a work of art that achieved the status of the monumental sublime, where elements of the extraordinary and the vast mingled to create expressions of awe and wonder and produced an indelible image that continues to hold an important place in realm of Romantic iconography now and for future generations.

Prominent Visitors to the Fonthill Abbey Estate in 1823

A'Court, Captain [Edward Henry], MP
Aberdeen, Earl of
Ackermann, [Rudolph]
Acland, Sir Thomas and Lady
Adare, Lord [Earl of Dunraven]
Alnutt, Mr
Althorpe, Colonel and Mrs
Arundel[l], Lord and Lady
Auckland, Lord
Bagshaw, Sir W.
Baker, Sir E. and Lady
Bankes, [Henry], Esq., MP, Corfe Castle
Barford, Lord
Baring, Alexander, Esq.
Baring, Francis, Esq., MP
Barnard, Mrs and Miss
Barry, Rev. Dr
Bath, Marquis of
Bebb, J[ohn], Esq. [Donnington Grove]
Belfour, J., Esq.
Bell, General
Belmore, Lord
Bench, William, Esq.
Bennet[t], Lady M.
Bennet[t], John, Esq., MP
Beresford, Lord
Biddulph, Captain
Bingham, Admiral and family
Bolton, Lord

Bosanquet, Mr and Mrs
Bradford, Earl and Countess of
Brecknock, [Earl of]
Brogden, [James], (Chairman of the Committees in the House of Commons)
Buckingham, Duke of
Burdett, Lady
Burford, Lord
Burgoyne, General
Burke, Colonel
Burrough, Sir James
Buxton, W., Esq., MP
Byng, G[eorge], Esq., MP and Mrs
Calcraft, [J. H.], Esq., MP
Callot, Rev. Dr
Calthorpe, Lord
Camden, Marquis
Cameron, General and Mrs
Carnarvon, Earl and Countess of
Cawdor, Lord and Lady
Chester, Bishop of
Cholmondeley, Mr
Clifford, Lord and Lady
Clive, Hon. Mr and Mrs
Clutterbuck, Mr and Mrs
Cobham, Mr and Miss
Cochrane, Hon. Mrs (purchaser by deputy)
Cockerill, John, Esq. and family
Cocks, the Hon. Somers and family

Coffin, Colonel [Pine]
Coffin, Rev.
Cohan, Rev. W. B.
Coventry, Hon. Mr and Mrs
Cuff, Rev. Mr
Cullum, Sir T[homas] and Lady
Currie, E.
d'Aglie, Count
Dalrymple, Sir H[ew]
Dashwood, Captain
Davis, Richard [Hart], Esq., MP
Delmar, Baron
Dering, Sir Edward, Bart.
Dibdin, Thomas F.
Digby, Lord
Dorchester, Lord
Drew, Colonel
Ducie, Lord and family
Duff, A., Esq.
East, Augustus and Lady
Ebrington, Lord and Lady
Egerton, Francis Esq., MP and Mrs
Ellenborough, Lord
Elston, Colonel
Essex, Earl of
Fawkes, Lady
Finch, Hon. Mr and Mrs
Fingall, Earl of
Fisher, [John, M. A.], Archdeacon [of Salisbury]
Fitzgerald, Sir James and Lady
Fitzhugh, Mr and Mrs
Forbes, Captain
Forbes, Hon. Mr
Foster, Major
Foulkes, Rev. Dr
Franchi, Gregorio
Franklyn, Sir William
Freemantle, Sir Thomas, MP
Gardner, Lady
Gordon, W[illiam], Esq., MP and Mrs
Gower, Lord F[rancis] Leveson, MP

Grant, Hon. Charles
Greenaway, G. C. and family
Grenfell, P[ascoe], Esq., MP
Grenville, Lord
Greville, Sir Charles
Grosvenor, Earl
Guildford, Countess of
Halden, General
Hammersley, Mr and Mrs
Hampson, Sir George and Lady
Harrison, Rev. Dr
Harvey, General
Harwood, Rev. Dr
Hasleigh, Lady
Haviland, Captain
Hawkins, [J. H.], Esq., MP
Haylett, MP
Hazlitt, William
Head, Rev. Sir John
Heber, Richard, Esq., MP
Herbert, Lady
Hereford, Bishop of
Heysham, Mr
Hoare, Henry
Hoare, Sir Richard Colt
Hodges, Mr (of Milbank)
Hodgson, General
Hoffender, Mr and Mrs
Homfrey, Captain
Howard de Walden, Lord
Hotham, Lord and Lady
Howard, Lady
Hurd, Philip
Hutchinson, Captain, RN
Ilchester, Lord
James, Sir Walter
Jolly, Colonel, the Recorder of London
Jones, I., Esq.
Kaye, Colonel
Kerr, Lord Henry
Kerry, Lord
Killeen, Lord and Lady

Kinnaird, D[ouglas]

Lansdowne, Marquis of (purchaser by deputy) and the Marchioness

Lennard, Sir T. B. and Lady

Leycester, Hugh, Esq.

Liverpool, Earl and Countess of

Lockhart, [John G.?] Mr and Mrs

London, Bishop of

Lucy, [George], Esq., MP

Macclesfield, Earl of

Mackintosh, Sir James

Macqueen, [Thomas] P., Esq., MP

Malet, Sir Alexander

Marryatt, [Joseph], Esq., MP

Marsett, Rev.

McDonald, Colonel

Mengden, Countess

Miles, P[hilip J.], Esq., MP [Leigh Court]

Miles, W[illiam] (from Bristol)

Millman, Lady

Montgomery, Mr (nephew of Earl of Pembroke)

Montmorency, Baron and Baroness

Moody, Captain

Moore, Thomas (the Poet)

Moorsom, Captain

Morgan, Sir Charles, Bart., MP

Murray, Hon. [John] and Mrs

Nepean, Sir Molyneux and Lady

Northcote, Sir Stafford

Northwick, Lord

Ogleby, Sir G.

Oldham, J. Esq.

Onslow, Sir Henry and Lady

Orde, General and Beckford's grand-daughters

Palmerston, Lord

Pares, Mr (business partner of Lord Mayor of London)

Parkinson, Colonel

Paulett, Lord H. and Lady

Paxton, Sir W[illiam], MP

Payne, Colonel and Mrs

Peel, Mr [Robert], (Home Secretary)

Peel, W[illiam, Esq. M. P.]

Pembroke, Earl and Countess of

Penruddock, J. H., Esq., MP

Percival, Rev. A.

Petty, Lord

Peyton, Captain

Phipps, Mr

Pole, Rev. Dr

Pole, Sir W[illiam Wellesley], Bart.

Pontesso, Marquis (from Madrid)

Porchester, Lord

Portman, [Edward Berkeley], Esq., MP

Powlett, General

Prevost, Rev. Dr

Price, Captain

Pringle, Sir J[ohn]

Prudhoe, Lord

Redesdale, Lord

Ricardo, R. Mr and Mrs

Rivers, Lord and Lady

Riversdale, Lord and Lady

Rochford, Earl of

Roden, Earl and Countess Dowager of

Rogers, [Samuel] (the Poet)

Ross, Sir P.

Roxburgh[e], Duchess of

Rumbold, [Charles E.], Esq., MP

Russell, [J.] Watts, Esq., MP

Sadler, Lt., RN

St. Germain, Lord and Lady

St. Quintin, E. H. Esq. and Mrs

Salisbury, Dean of [Hugh Nicolas Pearson]

Salisbury, Lord Bishop of [John Fisher, D. D.]

Sanganskow (two Russian Princes)

Scott, Sir Claude (purchaser by deputy)

Shuckburgh, Mr

Smith, Rev. Mr

Somerset, Duke and Duchess of

Somerset, the Ladies

Somerville, Lord and Lady.
Stair, Earl
Stanhope, Colonel
Steward, Captain
Steward, Lt. Colonel and Mrs
Stopford, Hon. I.
Stormont, Viscount
Stowell, Lord
Strode, Captain
Stuart, Hon. C.
Sturt, [Charles E.]
Symons, Major
Talbot, Sir George
Theobald, Mr, Esq.
Thynne, Lord John, MP
Torrens, Count and Countess
Trench, [Frederick W.], MP

Trotter, Sir Coutts and Lady
Ulston, Colonel
Verdunin, Count
Vivian, Colonel H.
Warren, Rev. Dr
Way, Rev. J.
White, Colonel
Wilder, Sir F[rancis] and Lady
Williams, Lady Hampden
Wilson, Sir Henry
Winchester, Bishop of
Woodcock, Rev. Dr
Wray, Sir. B., Bart.
Wrottesley, Sir John, MP
Wyndam, Wadham, Esq., MP
Wynn, Sir W. W., Bart. and Lady

The *Morning Chronicle* Articles on Fonthill by J. Sidney Taylor, 1823

J. Sidney Taylor (1795–1841) was born in Dublin in 1795, educated at Samuel White's academy in Dublin and then Trinity College, Dublin, where he gained some renown as a member of the college historical debating society and praised for his rhetorical abilities and deep knowledge of the great authors of English literature. He decided to pursue the legal profession and moved to London where he was called to the English bar by the society of the Middle Temple in 1824. To support himself initially, he became associated with the *Morning Chronicle* as a reporter under the editorship of John Black. He then went on to become editor of the *Morning Herald* before devoting his full-time interest to the legal profession where he distinguished himself.

As a journalist for the *Morning Chronicle*, he was assigned the task of covering the Fonthill sale of 1823 and wrote most of the articles that appeared in this newspaper during the period of the auction with the exception of the commentary by William Hazlitt, Thomas Dibdin [Isaac Littlebury], submissions from various readers, and two essays from an intriguing writer identified simply as 'An Artist'. Some of Taylor's articles on Fonthill were reprinted in part in *Selections from the Writings of the Late J. Sidney Taylor*, London, 1843, pp. 338-49. I have examined all of the articles in the *Morning Chronicle* published during this period, beginning with Taylor's arrival at the estate on 9 September 1823 to the conclusion of the sale in October. I provide here a selection of the more important critical observations he wrote, identifying my attributions with his name in square brackets to distinguish them from those that were identified shortly after his death in 1843. The process of identification was not difficult since Taylor had a very distinctive writing style, highly literate in character and usually combined with references to or quotations from the great writers of the past who inspired him. His collection of essays join the works of other contemporary writers—Hazlitt, Dibdin, Macquin, and Charles Knight—as some of the most important records of the sights and sounds of the experience of being there when Phillips raised his hammer to disperse the riches of Fonthill.

FONTHILL ABBEY, Sept. 9 1823 [By J. Sidney Taylor]

Today the sale of the superb Effects of this magnificent Establishment commenced. The fineness of the weather was highly favourable to the display of all the circumstances which invest the Abbey with so much interest and attraction. The serene and mellow radiance of a clear autumnal sun gave to the solemn architecture of Fonthill, and the deep scenery in which it is embosomed, the highest richness and variety of effect. At this season, while the luxuriant foliage of the trees is slightly receiving the tints of autumn, without exhibiting any of the appearance of decay, the impression made by the deep green solitudes, the mazy walks, the wild and sylvan retreats, is more in unison with the sombre and religious grandeur of the pile which they surround, than the livelier effects of a gayer period of the year. Notwithstanding the beauty of the morning however, the concourse of visitors was not so great as had been expected; but it was accounted for on the ground that an erroneous opinion had gone abroad of the view having closed in consequence of the commencement of the sale. There is no doubt, that had it not been for such a supposition, the number of equipages, which added brilliance and animation to the scene, would have been much augmented, and there would have been a greater profusion of beauty to give its last and consummate grace to a creation of human art, which seems to realise the fictions of Arabian enchantment. The public were informed that the Library would be taken first, but the rare and curious works were not among those enumerated for the first day's sale .... .

[Published 11 September 1823, p. 3. This is Taylor's first day on the estate. What followed in this first essay were some instructions from Phillips and some details about the books sold on the first day].

FONTHILL ABBEY, Sept. 10.—

Having reached this yesterday but a short time before the sale commenced, I had but a slight and imperfect glimpse of the Abbey and its curiosities, and had no opportunity of stating more than the general impression conveyed by a first and hasty view. I have seen but a small part yet of that which must be seen carefully to be well described. There have been so many loose and vague accounts of this extraordinary place published, that very conflicting opinions with respect to the merits of the building itself, and the value of its contents have been the result, as some have praised every thing without discrimination, and others have indulged in as lavish an expression of censure. Both parties err themselves, and their representations are calculated to lead others astray. There is here much indeed to be admired, much to feed and gratify curiosity, and even a more enlightened spirit of inquiry beyond the most sanguine expectation; but there is also room in the exercise of candid criticism, for the detection of occasional blemishes. But of these hereafter.

The country about this mansion of *vertû* would be worthy of the Temple of the Muses. It is not, indeed, of a bold and striking character. Its features are those of beauty, richness, and repose. It has an Arcadian aspect. The ground undulates in the most pleasing varieties: covered as it is with corn-fields and lawny prospects, skirted by plantations picturesquely disposed—the whole region prepares the traveller for the central attractions of the magnificent shrine of taste, to which so many lovers of art and votaries of fashion make a devoted pilgrimage, or a romantic excursion. At the present moment, the busy and glad occupations of the harvest give peculiar vivacity and interest to the adjacent scenery. Every where industry, animated by the unexpected benignity of the weather, is seen putting his sickle into the golden blade, or carrying away his sheaves rejoicing. There is on all sides cheerfulness, and the promise of abundance. It is under such circumstances that all who now visit the Abbey, approach its solemn battlements and mysterious shades. The distant view of its tower, rising majestically above dense ramparts of foliage, is a very imposing feature in the prospect. It wants, however, on a nearer view, the colouring of time, and the ivy wreaths, without which Gothic structures, however well executed, can never produce complete delusion. The whole building, when seen close, appears naked in contrast with the dark luxuriance of verdure that surrounds it, and does by no means harmonise with either the richness or the gloom, which sunshine or clouds throw upon the masses of wood, that overhang all its avenues.

The approach from Salisbury is through what is called, the Old Park, where stood the mansion of the late Alderman Beckford, one wing of which is still in existence, and, under the denomination of the Pavilion, furnishes accommodations to visitors. The carriage road through this park runs for some distance along the border of a very handsome lake, the sylvan scenery of which does great credit to the taste of the late proprietor. Indeed all the pleasure-grounds afford beautiful specimens of landscape gardening, in which nature has been as faithfully emulated as could be done by the combined efforts of judgment and expense. This route touches on the best points of view for seeing the Abbey by sudden and picturesque glimpses, allowed by the inequality of the ground, and the diversity of lawn and plantation. It also allows an opportunity of admiring what are called, the American Gardens, which give an idea of as deep and wild a solitude for their extent, as Pennsylvania itself could afford. But as the sale is now about to commence, and the black-letter spectacles are put on, I must turn from the peacefulness of lakes and woods to the amicable contents of the votaries of erudition, and reserve other remarks to my next communication.

[Published 12 September 1823, p. 3. Taylor's account of the second day's sale with selected details followed this article, bearing the title 'The Sale']

FONTHILL ABBEY, Sept. 11.—

How little and contemptible is the taste displayed in the vaunted Gardens of Versailles, compared with that which has formed these beautiful grounds, where the only ambition of art has been to follow nature. Here no absurd artifices remind us of the geometrical gardener, with his compasses and his diagram, binding and torturing all native charms, in one chain of ostentatious formality. Nature has not here, by barbarous refinement, been dislocated out of her proper graces; she does not appear tight-laced and in a hoop petticoat, without the merit of simplicity, or the fascination of true elegance. In the grounds of Fonthill, all beauty has been cultivated on so just a principle, that it seems the spontaneous effect of natural fertility. From the lighter sprinkling of verdure, to the deepest gloom of almost impervious foliage, all partakes of the freedom of untrained productions ; and whether 'by hill, or valley, fountain, or fresh shade', the votary of nature may feel himself under the influence of her acknowledged supremacy.

The diversity of situation and circumstance is also very great. Here are extent, repose, and majesty for the pencil of Claude; the rugged grandeur that would attract Rysdael, and the deep and savage wildness which suited the genius of Salvator. Here might Collins indulge in the dreams of fanciful enchantment; Gray soar upon the eagle wing of an ardent ambition; and the classic Thomson 'lie at large, and sing the glories of the circling year'. Though such is the character of the grounds, they do not seem to be known to the visitors in general, farther than they are compelled to become acquainted with them, in their drive to the Abbey. The latter is the great object of the public attention. *There* is the shrine of their idolatry, and for one person who would penetrate the romantic recesses of the woods, there are one hundred who express an exclusive anxiety with respect to the old china. A great number of the latter class of virtuosi have indeed been converted to an admiration of the books; but that is merely on the score of their exquisite binding, and in this respect, we have seen many old friends with new faces, so new and so handsome, that we doubt if Plato, or Tully, or Virgil came on earth again, they could be made to believe that their philosophy, eloquence, or poetry, which they sent into the world so unadorned, could ever have been so arrayed in purple and gold as to gain more converts by their outward glory, than by the spirit that animated them.

The Abbey is in the middle style of architecture, and its external character gives the impression that it was never originally contemplated as a whole, but is made up of parts, combined without much reference to general proportion and symmetry. The character is that of the Gothic Cathedral; but its martial battlements are at variance with the religious solemnity of the structure, and impair its otherwise tranquil effect. The style of execution is that of the middle Gothic—but to be in unison with the embellishments of the interior, it should have been finished in the florid style, and have been enriched with the most elaborate decorations of quaint devices and antique imagery. In fact any person who, being acquainted with the splendid remains of the Gothic style which still exist in this country, expects any thing admirable in the external view of Fonthill Abbey, will be disappointed. The workmanship of Westminster Abbey leaves it beyond all comparison in the background: and Salisbury Cathedral, in symmetry and execution, leaves it little claim to admiration But it is the charm of its grounds, and the embellishments of its interior, which are its real and exquisite sources of attraction. The former are at least equal to any of the kind which I have seen; the latter surpass all I could have conceived: but as the sale now commences, I shall again take up the subject....

A new attraction has been added to the Abbey by the erection of a fine organ, which is played during part of the day, and the effect is grand and impressive beyond description. The sounds revelling along the vaulted galleries and corridors give the sublimest aid of harmony to the other fascinations of the place. Last night the Marquess and Marchioness of Lansdown, Lord Petty, and a few private friends formed a party in the octagonal or grand saloon, and enjoyed, to a late hour, the full effect of music, under circumstances the most favourable to the highest pleasures of sense and imagination.

The organ was played by Mr. Goodall, who executed with great ability and success some of the pieces best adapted to this instrument for volume and variety of expression; 'The Storm', in particular, excited admiration; and the music of the witch scene in *Macbeth*, gave to the romantic character of the Abbey all the magic of 'sweet sounds'. The Noble Marquess and his friends passed the night in this place of ascetic seclusion … .

[Published13 September 1823, p. 3]

FONTHILL ABBEY, Sept. 13.—

It is now nearly ten o'clock at night—I am sitting alone in the Latimer Turret of Fonthill Abbey, the night dark, the wind high, and the trees disturbed by the hoarse spirit of the coming storm. In this sullen and starless night, my solitary candle, shooting its rays across the gloom from this elevated place, is, perhaps, the only luminous object that some benighted traveller sees above the leafy wilderness that once separated this mansion from the vulgar intrusion of the world; it is an extraordinary place to be erected in the short term of one man's existence, and be abandoned by him as a child satiated with a toy—a plaything which absorbed all his faculties, and absorbed nearly all his opulence. He is, indeed, an instance of the instability of human affections, where they are not connected with any principle of rational desire or moral improvement; he realises the oriental tale which you lately read of the monarch, who devoted his great power and inexhaustible treasures to the pursuit of happiness, but found that the effort to be happy only confirmed the insufficiency of all human enjoyment.

For my part, the grounds are the most gratifying, of all the objects of curiosity which this place contains, although the arrangements of the interior of the Abbey, the richness and variety of its decorations, the superb furniture, books, and above all, the profusion of exquisite *bijouterie* surpass all I ever saw, or could previously have conceived. After all, I prefer domestic comforts and its unobtrusive circumstances, to all the dreary magnificence of Fonthill. There are some views of the Abbey by moonlight, which are certainly of a very fine character. Last night we had a furious thunderstorm, which rocked the battlements, but this is a fine day, and full of autumnal effects.

[This appears to be a letter to unidentified friend and not one of the published articles]

FONTHILL ABBEY, Sept. 15.—

Having taken up my abode in the Pavilion, I soon found that I had put myself within that most direful implement of torture, a termagant woman's tongue—in fact, the landlady's voice was to be heard in the shrillest key of discord from the time that she got out of bed, until sleep again suspended the voluble engine of perpetual commotion. I have sat for hours trying to write about scenes of tranquil beauty and romantic solitude, during which, every idea that woods and glens could inspire was put to flight by an incessant rattle, worse to my ears than the tail of the rattle-snake: at last, I came in for my share, as one day the bed I had engaged in the morning was given to another, and on my return at night and remonstrating upon such conduct, I was saluted with such a volley of sounds as made me feel that nature had given the supremacy to the female sex, whenever they choose to exert it. This will account to you for what I state in the commencement of my letter, of writing in the Latimer Turret; for it is there I now sleep, and there I can look down, like a crow from the topmost branch of some lofty elm.

[The above paragraph is another private letter, followed below by an article that appeared in the *Morning Chronicle*]

Yesterday being Sunday, the barrier gates were closed to all public visitors. However the vicinity of the grounds was greatly enlivened by numerous parties of the inhabitants of Hindon, Tisbury, and other circumjacent places, who having been liberally admitted by Mr. Phillips on a former occasion to explore the windows of the Abbey, and to feast all the longings of their rustic curiosity, expected a repetition of the indulgence. The gates of Paradise were, however, closed against them. The solemn sentence was not to be revoked; yet, from the rising to the setting of the sun, many were the parties of lads and lasses, the hale and ruddy children of rural labour, with their shining Sunday faces and best apparel and looks of anxious interest, who wandered about the verdurous fence of this the Eden of their pilgrimage, without obtaining a glimpse of the treasures which they came prepared to stare at with all the eyes of an idolatrous astonishment. The groups which gave animation to the sylvan borders of the demesne, would have afforded much agreeable employment to the pencil of Teniers or Jan Staen, as they consoled themselves for their disappointment by various *fêtes champêtres*, in which cheese, ale and glances of tender meaning were the principal ingredients of pleasure, and no doubt to Sancho Panza himself, even in his way to the government of Barrataria, would have brought Dapple to a dead stop in admiration of a scene of such rational enchantment. The day shone about them with steady lustre. They made themselves as happy as they could be outside the bounds of Fonthill, whose sullen towers overlook the green retreats of their frugal hilarity, and the evening sun saw them depart in peace, not without 'casting many a longing lingering look behind'.

   At night I had an opportunity of seeing the effect of a serene and beautiful moonlight sky upon the Abbey, and the surrounding scenery. The objections to which the building is exposed, when lighted by the open day, no longer detracted from the full beauty of the prospect. The best point of view, I think, is from the opposite border of the lake in the American Gardens, where there is a better combination of circumstances for well composed picture of this kind, than any I have yet seen. The mellow lustre and broad shadows which fall upon the majestic towers, the rugged battlements, the shafted oriels, and arched recesses of the Abbey, destroy all the detail of those parts which, in the broad-day, appear confusedly heaped together, and force upon the spectator the idea of disproportion and incongruity. The antique form of the edifice takes its full effect both on the eye and the imagination. The newness of its colour is not then at variance with the ancient character, which its formation assumes. It does not seem to be an usurper upon the realms of antiquity, but a legitimate inheritor of the honours that are paid her. Entrenched in gloomy grandeur in its woody heights, tinged with the silvery flickering lights, which give a deeper tone to its solitude, and reflecting its broad masses in the calm transparency of the lake below, on which sometimes the wild bird raises his lonely cry—it seems the throne of ancient superstition, which has stood amid the storms of ages, and overlooked the revolutions of time.

In beholding this scene, I was reminded of the advice which the author of *The Lay of the Last Minstrel* gives to those who turn aside, for a moment, from the ordinary world to converse with the spirit of past times, in the ruins of Melrose Abbey :—

> If you would view fair Melrose aright,
> Go visit it by the pale moonlight;
> For the gay beams of lightsome day,
> Gild but to flout the ruins gray.

And surely if Melrose, with all the associations of romantic history clinging to its relicts, and interwoven with the verdure of its decay, *be too old* to be seen to advantage by the glare of daylight, Fonthill is *too new*. If such a light exhibits the venerable misery of the former too plainly, it also gives too palpable an exposure to the splendid novelty of the latter: moonlight invests both with a poetic attraction, which the day partly dissipates. It is under the softened radiance of such an hour as I describe, that cold philosophy will forget to triumph over the ruins of the one, or severe criticism abate the proud pretensions of the other.

Abbeys or the ruins of Abbeys are generally situate in valleys, or at least on plains surrounded by luxuriant woods. The view of them, as is the case with Vale Crucis, Tintern, and others, is romantic, tranquil, rich, but not commanding. In this respect the Abbey of Fonthill, when you once allow it the name, has a singular character and a decided advantage. The elevation on which it stands, makes it the great and prominent object in the midst of scenery which consists of many fine parts. It thus unites, as it were, seclusion with authority; and while it seems to withdraw from the surrounding world, as in conscious superiority, looks down upon it. Thus, a lofty sternness appears blended with a mysterious retirement, and—as in the character of Becket or Wolsey—the spectator does not know whether to admire most the real ambition, or the assumed sanctity.

I speak now of the Abbey as its impression was made under the influence of the moonlight, without retracting any objection which the view of its exterior presented to my mind in the plain light of day.

I also enjoyed the benefit of contrast last night in a high degree, as a violent thunderstorm came on, which shook the battlements of the abbey and overcast them with a depth of gloom sufficiently awful. The lightning flashing on the stained windows, and the rain falling in torrents, while the multitude of trees fluctuated like the ocean, produced a scene of terrific interest. Today is however very fine, and the number of visitors, mostly of the higher class, are taking advantage of the restored tranquillity of the elements, by traversing the galleries and pleasure grounds of Fonthill....

[Published 17 September 1823, p. 3. A paragraph followed listing the names of a few of the prominent visitors]

FONTHILL ABBEY, Sept. 19.—

I have had a moonlit walk some of the grounds which I had not seen before. Without much effort of the imagination, I might have supposed myself in the realms of King Oberon, and the delightful haunts of his aerial population. I confess myself an inordinate lover of such scenes. If my fair friend C—, and her sisters were here, I would teach them one accomplishment—that of gathering nuts in profusion.

M.—kindly lent me a horse, or rather a poney, and away I went, with one companion, to Shaftesbury. The road was very bad, full of loose stones, and the animal suddenly went into a devout posture upon the highway:—not content with kneeling, he absolutely prostrated himself with his forehead to the earth, in the true style of oriental adoration. I could not but follow so laudable an example, and over I went upon my head, with a spirit of humility which an Indian Faquir might view with admiration. Both of us suffered from the exploit—the poney's knees bore ample testimony to the fact—and I received a scratch across my forehead, an awkward injury on the bridge of the nose, and a contusion near my hip. There was a troop of Wiltshire people, men and women, coming up. I was rolled over and over in dust, and my face disfigured with blood,—yet they passed with the most perfect indifference, and I did not know where to get water to wash my face, until a travelling pedlar assisted me to it. A stranger under such circumstances would not have been so treated among the 'savages' of Ireland. Since then, I most narrowly escaped being bitten by an adder in the delightful American Gardens.

[Another private letter]

FONTHILL ABBEY, Sept. 24—[By J. Sidney Taylor]

... Although among the books already disposed of a Fonthill there were not many to gratify the mere bibliomaniast, yet there were some which antiquarianism cold not fail to reverence. Pope's sarcasm could not, indeed, be applicable to Mr. Beckford, as a collector—'In books, not authors, curious was my Lord'. Still he had some works, the names of whose authors the world did not trouble its memory with, and yet their contents were no destitute of interest. The most remarkable were the illuminated Manuscripts, Missals, &c., one of which, for instance, contains the military ordinances of Charles the Bold, Duke of Burgundy, and Brabant, the fierce rival in arms and policy of Louis the Eleventh of France. This code of military regulations appears to have been drawn up under his immediate direction, and was no doubt a work of considerable importance in that day. It has all the appearance of having been deposited with peculiar care in the archives of a palace. It contains a very superior specimen of illuminated illustration, evidently the work of one of the most ingenious artists in that style of decoration.

The subject seems to be Charles the Bold, sitting in state in the midst of his Peers, great Officers, and Clergy, receiving the presentation of a book, which, from the peculiarity of its binding and shape, appears to be the very one which contains the picture. The design and execution of this subject is superior to what I have generally seen in illuminated writings. The figures have some claim to drawing; the expression, though in the most minute style of miniature, has a great deal of character, and the rich and elaborate finish has still a sparking freshness, which unhappily many of the nobler works of art since that period have totally lost. Charles himself is arrayed in cloth of gold, and the various robes of office and distinctions of costume are given with as nice a fidelity as they could receive from the pencil of Gerard Douw or Wilkie, The cieling [*sic*] of the chamber afforded Mr. Beckford the model of that of one of his splendid rooms.—

The book is upon fine vellum, richly bound in crimson velvet, with embossed gildings, and in excellent preservation. Among the *Missals*, there is one, the labour expended in the ornamenting of which may be easily supposed to have consumed the whole life of an artist, though it were extended to that of an ancient Patriarch. Here are the lives of the Saints and the whole of the mysteries of the Gospel set forth as a painted sermon, in which the rhetoric of the pencil glows in the most florid style of captivation. It presents, in fact, a Gallery of Scriptural Paintings on a miniature scale, in which, setting aside drawing, perspective, design, and all the heathenish graces of composition, there is much to gratify the inspection of the curious. The[re] is also a contempt of chronological order, which shews that the work was intended for something very different from a religious almanack. For instance, Christ appears before Pilote, and is afterwards seen in the Manger; and the Crucifixion precedes the Slaughter of the Innocents. Useful hints might, however, be derived by mythological painters, from the manner in which the subjects are treated. In the Nativity we see the Holy Virgin in the stable-yard of an inn, clothed in a superb dress of ultra marine and gold, kneeling with her hands clasped, contemplating the mysterious child that lies uncovered on the verdant grass. Joseph, attired in blue and purple, is also in the attitude of adoration; behind him are a donkey and a cow, much more original than those of Cuyp or Paul Potter, regaling themselves at the manger; and from the part of the stable behind the Virgin is suspended a curtain of scarlet richly embroidered with gold. From the child's body golden rays emanate, which may have suggested to Corregio the idea of making the body of the infant Christ luminous, which he has done in his *Nativity*. Here is also given the combat between the Archangel Michael and Satan, in a manner far more unique that that in which Milton sung or Flaxman sculptured the same terrific subject. The Devil is represented not black according to the vulgar notion, but of a delicate brown, as if but half roasted; he has neither horns nor tail, but shakes an enormous length of ears, and, extended on the green turf, receives with remarkable quietness the spear of Michael in his obdurate heart. He is naked, while Michael has on the whole armour of righteous, consisting of a Dutch breeches, gold epaulettes, and pink wings.

In another design St. Peter is represented walking on the sea, and endeavouring to preserve his equilibrium by balancing a long pole like a rope-dancer. Another Apostle is standing on the shore, and in the middle of the noon day kindly holding out to his sinking brother the light of a lanthorn. Our Saviour is seen behind St. Peter, with something like a black velvet mitre on his head, emblazoned with gold, carrying in his hand the orb, and apparently leaving the incredulous apostle to sink or swim. Peter wears a turban surmounted by a golden halo, and appears to have been more the favourite of the Artist than his divine master. He is clothed in the flowing drapery of a rich blue mantle, such as would become Peter the Great instead of Peter the Fisherman, and his scarlet surcoat, richly embroidered, is in danger meeting the fate of Sterne's wig—that of being dipped in the Ocean. Another illustration represents a dead Christ supported in the arms of a personage wearing the insignia for the Pope, and in a palace rich as that which Sardanapalus inhabited.

We have likewise the renowned encounter between St. George and the Dragon, in which the military saint appears mounted on a snow-white Rosinante, in trappings of purple and gold that seem to give sufficient exercise to the ponderous gilt spur of Knighthood. The saint bestrides a saddle of ultramarine and gold, an olive scarf floats from his right arm, which urges the spear with resistless force into the back of the monster, that lolls out its fiery tongue and expires. In the verdant plain in which the exploit is performing, a pious king is kneeling at a respectful distance, and telling his beads as a devout Sovereign ought, and from a tower behind, two other kings are seen to pop out their heads and glittering crowns, to see the combat, trusting more to stone walls that to beads and rosaries. There are great number of other curious illustrations, but *ex uno disce omnes*.

[Published 24 September 1823, p. 2]

FONTHILL ABBEY, Sept. 26—[By J. Sidney Taylor]

In the history of human vicissitude, there is no more signal instance of mutability than the fate of Fonthill. Created by an individual of enormous wealth, whose opulence enabled him to construct a line of circumvallation around his abode against all the world, and to reign the absolute sovereign of his isolated territory, with the stately seclusion of the Lama of Thibet, it all at once became the scene of crowded resort, and the gay haunt of eager curiosity. It is but a short time since a mysterious gloom hung over all this region, deep as the forest shades 'that gird the wild domain', but now, business, pleasure, fashion, and popular wonder, all meet on these once forbidden grounds, and roam as it pleaseth them through all that had so long excited inquiry and baffled examination. I have been much struck with this reflection when beholding the variegated groupes of visitors who now revel in the indulgence of unlimited curiosity on the soil which had been as strictly guarded from the foot of human intrusion as the fabled garden of the Hesperides. But the dragon vigilance that protected both was obliged to yield to overpowering necessity. In the midst of his unfinished projects, the creator of his place, who designed yet greater things than all which he has accomplished, has been completed to abandon the little world on which he had put the stamp of his own genius and the mystery of his own life, and to see it in a moment divested of the air of sullen romance which it was his constant study to preserve inviolate.

The vast wealth which he expended here, one would have thought, was a stream from an exhaustless source; but the golden tide has had its ebb; the uncalculated treasure, which in its effects rivalled the power of enchantment, is dissolved like Cleopatra's pearl. The spell which separated this magnificent abode of a lordly anchorite from the rest of the Creation, is gone, and full exposure succeeds to inexorable concealment. The prancing of steeds and the rattling of wheels coming and departing, must cause strange alarm to the Fauns and Dryads who had so long enjoyed their green retreats and delicious solitudes in undisturbed seclusion. The Naiades are scared from their native lake by the adventurers for pleasure upon the liquid element, who launch the white sailed boat upon the waves, where, except the snowy plumage of the swan, the expanding sail of navigation was never seen before. The deep and leafy alleys and romantic glades, whose soft, green turf, fancy would consecrate to fairies and their moonlight revels, are now enlivened by the graceful forms of mortal beauty, and glitter with the radiant looks of earthly fascination.…

[Published 26 September 1823, p. 3]

FONTHILL ABBEY, Sept. 30.—

You ask how I get on in the Latimer Turret.—I removed from that a few days ago, and am now in the Nunneries of the great tower. My present apartment is much higher than the one I lately occupied, which is now in the hands of the fair sex; while I being, as you know, a saint or nobody—which in the eyes of the ladies is all the same—am sent to vegetate among the Nuns. I have now to ascend by 202 steps to my apartment, but the splendour of the view that bursts upon me, amply compensates for the labour of mounting to it at night. I have nearly the whole circuit of the grounds under my eye—and a vast horizon beyond them—which, under the rising or the setting sun, have a magnificence that language cannot communicate.

I have been reading Mr. BECKFORD'S own work, *Vathek*, and there I find that Lord BYRON has not disdained to borrow a good deal from his invention, and, perhaps, the first idea of *The Giaour* was suggested to the poet by the perusal of that singular story. Hazlitt has sent up some critical observations on the work, which I have not yet seen, but we had a previous conversation about it. [Hazlitt's review of *Vathek* appeared in the 10 October issue of the *Morning Chronicle*] Thomas MOORE has also been indebted to Vathek for the ideas of his most luxuriant oriental descriptions—more particularly in his poem, *The Garden of Roses*, and I think if you look over both, you will trace the strong resemblance.

[Private letter]

FONTHILL ABBEY, Oct. 4, 1823—[By J. Sidney Taylor]

... a Pannel of Tapestry for a large room, 20 feet 6 inches, by 13 feet, which the catalogue says represents the Feast of the Gods, but I rather thing the subject is Apollo and the Nine Muses engaged in a vocal and instrumental concert, while the Court of King Admetus, for whom he acted as a shepherd, in his banishment from Olympus, are partaking of a collation under the canopy of a spreading tree, and are surprised by the revealed glories of the God of Song, in the midst of his choir of intellectual beauties. The painter of this subject must certainly have been a native of Cremona, or some such harmonious neighbourhood, though he runs very discordant notes in chronology, for he has introduced violins and music-books into the hands of the Muses, which appear to master with all the graces of an opera band. He has also set up an organ, of which I suppose Boreas is the bellows-blower and I think there is something like a harpsichord dimly visible. In the foreground is a lady of most robust dimensions, with her back to the spectator, earnestly operating upon the double base, the sounds of which, no doubt, form an admirable substitute for their Music of the Spheres. The Muses are all taken our of their antique habiliments, and attired in the more modest costume of the day; so far the fashion of their dress and their fiddles are in unison. The workmanship of the embroidery is rich and bold, and in excellent preservation The piece was knocked down for 421[£].

The Tent of Darius, 19 feet 6 inches by 13 feet. The subject is from the Picture by Le Brun, and is at least as true and spirited a copy of that painting, as Thornhill's copies of the Cartoons of Raphael in Somerset House are of their originals. This is perhaps the happiest of the efforts of Le Brun, on a subject of so much moral and historical interest. What a contrast between the voluptuous weakness of all that remains of the empire of Darius, and the simple grandeur of the conqueror. The females of a barbarian monarch are, with the accustomed gallantry of despotism, abandoned to their fate, while the victor, who had learned the institutions of a free people, approaches their gaudy, yet forlorn abode, more like a visitor to his equals than a conqueror to his slaves. What a glorious retribution had the spirit of Greece here over the haughty power that carried fire and sword, and every form of desolation into her territory, and fell vanquished as much by her generosity in conquest as by her courage in the field. In one point the design is defective; it does not sufficiently mark the mistake made by the females who prostrated themselves to Hephaestion, the favourite, who was taller than Alexander, and assumed more external royalty than his master. The colours of this piece are in good preservation; it sold for 39l. 7s 6d....

[Published 4 October, 1823, p. 3]

FONTHILL ABBEY, Oct. 6, 1823.—

The Abbey is full of company, and all the places of accommodation in the neighbourhood full of guests. The approaching close of the view and of the season makes every fine day be taken advantage of by parties whose fashion or curiosity invites to a place of such popular fame and singular attractions. Here are now mingled in picturesque confusion the lovers of erudition and the admirers of old china—the adorers of antique relics and the fanciers of splendid novelties—the pale aspects that pore over illuminated manuscripts, and the pretty eyes that reflect the brilliancy of the jewels they admire—the connoisseur, whom a painting of Teniers or Dow throws into an ecstacy, and the exquisite beau, who, Narcissus-like, worships the picture of himself in every mirror. Here you may see the admirer of sylvan scenery, who traverses every mazy walk, and explores every romantic glade. There the steady man of business, who keeps his even course to the sale-room, and never looks at a tree unless it be furnished with a painted board, directing him to the right hand or the left. In one place the man of military experience considers how long this position could hold out against a besieging force, while the lawyer calculates how long it could resist an array in Chancery. The divine wishes the ground consecrated, and the Abbey a cathedral. The collector cares little what becomes of the grounds so the Abbey be made a museum. The painter leaves both to their speculations, and luxuriates through the prints of costly folios within, or indulges in all the varieties of form and colour without. The poet throws himself at the mossy foot of some fantastic oak, views the effect of the setting sun from the laurelled terrace, or listens to the organ pealing through the religious gloom of saint-adorned galleries, like the living voice of inspiration. His contrast—the portly oracle of some generous corporation inquires after the dimensions of the kitchen-range, and all the conveniences for substantial enjoyment. The crimson and purple moreen, lace, quilts, &c. catch the eyes of elderly maiden ladies, and more dazzling tints and animated forms engage a portion of younger admiration. To every taste there is something appropriate. The man of science may ascend the lofty tower and inspect the stars, the scholar peruse the Elzevirs, the dramatist observe all sorts of character, but the antiquarian in vain looks for *rust*. There is neither a mouldy relic nor a time-encrusted monument of former days in the whole collection; even the oldest books are modernised by the splendour of their bindings, and could hardly be known by their own authors, in their costume of gold and morocco; and whatever antiquity presents to the eye of the curious, is embellished like the ornaments of a Persian caliph.

Among the Books in this Collection is one entitled *Le Histoire de Bretagne composée sur les titrés et les auteurs originaux par Dom Guy Alexis Lobineau prestre religieux Bénédictins de la Congregation de St.Maur*. In this Book there is much pencilled writing in French by Mr. BECKFORD, consisting of references chiefly to the more curious parts of the text. But there is one note in the first volume, which I think deserving of being copied, and from which, by collation with the original text, I think I have discovered the Origin of the Romance of Vathek.

The note is as follows :

> Brutalité cruentés, extravagances, horreurs inouïes de Gilles de Laval, Mareschal de Raiz. Sa naissance étoit des plus illustres, ses talens militaires trés distinguées, sa fortune immense, sa prodigalité sans bornes—il se faiséoit suivre partout d'une chapelle composée de 25 ou 30 personnes en grands habits d'écarlette fourrés de petit griz et de menu vair. Rien de si magnifique que les ornamens de autel qu'on portoit avec lui, ainsi qu'un jeu d'orgues, sa table, toujours ouverte pour tout le monde, etait couverte de mets le plus exquis—A ces dépenses excessives il joignoit cette de donner la *Comèdie*, si l'on peut appeller de ce nom les farces que se jouoient alors aux grands festes de l'année et que l'on appelloit *Mystères*—ses debauches font fremir—Par un dereglement inconcevable, les malheureuses victimes de sa lubricité n'avoient des charmes pour lui que dans le moment quelles expiroient!—ou prouvé qui'l avoit fait perir plus de cent enfans toutes en les accablant de ses infernelles caresses—Jamais personne s'est rendu plus agréable au Prince des Ténèbres que Gilles de Laval—Abominations, sacrifices,encensemens sont mis en suivre pour captiver l'attention de cette créature ennemi de Dieu—Le Mareschal faisoit tout et ne voyoit rien—Enfin son procès fut entamé pour les triples crimes d'hérésie, de sortilége et de—, il fut condamné au feu et supplice, le Diable emporte son ame! son corps, après des obsèques que fort honorables, fut inhumé solemnellement.

The Gilles de Laval, who forms the subject of the above note, was one of those personages who sometimes, in a rude age, alarms all ordinary barbarism, by singular acts of audacity and crime. In him the human form seemed truly but a mask, under which the incarnate Spirit of Evil degraded the image of the Deity, and realised on earth all the imaginable scenes of horror which are supposed peculiar to his infernal abodes. He was a man, than whom, if ancestry could confer virtue, few would have merited a more illustrious reputation. He was allied to the first ranks of the nobility; and the ancient houses of Laval, Montmorency, de Ronci, Craon, and others, combined in his extraction. At twenty years of age, the death of his father left him in possession of a vast inheritance and an unbridled liberty; for although his uncle, Jean de Craon, was appointed his guardian, yet he had no control that his licentious mind did not readily shake off. To his extensive landed possessions he received a great accession by marriage with Catherine de Thouars; he was received into the friendship of the Due de Bretagne, who made him his Lieutenant-General; and having distinguished himself by exemplary valour in the field, was honoured for his services with the exalted rank of Mareschal de France—a distinction then conferred upon very few, even of those who united warlike fame with a splendid origin. So ample were his resources at this time, that his moveable property alone was, even in that age, computed at 100,000 crowns of gold. His lands returned him a rent of 30,000 livres—an income which was equal in value to 300,000 livres at the commencement of the last century,—and this wealth was exclusive of the profits of his fief, and his emoluments as a Marshal of France. His riches, however, were surpassed by his extravagance. In personal pomp and the state of his household, he vied with the most powerful Princes of the time. He went about distinguished by a retinue of 200 attendants on horseback, and, wherever he travelled, was always followed by the priests and choir of his chapel, amounting to about 30 persons.... His chief confidant and most audacious adviser was Francois Prelati, an Italian, who was endeared to him by a supposed personal and very close intimacy with the Prince of Darkness. From such an instructor, Gilles do Laval, who was passionately addicted to magic, hoped to obtain a knowledge of all the mysteries of the art, and even to be admitted to the honour of a conference with Satan himself. Prelati affected to hold very agreeable soirees with his sable Majesty, and, in order to merit the same distinction, his master made daily adorations to the infernal spirit. He endeavoured to propitiate him by incense and sacrifices. He wrote a deed with his own blood, in which he agreed to give him whatever he would demand, except his life, which he wished to enjoy somewhat longer, and his soul, which he was putting at his disposal as rapidly as possible. To consummate the horrid ceremonies and barbarous incantations, the lives of children were understood to be the most grateful sacrifice, and Laval had a spirit which no compunctious visitings of nature prevented from operating as chief priest at the altar of such bloody and ferocious superstition. Still the dark Being, to which his passions were so subservient, did not gratify him with his visible presence. The impostors in magic by whom he was surrounded, were each of them afraid to carry the trick so far as to personate the arch fiend, lest Laval, who was a man of the most desperate intrepidity, might try an experiment with his sword upon the ribs of the apparition; and they pretended that the devil would not come, because he had either made the sign of the cross, or muttered a prayer on entering the magic circle. In the meantime he went on with his abominations, and reached such atrocious perfection that he was in the habit of decoying children into his castles, and after gratifying his brutal purposes, enhanced the pleasure by the torture and destruction of his victims.

He was, however, determined to try an experiment with his sword upon the ribs of the mimic apparition. To account for the moroseness of the sense of religion to be qualified for a personal interview with the Great Enemy of mankind, and that he instinctively muttered a prayer, or made the sign of the cross on entering the magic circle, which was an insult that Satan could not overlook.—Laval went on to qualify himself to overcome the most fastidious scruples of this kind, by putting off all the vestiges of the human character. He arrived at the most diabolical perfection in debauchery and cruelty, and it was proved on his trial that he had destroyed in his castles of Machecon and Chontoci near a hundred children, besides several in other places, on most of whom he inflicted death with his own hand, and expressed a horrible joy over the convulsive pangs of his innocent victims. This monstrous iniquity, his great power enabled him to practice for some time with impunity, under that feudal system, the extinction of which Burke so eloquently laments as the departed glory of Europe ! His crimes at length brought down the avenging sword of justice. He was arrested by order of the Duke of Bretagne, along with Prelati and others of his accomplices. He at first behaved before his Judges with the most insolent contumacy: but Prelati and others having made a full confession, he was induced to acknowledge his enormities, and avowed that he had perpetrated crimes enough to forfeit the lives of ten thousand men. He concluded his dreadful and appalling career by undergoing the infamous punishment of fire, at Nantes, on the 25th of October, 1440.

In the being whose extraordinary habits and fate form the subject of the preceding narrative, are discernible the original lineaments of the character of the Caliph Vathek. However the subject may be disguised or relieved by the circumstances of Eastern fiction, it is the story of Laval de Raiz, embellished with the accessories of Arabian invention. From the situation of a feudal lord in the 15th century, he was easily transplanted to the Throne of the Caliphate of the East, preserving essentially all the qualities in his feigned existence which made his real life so singular, so terrific, and so infamous. Like Vathek, his prototype, De Raiz, had some tincture of letters, and some tendency to religion, with a contempt of its obligations; like him he was inordinately fond of princely pomp and vulgar associations; like him, in danger intrepid; in pleasure, frantic; in ambition a dupe, and in malice a demon. The one, in a subordinate station, set at defiance the laws of God and man; the other, with supreme power on earth, wished to scale the barriers of heaven, or descend into the gloomiest recesses of despair. Both burned with intense desire to penetrate the secrets of a mysterious world; both ardently desired a personal and familiar knowledge of the visible Spirit of Evil. To this dreadful passion they made every sacrifice at which the human heart recoils, and imagination shudders. To propitiate the Infernal Power, they are told that they must steep themselves in crime beyond the possibility of expiation or repentance, and the very necessity of committing more crime in aid of their criminal ambition, is in itself a source of poignant gratification. The very nature of their oblations on the altar of the Demon is the same—one decoys a crowd of children from their parents, and with the smile of a fiend, flings them down to Eblis; the other, with similar mirth, sheds their blood to Satan. The Counsellor of Vathek is a sorceress; the adviser of De Raiz is a pretended magician. Both combine jocularity with the most savage cruelty—if the one calls for the 'Koran and sugar', the other with a like spirit says, that 'the Devil is such a low fellow, he has no taste for the conversation of gentlemen'. Thus they commit magic, murder, heresy, and jests. But just before the close of their career, there is a pause in the wickedness of both—Vathek turns aside from his profligate course under the influence of the song of the good genius, and a sudden illumination of conscience makes De Raiz resolve to abandon his vices, and make a pilgrimage to the Holy Land; but with the one and the other it was but the momentary recoil of the soul from the verge of the last precipice before it plunged into headlong perdition.

[Published 8 October 1823, p. 4]

Note in Response to Taylor's Article in the *Salisbury and Winchester Journal*, 20 October 1823, p. 4

THE CALIPH VATHEK—The author of this extraordinary tale has at all times been anxious to throw a covering of originality over this production. The shroud of mystery in which it has been heretofore enveloped appears now however to be completely removed, as we find by the statements in several papers in this city (said to be founded on the actual manuscript of the author), which, if true, would leave little doubt as to the real character the author had in view when he wrote it. As we have frequently read the book with much pleasure, we own we should have been much better pleased to have learned that this story derived its origin from some more amiable source than the character referred to, which at best evinces a most extraordinary taste in its selection, as we cannot but pronounce this Gilles de Lard [*sic*] to be one of the most atrocious beings in the shape of human that was ever suffered to disgrace society, and we should rejoice to find that our 'Savants' were utterly mistaken in their discoveries.

[Published 20 October 1823, p. 4}

FONTHILL ABBEY, Oct. 13.—

I have, since I wrote, had a message conveyed to me from Mr. BECKFORD through his agent, and it was to assure me 'upon his honour'—that the character in which I traced the resemblance to Vathek (Gilles de Raiz), and gave my opinion that it was the original of that fanciful story—he was not acquainted with at the time he wrote it. He acknowledges that the points of coincidence are very strong, and as he said, made out with an ingenuity that would lead most to believe it; but he was anxious that I should understand the book was not in his possession at the time. I don't know, however, if you read the article I allude to in the Chronicle—it has caused some conversation here. Mr. HEBER, the member for Oxford, mentioned in the sale room the other day, that it was much debated at Pitt House, the seat of Mr. BENET, and that the company were all converts to the opinion I had advanced.

[Private letter]

FONTHILL ABBEY Oct. 16.—

Some paintings which formed the flower of the collection, were disposed of to-day. The Abbey has a most brilliant appearance, as the weather is fine and the ladies have again assumed the sceptre of taste in deciding on the merits of the furniture and ornaments; at this moment the appearance of the two yellow damask drawing rooms makes indeed a brilliant coup d'oeil—so much is the costly appearance of the rooms enlivened by the presence of beauty and fashion. The state of Spain—which I see by the paper to-day—how deplorable ! The eye of the Almighty is still upon the world, and that is enough to know.

[Private letter]

FONTHILL ABBEY, Oct. 23.—

At length the sale approaches its final close—long as I have been here, there are a great many of the beauties of the place which I have not yet seen; only yesterday I was lost in a part of the grounds where I had not been before. I would gladly have accepted the service of a fairy to replace me in the right road, but alas ! those benevolent attendants upon knights-errant, did not consider me worthy of their special interference, and I was obliged to resort to mere human efforts to escape from the mazes of enchantment. What a place for dear little E to hop about, and pick up berries like one of the sportive train of Titania. She and M would soon forget the Temple Gardens.

[Private letter]

ILLUMINATION OF THE ABBEY, Oct. 24—[By J. Sidney Taylor]

Last night, according to notice, the Abbey was illuminated. The public curiosity to witness the spectacle was so great, that the lower apartments of the building were crowded long before the time at which it was specified the arrangements would be completed. A great number of those who attended during the day had not left the Abbey at all, but waited during the evening with the grave impatience of Chinese expecting the solemn opening of their *Feast of Lanthorns*. There were few present who had ever seen an illuminated Abbey, and the novelty of beholding the sullen grandeur of this edifice invested with a dazzling brilliancy, and exchanging for a transient brightness, its mysterious gloom, excited undefined anticipations. Many groups stationed themselves soon after sun-set in the lawn, and anxiously watched every light that passed across the windows of the tower, and gazed as intensely as Leander when he looked up to the turret of Hero for the signal-torch which was to guide him to the possession of happiness. The brightest stars shone in vain on eyes that looked but for waxen tapers, and had no vision for celestial objects; even that sparkling planet dedicated to the hallowed influence of the divinity of love was neglected of its young votaries, and looked down on a deserted shrine! At length the lanthorn of the tower streamed a sudden blaze of radiance, and the beholders were struck with silent delight, as when:

> Unnumber'd lamps proclaim the feast
> Of Bairim through the boundless East.

The portals of thee galleries were thrown open, and the visitors passed with the ardour of fire-worshippers into the temple of their refulgent Deity. At the same time the organ, from its lofty station, began to 'swell forth its high and holy harmony', now swelling in a volume of sound—now dying in distant cadences. The grand octagon saloon exhibited at this time a magnificent spectacle. The light playing along the shafted arches which lead off to various parts of the structure, and flickering upon the enriched work of the interior of the tower, the height and symmetry of the poetic architecture—the splendour of the lanthorn—all whose stained windows were in a blaze of coloured radiance—the clear brightness of the circular windows beneath, and the deep relief of draperies of solemn richness, all produced the effect of a magical illusion. The view on either side, from the octagon, down St. Michael and King Edward's galleries, was novel and imposing. The lengthened streams of light, along which the eye had an indistinct vision of glittering and accumulated ornaments which yet decorate the walls, gave the impression of a place where genii held their fanciful dominions, or reminded one of those depositories of the treasures of Eastern Caliphs, in which gold and jewels are surrounded by spells, mystery, and enchantment. All was uncommon, strange, and romantic. The view from King Edward's oratory was in particular very interesting, when the eye, glancing through the solemn gloom of the sanctuary, saw the brilliant and animated scene beyond, heightened by contrast. The oratory itself is now stript of the image of St. Anthony, which once presided there on an altar, surrounded by silver candlesticks, and illumined by one elegant and solitary antique lamp: his place is now supplied by a large mirror which, although it, on this occasion, multiplied many agreeable images and sparkling eyes that would have become the 'garden of roses', yet its glare banished the repose, and distracted the solemnity of this beautiful and regal retreat of Gothic devotion. The crimson and blue saloons had a rich effect of a very different character. Their style and furniture are more adopted to the interior of a Palace than an Abbey, and they had less of a romantic, than a superb appearance. The view on the exterior was not as striking, as, under different circumstances, it might have been, for the moon shone with all her lustre, and robbed the mimic galaxy of half its attractions. The night was serenely beautiful, and soon after ten, the lights were extinguished, and the company rejoiced, that there still remained the illumination of the Heavens to guide them to their homes....

[Published 24 October 1823, p. 4]

Endnotes

Chapter 1

1. Redding, *Memoirs of William Beckford of Fonthill* (1859), 2: 146 and the unpublished manuscript of Redding's Memoirs, MS Beckford, Bodleian Library, c.86, f. 33b.
2. *Leeds Intelligencer*, 3 July 1770, p. 2.
3. *The Manchester Mercury and Harrop's General Advertiser*, 3 July 1770, p. 1.
4. *Kentish Gazette*, 3 July 1770, p. 4.
5. [W.B. to Alexander Cozens], 24 November 1777, Melville, *The Life and Letters of William Beckford of Fonthill* (1910), p. 40.
6. *Hamilton Palace Sale Catalogue of the Beckford library* (1882–83) 2: 2465; hereafter referred to as *H.P.S.*
7. [W.B. to Cozens], 3 October 1777, Melville, p. 32.
8. [W.B. to Cozens], 5 June 1778, *Ibid.*, p. 52.
9. Alexander examined this document in unpublished form when he was custodian of the Beckford Papers. He gave it a working title of 'Fonthill Foreshadowed' and quoted from it in *England's Wealthiest Son*. The complete text has now been made available as an edited manuscript on the internet by Dick Claésson with a different title, 'The Transport of Pleasure' (1996) to reflect the broader characteristics of the work than did Alexander's title. This quotation is from p. 26 of the text. All quotations hereafter are from this text. Available: http://www.hum.gu.se/~litwww/TransportOfPleasure.pdf.
10. 24 November [1777], Melville, p. 37.
11. *Idem.*
12. 25 December 1777, *Ibid.*, p. 41.
13. *The Vision* [and] *Liber Veritatis*, ed. Chapman (1930), p. 85.
14. For a further discussion of Beckford's writing within the tradition of picturesque aesthetics, see the Introduction, *Dreams, Waking Thoughts and Incidents*, ed. Gemmett (2006), pp. 14-34. All references hereafter are to this edition.
15. Beckford's record of this experience is included as *An Excursion to the Grande Chartreuse* in my edition of *Dreams, Waking Thoughts and Incidents*, pp. 211-30.
16. Redding, 'Recollections of the Author of *Vathek*', *The New Monthly Magazine*, 61 (June 1844): 153.
17. 'William Beckford', *Dictionary of National Biography*, II: 84.
18. Sloan, *Alexander and John Robert Cozens* (1986), pp. 138-57. For a more extended application of Sloan's findings to Beckford, see Shaffer's essay '"To remind us of China"— William Beckford, Mental Traveller on the Grand Tour: The Construction of Significance in Landscape', in *Transports: Travel, Pleasure, and Imaginative Geography, 1600–1830*, ed. Chard and Langdon (1996), pp. 207-42.

19. *Dreams, Waking Thoughts and Incidents*, p. 150.
20. As quoted by Oliver, *The Life of William Beckford* (1932), p. 89.
21. *Vathek*, ed. Lonsdale (1998), p. 4.
22. *The Travel-Diaries of William Beckford of Fonthill*, ed. Chapman (1928), 2: 272
    All references to *Recollections of an Excursion to the Monasteries of Alcobaça and Batalha* hereafter are to this edition.
23. Redding, *The New Monthly Magazine*, 61: 146.
24. In addition to the accusation of apostasy, this article, which ran for two consecutive issues of the *Sunday Times*, ranks among the severest attacks on Beckford and his father ever published. It charged his father with deriving his wealth from a 'traffic in negro slaves', which, it said he 'pursued with more persevering ardour than those who laboured with him in the same wretched field'. Once the Lord Mayor died, the article continued, the 'whole mass of this evil-speaking gold devolved upon the present Mr. Beckford', who then squandered it on building Fonthill for the purpose of astonishing the world with the 'extent of his resources'. 'Fonthill Abbey—Mr. Beckford—and Vathek', *Sunday Times*, 28 September 1823, p. 4 and 5 October 1823, p. 1. For Beckford's extended reaction, see Gemmett, 'The Two Faces of William Beckford', *History Today* (October 2011), pp. 23-8.
25. 'Conversations with the Late W. Beckford, Esq.', *The New Monthly Magazine*, 72 (November 1844): 419-20.
26. *Ibid.*, (December 1844): 518.
27. *England's Wealthiest Son*, p. 135.
28. Quest-Ritson, *The English Garden Abroad* (1992), pp. 160-1.
29. W.B. to Charlotte Courtenay, 22 February 1781, Chapman, *Beckford* (1952), p. 82.
30. Written in 1838. *Ibid.*, p. 69.
31. W.B. to Count Benincasa, 21 October 1780, *England's Wealthiest Son*, p. 76.
32. 11 December [1780], Oliver, p. 52.
33. 29 December 1780, *Ibid.*, p. 54.
34. 9 January 1781, *Ibid.*, p. 55.
35. 28 January 1781, *Ibid.*, p. 59.
36. For press citations on the scandal, see Chapman, pp. 185-6.
37. 'Thoughts on a Late Biography', *The Monthly Visitor*, 2 (October 1797): 343.
38. Draft to Lady Craven, undated [between 1793 and 1796], *England's Wealthiest Son*, p. 122.
39. *The Journal of William Beckford in Portugal and Spain 1787–1788*, ed. Alexander (1955), p. 100. All references hereafter are to this edition.

Chapter 2

1. 'Conversations with the Late W. Beckford, Esq. Contributed by Various Friends', *The New Monthly Magazine*, 72 (November 1844): 419. This is the second of three articles signed 'H.' The author remains unidentified.
2. Lees-Milne, *William Beckford* (1976), p. 41.
3. *H.P.S.*, I: 1788.
4. Gregory, *The Beckford Family. Reminiscences of Fonthill Abbey and Lansdown Tower*, 2nd ed. (1898), p. 139.
5. *Dreams, Waking Thoughts, and Incidents*, pp. 54, 59.
6. *Travel-Diaries*, 2: 18.
7. For a discussion of this subject, see the Introduction to *Biographical Memoirs of Extraordinary Painters*, ed. Gemmett (1969), pp. 26-31. All references hereafter are to this edition. See also Gemmett, *William Beckford* (1977), pp. 61-2.
8. *Dreams, Waking Thoughts, and Incidents*, pp. 50; 52.
9. *Ibid.*, p. 206-7.

10. (1772), p. viii. Beckford's reaction to Chambers's essay was that it was 'florid' and 'exaggerated', but it is not clear that he understood that the architect's real purpose for writing this essay was to present his own views on English landscape gardening rather than to extol the virtues of Chinese gardening. For Beckford's comments, see *Travel-Diaries*, 2: 265-6.
11. *Travel-Diaries*, 2: 246.
12. *Memoirs*, 2: 147.
13. *Ibid.*, 2: 206-7.
14. For the catalogues of Beckford's library, see *The Sale Catalogues of Libraries of Eminent Persons*, Vol. 3, William Beckford, ed. Gemmett (1972). I provide a more extensive list of books on gardening in Beckford's library in my unpublished doctoral dissertation 'William Beckford and the Picturesque: A Study of Fonthill', Syracuse University, 1967, pp. 252-6.
15. *England's Wealthiest Son*, pp. 177-8.
16. These citations appeared in chapter 4 of John Rutter's *Delineations of Fonthill and its Abbey* (1823), pp. 83-4. Boyd Alexander believed that these and the other poetical citations in Rutter's book came directly from Beckford. *England's Wealthiest Son*, p. 173.
17. For an excellent discussion of the gardening movement in the eighteenth century, see Chase, *Horace Walpole: Gardenist* (1943), pp. 135-67; 178-9.
18. *Memoirs*, 2: 147.
19. *Journal in Portugal and Spain*, p. 127.
20. *The New Monthly Magazine*, 71 (June 1844): 149.
21. *Travel-Diaries*, 2: 343. See also *England's Wealthiest Son*, p. 152.
22. This book was in the Beckford collection of James T. Babb, and is now in Yale's Beinecke Library.
23. Oliver, p. 295.
24. *Dreams, Waking Thoughts and Incidents*, p. 68.
25. *Ibid.*, p. 120.
26. *Travel-Diaries*, 2: 239.
27. *Journal in Portugal and Spain*, p. 111.
28. *Modern Novel Writing, or the Elegant Enthusiast*, ed. Gemmett (2008), p. 130. Hervey wrote: 'In the distribution of the grounds, the hand of Brown had assisted, but not forced nature; each masterly stroke of his art had only served to bring to light beauties that lay concealed before'. (1788), 2: 204.
29. See Hervey, 2: 204-11 for the full description of the grounds that Beckford used as the source for describing Lord Mahogany's estate.
30. *Azemia, A Novel*, ed. Gemmett (2010), p. 74.

Chapter 3

1. *England's Wealthiest Son*, pp. 172-3.
2. *William Beckford Composing for Mozart* (1998), p. 37.
3. MS Beckford, Bodleian Library, c. 15, f. 12. This is the collection of Amelia Sophia Eleanor Hanover (1711–1786), who died the previous year.
4. *The European Magazine and London Review*, 31: 104-7. The identity of the editor during this period of time has not been certain. James Perry (1756–1821) was the founding editor, but he left the magazine in 1783. One likely possibility is Isaac Reed (1742–1807), who was a proprietor of the magazine at this time. While it is known that he denied being an editor (J. B. Nichols, *Illustrations of the Literary History of the Eighteenth Century* (1848), 7: 48), he was a contributor and Lettice seemed to address him as the editor in a subsequent letter requesting an editorial change in an article on Beckford which appeared in the September 1797 of this magazine. Lettice wrote to Reed: 'In the last period of my Account of Mr.

Beckford sent to you Yesterday, I much wish the word valued to be substituted for regarded. To say the Laws of Nations might possibly be little regarded by the French Plenipotentiaries would admit a bad Construction; I mean an unsafe one'. Beinecke Library, Beckford Collection, Box 4, f. 96. Reed did incorporate the correction. The fact that Lettice authored this account of Beckford points to the possibility of Lettice being the 'correspondent' of the article on the Christmas festivities at Fonthill published in January, 1797 and to Lettice being the source of information for the article in the February issue.

5. 'Account of the Christmas Festivities at Fonthill by a Correspondent Who Was Present', *The European Magazine and London Review*', (January 1797), 31: 4-6.

6. Rutter, pp. 92-3.

7. *Observations on the Western Parts of England Relative Chiefly to Picturesque Beauty* (1798), p. 116.

8. Rutter, p. 107.

9. *The European Magazine and London Review*, 31: 105.

10. *Ibid.*, p. 104.

11. John Britton indicated that the bridge was removed in 1781, the year Beckford reached majority. *The Beauties of Wiltshire* (1801), 1: 248.

12. *The European Magazine and London Review*, 31: 105.

13. W.B. to Sir William Hamilton, 15 April, 1796, Alfred Morrison, *Collection of Autograph Letters and Historical Documents, The Hamilton and Nelson Papers* (Second Series), Printed for private circulation, 1893-4, 1: 219. Hereafter referred to as *Hamilton and Nelson Papers*. Beckford is referring to the interior of Fonthill Splendens in this letter ('harmony is everything in pictures, furniture, &c. I have been trying to harmonise Fonthill—no easy attempt, I can assure you—wealth have done a confounded deal of mischief'.), but his remark applies to his exterior work as well.

14. *The European Magazine and London Review*, 31: 105.

15. 'Fonthill Property', *The Times*, 4 October 1822, p. 3.

16. MS Beckford, Bodleian Library, c. 84, f. 110.

17. Beinecke Library, Beckford Collection, Gen MSS 102, Box 6, f. 111.

18. *The Beauties of Wiltshire*, 1: 246.

19. *Ibid.*, 1: 240.

20. W.B. to Samuel Henley, 19 May and 10 July 1784, Alfred Morrison, *Collection of Autograph Letters and Historical Documents* (Second Series), Printed for private circulation, 1893, 1: 192. Hereafter referred to as *Morrison Collection*.

21. Fraser Neiman, 'The Letters of William Gilpin to Samuel Henley', *Huntington Library Quarterly*, 35 (February 1972): 159-69.

22. *The European Magazine and London Review*, 31: 105.

23. *Idem.* See also Redding, *Memoirs*, 2: 80 for corroborative information regarding the Alderman's work.

24. *The European Magazine and London Review*, 31: 105.

25. *The Beauties of Wiltshire*, 1: 242. It should be noted that Britton's phrasing here is somewhat ambiguous on the matter of when Beckford became involved in planting. One could interpret his wording to mean he began before 1781, during his 'minority'. However, Britton may have intended a separation of time between the development of Beckford's 'feeling for the picturesque' which he discovered 'in a very early stage of his minority', and the major landscaping activities conducted later in the area of the Alpine Garden. The account provided in *The European Magazine and London Review* is clearer in identifying 1781 as the year Beckford's land improvements began.

26. Redding wrote: 'Soon after Mr. Beckford's return from seeing Aranjuez, his old tutor was at Fonthill, instructing the Misses Beckford, and he suggested that walks should be made of nearly a mile in extent, in order to render that wild spot pleasanter for the ladies, who seemed to have a partiality for it. Mr. Beckford, struck with the capabilities of the place,

ordered the necessary workmen to be busy; and the end was achieved in what afterwards had the name of the "Alpine Garden". *Memoirs*, 2: 81. It should be noted that this published version differs from the Redding's manuscript account of the *Memoirs*. In the manuscript he overstated Lettice's role in the production of the Alpine Garden by saying that it was 'formed by Dr. Lettice' and then modified it before publication. MS Beckford, Bodleian Library, c. 86, f. 33 and 34b. While Lettice played a role, it is clear from Britton's account and *The European Magazine and London Review* that considerable work had been done before Lettice's involvement. See also Laurent Châtel's reconstruction of the development of this landscape element in 'The Mole, the Bat, and the Fairy of the Sublime Grottoes of "Fonthill Splendens"', *The Beckford Journal*, 5 (Spring 1999): 58-60.

27. *Beauties of Wiltshire*, 1: 242-3.
28. MS Beckford, Bodleian Library, c. 33, f. 73.
29. *Beauties of Wiltshire*, 1: 243-5.
30. 'Modern Gardening', *Anecdotes of Painting in England*, ed. Wornum (1849), 3: 807.
31. *Memoirs*, 1: 148.
32. Redding wrote: 'A grotto was made by a workman named Lane, in imitation of one constructed many years before for Mrs. Beckford's uncle, the Hon. Charles Hamilton, of Pain's Hill, Surrey', *Ibid.*, 2: 81. Josiah Lane is often wrongly identified as the person responsible for creating the grotto at Painshill. See Kitz, *Pains Hill Park* (1984), p. 73. When the construction of it began in 1763, Josiah (1753–1833) was only ten years old. It therefore had to be the work of his father, Joseph (1717–1784), who died the year Josiah began to create Beckford's grotto on the east side of the lake.
33. 13 October 1784, *Morrison Collection*, 1: 192-3.
34. *The Times*, 4 October 1822, p. 3.
35. *Beauties of Wiltshire*, 1: 247.
36. Lot 255, Jamaica Letter Books, Manuscript, Christie, Manson, Woods sale catalogue, Important Autograph Letters, 2 April 1975.
37. *Historic Gardens of Wiltshire* (2004), p. 89.
38. MS Beckford, Bodleian Library, c. 86 f. 18.
39. It is difficult to know with certainty that Lane was responsible for this inscription, particularly since this grotto, as I examined it, contains numerous carvings of initials and dates in the stone. The fact that it is a roundel, however, sets it apart from the others. Châtel, p. 58, has pointed out the initials J. L. could also stand for John Lettice, but it is difficult to see how Lettice's interest in overseeing the development of walkways in the Alpine Gardens could be associated with the construction of a grotto.
40. *Letters Written during a Residence in England* (1799), pp. 304-5. [letter XIX devoted to Fonthill]. There have been some differences of opinion concerning the year Meister visited Fonthill. He does mention Beckford's age in this account as thirty-three which would place the year of the visit as either 1793 or 1794. However, Meister's description indicates that he actually met Beckford which would make 1794 impossible since he was in Portugal during that year. Internal evidence, involving seasonal references, suggests that Meister was there in the summer of 1793, a matter of months before Beckford's thirty-third birthday on 29 September.
41. Rutter described this feature as a 'building called a Hermitage, whose ruinous state indicates that the taste which presided over such erections is gone by'. Rutter, p. 95. A handbook for travellers published in 1869 recorded that the 'Hermit's Cave' was made by the 'younger Beckford' and described it as a 'circular cavern with 2 dark recesses in one of which lies the mutilated figure of the hermit'. *Handbook for Travellers in Wiltshire, Dorsetshire, and Somersetshire* (1869), p. 153.
42. Mowl believes that this cromlech was really a viewing tower, 34-5. Châtel argues that this monolith is really a cromlech after all. *The Beckford Journal* (Spring 1999), 63-4.
43. Rutter, p. 96.

44. *The English Garden Abroad* (1992), p. 160.
45. *Sintra A Landscape with Villas* (1989), p. 67.
46. Da Silva and Luckhurst slightly misquote the poem. These and the following lines are from Thomas Cargill, *Fairylife and Fairyland A Lyric Poem* (1870), pp. 279; 305.
47. *Ibid.*, A photograph of the stone arch appears on p. 66.
48. Quest-Ritson, p. 160.
49. As quoted by Gerald Luckhurst, 'Gerard de Visme and the Introduction of the English Landscape Garden to Portugal (1782–1793)', *Revista de Estudos Anglo-Portugueses*, 20 (2011): 143.
50. 'Description of the Village of Cintra, in Portugal, 1818', *The European Magazine and London Review*, 44 (July 1818): 37. See also Luckhurst, 'Here didst thou dwell … William Beckford at Monserrate', *The Beckford Journal*, 18 (2012): 56-71.
51. As quoted by Rose Macaulay, *They Went to Portugal* (1946), p. 137.

Chapter 4

1. Rutter, p. 108.
2. *England's Wealthiest Son*, p. 157.
3. *Idem.*
4. *The European Magazine and London Review*, 31: 105.
5. This draft letter is undated, but in view of a reference in it to the recently completed wall it was likely written in the year 1795. See Oliver, pp. 257-8.
6. Reproduced for the first time in *England's Wealthiest Son*, p. 118.
7. Melville, p. 214.
8. *Ibid.*, 214-15.
9. This passage was omitted by Melville. *England's Wealthiest Son*, p. 282, n. 6.
10. Rutter, p. 109.
11. *The European Magazine and London Review*, 31: 106 and Beckford's letter to Sir William Hamilton of 2 February 1797, *Hamilton and Nelson Papers*, 1: 227.
12. *The Diary of Joseph Farington*, ed. Garlick and MacIntyre (1978) 2: 612.
13. *The Gentleman's Magazine*, 66, pt. 2: 784.
14. To John Lettice, Melville, p. 243.
15. To Nicholas Williams, 12 October 1796, *England's Wealthiest Son*, p. 159.
16. 29 November 1796, Melville, pp. 221-2.
17. W.B. to Sir William Hamilton, *Hamilton and Nelson Papers*, I: 227.
18. *The European Magazine and London Review*, 31: 105.
19. Rutter, p. 109.
20. See John Ely-Wilton, 'Beckford, Fonthill and the Picturesque', in *The Picturesque in Georgian England*, ed. Arnold (1995), pp. 37-9, and his earlier work 'The Genesis and Evolution of Fonthill Abbey', *Architectural History*, 23 (1980): 40-51 and plates 28b, 30a, b, c, 31, 32a, b.
21. Ely-Wilton, 'Beckford, Fonthill Abbey and the Picturesque', p. 37. Wyatt's exhibit was no. 1143 'Design for a building now executing at Fonthill, the seat of William Beckford, Esq. in the style of a Gothic abbey'.
22. *Farington Diary*, 3: 880 and 918.
23. Rutter, p. 110. There has been some question about how many times the tower collapsed under construction. We do know for certain that a dramatic collapse of the tower occurred in May 1800, and Cyrus Redding indicated that the tower was rebuilt three times. Redding, *Memoirs*, 2: 158. Beckford's secretary and librarian Abbé Macquin also reported in his series of articles on Fonthill that the tower was once destroyed by fire, but he provides no date. Redding also recorded a fire at the summit of the tower, noting that a 'considerable expense

was incurred in its restoration'. Redding, *Memoirs*, 2: 156. Finally, John Britton reported that the tower had been raised three times. See 'Visit to Fonthill', *The Literary Gazette and Journal of Belles Lettres*, 24 August 1822, p. 527, and Britton's *Graphical and Literary Illustrations of Fonthill Abbey* (1823), p. 52. In short, the evidence supports the occurrence of two collapses (one in 1797 and the other in 1800) and a fire at some indeterminate date during construction—all three occasions requiring raising the tower. But even after these three events, problems continued because Wyatt used a synthetic material called 'compo-cement' which had to be re-encased in 1806—hence a fourth restoration. See *England's Wealthiest Son*, p. 14.

24. MS Beckford, Bodleian Library, c. 86, f. 19.
25. This could have been the occasion for Redding's comment that the Octagon Hall was 'twice built'. *Memoirs*, 2: 158.
26. Linstrum, *Catalogue of the Drawings of the Royal Institute of British Architects Wyatt Family* (1974), p. 38.
27. The contemporary label information kindly provided by Scott Wilcox, Curator of Prints and Drawings, Yale Center for British Art.
28. Linstrum reproduces all three early-stage drawings by Wyatt in figures 32, 33, and 34.
29. 'Fonthill Abbey', *Morning Chronicle*, 3 October 1823, p. 3.
30. *Farington Diary*, 3: 916.
31. *Ibid.*, 3: 1091.
32. 'Visit to Fonthill', *Literary Gazette and Journal of Belles Lettres*, 14 September 1822, p. 585.
33. Oliver, p. 235.
34. *The European Magazine and London Review*, 31: 106. The editor indicates that the medieval church was demolished after Fonthill house burnt down in 1755. Actually, records show that the removal of the church took place earlier, sometime between 1747 and 1749. D. A. Crowley, *A History of Wiltshire, Southwest Wiltshire* (1980), XIII: 168. The church was already in a state of ruin by 1747. The foundation stone of the church he built still exists and is incorporated in the vestry of the current Fonthill Gifford church on the same site. It reads: '18 May 1748/ WILLm.BECKFORD/ESQR FOUNDER'.
35. ALS, 4 January 1797, MS Beckford, Bodleian Library, b 8, ff. 10-1.
36. *The Gentleman's Magazine*, 68, pt. 2 (July 1798): 639.
37. As cited by H. A. N. Brockman, *The Caliph of Fonthill* (1956), p. 111. Farington recorded in his diary on 16 November 1798 that the spire would be '17 feet higher than the top of St. Peter's at Rome', 3: 1091.
38. *Farington Diary*, 3: 1117.
39. A suggestion first made by Nancy L. Pressly, *Revealed Religion: Benjamin West's Commissions for Windsor Castle and Fonthill Abbey* (1983), p. 58.
40. Draft copy, MS Beckford, Bodleian Library, c. 16, ff. 21-2. Robert Bowyer (1758–1834), bookseller and miniature painter, Historic Gallery, Pall Mall.
41. Rutter, 31. Pearson (*c*. 1742–*c*. 1840) is identified in the *Dictionary of National Biography* as having died in 1805, but he lived well into his nineties and in 1815 published a letter in *The Gentleman's Magazine* in which he cited Beckford as one of a number of authorities who could confirm that the 'art of staining glass has been brought to perfection in England'. See 85, pt. 2 (July 1815): 28. Pearson's window of Thomas à Becket has survived and is now in the Lord Mayor's chapel in Bristol. See the *Bath Journal & Weekly Gazette*, 21 September 1797, p. 3 for Pearson's additional involvement in reproducing eight of West's paintings.
42. 'Progress, &c. of Stained Glass in England', *The Gentleman's Magazine*, 87, pt. 1 (April 1817): 315. Dallaway (1763–1834), topographer and antiquarian, was the author of numerous works, including *Anecdotes of the Arts in England* (1800) and *Observations on English Architecture, Military, Ecclesiastical, and Civil ... including Historical Notices of Stained Glass, Ornamental Gardening, etc.* (1806). This important essay was published anonymously, but it is obviously Dallaway's work. It is signed with the initials 'E.M.S.', which he often used

for his anonymous pieces and which stood for Earl Marshal Secretary, a position which he was appointed to in 1797 and held for the rest of his life.

43. *A Description of Fonthill Abbey, Wiltshire* (1812), p. 11.
44. MS Beckford, Bodleian Library, c. 16, f. 20.
45. Rutter, p. 55. Francis Eginton (1737–1805) owned a shop on Newhall Street, Birmingham. His son William Raphael Eginton took over the business when he died. William placed an advertisement in *The Salisbury and Winchester Journal* during the 1822 sale announcing that the stained glass windows in the Abbey were executed by 'Mr. Eginton' to attempt to attract further business as a supplier of stained glass in 'Vitreous Colours'. See issue of 16 September 1822, p. 4.
46. MS Beckford, Bodleian Library, c. 30. f. 115.
47. See Clive Wainwright's essay on the interior of Fonthill Abbey in *The Romantic Interior* (1989), p. 117.
48. See also E. G. Cundall, 'Turner Drawings of Fonthill Abbey', *Burlington Magazine*, 29 (April 1916): 16-21.
49. *Farington Diary*, IV: 1277.
50. MS Beckford, Bodleian Library, c. 86, f. 21.
51. *The Times*, 27 May 1800, p. 3.
52. *Morning Chronicle*, 3 October 1823, p. 3.
53. *The Times*, 20 May 1800, p. 3.
54. *Ibid.*, 27 May 1800, p. 3.
55. *Morning Chronicle*, 22 May 1800, p. 3. The tower actually fell on Saturday, 17 May 1800.
56. *Ibid.*, May 29, 1800, p. 3.
57. Oliver, p. 238.
58. 21 May 1800, Oliver, p. 237. There is some evidence to suggest that he never gave up entirely the notion of a spire that would be added to the tower. An article that appeared in the *Morning Herald* in 1822 noted that the tower 'lofty as it is, it is yet unfinished; the spire remains to be added, which, from the proportion, must be raised to least a hundred and twenty feet. It is to be surmounted by a cross, and the whole, when finished, will present a tower and spire, whose highest point will be four hundred feet from the ground. Some idea may be formed of the extensive view which the highest galleries will afford, when it is observed that the base of the tower is as high as the top of the spire of Salisbury Cathedral, which is remarkable for its altitude'. 'Fonthill, October 4', *Morning Herald*, 7 October 1822, p. 2.
59. Nicholas Williams to W.B., 11 September 1801, Melville, p. 263.
60. 'Letter from a Gentleman, Present at the Festivites at Fonthill, to a Correspondent in Town', *The Gentleman's Magazine*, 89, pt. 1 (March, April 1801): 206-8; 297-8.
61. To Nicholas Williams, 5 January 1801, Melville, p. 238.

Chapter 5

1. 24 July 1799, Melville, p. 256.
2. Letter to his mother, 29 November 1796 and to Sir William Hamilton, 2 February 1797, Oliver, pp. 234-6.
3. *The European Magazine and London Review*, 31: 106.
4. Rutter, p. 83.
5. *Idem.*
6. 'Sketches and Hints on Landscape Gardening' in *The Art of Landscape Gardening*, ed. Nolens (1907), p. 26.
7. *Essays on the Picturesque* (1798), 2: 160.
8. 'A Day at Fonthill Abbey', *New Monthly Magazine*, 8 (1823): 370. See also Boyd Alexander, 'William Beckford, Man of Taste', *History Today*, 10 (October 1960): 693-4.

9. Repton, p. 132. See also *William Chambers, Dissertation on Oriental Gardening* (1773), pp. 18-9; Horace Walpole, 'On Modern Gardening', 3: 805; Price, (1798), 2: 177.

10. Loudon, pp. 442-3.

11. (1798), 2: 134-5.

12. 'Fonthill Abbey', *The Gazette of Fashion*, 31 August 1822, p. 65.

13. (1794), pp. 50-1.

14. *Past Celebrities Whom I Have Known* (1866), 1: 315-6.

15. *The European Magazine and London Review*, 31: 107.

16. Based on Rutter's description in 1823.

17. Rutter, p. 86.

18. *Ibid.*, p. 88.

19. This was Sir Richard Colt-Hoare's description of the Abbey from this vantage point. It appeared in an article he published under the pseudonym 'Viator'. 'Fonthill Abbey. On its Close', *The Gentleman's Magazine*, 92, pt. 2 (October 1822): 291. This article has often been erroneously attributed to Beckford.

20. Rutter, p. 89.

21. *Life at Fonthill*, p. 158.

22. As described by Storer in 1812, pp. 4-5. Rutter omits these details.

23. The lake was created before 1639 by the Cottington family by damming a stream which flowed eastward to the Nadder River. Crowley, 13: 155-6. Beckford made clear his own involvement in the development of the 'sublime effect' of the lake in a letter of 1817, explaining that it was accomplished by 'tree felling' and by 'the particular shape I have given to the shore on a grand scale'. *Life at Fonthill*, p. 234. The lake also had a utilitarian purpose. At the southern extremity of the lake, Beckford had an ingenious hydraulic system installed, involving a water wheel, a wooden trough and a series of underground pipes, that provided water to the Abbey.

24. *Illustrations of Fonthill Abbey*, pp. 35-6.

25. Storer, p. 5.

26. 'Fonthill Abbey', *Morning Chronicle*, 17 September 1823, p. 3.

27. *Life at Fonthill*, pp. 97-8.

28. Lady Anne Hamilton's diary mentions the existence of the American garden in 1803. MS Beckford, Bodleian Library, e. 4, f. 10. Milne could have been involved in additional planting here for the purpose of expanding it from when she saw it.

29. Redding, *Memoirs*, 2: 127-8.

30. (1794), pp. 20-1.

31. *Ibid.*, p. 277.

32. *The New Monthly Magazine*, 71: 149.

33. *Literary Gazette*, 24 August 1822, pp. 527-8.

34. To Dr. Mitford, 29 August 1808, ed. L'Estrange, *The Friendships of Mary Russell Mitford* (1882), pp. 30-1.

35. Oliver, pp. 272-3.

36. MS Beckford, Bodleian Library, e. 4, f. 11.

37. *The European Magazine and London Review*, 31: 105.

38. J. C. Loudon, 'Notes on Gardens and Country Seats—Fonthill', *The Gardener's Magazine*, 11 (September 1835): 444.

39. Storer, p. 6.

40. Loudon, 11: 444.

41. Storer, p. 3.

42. Rutter, 90.

43. *Life at Fonthill*, p. 90.

44. Loudon, 11: 443.

45. Henry V. Lansdown, *Recollections of the Late William Beckford of Fonthill*, Wilts. and Lansdown, Bath, ed. Lansdown (1893), p. 47.

46. 'A Day at Fonthill Abbey', *The New Monthly Magazine*, 8 (1823): 379.
47. 'Fonthill Abbey', *Morning Chronicle*, 13 September 1823, p. 3.

Chapter 6

1. For a detailed discussion of Beckford's financial problems, see *England's Wealthiest Son*, 200-25.
2. *The Times*, 24 July 1801, p. 3.
3. 'Fonthill Abbey', *Morning Post*, 3 September 1801, p. 4.
4. Beckford's biographers do not mention the October sale, nor was I aware of it when I compiled a census of sales in 1972. *Sale Catalogues of Libraries of Eminent Persons*, 3: 6-8. Further research has revealed that Sir Richard Colt Hoare recorded its existence writing in *The History of Modern Wiltshire* (1828), p. 26, that 'the second sale took place 7th October 1801, and continued for two days, consisting chiefly of furniture and eight fine marble chimney-pieces'. John Britton also mentions it; see Jones, *A Descriptive Account of the Literary Works* of *John Britton Being a Second Part of His Auto-Biography* (1849), p. 24.
5. Melville, 263.
6. I have located one in the Beinecke Library, Yale University. Although not listed in William Finley's description of the Beckford collection, there is a copy bound up with two other Fonthill catalogues once owned by Rowland Burdon-Muller. (Beckford, Gen Mss 102, 2007 + 60). The other is in the Soane Museum; it is Soane's personal copy which contains some markings by him.
7. *The Times*, 26 September 1801.
8. Philip Hewat-Jaboor reported that in 1801 'the east wing was demolished … leaving the remaining structure unbalanced', but it is more likely that it was left standing empty and then taken down completely in 1807 or thereafter. John Buckler's painting of Splendens *c*. 1806 shows both wings and at least one colonnade still intact. It is also clear from the title page of the building materials catalogue of 1801 that Beckford was in the process of dismantling both wings of the building and not just the east wing. The complexity of the task was such that removal of the building materials had to take place over a period of time after the respective sale. See Hewat-Jaboor, 'Fonthill House: 'One of the most Princely Edifices in the Kingdom'', in *William Beckford, 1760–1844: An Eye for the Magnificent*, ed. Ostergard (2002), p. 66.
9. A special thanks to Andrea Gilbert, Librarian and Archivist of the Wallace Collection for providing me with a photocopy of the original catalogue.
10. 'Fonthill Auction', *Morning Chronicle*, 25 August 1801, p. 2.
11. 'Fonthill Auction', *The Times*, 26 August 1801, p. 3.
12. *The Times*, 21 August 1801, p. 2.
13. 'Fonthill Auction', *Morning Chronicle*, 25 August 1801, p. 2. This article was reprinted in other newspapers, including *The Times* on the following day (slightly revised) and *The Gentleman's Magazine*, 71 (September 1801): 853-54.
14. This identification is made possible by press notices about the sale indicating the presence of 'Rev. Mr. Ogle' and further identifying him as the brother-in-law of 'Mr. Sheridan, M.P.'. Ogle's sister married Richard Brinsley Sheridan in 1795. See *Morning Chronicle*, 25 August 1801, p. 2 and *The Gentleman's Magazine*, 71, pt. 2 (September 1801): 854.
15. It is difficult to identify many of the buyers at this sale but occasionally Phillips helps by specifying the name of the town where the individual resides. In these two cases, Phillips lists 'Ames Hindon' followed immediately by 'Dr. Lambert D[itt]o'. See also *The Universal British Directory of Trade, Commerce and Manufacture* (London, 1791), 3: 274.
16. For this identification, see *The Salisbury and Winchester Journal*, 28 October 1805, p. 2.
17. My thanks to Trevor Fawcett for providing information about William Evill. See also

Woodward, 'William Beckford and Fonthill Splendens Early Works by Soane and Goodridge', *Apollo*, 147 (February 1998): 37-8.

18. Meistre, pp. 306-7.

19. Melville, 99.

20. Eric Darton suggested the possibility that Beckford bought a Stein harpsichord in his article 'William Beckford and Music. 4. The Harpsichord and Pianoforte', *Beckford Newsletter* (spring 1988), p. 5.

21. Darton believes this instrument was a 'square piano, as it was usual to refer to these as just a pianoforte'. He adds that 'an early model ... is indicated by the selling price', which he identifies inaccurately as £7. He also misidentifies 'Burlton' as the buyer when it was Penleaze who bought it for £21 10s 6d. *Ibid.*, p. 6.

22. 'Fonthill Auction', 25 August 1801, p. 2.

23. This could possibly be James Penleaze who had bought the High Cliffe estate in Hampshire in *c.* 1800 from the 3rd Earl of Bute. The sale of the estate was prompted by the necessity of dismantling the mansion house due to erosion of the cliff where it was located. Penleaze erected a new house in a different location on the estate. 'Introduction, Castles and Manors', *A History of the County of Hampshire*, ed. Page (1912), p. 5, n. 25.

24. Holford's table passed through a number of owners and most recently was sold as part of Saul P. Steinberg's auction at Sotheby's, New York, 26 May 2000, lot 205, for the sum of $2,205,750, a world auction record for English furniture. The Steinberg catalogue describes the writing-cabinet as an 'important George III ormolu-mounted and brass-inlaid mahogany dressing and writing commode attributed to John Channon *c.* 1765. The present commode ... is one of the most richly conceived objects of case furniture surviving from this period. The strong serpentine form with its central recess mirrored at each side with further arches in the gothic manner is veneered in mahogany with an unusual lustrous figure which appears to shimmer as light plays across its surface. In flickering candlelight this must have resembled flowing water....' The commode did not meet Sotheby's high estimate of four million dollars. For attribution to the workshop of John Channon, see Gilbert and Murdoch, *John Channon and Brass-Inlaid Furniture 1730–1760* (1993), pp. 91; 94.

25. Phillips identifies the buyer as 'Mrs. Wyndham Marshwood H'.

26. Phillips lists 'Vidler Salisbury'. Joseph Vidler is listed in *Universal British Directory* (1791), 4: 562 as upholsterer and cabinet-maker (his name is misspelled 'Vilder'); and by 1805, he was operating as an auctioneer in Salisbury. Various auction announcements appear in *The Salisbury and Winchester Journal* for that year carrying his name.

27. *Morning Chronicle*, 25 August 1801, p. 2. The reporter does not specifically identify the Turkish Room, but these furnishings belong to it rather than to the Grand Entrance Hall.

28. *The Beauties of Wiltshire*, 1: 213-14.

29. *Morning Chronicle*, 25 August 1801, p. 2.

30. Suggested by Hewat-Jaboor, 61.

31. Christopher Hussey provides a picture of the Fonthill wrought ironwork at Dodington Park in *English Country Houses Late Georgian 1800–1840* (1958), pp. 48; 53-4. Codrington sent eleven carriages to Fonthill in 1808 to pick up the Grand Staircase.

32. Redding, *Memoirs*, 2: 131.

33. Michael I. Wilson, *The Chamber Organ in Britain, 1600–1830* (2001), p. 128.

34. *The Gentleman's Magazine*, 71, pt. 2 (September 1801): 854.

35. See Philippa Bishop, 'Settees from Fonthill Splendens', *The Beckford Journal*, 1 (Spring 1995): 15-17.

36. One of these pairs was sold in the sale 'Important English Furniture and Carpets including The Kedleston Bookcase', Christie's, London, 9 June 2005, lot 270, for £232,000. According to the catalogue, the carved medallion back contains the Beckford heraldic crest of a heron with a fish in its beak. This set came by descent to Miss Edmée Southey, who sold them at Christie's in November 1994. It is suggested in the catalogue that they came to the Southey family by way of the poet Robert Southey who was living in the Bristol area in 1801.

Another pair found in St Andrew's Church in Trent was sold by Duke's of Dorchester on 17 April 2003 for £276,000 (lot 918).

37. This information was obtained from the *International Genealogical Index*.

38. *Excursions from Bath* (1801), p. 121.

39. Rupert Gunnis, *Dictionary of British Sculptors 1660–1851* (1968), p. 436.

40. *Morning Chronicle*, 25 August 1801, p. 2.

41. David Watkin, 'Beckford, Soane, and Hope The Psychology of the Collector', in *William Beckford, 1760–1844: An Eye for the Magnificent*, pp. 39-41. Watkin explores and provides some important insights into the parallel characteristics of these three complicated personalities.

42. *Universal British Directory* (1791), 2: 274-75. 'Mr. Cox's gardens and pleasure-grounds are deserving the attention of the curious traveller'. Cox's son, Samuel, Jr, was a sail-cloth manufacturer in the same town. Phillips identifies Cox in the catalogue as 'Cox Beaminster'.

43. Information about the restoration of these paintings and a brief sketch of their history can be found in the Bath Royal Literary and Scientific Institution Proceedings available on-line: www.brlsi.org/collections/casali.htm. A photograph of The Banquet of the Gods can be seen in John Harris, 'Fonthill, Wiltshire I Alderman Beckford's Houses', *Country Life*, 24 (November 1966): 1372.

44. Hewat-Jaboor, 56, describes this painting as 'Apollo with his harp, Fame her trumpet and the Muses with instruments of ancient and modern music'.

45. *Beauties of Wiltshire*, 1: 215.

46. Woodward, 38-9.

47. Warner, 126.

48. Phillips records the buyer's name as as 'Randalls Wilton'. See *Universal British Directory* (1791), 4: 762.

49. Woodward, 35-6. This article includes pictures of two designs for the bed.

50. *The Times*, 23 October 1801, p. 3.

51. *Morning Post*, 21 December 1801, p. 2; *Chester Chronicle*, 1 January 1802, p. 4; *Hampshire Chronicle*, 4 January 1802, p. 3.

52. Morell is likely the furniture maker who was employed at this time by the brewer Samuel Whitbread II (1796–1803), owner of the Southill estate, Bedfordshire to which he succeeded in 1796. The architect Henry Holland started reconstructing the mansion in 1800. Hussey, 33. Morell bought the double-plated pier mirror in the State Bed Chamber for £115 10s. The bottom section measured ninety-five by fifty-one inches; the top fifty-one by twenty-two inches. He also bought eight pictures in *chiaro obscura* by Du Hamel that were in the upper tier of the Grand Entrance Hall for £26 5s (lot 58, third day) and the bronze statue of the *Rape of Proserpine* from the Great Saloon for eighteen guineas (lot 147, fourth day). All three lots could have been purchased for Southill. Lord Ilchester bought the carved framed pier glass, 101 by 49 inches, from the Cabinet Anti Room [*sic*] for £162 15s (lot 154) and Shute took in the plate glass, sixty-three inches in diameter, from the Small Anti Room [*sic*] for £73 10s (lot 208).

53. Phillips lists the buyer for this lot as 'Moody'; lots 106 and 109, fourth day designate him as 'Wm Moody' and 'W. Moody'.

54. 25 August 1801, p. 2.

55. Fonthill Abbey', *London Magazine*, November 1822, in *The Complete Works of William Hazlitt*, 18: 176.

Chapter 7

1. Redding, *Memoirs*, 2: 132-4.

2. MS Beckford, Bodleian Library, c. 86, f. 32.

3. MS Beckford, Bodleian Library, e. 4, ff. 1-15.

4. Rutter, p. 11.

5. The letter was signed 'Observator' in *The Gentleman's Magazine*, 76, pt. 2 (December 1806): 1127-8. This repair of the tower confirms Redding's statement that the central tower was rebuilt 'three times'. *Memoirs*, 2: 158.

6. Hoare, p. 26.

7. *The Farington Diary*, 4: 197.

8. *The Times*, 29 September 1807, p. 3.

9. For the proposed agreement, see Bodleian Library, MS Beckford, c. 30, fols. 175-6. The advertisement on the first page of *The Times* for 16 September 1807, reads: 'The Building Materials of Fonthill House, Wilts.—By Mr. H. Phillips, on the Premises, on Wednesday, Sept. 16, and following days, at 11 o'clock each day, unless an acceptable offer is previously made for the whole'.

10. Gunnis, p. 149. Flaxman joined the Wedgwood firm in 1775 and from 1787 to 1794 directed the Wedgwood Studio in Rome.

11. *The Journal of William Beckford in Portugal and Spain*, p. 124.

12. Gunnis, p. 27. The Satin Drawing Room in 1801 and earlier was known as the Tapestry Room. Christopher Woodward notes that John Soane supplied designs for ornamental chimney-pieces for Fonthill in 1787-88 that were executed by Banks. Relying on the existence of Soane's original drawings now in the Soane Museum and in the Bodleian Library, Woodward indicated that one was supposed to be placed in the Tapestry Room and the other in the Southeast Parlour. This would contradict Phillips's attribution that the chimney-piece in the Satin Drawing Room (Tapestry Room) was by Bacon. I would have to assume that Beckford provided Phillips with the correct name of the sculptor. A Banks chimney-piece did show up in the State Bed Chamber, suggesting that Beckford may have changed his mind from the original plan. Woodward, pp. 34; 39, n. 18.

13. Using almost the same description, Phillips offered this chimney-piece in the building materials sale of 1801, third day, lot 72.

14. It could have been sold in the building materials sale of 1801. The final lot of the first day of the sale (lot 26) describes 'A fountain and bason of marble'.

15. This chimney-piece was also offered in the building materials sale, of 1801, third day, lot 74.

16. Hewat-Jaboor, p. 57.

17. Hewat-Jaboor, p. 69, n61.

18. See 'Sale at Fonthill', *The Gentleman's Magazine*, 77, pt. 2 (September 1807): 880. This person might be W. Abbott, the auctioneer and appraiser, whose place of business was on Sackville Street, Piccadilly.

19. Offered in the building materials sale of 1801, as from the State Dressing Room, third day, lot 70.

20. George Robins, *Hafod Estate* [sale catalogue] Which will be sold by Auction at the Auction Mart, London, 6 September 1832, p. 6.

21. *Idem.*

22. Christie's *The Remaining Contents of the Mansion of Clumber the Property of the Honourable the Earl of Lincoln*, 19 October 1937 and three following days. Lot 289 describes the Moore piece as 'A WHITE MARBLE MANTELPIECE, the centre of the breast designed with a panel with two female figures in a landscape and with oak branches at the sides, and the jambs with male nude figures in high relief on a background of giallo marble—about 8 ft. 2 in. wide, 5 ft. 7 in. high; and the Marble Curb the same'. John Harris traces the various owners of this chimney-piece down to 1989. It is now in a private collection. *Moving Rooms*, (2007), p. 17.

23. *The Consummate Collector William Beckford's Letters to His Bookseller*, ed. Gemmett (2000), p. 190.

24. *A Land of Pure Delight Selections from the Letters of Thomas Johnes of Hafod 1748–1816*, ed. Moore-Colyer, (1992), p. 226; *The Salisbury and Winchester Journal*, 31 August 1807, p. 4.

25. 'Fonthill Sale', *The Times*, 29 August 1807, p. 3.

26. *The Gentleman's Magazine*, 77, pt. 2 (September 1807): 880.

27. *The Gentleman's Magazine*, 67, pt 2 (October 1797): 816.

28. *Farington Diary*, 3: 921.

29. *The Beauties of Wiltshire*, 1: 233-4.

30. For additional information, see Norman Kitz, 'The Search for a Lost "Greek" Statue', *The Beckford Journal*, 11 Spring 2005): 14-19. Kitz writes that 'current scholarly opinion believes it to be a first century Roman marble after a lost Greek original', which would justify Charles Hamilton's confident assessment of its importance and value.

31. *The Salisbury and Winchester Journal*, 31 August 1807, p. 4.

32. Wilson, p. 129.

33. *The Travels through England of Dr. Richard Pococke*, ed. Cartwright (1889), 2: 47.

34. *The Gentleman's Magazine*, 25 (February 1755): 90.

35. See advertisements in *The Salisbury and Winchester Journal*, 6 May 1805, p. 4 and 24 August 1807, p. 4. In the latter, he lists thirty-two paintings by major artists for sale along with 'A very fine Copy of the Seven celebrated Cartoons of RAPHAEL, painted by SIR JAMES THORNHILL, from the originals in the KING'S collection, and supposed to be the only copies in oil, except those by the same Painter, lately presented by the DUKE OF BEDFORD to the Royal Academy; also the SAINT JOHN of Raphael, and the original Portraits of Raphael and his Sister, by PIETRO PERUGINO'.

36. Notices appeared in issues of 3 August 1807, p. 3 and 17 August 1807, p. 4.

37. The d'Hondecoeter painting was not noted in the press, but it showed up in Jeffrey's gallery in May 1809. See Jeannie Chapel, 'William Beckford: Collector of Old Master Paintings, Drawings, and Prints', in *An Eye for the Magnificent*, 249, n. 145. Chapel is relying on the catalogue Jeffrey issued now in the possession of Philip Hewat-Jaboor.

38. Alex Kidson, *George Romney 1734–1802* (Exhibition catalogue), (2002), p. 226.

39. *The Beauties of Wiltshire*, I: 232.

40. *The Gentleman's Magazine*, 72, pt. 1 (March 1802): 218.

41. Beinecke Library, Yale University, Beckford, Gen Mss 102, Box 6, f. 109. Beckford's statement of expenses for Soane's work at Fonthill mentions 'making fair drawings of a design for forming the Gallery and introducing the Prints of the Vatican'.

42. For useful biographical information on both Elwin, Sr and his son, Hastings Elwin, Jr, see Hugh S. Torrens, 'The Life and Times of Hastings Elwin or Elwyn (1777–1852) and His Critical Role in Founding the Bath Literary and Scientific Institution in 1823', *The Geological Curator*, 8 (December 2005): 141-68.

43. *The Salisbury and Winchester Journal*, 31 August 1807, p. 4 and *The Gentleman's Magazine*, 77, pt. 2 (1807): p. 880, specified that it was 200 guineas.

44. Chapel, p. 247, n84.

45. *Excursions from Bath*, p. 122.

46. Giovanni Morelli, *Italian Painters Critical Studies of their Works*, trans. Ffoulkes (1893), p. 91.

47. *Excursions from Bath*, p. 123. Beckford bought this painting together with the Altieri Claudes in 1799 with the assistance of Henry Tresham (1749?–1814). *Farington Diary*, 4: 1218-19.

48. *Ibid.*, 3: 197.

49. *The Gentleman's Magazine*, 77, pt.2 (1807): 880.

50. Chapel, p. 240.

51. *Excursions from Bath*, p. 122.

52. First day, lot 63: 'Two pastoral pictures, by Casali' and lot 64: 'A painting, in a gilt frame, by ditto'.

53. *Life at Fonthill*, p. 42.

54. First day, lot 96: 'A painting on the cieling [*sic*] in the great hall'.

55. Phillips's handwriting is sometimes difficult to decipher, but the buyer's name appears to be 'Dennys by Lincoln', whom I have not been able to identify.

56. Hewat-Jaboor, p. 64.

57. *The Beauties of Wiltshire*, 1: 234 and Woodward, p. 34. The cabinets in the Soane niches were sold in 1802 for £84 each to Henry Woodford, a London cabinet-maker located at 26 New Street Square, Shoe Lane. James Christie, *A Catalogue of the most superb, capital, and valuable collection of Italian, French, Flemish and Dutch pictures* [owned by Beckford], 27 February 1802, lots 51-2.

58. Sir Ambrose Heal, *The London Furniture Makers from the Restoration to the Victorian Era 1660–1840* (1953), p. 126.

59. Moitte had also sculpted a marble statue of Ariadne for Beckford. Gisela Gramaccini, *Jean-Guillaume Moitte Leben und Werk* (1993), 2: 62.

60. *The Salisbury and Winchester Journal*, 31 August 1807, p. 4.

61. *Idem.*

62. *The Times*, 29 August 1807, p. 3.

Chapter 8

1. *Life at Fonthill*, p. 41.

2. *Idem.*, pp. 41-2.

3. 28 November 1806, Oliver, pp. 247-8.

4. John Wilton-Ely provides photographs of this model and discusses aspects of it in 'A Model for Fonthill Abbey', in eds. Colvin and Harris, *The Country Seat: Studies in the History of the British Country House* (1970), pp. 199-204. The model is currently on loan to Beckford's Tower and Museum in Bath. See also Amy Frost, 'Beckford's House of Card: An Analysis of the Fonthill Abbey Model', *The Beckford Journal*, 16 (2010): 114-123.

5. Steven Blake, 'William Beckford and Fonthill Abbey: A Victorian Showman's Account', *Bath History*, 9 (2002): 126-37. The Fonthill Abbey model, along with seventeen others, were ultimately donated to the Walters Art Gallery but they can no longer be traced and are assumed to have been destroyed during the Second World War.

6. Special thanks to Andrea Gilbert, Librarian of the Wallace Collection, for providing me with a copy of the catalogue.

7. *Salisbury and Winchester Journal*, 9 May 1808, p. 4 and 30 October 1809, p. 3.

8. Notices appeared in 3 August 1807, p. 3, and 17 August 1807, p. 4.

9. I have attempted to determine if the floors did go to Cappoquin House, but it burnt down in 1922. According to Charles Keane, the current proprietor, the family records and books are believed to have been destroyed in the fire.

10. See 'Diaries of the estate agent to the Earl of Pembroke' (1810–1840). These thirty-one diaries are in the Wiltshire and Swindon Archives, Salisbury and South Wiltshire Museum. There is a possibility the flooring went to Wilton House, which was undergoing renovations at the time, but I have not been able to determine if Ford was the estate agent as early as 1807.

11. There is an ms note in the margin: 'with the copper on it'. This lantern does not appear in any of the engraved views of Splendens I have seen.

12. Derek Lindstrum, *Sir Jeffry Wyattville Architect to the King* (1972), p. 54.

13. 17 August 1807, p. 1.

14. Anne Warren, 'The Building of Dodington Park', *Architectural History*, 34 (1991): 177.

15. Hoare, p. 26

16. Arthur M. Templeton, jun. (pseudo.), *New European Magazine*, 3, August 1823, pp. 135-42, as cited by Gemmett, *Beckford's Fonthill The Rise of a Romantic Icon* (2003), p. 308. De Cort's painting of Splendens contains an inscription in Latin on the back, apparently in the artist's own hand. The translations reads: 'The Fonthill Mansion That which he was able to accomplish by his genius and his own good right hand To the Most Noble, Most ingenious

lord, Lord William Beckford. The Judge, cultivator and Patron of the liberal arts, Henry de Cort dedicates: A native of Antwerp, Painter of the Royal French Academy, and of the most serene Price of Condé, 1791'. My thanks to Jean Bray, Sudeley Castle archivist, for supplying this inscription.

Chapter 9

1. Based on letters to Isaac Heard of 11 September and 11 October, 1808, Oliver, pp. 249-50. See also letter of 25 September, 1808, *Life at Fonthill*, pp. 83-5.
2. Based on a draft letter to Lady Craven, 22 July 1809, *England's Wealthiest Son*, p. 165.
3 . W.B. to Franchi, 22 June 1810, *Life at Fonthill*, p. 91.
4. Letter dated 23 December 1811, *The Beckford Journal*, 1 (Spring, 1995): 47-50. Bankes (d. 1855), the eldest son of Henry Bankes of Kingston Hall, Dorsetshire, represented the borough of Truro in Parliament from 1810 to 1812. A close friend of Byron, he later became MP for the University of Cambridge and the county of Dorset.
5. *A Description of Fonthill Abbey* (1812), p. 8.
6. *Life at Fonthill*, p.128.
7. *Idem.*
8. *Ibid.*, p. 150.
9. *Ibid.*, pp. 226, 230.
10. *Ibid.*, p. 226.
11. These figures represent exterior measurements as provided by Britton, p. 13.
12. MS Beckford, Bodleian Library, c. 86, f. 28.
13. Brockman, p. 112.
14. Britton, p. 11.
15. *Ibid.*, p. 12.
16. The exact dimensions, according to Rutter, were 112 ft. 4 in. long, 13 ft. 7 in. wide, 15 ft. 4 in. high. Rutter, p. 55.
17. Brockman, p. 112.
18. Storer, p. 15.
19. *Magnificent Effects at Fonthill Abbey to be Sold by Auction by Mr. Christie* (1822), lots 58, 85.
20. Rutter gives the dimensions of the Gallery as 68 ft. long, 16 ft. 10 in. wide, 17 ft. 10 in. high; the Sanctuary as 13 ft. long, 14 ft. wide, 16 ft. high; the Oratory as 12 ft. long, 14 ft. wide, 17 ft. high. He neglected to mention the measurements of the Vaulted Corridor. My estimate is that it was approximately 34 ft. long, 14 ft. wide, 17 ft. high. Rutter, p. 36. Neither Rutter nor Britton identified the length of the vestibules leading into King Edward's and St Michael's galleries. Each of these, utilising the extant floor plans of the Abbey, appears to have been approximately 16 ft, 6 in. long. Thus, combined with the 35 ft. diameter of the Grand Saloon or Octagon Hall, the length of the vista from one end of the two galleries to the other would be 307 feet, as Rutter recorded.
21. *Ibid.*, p. 33.
22. *Memoirs*, 2: 53-4.
23. *Journal in Portugal and Spain*, p. 301.
24. Wainwright, pp. 117-18. A photograph of the table appears on p. 217.
25. Rutter., p. 36.
26. *Ibid.*, p. 37.
27. Goldsmiths identified by Lady Anne Hamilton; she also identified the '36 wax lights in Gold Branches and Candlesticks' that surrounded the statue of St Anthony in 1803 as by goldsmith Henri Auguste of Paris. MS Beckford, Bodliean Library, e. 4, f. 4.
28. Britton, p. 47.
29. Rutter, p. 40.

30. MS Beckford, Bodleian Library, c. 86, f. 28.

31. Rutter, p. 28.

32. *Ibid.*, p. 8.

33. Storer, p. 18.

34. Redding MS, c. 86, f. 18.

35. Rutter, p. 24.

36. MS Beckford, Bodleian Library, c. 86, f. 28.

37. Storer, p. 17.

38. *The New Monthly Magazine and Literary Journal*, 8 (1823): 372. The poet Thomas Campbell (1777–1844) was the editor at this time. Cyrus Redding was serving as the sub-editor.

39. Rutter, p. 21.

40. *The New Monthly Magazine*, 8 (1823): 373.

41. 'A Visit to Fonthill Abbey', *Literary Gazette*, 17 August 1822, p. 520.

42. For details of his offer to the Duke of Hamilton, see *Life at Fonthill*, pp. 326-31.

43. 'Fonthill Abbey', *Morning Chronicle*, 26 September 1823, p. 3.

Chapter 10

1. 14 December 1807, *Farington Diary*, 8: 3166-7.

2. 26 July 1810, *Life at Fonthill*, pp. 93-4.

3. MS Beckford, Bodleian Library, c. 86, f. 40c. A press report matches almost word for word Redding's account of Beckford's initial intention to continue to live on the estate in a separate cottage by Bitham Lake. 'Mr. Beckford', *Morning Herald*, 18 September 1823, p. 1.

4. *Magnificent Effects at Fonthill Abbey* (1822), pp. iii-v.

5. For a further discussion of Beckford's book collecting tastes and interests, see *The Consummate Collector*, pp. 13-20.

6. 'Fonthill Abbey', *Morning Herald*, 7 October 1822, p. 2.

7. 'Fonthill Abbey', *The Gazette of Fashion*, 31 August 1822, p. 65. See also Gemmett, 'The Critical Reception of William Beckford's Fonthill', *English Miscellany*, 19 (1968): 133-51.

8. 7 August 1822, *Life at Fonthill*, p. 336.

9. Author attribution derives from Britton, *Graphical and Literary Illustrations of Fonthill Abbey*, who identified these articles as 'written by the lively and versatile pen of the learned author of several volumes on bibliography and bibliomania; and who, by his writings on the latter subject, has contributed more to increase than to cure the disease'(p. 15). Furthermore, a piece on Stourhead extracted from this extended review appeared under the pseudonym Cuthbert Tonstall in *The Gentleman's Magazine*, 92, pt. 2 (1822): 388-91. These quotations are from the first and sixth essays. *The Museum, or Record of Literature, Fine Arts, Science, Antiquities, the Drama*, etc., 5 October 1822, p. 379 and 9 November 1822, p. 456.

10. Rutter's book, a precursor to his more extended and elegant book on Fonthill published the following year, appeared under the title *A Description of Fonthill Abbey, and Demesne* (Shaftesbury, 1822); Whittaker's book appeared as *A New Guide to Fonthill Abbey* with an engraved frontispiece by William Read (Witham, Essex, 1822) and in a London edition with a frontispiece by Thomas Higham; Storer's book published originally in 1812, *A Description of Fonthill Abbey* was published again in London by Sherwood, Neely, and Jones and in Salisbury by Brodie and Dowding in 1822 and 1823. The first issue of *The Portfolio* (1823) contained Storer's description and interior views of the Abbey. Earlier editions of Easton's book, *The Salisbury Guide*, provided only a brief description of Fonthill Abbey.

11. For a census of the various engravings that appeared, see Jon Millington, 'Engravings of Fonthill', *The Beckford Journal*, 7 (Spring, 2001): 47-58.

12. 24 August 1822, p. 540. Signed with the initials M. J.

13. The following list includes individuals who visited Fonthill in 1822 but whose names did not appear again in the press notices for the 1823 sale: Lord Andover, Lord Apsley, Lord Ashley [Earl of Shaftesbury], Duke of Beaufort, Lord G[eorge] Bentinck, the Right Hon. Sturges Bourne, Lord Braybrooke, Earl of Bridgewater, Lord and Lady Bridport, Earl of Carlisle, Lord Carrington, Romeo Coates, Mrs Coutts [Harriet Mellon], Earl Cowper, Earl of Craven, Earl of Darnley, Countess de Rolle, Duke of Devonshire, Countess of Effingham, Lord George Fane, Lady Fraser, His Royal Highness the Duke of Gloucester, Earl Harcourt, Lord Holland, Countess Howe, Sir Thomas Lawrence, Sir Charles Long, Lord and Lady Murray, Lord and Lady Northcote, Lady E. Palk, Lady Pollen, Lady Mary Vaughan, Duke of Wellington, Earl of Westmorland. Appendix I provides a compilation of the names of some of the prominent visitors to the estate in 1823.

14. 'Fonthill', *Morning Herald*, 7 October 1822, p. 2.

15. *The Times*, 14 September 1822, p. 2.

16. *The Times*, 30 September 1822, p. 3.

17. *Idem.*

18. *Once Upon a Time* (1865), p. 506.

19. 2 September 1822, *Life at Fonthill*, p. 337-8.

20. Beginning with the *Literary Gazette* issue of 17 August 1822. These five contributions appeared anonymously. I have based this attribution on Jerdan who recorded that 'from Fonthill, in the autumn of 1822, he [Macquin] contributed … a series of papers giving an historical account of the Abbey, a biography of the family of Beckford, the author of "Vathek", and a fine description of the place and its contents previous to its sale. The second paper was illustrated by a drawing, of which I published a neat engraving. The fifth is in verse.…'. The *Autobiography of William Jerdan* (1853), 3: 107-8. The poem appeared in the issue of 21 September 1822, pp. 602-3. The four essays are reprinted in *Beckford's Fonthill The Rise of a Romantic Icon*, 240-55; the complete poem with notes is reprinted on pp. 390-94.

21. 'Armorial Decorations at Fonthill Abbey', *The Gentleman's Magazine*, 92, pt. 2 (September, October, November, 1822): 201-4; 317-20; 409-14.

22. 7 August 1822, *Life at Fonthill*, pp. 337-8.

23. MS Beckford, Bodleian Library, b. 8, ff. 19-20.

24. The sale document lists only the lot numbers from A Catalogue of the Magnificent Effects At Fonthill Abbey, Wilts. to be sold by Auction, by Mr. Christie (1822). The lots Beckford selected were First day, Lots 18 'Two extremely rare BLACK AND GOLD JAPAN SALVERS with the Fung-Hoang and foliage.—N.B. These fine pieces came from the collection of the Duc de Bouillon'; 52 'A very singular [Japan tray], the ground of a curious wood artificially waved, with storks in various attitudes on the shore, mosaic border and avanturine back, from the museum of the Duchess of Portland'; 73 'Two fine illumined missal drawings in one black and gold frame'; 87 'An extremely curious enamel on copper, in three divisions, the centre representing the Descent from the Cross, and Daniel and St. Paul in the side compartments, in an ebony frame'; Second day, Lots 61 'BAUER. A fine and elaborate small drawing of figures disembarked, and architecture'; 62 'Three curious illumined miniature paintings of Saints of the Greek Church, in a black and gold frame, in 3 compartments'; 71 'A MINIATURE PORTRAIT, in water-colours of LOUIS XII. at his Devotions, with St. Louis, St. Michael, Charlemagne, and St. Denys'; 93 'A fine miniature drawing of Saint Charles Borromeo, in a very richly carved and gilt frame'; Third day, Lot 26 'A round CUP and COVER of ORIENTAL MAMMILLATED CALCEDONY undulated, mounted in sliver gilt, delicately engraved in the Persian style, the stem enriched with oriental rubies, set in gold, most singularly beautiful'; Fourth day, Lot 58 'A pair of beautiful silver gilt candlesticks, executed by VULLIAMY, from an original design by Holbein'; Fifth day, Lots 41 'A Circular Deep SALVER of LIMOSIN ENAMEL, on copper, embellished with a Procession of Diana and Nymphs returning from the Chace; the border of Raffaellesque device, the bowl of the salver also externaly [*sic*] decorated with masks and ornaments.

The date is inscribed in enamel, 1563, P. R. It was made for Henry II. Of France, and was presented by him to Diane de Poictiers. It is mounted with a central boss bearing her cypher, a triple crescent, and inscription; and the border also enriched with monograms'; 46 'A VESSEL, of compressed oval shape, formed of a LARGE BLOCK of SARDONYX hollowed out, and the surface incrusted with vine leaves of good design and sharpest execution. A pair of Satyr's Heads are sculptured as Handles to the Vase; the bottom is externally carved with foliage, and affords reason for believing, that this rare and very curious article must have been executed by a GREEK ARTIST in ASIA MINOR. It is protected at the top by a rim of fine gold'; 58 'A Magnificent Large Oval CASSOLETTE, of Hungarian Agate, massively mounted in silver, engraved, chased and gilt, ornamented with masks of satyrs admirably modelled, and of the first workmanship'; Seventh day, Lots 5 'Flemish A small Portrait of a Lady, with the date 1662'; 9 'Stothard Tom O'Shanter: from Burns's Poems'; 10 'Steenwyck Interior of a Cathedral, with figures'; 15 Holbein A small Portrait of a Man with the Hands joined in Prayer—very beautifully finished'; 16 'Walckenberg The Building of the Tower of Babel, with a Multitude of small Figures. See the Catalogue of King Charles's Collection'; 25 'Breughel A Landscape with numerous Figures, and Christ bearing his Cross, with distant View of Jerusalem and Mount Calvary'; 34 'Siqueira The Reposo in Egypt, with Infant Angels—a very pleasing specimen of a distinguished Portuguese Artist'; 41 'Cima di Conegliano The Virgin, in richly coloured Drapery, holding the Infant in her Lap. In the distance, is a Landscape with view of part of the buildings of a fortified town, with a clear and brilliant sky. This beautiful specimen of one of the scarcest Masters of the early Venetian School, formerly belonged to Mr. Strange, and was originally in the collection of the Nuncio di Verona'; 53 'Breughel A small River Scene with Boats and Figures'; 76 'Wilson A small Landscape, View on the Tiber, with a Figure on a Timber Raft, and a Female reposing on the Front Ground. 13 From Mr. Knight's Collection, undoubtedly, one of the most beautiful productions of the Master'; 81 'Peters A View of Ostend, and the Mouth of the Harbour, with Boats putting out—very fine and spirited'; 97 'West A Grand Mass in the Interior of St. George's Chapel at Windsor, in which are introduced the Kings of France and Scotland, when Prisoners at Windsor: cabinet size'; 98 'Poelemborg A Landscape, with Two elegant draped Female Figures; beyond which are others in a Pool of Water, half-concealed by the rising front-ground; rocky Masses and Ruins, with Wood, crown a Bank in the distance'; 99 '[Poelenburgh] A [Landscape] with Ruins, and Pastoral Figures, and an elegant Group of Half-draped Females in the front-ground; finished with great delicacy'; 112 'G. Poussin A grand Landscape, composed of fine mountainous Scenery, and at the foot of it a woody Glade, where Figures are Reposing; a Conflagration of some Buildings on the half-ascent of the hills, is represented with great spirit, and gives a lively interest to the scene'; 'either Lot 106 or 113 option, as to the said John Farquhar', Lot 106 'Berghem A small Landscape with Cattle feeding and reposing on a rising Pasture Ground; a Shepherd and Shepherdess piping on the left; with a hilly distance, and a very brilliant sky. This pure and exquisite bijou was formerly in the Cabinet de Praslin. Where it ranked high, as the Diamant de Berghem'; Lot 113 'Berghem The very celebrated Sea Port of the PRASLIN CABINET, termed the Embarquement des Vivres; and noticed in the Catalogue as one of the three principal ornaments of that Collection. It represents a group of Figures and Cattle on the Shore of the Gulf of Genoa, which is enlivened with Buildings and Shipping, painted in the finest style of the Master'.

25. MS Beckford, Bodleian Library, b. 8, ff. 19-20.
26. *The Salisbury and Winchester Journal*, 14 October, 1822, p. 4.
27. *Morning Post*, 8 October 1822, p. 3.
28. *Observer*, 13 October 1822, p. 4.
29. 7 October 1822, *Life at Fonthill*, p. 340.
30. [December], 1822, MS Beckford, Bodleian Library, c. 30, ff. 122-3.
31. *New European Magazine*, 2 (January 1823), p. 83.

32. Draft copy, Tuesday 25 March 1823, MS Beckford, Bodleian Library, c. 14, f. 55.
33. W.B. to George Clarke, 1 April 1832, *Consummate Collector*, p. 134.
34. 'Fonthill Abbey', *Morning Chronicle*, 24 September 1822, p. 3.
35. 'Wiltshire', *The Times*, 10 December 1830, p. 4.
36. 9 January 1823, Oliver, p. 289.
37. *The Gentleman's Magazine*, 92, pt. 2 (October, 1822): 291.

Chapter 11

1. 'Fonthill', *Morning Herald*, 9 September 1823, p. 3.
2. 'Fonthill', *Ibid.*, 3 October 1823, p. 3.
3. *Idem.*
4. Based on information provided in Phillips's 1823 sale catalogue, I indicated in Beckford's Fonthill (p. 138) that a separate sale of the wines and liqueurs in the Abbey cellars took place on 30 and 31 October 1823. However, I have since determined that Phillips re-scheduled this sale. It actually occurred on Saturday, 15 November. He also issued a separate catalogue for the occasion, a copy of which has not been located.
5. 'A Day at Fonthill Abbey', *The New Monthly Magazine*, 8 (1823): 371.
6. 'Fonthill Abbey', *Morning Post,* 8 September 1823, p. 3.
7. 'Fonthill Abbey', *Ibid.*, 10 September 1823, p. 3.
8. *The Salisbury and Winchester Journal*, 4 August 1823, p. 4.
9. 'Fonthill Abbey', *Morning Herald*, 29 August 1823, p. 3.
10. 'Fonthill', *Morning Chronicle*, 30 August 1823, p. 3. This attribution is based on Beckford's identification of Littlebury as Dibdin, or 'P.D.', for 'Puppy Dibdin', as he commonly referred to him. The occasion was Dibdin's second visit. The account of his first visit in 1822 appeared in five succeeding numbers of *The London Museum* under the pseudonym of Cuthbert Tonstall. See fn 12 for Beckford's identification.
11. 'Fonthill Abbey', *Morning Herald*, 8 September 1823, p. 3.
12. *Morning Chronicle*, 26 August 1823, p. 3. In a manuscript note to this article, Beckford reacted: 'Poor P.D. treated with very little ceremony. Woeful disappointments—probably an effusion of P.D. himself under the signature of Isaac Littlebury'. MS Beckford, Bodleian Library, b. 6, ff. 65-6.
13. *The New Monthly Magazine*, 8 (1823): 368.
14. 'Fonthill', *Morning Herald*, 10 September 1823, 2.
15. 'Fonthill', *Ibid.*, 12 September 1823, 3.
16. 'Fonthill', *Ibid.*, 27 September 1823, 3.
17. 'Fonthill Abbey', *Morning Post*, 13 October 1823, p. 3.
18. 'Fonthill Abbey', *Morning Chronicle*, 26 September 1823, p. 3.

Chapter 12

1. *The Times*, 12 September 1823, p. 2.
2. See Appendix I for a list of prominent visitors to the estate as identified in press notices.
3. As quoted by the *The Times*, 30 September 1823, p. 3.
4. *Literary Gazette*, 20 September 1823, p. 602 and 27 September 1823, pp. 617-8.
5. *The Times*, 26 September 1823, p. 3.
6. First published in the *Literary Museum and Register of Belle Lettres*, 1 November 1823, pp. 701-2, under the title 'The Sale at Fonthill A Fragment'. This periodical is extremely rare. Fortunately, Beckford, as was his habit, saved a clipping of the poem, which I found among his papers at the Bodleian Library. This poem was also issued separately as a broadside

under the title 'Fonthill Sale A Parody' and signed with the initials 'A.A.W.', which stands for Alaric A. Watts (1797–1864), author of *Poetical Sketches* (1822) and editor of the *Leeds Intelligencer*, the newspaper that launched the attack against Harry Phillips for including books and works of art in the sale that were not considered to be genuine Fonthill items. I have used the broadside here since Watts revised the first printing with textual variations and punctuation. Author attribution derives from Watts's own admission in a copy of the broadside on file in the Beinecke Library, Yale University. Watts sent the broadside to John Britton, noting on the verso that there were errors in the first printing that were corrected in the broadside. The broadside also contains a hand-written date at the top as '19 Jan 1824'. Beinecke Library, Beckford Collection, GEN MSS 102, Box 4, f. 100. Lewis Melville reproduced the broadside for the first time, but without author identification, pp. 315-19.

7. AL, to John Britton, 6 October 1823, Beinecke Library, Beckford Collection, GEN MSS 102, Box 4, f. 71. Adams's letter also provides the details regarding Phillips's reactions.

8. *The Salisbury and Winchester Journal*, 27 October 1823, p. 4.

9. *The Times*, 5 November 1823, p. 3. Interestingly, Lewis paid for the publication of his response as an 'Advertisement', probably to ensure its appearance.

10. The individuals identified in Lewis's provenance of the vase were George Stanley, auctioneer, 21 Old Bond Street, George Winyett Farmer, jeweller and silversmith, 32 Tavistock Street, Covent Garden, and either Edward Foster, 14 Greek Street, Soho, or Charles Foster, 6 Angel Court, Throgmorton Street, both London auctioneers. The other dealers Lewis mentions as supporters of his assessment included the firm of J. T. & C Hawley, 75 Strand, goldsmiths and watch-makers and John Boykett Jarman, goldsmith and jeweller, 30 St James's Street.

11. MS Beckford, Bodleian Library, b. 8, f. 7. On the verso of this document is written in Beckford's hand 'Acct of the Topaz Vase'. There is no date, but the paper is watermarked 1810.

12. 'The Hungarian Topaz Cup', *The Salisbury and Winchester Journal*, 17 November 1823, p. 4.

13. See Joseph Alsop, 'The Faker's Art', *New York Review of Books*, 23 October 1986, pp. 25-31 and Richard E. Stone, 'A Noble Imposture: The Fonthill Ewer and Early-Nineteenth-Century Fakery', *Metropolitan Museum Journal*, 32 (1997): 175-206.

14. 29 October, 1819, *Life at Fonthill*, p. 324.

15. 28 October 1819, *Ibid.*, pp. 323-4.

16. *The Times*, 17 November 1823, p. 3.

17. 'Drury Lane', *The Guardian*, 28 December 1823, p. 413.

18. 'The Drama', *The New Monthly Magazine and Literary Historical Register*, 12 (February 1824): 56.

19. 'Drury-Lane Theatre', *The Times*, 27 December 1823, p. 3; 'The Drama', *The London Magazine*, 9 (February 1824): 201.

20. 'Fonthill Abbey', *London Magazine*, 6 (November, 1822): 405.

21. *New European Magazine*, 3 (August, 1823): 135-42. This magazine was published under this title by John Letts, Jr. 32 Cornhill, London, from July 1822 to June 1824. The editor and most of the contributors remain unknown. Arthur M. Templeton, Jun. is a pseudonym, a name that was used in the earlier *European Magazine* with the addition of 'Jun.' at the end of the name. Percival G. Somerset is the editor's pseudonym. *British Literary Magazines The Romantic Age*, 1789–1836, ed. Sullivan (1983), pp. 327-30.

22. *Morning Chronicle*, 8 October 1823, p. 4. See also Appendix II for details.

23. *The Salisbury and Winchester Journal*, 20 October 1823, p. 4

24. *Selections from the Writings of the Late J. Sidney Taylor* (1843), p. 349.

25. 'Illumination of the Abbey', *Morning Chronicle*, 24 October 1823, p. 4.

26. 'Fonthill Abbey', *Morning Post*, 1 October 1823, p. 3.

27. 10 February 1815, *Life at Fonthill*, pp. 173-4.

28. *Passages of a Working Life During Half a Century* (1865), I: 311.

29. Signed 'A Passerby', *The Gentleman's Magazine*, 91, pt. 2 (December, 1821): 495-6.

30. *The Diary & Memoirs of John Allen Giles*, ed. Bromwich (2000), pp. 41-2.

31. Signed 'H' 'Fonthill Abbey in Ruins', *The Gentleman's Magazine*, 96, pt. 1 (February, 1826): 123. See also the letter, dated 21 December 1825, from a person on the scene, published in *The Gentleman's Magazine*, 95, pt. 2 (December, 1825): 557.

32. Loudon, 2: 446-7.

33. *Memoirs*, 2: 258.

34. Crowley, XIII, 161; Hoare, p. 24. For additional details of these complex transfers, see John B. Nichols, *Historical Notices of Fonthill Abbey, Wiltshire* (1836), pp. 32-4.

35. *Catalogue of the Entire Astronomical, Chemical, and Philosophical Library of the Late John Farquhar, Esq. of Fonthill*; including Six Volumes of Elaborate and Splendid Patna Drawings. Which will be Sold by Acution by Mr. Sotheby … on Thursday, the 1st of March, 1827 and four following days.

36. Letter signed 'T. A. jun.' and dated, 'Shaftesbury, May 15', *The Gentleman's Magazine*, 96, pt. 1 (May, 1826): 424. Adams was a bookseller from Shaftesbury and author of *History of the Ancient Town of Shaftesbury from the Founder, Alfred the Great* (1809). In an unpublished letter to John Britton, dated 13 November 18[2]3, Adams provided a description of the interior of the Abbey, following his own visit: 'I have been asked[?] to describe the effect of the illumination at that place, or rather the lighting up of it—illumination carries with it an idea of brilliancy, nothing could be more different. It had the appearance of a gentleman laying in state only wanting the sarcophagus to complete it, for the purple curtains by candle light appearing black and the crimson ones not very light together with Mr. Goodell's performance on the organ of some of the heavy choruses of Handel and the service of the dead … Many were disappointed but Mr. Heber, my Ld Arundell's party were delighted. So were others.' John Hodgkin MS, Eng. Misc. 222, ff. 44-5, Bodleian Library, Oxford University.

37. MS Beckford, Bodleian Library, c. 14, f. 81.

38. Richard Gatty, *Portrait of a Merchant Prince, James Morrison 1789–1857* (1976), p. 111.

39. Lansdown, pp. 38-48.

40. It still exists today, though in a badly weather-worn condition, and can be seen in the garden of Wardour Castle.

Chapter 13

1. 'Foreword' Brockman, p. xii. Jon Millington has compiled an interesting exhibition catalogue of Fonthill souvenirs that demonstrates the keen interest in the Abbey during Beckford's lifetime. *Souvenirs of Fonthill Abbey* (1994).

2. 'Fonthill Abbey', *Morning Chronicle*, 17 September 1823, p. 3.

3. 'A Day at Fonthill Abbey', *The New Monthly Magazine and Literary Journal*, 8 (1823): 376.

4. 'Fonthill Abbey', *The Literary Chronicle and Weekly Review*, 19 October 1822, p. 666.

5. Rutter, pp. 83-4.

6. *The Gentleman's Magazine*, 92, pt. 2 (October, 1822): 291.

7. *Gazette of Fashion*, 31 August 1822, p. 65. See also [John Britton], 'Fonthill Abbey', *The Museum; or Record of Literature, Fine Arts, Science, Antiquities, the Drama, &c.*, no. 19 (1822): 300-1.

8. *Morning Post*, 22 August 1823, p. 3.

9. *Morning Chronicle*, 21 August 1823, p. 2.

10. 'Fonthill Abbey', *Morning Chronicle*, 20 August 1823, p. 3.

11. Based on a transcription of the original letter of 29 August 1823 by Ian Fleming Williams and published in the *Beckford Newsletter*, ed. Millington (Spring, 1983), pp. 8-9.

12. Dated 21 August 1822. 'Written for the Second Edition of J. Rutter's Description of the Abbey', *The Gentleman's Magazine*, 92, pt. 2 (August, 1822): 102. William Lisle Bowles (1762–1850), divine, poet and antiquary, served as vicar of Bremhill, Wiltshire from 1804

to 1850. He published poetry, an edition of Alexander Pope and various ecclesiastical and antiquarian works.

13. 'Fonthill Abbey', *The London Magazine*, 5 (November 1822): 405-6.

14. 'Pictures at Wilton, Stourhead, &c.', *The London Magazine*, 8 (October, 1823): 359.

15. 'Fonthill Abbey', *The Examiner*, 10 August 1823, p. 514. Hazlitt has been recently identified as the author of this essay. See *New Writings of William Hazlitt*, ed. Duncan Wu (Oxford, 2007), 1: 444-49.

16. See Damian W. Davies and Laurent Chatel, '"A Mad Hornet": Beckford's Riposte to Hazlitt', *European Romantic Review*, 10 (Fall, 1999): 452-79. Macquin's letters in French are among the Beckford Papers. My quotations are from the translations provided in this article.

17. 'Fonthill and Its Late Owner', *New Times*, September 23, 1823, p. 2.
    Another condemnation ran in two consecutive issues of the *Sunday Times*. The editor at the time was Daniel Whittle Harvey, known for writing hard-hitting lead articles to capture reader interest. The first of the two articles noted about Beckford that 'the story of his past life is reviewed with unyielding rancour—the wild caprices of his restless mind are arrayed as sins, and a frightful stain upon his moral character has rung across the land'. 'Fonthill Abbey—Mr. Beckford—and Vathek', 28 September 1823, p. 4 and 5 October 1823, p. 1.

18. *History Today*, 10: 686-7.

19. Wainwright, pp. 121-7; 131-6; 141-2.

20. *Ibid.*, p. 143.

21. *A List of Carvings and other Works of Art* (1854), p. 26.

22. *Works of William Hazlitt*, 19: 280.

23. Stanley Jones, 'The Fonthill Abbey Pictures: Two Additions to the Hazlitt Canon', *Journal of the Warburg and Courtauld Institutes*, 41 (1978): 278-96.

24. F. W. Haydon, *Benjamin Robert Haydon: Correspondence and Table Talk* (1876), 2: 79.

25. 'Notices of Curious and Highly Finished Cabinet Pictures at Fonthill Abbey', *Morning Chronicle*, 20 August, p. 3; 22 August, p. 3; 25 August, p. 3; 1 September 1823, p. 2.

26. *Ibid.*, 20 August 1823, p. 3.

27. *Morning Chronicle*, 30 September 1823, p. 2.

28. 'Fonthill Abbey', *The Examiner*, 10 August 1823, p. 514.

29. 'The Main Chance', *The New Monthly Magazine*, 17 (February 1828): 120.

30. *England's Wealthiest Son*, p. 170.

31. *New Monthly Magazine*, 8 (1823): 404.

32. *The Gentleman's Magazine*, 92, pt. 2 (December 1822): 491-4.

33. 'I enclosed a few remarks on the Abbey written by my friend Garbett, an Architect of Winchester, & intended by him for Gents. Mag.' Copy of a letter to Beckford, 23 October 1822, Beinecke Library, Beckford Collection, GEN MSS. 102, Box 8, f. 181.

34. *The Salisbury and Winchester Journal*, 30 September 30, 1822, p. 4.

35. 'Fonthill Abbey', *Morning Chronicle*, 13 September 1823, p. 3.

36. John Harris, 'C. R. Cockerell's 'Ichnographica Domestica', *Architectural History*, 14 (1971): 15-16.

37. *The Salisbury and Winchester Journal*, 8 September 1823, p. 4.

38. 'Fonthill Abbey', *The Museum; or Record of Literature, Fine Arts, Science, Antiquities, the Drama, &c.*, no. 17 (1822): 264. Britton was identified as the author of this essay in the August 1822 issue of *The Gentleman's Magazine*, 92, pt. 2 where it was reprinted on pp. 100-3. See also Britton's abbreviated description of the Abbey in his *Beauties of England and Wales* (1814), 15: 265-8 for textual similarities. Beckford saw the manuscript before it was published and provided some emendations.

39. ALS, 13 July 1835. MS Beckford, Bodleian Library, c. 27, ff. 32-3.

40. ALS, dated 'Fonthill', 5 September 1822 to Beckford at the Clarendon Hotel, London, MS Beckford, Bodleian Library, c. 27, ff. 14-15a.

41. ALS, 30 July 1823, MS Beckford, Bodleian Library, c. 27, ff. 16b-17.

42. The Chinese vase, now in the National Museum of Ireland, dated from *c.* 1340 and is today considered to be one of the earliest documented pieces of Chinese porcelain to have reached Europe. The Limoges enamelled chasse Beckford wanted to include is now in the Metropolitan Museum. The rare Rubens vase is in the Walters Art Gallery in Baltimore. See Wainwright, 133-6 and Arthur Lane, 'The Gaignières-Fonthill Vase: A Chinese Porcelain of about 1300', *Burlington Magazine* 103 (April 1961): 124-32. The chasse Britton substituted was owned by the antiquary Thomas Astle (1735–1803). Ironically, Britton noted the similarity between the two reliquaries in *Illustrations of Fonthill Abbey*, p. 55. Marie-Madeleine Gauthier provides a full history of the Beckford chasse in Émaux méridioneaux: *Catalogue international de l'ouevre de Limoges*, I (1987): 181-2.
43. ALS, 5 September 1823, Beinecke Library, Beckford Collection, GEN MSS 102, Box 1, f. 8.
44. *Illustrations of Fonthill Abbey*, p. 39.
45. *Ibid.*, pp. 51-2.
46. 'Conversations of the Late W. Beckford, Esq.', *The New Monthly Magazine*, 62 (December 1844): 516.
47. The article he was responding to and quoted from here was 'Mr. Beckford Fonthill Abbey', *The Gleaner, or Weekly Historical Register*, 15 October 1823, pp. 407-9. For Wyatt's response, see *The Morning Herald*, 1 November 1823, p. 3.
48. Stephen Clarke addresses Britton's unhappiness with Cattermole's work in 'The Troubled Gestation of Britton's Illustrations of Fonthill', *The Beckford Journal*, 6 (Spring 2000): 58-74.
49. Copy of an ALS, W.B. to Britton, 3 October 1822, Beinecke Library, Beckford Collection, GEN MSS 102, Box VIII, f. 181.
50. ALS, 5 September 1823, Beinecke Library, Beckford Collection, GEN MSS 102, Box 1, ff. 7-8.
51. ALS, Franchi to Britton, 3 October 1822, bound in Britton's personal copy of *Graphical and Literary Illustrations of Fonthill Abbey* (1823), Devizes Museum Library, f. 133.
52. ALS, Franchi to Britton, 9 November 1822, *Ibid.*, f. 136.
53. ALS, [September, 1823], *Ibid.*, f. 145.
54. Beinecke Library, Beckford Collection, Gen Mss 102, Box 9, f. 189.
55. *Ibid.*, f. 189.
56. Le Keux was invited but never responded. All of the other artists were not invited. There is a Shaw on the list, but it may not be Henry Shaw, who did the drawing for the east window in St Michael's Gallery.
57. *Delineations of Fonthill and its Abbey*, pp. vii; ix.
58. *England's Wealthiest Son*, p. 284, n. 35.
59. *The Salisbury and Winchester Journal*, 29 September 1823, p. 4.
60. ALS, 22 November 1823, MS Beckford, Bodleian Library, c. 27, ff. 18-19; Beckford's draft, MS Beckford, Bodleian Library, c. 27, f. 20.
61. J. C. Loudon, *An Encyclopedia of Gardening* (1824), 2: 999.
62. *The Gardener's Magazine*, 11: 442.

Chapter 14

1   *The New Monthly Magazine*, 61: 308.
2. *History of the Gothic Revival*, ed. Crook (1970), p. 61.
3. *History of the Modern Styles of Architecture*, 2nd ed. (1873), p. 360.
4. *Pageantry of Life* (1900), pp. 212-13.
5. *Memories of Old Wiltshire* (1906), p. 116.
6. *The Drift of Romanticism* (1913), p. 14.
7. *Travel-Diaries*, I: xliv.
8. *The Rule of Taste* (1936), p. 85.
9. Katharine Ashworth, "Tisbury's Ancient Secrets," *Country Life*, 4 November 1954, p. 1592.

10. *The Gothic Revival* (1964), p. 75.

11. Redding MS, c 86, f. 39.

12. *The Gothic Revival*, p. 77.

13. Oliver, p. 229.

14. *James Wyatt, Architect: 1748–1813* (1936), p. 157.

15. Michael McCarthy, *The Origins of the Gothic Revival* (1987), p. 2.

16. James Lees-Milne, *William Beckford* (1976), p. 52; James Macaulay, *The Gothic Revival 1745–1845* (1975), pp. 148; 210; 297; David Watkin, *The English Vision The Picturesque in Architecture, Landscape, and Garden Design* (1982), p. 108.

17. It is surprising how few writers have noticed this resemblance in their descriptions of Fonthill. A special thanks to Henry Maitland Clark, who as a resident of Tisbury and familiar with Westminster as MP for North Antrim, wrote to me in 2005 to remark about this relationship. As he wrote, 'The only thing I find peculiar is that none of the many writers who have studied and described Fonthill seem to have noted the resemblance, but perhaps few of them knew the Palace of Westminster as well as I do'.

18. Reynolds, Donald M. et. al. *Fonthill Castle: Paradigm of Hudson-River Gothic*. Riverdale, 1976, pp. 13-15; 20-2; 24.

19. *England's Wealthiest Son*, p. 176.

20. *The History of Gardens* (1979), p. 221.

21. Most notably John Wilton-Ely in "Beckford, Fonthill Abbey and the Picturesque," pp. 35-44 and his essay "Beckford's Fonthill Abbey: a Theatre of the Arts," in *The Beckford Society Annual Lectures 1996–1999*, ed. Millington (2000), pp. 3-22. See also Wainwright, pp. 109-46.

22. *Memoirs*, 2: 146.

23. *Ibid.*, 2: 226.

24. *Works of Art and Artists in England*, 3 (1838): 129-30.

Bibliography

I Books, Guide Books, Catalogues

Alexander, Boyd, ed. *Life at Fonthill 1807–1822 … From the Correspondence of William Beckford*. London: Rupert Hart-Davis, 1957.

Britton, John. *Graphical and Literary Illustrations of Fonthill Abbey, Wiltshire; with Heraldical and Genealogical Notices of the Beckford Family*. London, 1823.

Brockman, H. A. N. *The Caliph of Fonthill*. London: Werner Laurie, 1956.

Catalogue Raisonné of the Collection of Paintings at Fonthill Abbey. London: J. Davy, 1823.

Christie Auction Catalogue. *A Capital and Truly Valuable Collection of Original High-Finished Drawings, the whole executed by that eminent artist the younger Cozens, during a Tour through the Tyrol and Italy, in company with an Amateur of distinguished taste, from whose cabinet they are now first brought forward to public inspection … to be sold by Mr. Christie … on Wednesday, April 10 … London, 1805.*

—————————. *All the Truly Elegant Household Furniture, Silver-Gilt and Silver Plate, Oriental and Modern Porcelain; Some Pictures and Drawings … of William Beckford, Esq. of Fonthill … Which will be Sold by Auction, By Mr. Christie, on the Premises, No. 6 Upper Harley Street … May 9, 1817, & Three following days.*

—————————. *A Most Superb, Capital and Valuable Collection of Italian, French, Flemish, and Dutch Pictures, the property of a Gentleman, highly distinguished for his fine taste in the Arts; the whole selected with unbounded liberality, and now brought from his Seat at Fonthill, in Wiltshire … to be sold by Mr. Christie … Feb. 27 … London, 1802.*

—————————. *A Small, Capital, Genuine, and Select Collection of Pictures, lately consigned from Paris … the property of a Gentleman, brought from his seat at Fonthill, Wilts., but which did not arrive in time for the former Sale … to be sold by Mr. Christie … on Friday March 26 … London, 1802.*

—————————. *The Magnificent Effects at Fonthill Abbey, Wilts. to be Sold by Mr. Christie, October 1822*. London, 1822.

Collection of Fonthill Prints and Drawings, Lewis Walpole Library, Yale University, Farmington, Connecticut.

Cundall, E. G. *Fonthill Abbey A Descriptive Account of Five Water-Colour Drawings by J. M. W. Turner, R. A.* Haughton Hall Tarporley: Private Printing for Ralph Brocklebank, 1915.

Easton, James. *The Salisbury Guide, Giving an Account of the Antiquities of Old Sarum: the Ancient and Present State of New Sarum, or Salisbury, and the Cathedral. Comprising also a Brief Description of Fonthill Abbey … With the Distances of the Principal Towns and Villages … from Salisbury*. Salisbury, 1818. [other editions followed]

Evans Auction Catalogue. *Catalogue of a Collection of Curious, Rare and Valuable Books … the Whole are in Fine Condition, and Many from the Fonthill Collection, which will be sold*

by Auction, by Mr. Evans, at his house, No. 93, Pall Mall, on Monday, February 11, and three
following days. London], 1828.

Gemmett, Robert J. *Beckford's Fonthill The Rise of a Romantic Icon.* Norwich: Michael Russell,
2003.

_____., ed. *Sale Catalogues of Libraries of Eminent Persons,* Vol. 3, *William Beckford.*
London: Mansell & Sotheby Parke-Bernet, 1972.

_____. 'William Beckford and the Picturesque: A Study of Fonthill', Ph.D. diss.,
Syracuse University, 1967.

Gotlieb, Howard B. *Willliam Beckford of Fonthill Writer, Traveller, Collector, Caliph 1760–1844
A Brief Narrative and Catalogue of an Exhibition to Mark the Two Hundredth Anniversary of
Beckford's Death.* New Haven: Yale University Library, 1960.

Jeffrey, H[enry]. A Catalogue of a Valuable Collection of Paintings … Now on Sale at Jeffrey's
Gallery, Market-Place, Salisbury, 1809. Includes paintings by d'Hondecoeter and Casali and
some selected furniture pieces from Splendens.

Leigh, Sotheby Auction Catalogue. *A Catalogue of a Valuable and Elegant Collection of Books
Selected with Superior Judgment and Taste … Being a Portion of the Library of a Very
Distinguished Collector brought from his Seat in Wiltshire … Which will be Sold by Auction by
Leigh and S. Sotheby … Thursday, 9th June, 1808 and Two following days.* London, 1808.

_____. *A Catalogue of the Select and Valuable Library of Scarce and
Curious Books of a Gentleman, lately deceased … Which will be Sold by Auction by Leigh,
Sotheby, and Son … Thursday the 24th and Saturday the 26th Day* of *May, 1804.* London, 1804.

Miller, Norbert. *Fonthill Abbey Die dunkle Welt des William Beckford.* Munich: Carl Hensen
Verlag, 2012.

Millington, Jon. *Souvenirs of Fonthill Abbey.* [Exhibition Catalogue] Bath: Bath Preservation Trust,
1994.

Neale, J. P. *Graphical Illustrations of Fonthill Abbey, the Seat of John Farquhar, Esq. with an
historical description and notices of works of Art formerly preserved there.* London, 1824.

Nichols, John B. *Historical Notices of Fonthill Abbey, Wiltshire.* London, 1836.

Ostergard, Derek E., ed. *William Beckford, 1760–1844: An Eye for the Magnificent.* [Exhibition
Catalogue] New Haven and London: Yale University Press, 2001.

Phillips Auction Catalogue. *All of the magnificent Household Furniture [Glass, Statuary, Pictures,
Drawings, China] … and other valuable and splendid Effects, of Fonthill Mansion, near
Salisbury, Wilts … to be sold by Mr. Phillips … on Monday, August 17, and 6 following days …*
London, 1807.

_____. *Catalogue of the Whole of the Massive and Valuable Materials of that
Noble and Modern Stone Mansion Called Fonthill … Which Will Be Sold by Auction, by Mr.
Phillips … on the 16th of September, and following Days, 1807.*

_____. *Collection of Antient & Modern Prints & Drawings, Principally
Formed by William Beckford, Esq. A Catalogue of the Collection of Rare and Estimable Original
Drawings, Ancient & Modern Prints, and Books of Prints … Which will be Sold by Auction by
Mr. Phillips … On Monday, 1st of March, 1824, & Three following Days.* London, 1824.

_____. *Part of the superlatively elegant and magnificent Household Furniture,
Fittings, Organ by Crang, Marble busts, Bronzes, Pictures, Objets d'Art … and a variety of rare,
curious, and valuable Effects, the genuine property of William Beckford, Esq. of Fonthill, Wilts …
to be Sold by Mr. Phillips … on August 19 and 3 following days …* London, 1801.

_____. *Second Part of Auction at Fonthill, Wilts. A Catalogue of the Valuable
Building Materials of the Wing Erections and Colon[n]ades of Fonthill Mansion … Which Will
Be Sold by Auction, by Mr. Phillips … the 7th of October, 1801, and Two following days.* London,
1801.

_____. *The Unique and Splendid Effects of Fonthill Abbey. Catalogue of
the Extensive Assemblage of Costly and Interesting Property Which Adorns this Magnificent
Structure … Which will be Sold by Auction by Mr. Phillips, at the Abbey on Tuesday, the 23d of*

September, 1823, and Seven following Days and on Thursday, 16th October, and Four following Days. London, 1823.

_____. *The Valuable Library of Books, in Fonthill Abbey … Which will be Sold by Auction by Mr. Phillips at the Abbey, on Tuesday, the 9th of September, 1823, and Nine following Days, on Friday, the 3d of October, & Four following Days, and on Thursday, 23d October, 1823, & Four following Days.* London, 1823.

Rutter, John. *Delineations of Fonthill and its Abbey.* London, 1823.

_____. *A Description of Fonthill Abbey and Desmesne, in the County of Wilts*: Including a List of the Paintings, Cabinets, &c. [six editions published for the year], Shaftesbury, 1822.

_____. *A New Descriptive Guide to Fonthill Abbey and Demesne, for 1823, Including a List of its Paintings and Curiosities.* Shaftesbury, 1823.

_____. *Delineations of Fonthill and its Abbey.* London, 1823.

Sotheby Auction Catalogue. *A Catalogue of a Portion of the Library of William Beckford, Esq. of Fonthill; Comprising Many Valuable Articles in Topography, History, and Antiquities … Which will be Sold by Auction by Mr. Sotheby … May 6, 1817, and Two following Days.* London, 1817.

Storer, James. *A Description of Fonthill Abbey, Wiltshire.* London, 1812.

_____. *A Description of Fonthill Abbey, Wiltshire.* London, 1822.

Summers, Peter and Philippa Bishop. *William Beckford Some Notes on his Life in Bath 1822–1844 and A Catalogue of the Exhibition in the Holburne of Menstrie Museum.* Privately Printed, 1966.

Thorpe, Thomas. *A Catalogue … Comprising Upwards of Thirty Thousand Volumes of Rare, Curious, and Useful Books … Selected from Fonthill and Other Sales … Now Selling by Thomas Thorpe, No. 38 Bedford Street, Covent Garden.* London 1824.

[Whittaker, G. and W. B.]. *A New Guide to Fonthill Abbey, Wiltshire, the Seat of William Beckford, Esq. Comprising a Description of the Park and Buildings; Together with Brief Notices of Most of the Remarkable Productions of Nature and Art, Which are Now Deposited There, and Which are Exhibited and Offered for Sale by the Proprietor.* London, 1822.

William Beckford Exhibition 1976. The Victoria Gallery. Bath, 1976.

Wischermann, Heinfried. *Fonthill Abbey Studien zur Profanen Neugotik Englands im 18. Jahrhundert.* Freiberg: Berichte, 1979.

II Articles on Fonthill

'A Day at Fonthill Abbey', *The New Monthly Magazine and Literary Journal*, 8 (1823): 368-80.

An Architect [John Carter]. 'The Pursuits of Architectural Innovation', *The Gentleman's Magazine*, 81, pt. 1 (May 1801): 417–18.

An Artist. 'Fonthill Abbey', *Morning Chronicle*, 2 September 1822, p. 3; 5 September 1822, p. 3.

A Passer By. [Fonthill Abbey], *The Gentleman's Magazine*, 91, pt. 2 (December 1821): 495-6.

'A Visit to Fonthill Abbey', *The Weekly Entertainer and West of England Miscellany*, 9 September 1822, pp. 150-3; 16 September 1822, pp. 177-8; 23 September 1822, pp. 193-6.

A[dams], T[homas] ['Abbey of Fonthill'], *The Gentleman's Magazine*, 96, pt. 1 (May 1826): 424.

Aldrich, Megan. 'William Beckford's Abbey at Fonthill: From the Picturesque to the Sublime', in *William Beckford, 1760–1844: An Eye for the Magnificent*, ed. Derek Ostergard. New Haven and London: Yale University Press, 2001, 117-135.

Alexander, Boyd. 'Fonthill, Wiltshire—II, The Abbey and Its Creator, *Country Life*, 1 December 1966, pp. 1430-4.

_____. 'Fonthill, Wiltshire—III, William Beckford as Collector' *Country Life*, 8 December 1966, pp. 1572-6.

_____. 'William Beckford Man of Taste', *History Today*, 10 (October 1960): 686-94.

_____. 'William Beckford of Fonthill', *Yale University Library Gazette*, 35 (April, 1961): 161-9.

Alsop, Joseph. 'The Faker's Art', *New York Review of Books*, 23 October 1986, pp. 25-31.

'Anecdotes of Mr. Beckford', *Morning Post*, 20 September 1823, p. 3; 22 September 1823, p. 2.

'Anecdotes of Mr. Beckford', *The Observer*, 21 September 1823, p. 2.

Ashworth, Katharine. 'Tisbury's Ancient Secrets', *Country Life*, 4 November 1954, pp. 1590-2.

[Bacchus Statue], *The Gentleman's Magazine*, 67, pt. 2 (1797): 816.

Bath and Cheltenham Gazette additional notices on Fonthill: 23 September 1823, p. 3; 30 September 1823, p. 3; 28 October 1823, p. 3.

Bath Chronicle notices on Fonthill: 22 August 1822, p. 4; 29 August 1822, p. 3; 17 October 1822, p. 2.

Bath Journal and General Advertiser [Keenes's] notices on Fonthill: 19 August 1822, p. 4; 14 October 1822, p. 4; 4 November 1822, p. 4; 25 August 1823, p. 4; 20 October 1823, p. 4.

Baylis, Sarah.'Knight's in Painted Glass', *Country Life*, 7 February 2002, pp. 64-7.

'Beckford and Fonthill', *Chamber's Edinburgh Journal*, 2 (August 1844): 101-3.

'Biography of Eccentric Characters. William Beckford, Esq', *The Ladies' Monthly Museum*, 19 (February 1824): 67-71.

Bishop, Philippa. 'Settees from Fonthill Splendens', *Beckford Journal*, 1 (Spring 1995), 15-17.

Blake, Steven. 'William Beckford and Fonthill Abbey: A Victorian Showman's Account', *Bath History*, 9 (2002): 126-37.

Blunt, Anthony. 'Fonthill Abbey', *The Venture*, (February 1929): 75-81.

Britton, John. 'Fonthill Abbey', in *The Beauties of Wiltshire*. London, 1825, 3: 328-31.

_____. 'Fonthill', in *The Beauties of Wiltshire*. London, 1801, 1: 208-49.

_____. 'Fonthill Abbey', *The Museum, or Record of Literature, Fine Arts, Science, Antiquities, the Drama &c.*, no. 17 (1822): 264-5.

Brulé, André. 'Une visite à Fonthill en 1792', *Revue Anglo-Americaine*, 10 (1933): 33-42.

Buckland, W[illia]m. ['The Topaz Cup'], *The Times*, 17 November 1823, p. 3.

Carso, Kerry Dean. 'The Theatrical Spectacle of Medieval World Edwin Forrest's Fonthill Castle', *Winterthur Portfolio: A Journal of American Material Culture*, 39:1 (Spring 2004): 21-41.

Chapel, Jeannie. 'William Beckford: Collector of Old Master Paintings, Drawings and Prints, in *William Beckford, 1760–1844. An Eye for the Magnificent*, ed. D. Ostergard , London: Yale, 2001, 229-45.

Châtel, Laurent. 'The Mole, the Bat, and the Fairy or the Sublime Grottoes of "Fonthill Splendens"', *Beckford Journal*, 5 (Spring 1999): 53-74.

Claésson, Dick. 'Staging and Adapting the Nelson Visit', in *The Narratives of the Biographical Legend: The Early Works of William Beckford*. Göteborgs Universitet: Dissertation Edition, 2001.

Clarke, Stephen. 'Abbeys Real and Imagined: Northanger, Fonthill, and Aspects of the Gothic Revival', *Persuasions*, 20 (1998): 93-105.

_____. 'The Dispersal of the Collection as Public Spectacle: The Fonthill Abbey Sale of 1822-23 and the Strawberry Hill Sale of 1842', *Beckford Journal*, 13 (Spring 2007): 2-18.

_____. 'Fonthill Abbey and a Poem', *Beckford Journal*, 12 (Spring 2006): 3-9.

_____. 'Some New Yet Familiar Views of Fonthill Abbey', *Beckford Journal*, 17 (2011): 56-67.

_____. 'The Troubled Gestation of Britton's *Illustrations of Fonthill*', *Beckford Journal*, 6 (Spring 2000), 58-74.

[Clarke, William]. 'William Beckford Esq. Fonthill Abbey', in *Repertorium Bibliographicum; or, Some Account of the Most Celebrated British Libraries*. London, 1819, pp. 203-30.

Cooke, George A. *Cooke's Topographical Library, or, British Traveller's Pocket County Directory, Wiltshire*. London, [c. 1830], pp. 119-35.

Courier notices on Fonthill: 23 September 1822, p. 4; 9 October 1822; 21 August 1823, p. 3; 11 September 1823, p. 2; 12 September 1823, p. 2; 17 September 1823, p. 3; 18 September 1823, p. 3; 20 September 1823, p. 3; 22 September 1823, p. 4; 29 September 1823, p. 4; 1 October 1823, p. 2; 2 October 1823, p. 2; 3 October 1823, p. 3; 4 October 1823, p. 4; 16 October 1823, p. 4; 18 October 1823, p. 4; 24 October 1823, p. 4; 28 October 1823, p. 2; 7 November 1823, p. 4.

Craft, Adrian. 'Subterranean Enlightenment at Fonthill', *Beckford Journal*, 3 (Spring 1997): 30-3.

Crockery, Jr. 'The Fonthill Mania', *The Literary Chronicle and Weekly Review*, 20 September 1823, pp. 603-4.

Cundall, E. G. 'Turner Drawings of Fonthill Abbey', *The Burlington Magazine*, 29 (1916): 16-21.

Darton, Eric. 'Fonthill: John Farquhar and After', *Beckford Newsletter*, (Spring 1987): 6-7.

_____. 'William Beckford and Music. 4 The Harpsichord and Pianoforte', *Beckford Newsletter*, (Spring 1988): 5.

Davies, Damian Walford and Laurent Chatel. '"A Mad Hornet:" Beckford's Riposte to Hazlitt', *European Romantic Review*, 10, 11 (Fall, 1999; Winter, 2000): 452-79; 97-99.

'Description of Fonthill Abbey' in *The Flowers of Literature; Consisting of Selections from History, Biography, Poetry, and Romance* ... Second Edition, Revised and Corrected from the Work of the Late William Oxberry, London: Thomas Tegg, 1824, 4: 10-20.

Dillenberger, John. 'Paintings for William Beckford and Fonthill Abbey: 1795–1810', in *Benjamin West The Context of his Life's Work with Particular Attention to Paintings with Religious Subject Matter*. San Antonio: Trinity University Press, 1977], pp. 106-209.

E. M. S. [James Dallaway]. 'Progress, &c. of Stained Glass in England', *The Gentleman's Magazine*, 87, pt. 1 (April 1817): 309-15.

'Editor's Excursion to Fonthill Abbey', *New European Magazine*, 1 (October 1822): 364-70.

[Egan, Pierce]. *Real Life in London, or the Rambles and Adventures of Bob Tallyho, Esq. and his Cousin, the Hon. Tom Dashall, through the Metropolis*. London, 1824, 2: 640-8.

E[lderton ?], J[ohn]. 'Mr. Urban', *The Gentleman's Magazine*, 92, pt.1 (April 1822): 325-7.

Elderton John. 'Tour into the Lower Parts of Somersetshire', *The Gentleman's Magazine*, 61, pt. 1 (February 1791): 229-31.

'Epitome of Public Affairs', *The Ladies' Monthly Museum*, 16 (November 1822): 284-5.

'Fonthill', *The Adventurer of the Nineteenth Century*, 28 June 1823, pp. 177-81.

'Fonthill', *The Crypt, or Receptacle for Things Past*, 19 December 1827, p. 220.

'Fonthill', *The Gazette of Fashion and Magazine of Literature, the Fine Arts, and Belles Lettres*, 19 October 1822, pp. 181-2.

'Fonthill', *The Gentleman's Magazine*, 71, pt. 2 (September 1801): 853-4.

'Fonthill', *Handbook for Travellers in Wiltshire, Dorsetshire, and Somersetshire*. London: John Murray, 1869, pp. 151-3.

'Fonthill', *Morning Herald*, 11September 1823, p. 3.

'Fonthill', *Morning Herald*, 12 September 1823, p. 3.

'Fonthill', *Morning Herald*, 19 September 1823, p. 3.

'Fonthill', *Morning Herald*, 24 September 1823, p. 2.

'Fonthill', *Morning Herald*, 27 September 1823, p. 3.

'Fonthill', *The New Times*, 10 October 1822, p. 4.

'Fonthill Abbey', *Dublin University Magazine*, 76 (August 1870): 196-9.

'Fonthill Abbey', *The Gazette of Fashion and Magazine of Literature, the Fine Arts, and Belles Lettres*, 31 August 1822, pp. 65-7.

[Fonthill Abbey], *The Gentleman's Magazine*, 66, pt. 2 (September 1796): 784.

'Fonthill Abbey', *The Gentleman's Magazine*, 93, pt. 1 (January 1823): 79.

'Fonthill Abbey', *The Gentleman's Magazine*, 95, pt. 2 (December 1825): 557.

'Fonthill Abbey', *The Gleaner, or, Weekly Historical Register*, 15 October 1823, pp. 385-7.

'Fonthill Abbey', *The Kaleidoscope, or, Literary and Scientific Mirror*, 3 (1822): 117.

'Fonthill Abbey', *The Mirror of Literature, Amusement, and Instruction*, 23 November 1822, pp. 49-52.

'Fonthill Abbey', *The Mirror of Literature, Amusement, and Instruction*, 28 January 1826, pp. 54-5.

'Fonthill Abbey', *Morning Chronicle*, 21 August 1823, p. 2.

'Fonthill Abbey', *Morning Chronicle*, 13 September 1823, p. 3.

'Fonthill Abbey', *Morning Chronicle*, 17 September 1823, p. 3.

'Fonthill Abbey', *Morning Chronicle*, 24 September 1823, p. 2.

'Fonthill Abbey', *Morning Chronicle*, 25 September 1823, p. 4.

'Fonthill Abbey', *Morning Chronicle*, 26 September 1823, p. 3.

'Fonthill Abbey', *Morning Chronicle*, 1 October 1823, p. 3.

'Fonthill Abbey', *Morning Chronicle*, 8 October 1823, p. 3.

'Fonthill Abbey', *Morning Herald*, 29 August 1823, p. 3.

'Fonthill Abbey', *Morning Herald*, 7 October 1822, pp. 2-3.

'Fonthill Abbey', *Morning Herald*, 8 October 1822, p. 3.

'Fonthill Abbey', *Morning Herald*, 16 October 1822, p. 3.

'Fonthill Abbey', *Morning Post*, 8 September 1823, p. 3.

'Fonthill Abbey', *Morning Post*, 10 September 1823, p. 3.

'Fonthill Abbey', *Morning Post*, 17 September 1823, p. 3.

'Fonthill Abbey', *Morning Post*, 24 September 1823, p. 3.

'Fonthill Abbey', *Morning Post*, 25 September 1823, p. 3.

'Fonthill Abbey', *Morning Post*, 27 September 1823, p. 3.

'Fonthill Abbey', *Morning Post*, 1 October 1823, p. 3.

'Fonthill Abbey', *The Museum, or Record of Literature, Fine Arts, Science, Antiquities, the Drama &c.*, no. 19 (1822): 300-1.

'Fonthill Abbey', *The Observer*, 19 October 1823, p. 3.

'Fonthill Abbey', *Scientific American*, 29 July 1893, p. 75.

'Fonthill Abbey', *The Times*, 5 October 1822, p. 2.

'Fonthill Abbey', *The Times*, 15 August 1823, p. 3.

'Fonthill Abbey' *The Times*, 30 September 1823, p. 3. Reprint of article in *Leeds Intelligencer*.

'Fonthill Abbey Description of this Wonderful Place, By a Gentleman in the Neighbourhood', *Morning Post*, 16 October 1823, p. 3.

'Fonthill Abbey Further Particulars', *Morning Post*, 12 September 1823, p. 4.

'Fonthill Abbey—Mr. Beckford—and Vathek', *Sunday Times*, 28 September 1823, p. 4 and 5 October 1823, p. 1.

'Fonthill Abbey. Second Day's Sale', *Morning Post*, 12 September 1823, p. 3.

'Fonthill Abbey, South East View', *The Mirror of Literature, Amusement, and Instruction*, 8 July 1826, pp. 25-6.

'Fonthill Abbey, Wilts. The Seat of Sir Michael Shaw-Stewart, Bart.', *Country Life*, 28 December 1901, pp. 840-6.

'Fonthill and Its Late Owner', *The New Times*, 9 September 1823, p. 2.

[Fonthill Auction], *The Gentleman's Magazine*, 71 (September 1801): 853-54.

'Fonthill Auction', *Morning Chronicle*, 25 August, 1801, p. 2.

[Fonthill Auction], *The Times*, 21 August 1801, p. 2.

'Fonthill Auction', *The Times*, 26 August, 1801, p. 3.

'Fonthill Fete', *The Times*, 20 January 1797, p. 4.

'Fonthill Grand Disappointment', *Morning Post*, 8 October 1822, p. 3.

'Fonthill Property', *Morning Herald*, 1 October 1822, p. 1.

'Fonthill Property', *The Times*, 30 September 1822, p. 3; 1 October 1822, p. 2; 4 October 1822, p. 3; 7 October 1822, p. 3.

[Fonthill Sale], *The Literary Gazette and Journal of Belles Lettres*, 30 August 1823, p. 555.

'Fonthill Sale', *The Literary Gazette and Journal of Belles Lettres*, 20 September 1823, p. 602.

'Fonthill Sale', *The Literary Gazette and Journal of Belles Lettres*, 27 September 1823, pp. 617-18.

'Fonthill Sale', *The Times*, 29 August 1807, p. 3.

'Fonthill Sale', *The Times*, 23 September 1823, p. 3.

[Fonthill Splendens], *The Gentleman's Magazine*, 25 (1755): 90.

[Fonthill Splendens], *The Times*, 24 July 1801, p. 3.

[Fonthill Splendens], *The Times*, 29 September 1807, p. 3.

[Fonthill Splendens Sale], *The Salisbury and Winchester Journal*, 31 August 1807, p. 4.

Frith, W. P. 'The Fonthill Story', in *My Autobiography and Reminiscences*. London, 1890, pp. 349-54.

Frost, Amy. 'Beckford's House of Card: Analysis of the Fonthill Abbey Model', *Beckford Journal*, 16 (2010): 114-123.

————. '" Oh what a scene of desolation!" A Further Insight into the Ruins of Fonthill Abbey', *Beckford Journal* (Spring 2008): 2-10.

G[arbett], W[illiam]. 'Candid Critique on the Architecture of Fonthill Abbey', *The Gentleman's Magazine*, 92, pt. 2 (December 1822): 491-4.

Gardner, Albert Ten Eyck. 'Beckford's Gothic Wests', *Bulletin of the Metropolitan Museum of Art*, 13 (October 1954), 41-9.

Gatty, Richard. 'Fonthill', in *Portrait of a Merchant Prince James Morrison 1789–1857*. Northallerton: Pepper Arden, 1976].

Gemmett, Robert J. 'An Architect's View of Fonthill Abbey', *Beckford Journal*, 9 (Spring 2003): 19-26.

————. 'Beckford's Fonthill: The Landscape as Art', *Gazette des Beaux*-Arts, 80 (December, 1972): 335-56.

————. 'The Critical Reception of William Beckford's Fonthill', *English Miscellany*, 19 (1968): 133-51.

————. 'Fonthill and Its Abbey: 'The Haunt of Eager Curiosity', *Beckford Journal* 11 (Summer 2004): 30-45.

————. 'The "Fonthill Splendens" Demolition Sale of 1807', *Beckford Journal*, 17 (2011): 10-20.

————. '"The old palace of tertian fevers" The Fonthill Sale of 1807', *Journal of the History of Collections*, 22, no. 2 (2010): 223-34.

————. '"The tinsel of fashion and the gewgaws of luxury": the Fonthill Sale of 1801', *Burlington Magazine*, 140 (June 2008): 318-88.

Giles, John Allen. *The Diary & Memoirs of John Allen Giles*, ed. David Bromwich. Somerset Record Society, 2000.

Goldsmith, Rev. J. [Sir Richard R. Phillips]. 'Fonthill Abbey', in *The Natural and Artificial Wonders of the United Kingdom*. London, 1825, 2: 321-6.

'Gothic Revival's Grand Showman', *The Times*, 24 September 1960, p. 7.

Hamilton-Phillips, Martha. 'Benjamin West and William Beckford: Some Projects for Fonthill', *Metropolitan Museum Journal*, 15 (1981): 157-74.

Harris, John. 'Fonthill, Wiltshire—I, Alderman Beckford's Houses', *Country Life*, 24 November 1966, pp. 1370-4.

Hauptman, William. 'Beckford, Brandoin, and the "Rajah" Aspects of an Eighteenth-Century Collection', *Apollo*, 143 (May 1996), 30-9.

Hayward, J. F. 'Royal Plate at Fonthill', *The Burlington Magazine*, 101 (April 1959): 145.

H[azlitt], W[illiam]. 'Fonthill Abbey', *The London Magazine*, 6 (November 1822): 405-10.

————. 'Extracts from Curious Books in the Fonthill Library', *The Examiner*, 24 August 1823, p. 550; 31 August 1823, pp. 563-4.

————. 'Fonthill Abbey', *Apollo Magazine*, 1 (1823): 203-6.

————. 'Fonthill Abbey', *The Examiner*, 10 August 1823, p. 514.

————. 'The Main Chance', *The New Monthly Magazine*, 17 (February 1828): 120.

Hazlitt, William. *New Writings of William Hazlitt*, ed. Duncan Wu, Oxford, 2007, 1: 444-68.

————. 'Notices of Curious and Highly Finished Cabinet Pictures at Fonthill Abbey, *Morning Chronicle*, 20 August 1823, p. 3; 22 August 1823, p. 3; 25 August 1823, p. 3; 1 September 1823, p. 2.

————. 'Pictures at Wilton, Stourhead, &c.', *The London Magazine*, 8 (October 1823): 357-60.

————. 'The Science of a Connoisseur', *Morning Chronicle*, 30 September 1823, p. 2.

Herrick, George H. 'Fabulous Fonthill', *College Art Journal*, 12 (1953): 128-31.

Hewatt-Jaboor, Philip. 'Fonthill House: "One of the Most Princely Edifices in the Kingdom"', in *William Beckford, 1760–1844. An Eye for the Magnificent*, ed. D. Ostergard , London: Yale, 2001, pp. 51-71.

H[oare, Sir Richard Colt]. 'Fonthill Abbey in Ruins', *The Gentleman's Magazine*, 96, pt. 1 (February 1826): 123.

'Illumination of the Abbey', *Morning Chronicle*, 24 October 1823, p. 4.

J. H. 'The Topaz Cup', *Morning Post*, 8 November 1823, p. 4.

Jervis, Simon Swynfen, 'Splendentia Recognita: Furniture by Martin Foxall for Fontill', *The Burlington Magazine*, 147 (June 2005): 376-82.

'John Constable's Visit to Fonthill Abbey in 1823', *Beckford Newsletter* (Spring 1983), pp. 8-9.

'John Farquhar, Esq.' [Obituary], *The Gentleman's Magazine*, 96, pt. 2 (September 1826): 278-80.

Jones, Stanley. 'The Fonthill Abbey Pictures: Two Additions to the Hazlitt Canon', *Journal of the Warburg and Courtauld Institutes*, 41 (1978): 278-96.

Jourdain, Margaret. 'William Beckford of Fonthill', in *Memorials of Old Wiltshire*. ed. Alice Dryden. London, 1906, pp. 116-27.

Kitz, Norman. 'The Search for a Lost "Greek" Statue', *Beckford Journal*, 2 (2005): 14-19.

[Knight, Charles]. 'Fonthill Abbey', *The Guardian* [London], 25 August 1822, p. 269; 8 September 1822, p. 287; 15 September 1822, p. 294; 22 September 1822, p. 301; 29 September 1822, p. 309; 13 October 1822, p. 325.

Knight, Derrick. 'Xanadu of a Wiltshire Hilltop', in *Gentlemen of Fortune*. London: Frederick Muller, [1978], pp. 113-26.

Lacy, J. 'The Topaz Cup', *The Times*, 6 November 1823, p. 3.

Laing, A. 'Bacchus the Wanderer. The Peregrinations of an Antique Statue between Painshill Park and Anglesey Abbey', *The National Trust Historic House and Collections Annual*, ed. D. Adshead (*Apollo*, 2008), 22-29.

L[ancaster Herald, George F. Beltz]. 'Armorial Decorations at Fonthill Abbey', *The Gentleman's Magazine*, 92, pt. 2 (September October, November 1822): 201-4; 317-20; 409-14.

Lane, Arthur. 'The Gaignières-Fonthill Vase; A Chinese Porcelain of about 1300', *Burlington Magazine*, 103 (April 1961): 124-32.

Lawford, G[eorge]. 'Fonthill Sale', *The Times*, 26 September 1823, p. 3.

Leben, Ulrich, 'The Waddesdon Manor Nautilus Shell and Triton: A Masterpiece from the William Beckford Collection', *Antiques*, 164 (October 2003): 114-121.

[Lettice, John?], 'Account of the Christmas Activities at Fonthill', *The European Magazine and London Review*, 31 (January 1797): 4-6.

Lewis, Kensington. 'Fonthill Abbey: The Topaz Cup', *The Times*, 5 November 1823, p. 3.

Littlebury, Isaac [Thomas F. Dibdin]. 'Fonthill Campaign. A Slight Sketch', *The Literary Gazette and Journal of Belles Lettres*, 4 October 1823, pp. 634-5.

_____. [Thomas F. Dibdin]. 'Fonthill', *Morning Chronicle*, 26 August 1823, p. 3; 30 August 1822.

Longbourne, David. 'A Painting of Fonthill Abbey Discovered', *Beckford Journal*, 3 (Spring 1997): 6-7.

Loudon, J. C. 'Notes on Gardens and Country Seats', *The Gardener's Magazine*, 11 (September 1835): 441-9.

Luff, S. G. A. 'The Romantick Abbey: A Consideration of Beckford's Folly', *The Aylesford Review*, 6 (Winter 1963): 26-32.

[Macquin, Abbé Ange Denis] 'A Visit to Fonthill Abbey', *The Literary Gazette and Journal of Belles Lettres*, 17 August 1822, pp. 520-1; 24 August 1822, pp. 527-8; 31 August 1822, pp. 555-6; 14 September 1822, p. 585.

Marr, Alexander. 'William Beckford and the Landscape Garden', in *William Beckford, 1760–1844: An Eye for the Magnificent*, ed. Derek Ostergard. New Haven and London: Yale University Press, 2001.

Mayhew, Edgar. 'A View of Fonthill Abbey', *The Register of the Museum of Art, University of Kansas*, 1 (December 1957): 151-6.

_____. 'William Beckford' Metamorphosis of Fonthill', *Berlin Architectural Journal*, 4 (June 1982): 33-53.

McGarvie, Michael. 'William Beckford, Gardener, at Witham and Fonthill', *Frome Society Yearbook*, 7 (1997): 112-21.

McLeod, Bet. 'Some further objects from William Beckford's collection in the Victoria and Albert Museum', *Burlington Magazine*, 143 (June 2001): 367-70.

Millington, Jon. 'A Reissue of Storer's Fonthill', *Beckford Journal*, 4 (Spring 1998): 71-5.

_____. 'Engravings of Fonthill, *Beckford Journal*, 7 (Spring 2001): 47-59.

_____. 'Fonthill After Beckford', *Beckford Journal*, 2 (Spring 1996): 46-59.

_____. 'Francis Danby', *Beckford Newsletter* (Spring 1985): p. 3.

_____. 'John Rutter's A Description of Fonthill Abbey and Demesne, 1822', *Beckford Journal*, 13 (Spring 2007): 42-53.

_____. 'Nichols' *Historical Notices of Fonthill Abbey*', *Beckford Journal*, 6 (Spring 2000): 75-8.

_____. 'Where Nelson Went in Fonthill Abbey', *Beckford Journal*, 8 (Spring 2002): 43-9.

'Mr. Beckford', *Morning Herald*, 18 September 1823, p. 1.

'Mr. Beckford', *Morning Herald*, 6 October 1823, p. 4.

'Mr. Beckford', *Morning Herald*, 10 October 1823, p. 3.

'Mr. Beckford', *The Observer*, 21 September 1823, p. 4.

'Mr. Beckford and Fonthill', *Chambers Journal*, 2 (August, 1844): 101-3.

'Mr. Beckford and the Fine Arts', *Morning Herald*, 27 September 1823, p. 3.

'Mr. Beckford. Fonthill Abbey', *The Gleaner, or, Weekly Historical Register,* 22 October 1823, pp. 407-9.

'Mr. Beckford's Critiques and Commentaries', *The Literary Chronicle and Weekly Review*, 20 September 1823, p. 602.

'Mr. Beckford—Several Anecdotes, Illustrative of this Gentleman's Character', *The Bath and Cheltenham Gazette*, 23 September 1823, p. 2.

'Mr. Farquhar and Fonthill', *The Times*, 11 October 1822, p. 3.

'Mr. Farquhar and Fonthill Abbey', *The Mirror of Literature, Amusement, and Instruction*, 16 November 1822, pp. 33-5.

'Mr. Farquhar and the Fonthill Estate', *The Observer*, 13 October 1822, p. 4.

M. J. 'Fonthill Abbey', *The Literary Chronicle and Weekly Review*, 19 October 1822, pp. 665-7.

Morning Chronicle additional notices on Fonthill: 20 September 1822, p. 4; 24 September 1822, p. 3; 10 October 1822, 3; 21 October 1822, p. 3; 1 November 1822, p. 3; 4 November 1822, p. 4; 22 August 1823, p. 3; 11 September 1823, p. 3; 18 September 1823, p. 2; 19 September 1823, p. 3; 20 September 1823, p. 2; 22 September 1823, p. 2; 27 September 1823, p. 2; 29 September 1823, p. 2; 2 October 1823, p. 4; 3 October 1823, p. 3; 4 October 1823, p. 3; 6 October 1823, p. 3; 9 October 1823, p. 4; 11 October 1823, p. 4; 13 October 1823, p. 4; 15 October 1823, p. 4; 16 October 1823, p. 4; 18 October 1823, p. 4; 20 October 1823, p. 4; 23 October 1823, p. 4; 25 October 1823; 27 October 1823, p. 4; 11 November 1823, p. 4.

Morning Herald additional notices on Fonthill: 11 October 1822, p. 3; 8 September 1823, p. 3; 10 September 1823, p. 2; 13 September 1823, p. 3; 16 September 1823, p. 2; 17 September 1823, p. 2; 18 September 1823, p. 3; 20 September 1823, p. 2; 22 September 1823, p. 3; 26 September 1823, p. 3; 29 September 1823, p. 3; 1 October 1823, p. 3;2 October 1823, p. 3; 3 October 1823, p. 3; 15 October 1823, p. 3; 16 October 1823, p. 3; 1 November 1823, p. 3; 17 November 1823, p. 3.

Morning Post additional notices on Fonthill: 8 October 1822, p. 3; 8 August 1823, p. 3; 20 August 1823, p. 3; 22 August 1823, p. 3; 29 August 1823, p. 3; 2 September 1823, p. 3; 11 September 1823, p. 3; 13 September 1823, p. 3; 15 September 1823, p. 3; 18 September 1823, p. 3; 19 September 1823, p. 3; 20 September 1823, p. 3; 22 September 1823, p. 3; 26 September 1823, p. 3; 29 September 1823, p. 3; 2 October 1823, p. 3; 4 October 1823, pp. 3, 4; 9 October 1823, p. 3; 11 October 1823, p. 3; 13 October 1823, p. 3; 21 October 1823, p. 3; 24 October 1823, p. 3; 25 October 1823, p. 3; 28 October 1823, p. 2; 29 November 1823, p. 3.

Mowl, Timothy. 'Inside Beckford's Mind', *Country Life*, 7 February 2002, pp. 60-3.

New Monthly Magazine and Literary Journal additional notices on Fonthill: 6 (October, 1822): 479-80; 18 (April, 1826): 169.

New Times additional notices on Fonthill: 5 November 1822, p. 3; 27 August 1823, p. 4; 12 September 1823, pp. 3, 4; 13 September 1823, p. 4; 18 September 1823, p. 4.

Nightingale, James E. 'Some Account of the Objects of Interest in the Fonthill Excursion', A paper read at the 17th annual meeting of the Wiltshire Archaeological and Natural History Society, at Wilton. Salisbury, 1870.

Observator. 'Letter to Mr. Urban', *The Gentleman's Magazine*, 76, pt. 2 (December 1806): 1127-8.

Parkins, J. W. 'Mr. Farquhar', *Morning Chronicle*, 5 November 1822, p. 3.

[Patmore, Peter G.]. 'British Galleries of Art—No. IX Fonthill', *The New Monthly Magazine and Literary Journal*, 8 (1823): 403-8.

Pearson, James. 'The Art of Staining Glass', *The Gentleman's Magazine*, 85, pt. 2 (July 1815): 28-9.

Pendragon, Charles [Charles Knight]. 'An Episode of Vathek', *Knight's Quarterly Magazine*, 1 (July, 1823): 309-14.

Pevsner, Nikolaus. 'Fonthill Abbey', in *The Buildings of England Wiltshire*. London: Penguin Books, [1976], pp. 246-9.

Phillips, H[arry]. 'The Topaz Cup at Fonthill', *Morning Post*, 17 November 1823, p. 3.

Pressly, Nancy. *Revealed Religion: Benjamin West's Commissions for Windsor Castle and Fonthill Abbey*. San Antonio, 1983.

[Reed, Isaac], 'Account of the Works Now Executing at Fonthill', *The European Magazine and London Review*, 31 (February 1797): 104-7.

Reitlinger, Gerald. 'Further Adventures of the Gaignières-Fonthill Vase', *The Burlington Magazine*, 104 (1962): 34.

Richter, Anne Nellis. 'Spectacle, Exoticism, and Display in the Gentleman's House: The Fonthill Auction of 1822', *Eighteenth-Century Studies*, 41, no. 4 (2008): 543-63.

Roberts, Hugh. 'Beckford, Vuillamy and Old Japan', *Apollo*, 124 (1986): 338-41.

Rogers, Millard F. 'Benjamin West and the Caliph: Two Paintings for Fonthill Abbey', *Apollo*, 83 (June, 1966), 420-5.

Ross, Marvin Chauncey. 'The Rubens Vase Its History and Date', *The Journal of the Walters Art Gallery*, 6 (1943): 9-39.

Rushton, Andrée. 'The Fonthill Barrier', *Beckford Journal*, 4 (Spring 1998): 65-70.

'Sale at Fonthill', *The Gentleman's Magazine*, 77, pt. 2 (September 1807): 880.

'Sale at Fonthill Abbey', *The Museum, or Record of Literature, Fine Arts, Science, Antiquities, the Drama &c.*, no. 14 (1822): 216-17.

'Sale of Effects at Fonthill Abbey', *The Observer*, 1 & 2 September 1822, pp. 3, 2.

'Sale of the Whole of the Fonthill Estate', *The Observer*, 13 October 1822, p. 4.

Salisbury and Winchester Journal notices on Fonthill: 26 August 1822, p. 4; 2 September 1822, p. 4; 9 September 1822, p. 4; 16 September 1822, p. 4; 23 September 1822, p. 4; 30 September 1822, p. 4; 14 October 1822, p. 3; 14 October 1822, p. 4; 28 October 1822, p. 2; 4 August 1823, p. 4; 18 August 1823, p. 3; 25 August 1823, p. 4; 1 September 1823, p. 4; 8 September 1823, p. 4; 15 September 1823, p. 4; 22 September 1823, p. 4; 29 September 1823, p. 4; 6 October 1823, p. 4; 13 October 1823, p. 4; 20 October 1823, pp. 3, 4; 27 October 1823, p. 4; 3 November 1823, p. 2.

Scott, John. 'The Rise and Fall of Fonthill Abbey', *British History Illustrated*, 2 (August 1975): 3-11.

Scott, T. G. 'Fonthill Buildings', *Country Life*, 24 January 1957, p.157.

Skoggard, Carl. 'William Beckford, Fonthill Abbey', *Nest: A Magazine of Interiors*, no. 4 (Spring 1999).

Smith, H. Clifford. 'The Van Diemen Box', *The Burlington Magazine*, 29 (1916): 299-303.

Snodin, Michael and Malcolm Baker. 'William Beckford's Silver I', *Burlington Magazine*, 122 (November 1980): 735-48.

————————————————. 'William Beckford's Sliver II', *Burlington Magazine*, 122 (December 1980): 820-34.

Stone, Richard E. 'A Noble Imposture: The Fonthill Ewer and Early-Nineteenth-Century Fakery', *Metropolitan Museum Journal*, 32 (1997): 175-206.

——————————. 'The Fonthill Ewer Reconstructing the Renaissance', *Metropolitan Museum of Art Bulletin*, 55 (Winter 1997): 46-56.

Strong, Roy. 'The Fall of Fonthill', in *Lost Treasures of Britain*. London: Viking Penguin, [1990], pp. 188-201.

[Taylor, John Sidney].'Fonthill Abbey', *Morning Chronicle*, 11 September 1823, p. 3.

_____. 'Fonthill Abbey', *Morning Chronicle*, 12 September 1823, p. 3.

_____. 'Fonthill Abbey', *Morning Chronicle*, 13 September 1823, p. 3.

_____. 'Fonthill Abbey', *Morning Chronicle*, 17 September 1823, p. 3.

_____. 'Fonthill Abbey', *Morning Chronicle*, 24 September 1823, p. 2.

_____. 'Fonthill Abbey', *Morning Chronicle*, 26 September 1823, p. 3.

_____. 'Fonthill Abbey', *Morning Chronicle*, 4 October 1823, p. 4.

_____. 'Fonthill Abbey', *Morning Chronicle*, 8 October 1823, p. 4.

_____. 'Illumination of the Abbey', *Morning Chronicle*, 24 October, 1823, p. 4.

Templeton, A[rthur] M., Jr. 'A Second Visit to Fonthill Abbey', *New European Magazine*, 3 (August 1823): 135-42.

Thacker, Christopher. 'England's Kubla Khan', in *William Beckford Exhibition 1976*. [Bath, 1976], pp. 63-76.

_____. 'Fonthill', in *The History of Gardens*. Berkeley: University of California Press, [1979], pp. 221-5.

_____, Steven Ashley and Julian Berry. 'Twin Towers', *The Georgian Group Journal* (1995): 115-18.

The Times additional notices on Fonthill: 20 May 1800, p. 3; 27 May 1800, p. 3; 24 December 1800, p. 3; 21 August 1801, p. 2; 29 September 1807, p. 3; 14 September 1822, p. 2; 17 September 1822, p. 2; 20 September 1822, p. 2; 2 October 1822, p. 3; 3 October 1822, p. 2; 8 October 1822, p. 2; 9 October 1822, p. 2; 21 November 1822, p. 2; 15 August 1823, p. 3; 12 September 1823, p. 2; 28 October 1823, p. 2; 30 October 1823, p. 2; 30 October 1829.

Thurley, Simon. 'Fonthill Abbey Gothic Dream or Gothic Nightmare', in *Lost Buildings of Britain* (London: Viking, 2004), pp. 41-74.

Tonstall, Cuthbert [Thomas F. Dibdin]. 'The Fonthill Fever', *The Museum, or Record of Literature, Fine Arts, Science, Antiquities, the Drama &c.*, 5 October 1822, pp. 379-80; 12 October 1822, pp. 393-5; 19 October 1822, pp. 410-12; 26 October 1822, pp. 428-30; 2 November 1822, pp. 441-2; 9 November 1822, pp. 455-6.

[Tresham, Henry]. 'Letter from a Gentleman, Present at the Festivities at Fonthill, to a Correspondent in Town', *The Gentleman's Magazine*, 89, pt. 1 (March, April 1801): 206-8; 297-8.

Viator [Sir Richard Colt Hoare]. 'Fonthill Abbey. On its Close', *The Gentleman's Magazine*, 92, pt. 2 (October 1822): 291-2.

'Virtu', *The Court Journal*, 19 October 1833, pp. 1-2.

Wainwright, Clive. 'Fonthill Abbey', in *The Romantic Interior: The British Collector at Home 1750–1850*. New Haven: Yale University Press, 1989, pp. 109-46.

_____. 'In Lucifer's Metropolis', *Country Life*, 1 October 1992, pp. 82-4.

_____. 'William Beckford and His Collection', *Arte Illustra*, 4 (January–April 1971): 106-12.

_____. 'William Beckford's Furniture', *Connoisseur*, 191 (1976): 290-6.

Watson, F. J. B. 'Beckford, Mme. De Pompadour, the duc de Bouillon and the Taste for Japanese Lacquer in Eighteenth Century France', *Gazette des Beaux-Arts*, 61(1963): 101-27.

Weeks, Donald. 'William Beckford and Fonthill Abbey', in *Pages The World of Books, Writers, and Writing*, ed. Matthew Bruccoli. Detroit: Gale Reseach, [1976], pp. 58-61.

Whitehead, John. 'Some French Purchases by William Beckford', *Beckford Journal*, 2 (Spring, 1996): 39-44.

Wilkinson, Gerald. 'Fonthill', in *Turner's Early Sketchbooks*. New York: Watson-Guptill, [1972], pp. 100-4.

'William Bankes' Account of his Surreptitious Visit to Fonthill', *Beckford Journal*, 1 (Spring 1995): 47-50.

Wilton-Ely, John. 'Beckford, Fonthill Abbey and the Picturesque', in *The Picturesque in Late Georgian England*, ed. Dana Arnold. London: The Georgian Group, [1995], pp. 35-44.

_____. 'Beckford the Builder', in *William Beckford Exhibition 1976*. The Victoria Gallery. [Bath, 1976], pp. 35-62.

_____. 'Beckford's Fonthill Abbey: a Theatre of the Arts', in *The Beckford Society Annual Lectures 1996-1999*, ed. Jon Millington. Bristol: The Beckford Society, 2000, pp. 3-22.

_____. 'The Genesis and Evolution of Fonthill Abbey', *Architectural History*, 23 (1980): 40-51.

_____. 'A Model for Fonthill Abbey', in *The Country Seat Studies in the History of the British Country House*, ed. Howard Colvin and John Harris. London: Penguin Press, [1970], pp. 199-204.

Wood, Min. 'Landscape as Biography: William Beckford's Fonthill', *Beckford Journal*, 16 (2010): 124-43.

Woodward, Christopher. 'William Beckford and Fonthill Splendens Early Works by Soane and Goodridge', *Apollo*, 147 (1998): 31-40.

Wyatt, Benjamin. 'Fonthill Abbey', *Morning Post*, 1 November 1823, p. 2.

Yamaguchi, Kazuhiko. 'The Fonthill Legend: William Beckford's Landscape Architecture, *Journal of Educational Research, Shinshu University*, 6 (2000): 97-112.

III Poems on Fonthill

Bowles, William Lisle. 'Lines on a First View of Fonthill Abbey', *The Gentleman's Magazine*, 92, pt. 2 (August 1822): 102.

E. K. 'Fonthill Abbey, Wilts, Seat of W. Beckford, Esq. in July 1827', Jaulnah, Bombay, July 1856, from the Scrapbook of Ezra Hunt (1809–1876), Bath Public Library.

'Fonthill', in *The Anniversary; or, Poetry and Prose for MDCCCXXIX*, ed. Allan Cunningham. London, 1829, pp. 214-16.

Jefferson, John. *Fonthill: A Poem*. Blandford, 1824.

[Lettice, John]. 'Written in an Arbour of the Alpine Garden Fronting the Lake', Fonthill 4 August 1800. MS Beckford, Bodleian Library, c. 33, f. 73.

[_____]. 'Written in the Grotto', 6 August 1800. MS Beckford, Bodleian Library, c. 33, f. 72.

[Macquin, Abbé Ange Denis]. 'Fonthill Abbey', *The Literary Gazette and Journal of Belles Lettres*, 21 September 1822, pp. 602-3.

M. J. 'Fonthill: A Sonnet', *The Literary Chronicle and Weekly Review*, 24 August 1822, p. 540.

[Pickering, Henry]. 'On the Alienation of Fonthill Abbey', in *Ruins of Paestum: and other Compositions in Verse*. Salem, Mass., 1822.

W[atts], A[laric] A. 'Fonthill Sale A Parody', Broadside dated '19 Jan 1824', Beinecke Library, GEN MSS, 102, f. 100, Alaric Watts to John Britton.

IV Secondary Sources

Aldrich, Megan. *Gothic Revival*. London: Phaidon Press, 1994.

Alexander, Boyd, ed. *The Journal of William Beckford in Portugal, 1787–1788*. New York: John Day, 1955.

_____. *England's Wealthiest Son: A Study of William Beckford*. [London]: Centaur Press, 1962.

_____. 'Shades of Beckford', *Apollo*, 104 (August 1976): 146-7.

Andersen, Jorgen. 'Giant Dreams: Piranesi's Influence in England," *English Miscellany*, 2 (1962): 49-60.

Argenteries Le Tresor du National Trust for Scotland. La Collection Beckford et Hamilton du Château de Brodick. National Trust for Scotland, 1992.

Bishop, Philippa. 'William Beckford 1760–1844 British Antiquarian and Connoisseur', *Encyclopedia of Interior Design*. ed. Joanna Banham. London: Fitzroy Deaborn, 1997, 1: 111-14.

Britton, John. *The Autobiography of John Britton*. 2 vols. London, 1850.

Chambers, William. *Dissertation on Oriental Gardening*. London, 1773.

Chapman, Guy. *Beckford*. London: Rupert Hart-Davis, 1952.

_____., ed. *The Travel-Diaries of William Beckford of Fonthill*, 2 vols. Cambridge: Constable, 1928.

_____., ed. *The Vision Liber Veritatis*. Cambridge: Constable, 1930.

Chase, Isabel. *Horace Walpole: Gardenist*. Princeton: Princeton University Press, 1943.

Clark, Kenneth. *The Gothic Revival: An Essay in the History of Taste*. London: Penguin Books, [1962].

Crowley, D. A. *A History of Wiltshire*, 11, *Downton Hundred*, 13, *Southwest Wiltshire*. Oxford: Oxford University Press, 1980.

Culme, John. 'Kensington Lewis A Nineteenth-Century Businessman', *The Connoisseur*, 190 (1975): 26-41.

Dale, Anthony. *James Wyatt, Architect: 1748–1813*. Oxford: Basil Blackwell, 1936.

Da Silva, José Cornélio and Gerald Luckhurst. *Sintra A Landscape with Villas*. Ediçoes Inapa: The Genius of the Place Collection, 1989.

Eastlake, Charles L. History of the Gothic Revival, ed. J. M. Crook. Leicester: Leicester University Press, 1970.

Farington, Joseph. *The Diary of Joseph Farington*, ed. Kenneth Garlick, Angus Macintyre and Katherine Cave. 16 vols. New Haven: Yale University Press, 1978–1984.

[Farquhar, John]. *Costly Furniture, Bronzes, Marbles ... A Catalogue of the Superlatively Elegant Assemblage of Furniture ... and Miscellaneous Objects, the Property of a Gentleman, Removed from His Mansion in the West of England*. Which will be Sold ... by Mr. Phillips ... 22d day of June, 1825 and following days.

Fergusson, James. *History of the Modern Styles of Architecture*. London, 1873.

Finberg, A. J. *A Complete Inventory of the Drawings of the Turner Bequest*. 2 vols. London, 1909.

Fothergill, Brian. *Beckford of Fonthill*. London: Faber, 1979.

Frith, W. P. *My Autobiography and Reminiscences*. London, 1890.

Gauthier, Marie-Madeleine. Émaux Méridionaux Catalogue International de L'oeuvre de *Limoges*. Tome I, *L'Époque Romane*. Paris: Éditions du Centre National de la Recherche Scientifique, 1987.

Gemmett, Robert J., ed. *Biographical Memoirs of Extraordinary Painters*. Rutherford, N. J.: Fairleigh Dickinson University Press, 1969.

_____., ed. *The Consummate Collector William Beckford's Letters to His Bookseller*. Wilby, Norwich: Michael Russell, 2000. New, revised edition, Stroud: Fonthill Media, 2014.

_____., ed. *Dreams, Waking Thoughts and Incidents*. Stroud: Nonsuch Publishing, 2006.

_____. *William Beckford*. Boston: Twayne, 1977.

Gilbert, C. and T. Murdoch, *John Channon and Brass-Inlaid Furniture 1730–1760*. New Haven, 1993.

Gilpin, William. *The Essay on Prints*. London, 1768.

_____. *Observations on the Western Parts of England, Relative Chiefly to Picturesque Beauty*. London, 1798.

_____. *Three Essays on Picturesque Beauty: on Picturesque Travel; and on Sketching Landscape*. 3rd ed. London, 1808.

Gower, Lord Granville Leveson. *Lord Granville Leveson Gower, Private Correspondence, 1781–1821*, ed. Castalia Countess Granville, 2 vols. London, 1916.

Gregory, William. *The Beckford Family: Reminiscences of Fonthill Abbey and Lansdown Tower*. London, 1898.

Harris, John. 'C. R. Cockerell's "Ichnographica Domestica"', *Architectural History*, 14 1971): 5-29.

_____. 'English Country House Guides, 1740–1840', in *Concerning Architecture*, ed. John Summerson. Baltimore: Penguin, [1968], pp. 58-74.

_____. *Sir William Chambers Knight of the Polar Star*. University Park: The Pennsylvania State University Press, 1970.

H[arrison], W[illiam] H[arrison]. 'Conversations of the Late W. Beckford, Esq', *The New Monthly Magazine*, 72, no. 6 (December 1844): 516-22.

Haydon, F. W. *Benjamin Robert Haydon: Correspondence and Table Talk*. 2 vols. London, 1876.

H. 'Conversations with the Late W. Beckford, Esq', *The New Monthly Magazine*, 72, nos. 3-5 (September-November 1844): 18-24; 212-21; 418-27.

Herrmann, Frank. *The English Collectors A Documentary Chrestomathy*. New York: W. W. Norton, 1972.

Hoare, Sir Richard Colt and James Everard, Baron Arundell. *The History of Modern Wiltshire*. Vol. 4, *Hundred of Dunworth and Vale of Noddre*. London, 1829.

Hodges, Alison. 'Painshill, Cobham, Surrey: The Grotto', *Garden History*, 3 (Autumn 1974): 23-8.

Hopkins, John H. *Essay on Gothic Architecture, with Various Plans and Drawings for Churches: Designed Chiefly for the Use of the Clergy*. Burlington, 1836.

Howe, P. P. *The Complete Works of William Hazlitt*. vol. 19. London: J. M. Dent, 1933.

Hussey, Christopher. *The Picturesque: Studies in a Point of View*. London: G. P. Putnam, 1927.

Jack, Malcolm. *William Beckford An English Fidalgo*. New York: AMS Press, 1994.

Jerdan, William. *The Autobiography of William Jerdan*, 3 vols. London, 1853.

Jones, Barbara. *Follies & Grottoes*. London: Constable, 1953.

Knight, Charles. *Once Upon a Time*. London, 1865.

_____. *Passages of a Working Life During Half a Century with a Prelude of Early Reminiscences*. 3 vols. London, 1864.

Knight, R. P. *The Landscape, A Didactic Poem in Three Books*. London, 1794.

Kuist, James M., ed. *The Nichols File of the Gentleman's Magazine*. Madison: University of Wisconsin, 1982.

Lansdown, Henry V. *Recollections of the Late William Beckford of Fonthill, Wilts.; and Lansdown, Bath*. Bath, 1893.

Lees-Milne, James. *William Beckford*. Tisbury: Compton Russell, 1976.

Leslie, C. R. *Memoirs of the Life of John Constable*. London: John Lehman, 1949.

Luckhurst, Gerald. 'Here didst thou dwell ... William Beckford at Monserrate', *Beckford Journal*, 18 (2012): 56-71.

Macaulay, James. *The Gothic Revival 1745–1845*. London: Blackie, 1975.

Macaulay, Rose. *They Went to Portugal*. London: Jonathan Cape, 1946.

McCarthy, Michael. *The Origins of the Gothic Revival*. London: Paul Mellon Centre for Studies in British Art, 1987.

Malins, Edward. *English Landscaping and Literature 1660–1840*. London: Oxford University Press, 1966.

Manwaring, Elizabeth. *Italian Landscape in Eighteenth-Century England*. New York: Oxford University Press, 1925.

Meister, J. Henri. *Letters Written During a Residence in England*. London, 1799.

Melville, Lewis. *The Life and Letters of William Beckford of Fonthill*. New York: Duffield, 1910.

'Memoirs of William Beckford, of Fonthill', *The Gentleman's Magazine*, 206 (March 1859): 255-60.

Millington, Jon, ed. *Beckford and His Circle in the Gentleman's Magazine*. Bristol: Beckford Society, 2001.

Mitford, Mary Russell. *The Friendships of Mary Russell Mitford as Recorded in Letters from Her Literary Correspondents*, ed. Rev. A. G. L'Estrange. New York, 1882.

Moore, Thomas. *The Journal of Thomas Moore*, ed. Wilfred S. Dowden, Vols. 1–3. Newark: University of Delaware Press, 1984.

Morrison, Alfred. *Collection of Autograph Letters and Historical Documents*. (Second Series). Printed for Private Circulation, 1893.

_____. *Collection of Autograph Letters and Historical Documents, The Hamilton and Nelson Papers* (Second Series). 2 vols. Printed for Private Circulation, 1893–94.

Mowl, Timothy. *Historic Gardens of Wiltshire*. Stroud: Tempus Publishing, 2004.

_____. *William Beckford Composing for Mozart*. London: John Murray, [1998].

Murphy, James Cavanah. *Plans, Elevations, Sections & Views of the Church of Batalha in the Province of Estremadura in Portugal*. London, 1836.

Neiman, Fraser. 'The Letters of William Gilpin to Samuel Henley', *Huntington Library Quarterly*, 35 (February 1972): 159-69.

Newby, Evelyn. 'A Dutchman's Visit to Some English Gardens in 1791', *Journal of Garden History*, 2 (January–March 1982), 41-58.

Oliver, J. W. *The Life of William Beckford*. London: Oxford University Press, 1932.

Oppé, A. P. *Alexander and John Robert Cozens*. Cambridge: Harvard University Press, 1954.

Peniston, John. *The Letters of John Peniston, Salisbury Architect, Catholic, and Yeomanry Officer 1823–1830*. ed. Michael Cowan. Trowbridge: Wiltshire Record Society, 1996.

Pettigrew, T. J. *Memoirs of the Life of Vice-Admiral Lord Viscount Nelson, K. B.*, 2 vols. London, 1849.

Pococke, Richard. *The Travels Through England*, ed. James J. Carwright. 2 vols. Westminster, 1889.

Powys, Mrs. Philip Lybbe. *Passages from the Diaries of Mrs. Philip Lybbe Powys*, ed. Emily J. Climenson. London: Longmans, 1899.

Price, Uvedale. *Essays on the Picturesque*. 2 vols. London, 1798.

Pückler-Muskau, Prince. *Tour in England, Ireland, and France, 1828–1829*. Philadelphia, 1833.

Quest-Ritson, Charles. *The English Garden Abroad*. London: Viking, 1992.

Redding, Cyrus. *Fifty Years' Recollections, Literary and Personal, with Observations on Men and Things*. 3 vols. London, 1858.

_____. *Memoirs of William Beckford of Fonthill*. 2 vols. London, 1859.

_____. *Past Celebrities Whom I Have Known*. 2 vols. London, 1866.

_____. 'Recollections of the Author of Vathek', *The New Monthly Magazine*, 71 (June, July 1844): 143-58; 302-19.

Reynolds, Donald M. *et. al. Fonthill Castle: Paradigm of Hudson-River Gothic*. Riverdale: College of Mount Saint Vincent-on-Hudson, 1976.

Robinson, John Martin. *James Wyatt, 1746–1813: Architect to George III*. New Haven: Yale University Press, 2012.

_____. *The Wyatts: An Architectural Dynasty*. Oxford: Oxford University Press, 1979.

Rogers, Samuel. *Recollections of Samuel Rogers to Which is Added Porsoniana*. New York, 1856.

Shaffer, E. S. '"To remind us of China"—William Beckford, Mental Traveller on the Grand Tour: The Construction of Significance in Landscape', in *Transports: Travel, Pleasure, and Imaginative Geography, 1600–1830*, ed. Chloe Chard and Helen Langdon. New Haven: Yale University Press, 1996, pp. 207-42.

Sheard, Norah. *The History of Hindon*. Shaftesbury: The Shaston Printers, 1979.

Sherbo, Arthur. 'Isaac Reed and *The European Magazine*', *Studies in Bibliography*, 37 (1984): 210-27.

Simpson, Duncan. *Gothick 1720–1840* [Exhibition catalogue]. Brighton: Royal Pavilion, Art Gallery and Museums, 1975.

Sloan, Kim. *Alexander and Robert Cozens The Poetry of Landscape*. New Haven: Yale University Press, 1986.

Smeeton, George. *The Unique*. London, 1824.

Steegman, John. *The Rule of Taste from George I to George IV*. London: Macmillan, 1936.

Sullivan, Alvin, ed. *British Literary Magazines: The Romantic Age, 1789–1836*. Westport, CT: Greenwood Press, 1983.

Summerson, John. *Architecture in Britain, 1530–1830*. London: Penguin Books, 1953.

'Thoughts on a Late Biography', *The Monthly Visitor*, 2 (October 1797): 343.

Thrale, Hester Lynch. *Thraliana, The Diary of Mrs. Hester Lynch Thrale (Mrs. Piozzi), 1776–1809*, ed. Katherine Balderston. 2 vols. Oxford: Clarendon Press, 1951.

Tuohy, Thomas. 'William Beckford's Three Picture Collections Idiosyncrasy and Innovation', *The British Art Journal*, 2 (Autumn 2000): 49-53.

Waagen, G. F. *Works of Art and Artists in England*. 3 vols. London, 1838.

Walpole, Horace. *Anecdotes of Painting in England*. ed. Ralph Wornum. 3 vols. London, 1849.

Ward, William S. *Literary Reviews in British Periodicals 1789–1797 A Bibliography*. New York: Garland Publishing, 1979.

Wardle, Ralph M. *Hazlitt*. Lincoln: University of Nebraska Press, 1971.

Warner, Richard. *Excursions from Bath*. Bath, 1801.

Watkin, David. *The English Vision The Picturesque in Architecture, Landscape, and Garden Design*. New York: Harper & Row, 1982.

_____. *Thomas Hope 1769–1831 and the Neo-Classical Idea*. London: John Murray, 1968.

Watts, Alaric Alfred. *Alaric Watts. A Narrative of his Life*. 2 vols. London, 1884.

Whibley, Charles. *The Pageantry of Life*. New York: Harper, 1900.

Wilson, M. I. *The Chamber Organ in Britain, 1600–1830*. Aldershot, 2001.

Wilton, Andrew. *J. M. W. Turner His Life and Art*. New York: Rizzolli, 1979.

Index